D0764093

BENEDETTA PARODI

EVERYDAY COOKING FROM ITALY

First published in the United States of America in 2014
by Rizzoli International Publications, Inc.
300 Park Avenue South
New York, NY 10010
www.rizzoliusa.com

Everyday Cooking from Italy © 2014 Benedetta Parodi

Photographs © Benedetta Parodi

Pages iv, vi, 68, 200, 300, 338 © Matteo di Nunzio

Cover photograph © Pigi Cipelli

Contains material originally published in Italian as *I Menù di Benedetta* (Rizzoli, 2011) and *Mettiamoci a Cucinare* (Rizzoli, 2012).

English translation by Natalie Danford

2014 2015 2016 / 10 9 8 7 6 5 4 3 2 1

Distributed to the U.S. trade by Random House, New York

Printed in China

ISBN-13: 978-0-8478-4266-7
Library of Congress Control Number: 2013952649

CONTENTS

Publishing a cookbook in the United States is a dream come true for me. My native Italy, while a small country, has so many wonderful dishes to offer. There are hundreds of delicious pasta sauces, pizzas, risottos, and frozen desserts in these pages, and I'm so excited to share them with you. The ingredients that I use in my own kitchen in Italy are widely available in other countries, so you can make these in New York just as easily as in Milan. And they're so simple! I'm not a professional chef. I'm just a working woman with a big family and a love for cooking. My recipes are fast and easy. They'll help you make a good impression without much effort. With my tips and tricks, you can prepare a delicious Italian lunch in fifteen minutes. No kidding—we Italians joke about everything but food. Please join me in the kitchen and at the table.

Buon appetito!

Benedetta

ANTIPASTI

Note: Throughout the book you'll encounter a quintessentially Italian phrase, *quanto basta*, literally "enough." Since so many of my recipes combine fresh ingredients with common pantry staples, this means to use "as much as you need" or "as much as you like" of everyday ingredients you're likely to have on hand.

« PINZIMONIO CON TRIS DI SALSE »
CRUDITÉS WITH THREE SAUCES

Pinzimonio, a raw vegetable and olive oil starter, is always a good fallback, because it's light and lends itself to variation. The challenge is creating tasty dipping sauces, so here I've included not one but three! The proportions are merely suggestions. When it comes to the sauces, taste and decide whether you want to adjust the ratios.

SERVES 4

Crudités cut into sticks (carrots, bell peppers, celery, fennel, radishes, zucchini)

Anchovy Sauce
2 anchovy fillets in olive oil, drained
2 teaspoons white wine vinegar
1/4 cup plus 1 tablespoon extra-virgin olive oil

Yogurt-Mustard Sauce
2 to 3 tablespoons plain yogurt
1 to 2 tablespoons grainy mustard
Salt and pepper to taste

Cheese Sauce
1/2 cup (100 milliliters) heavy cream
Juice of 1/2 lemon
2 tablespoons ricotta
6 ounces (150 grams) stracchino or other creamy, spreadable cheese
Paprika to taste
Minced chives to taste
Salt to taste

To make the anchovy sauce, puree the anchovies in a blender with the vinegar and oil. For the yogurt-mustard sauce, mix the yogurt and mustard by hand and season with salt and pepper. For the cheese sauce, combine the cream and lemon juice and set aside for 10 to 15 minutes to sour. Add the ricotta and stracchino cheeses to the cream mixture and stir until smooth. Stir in the paprika and chives and salt to taste. Serve the crudités on a platter with the sauces in small bowls for dipping.

« BAGNA CAUDA »
CRUDITÉS DIPPED IN ANCHOVY-GARLIC SAUCE

Literally translated as "warm bath," bagna cauda is a dipping sauce from Piedmont made with abundant anchovies, oil, and garlic. Diners dip raw vegetables into the warm sauce, which is ideally served in special pot over a heating apparatus—like an Italian fondue. This isn't the traditional recipe for this Italian classic, but a lighter version that is just as good. I want to thank Mino Ambrosiani, who gave me his secret for a light and easy-to-digest bagna cauda.

SERVES 6 TO 8

2 heads garlic, cloves separated and peeled
1 pint plus 1 $^1/_2$ tablespoons ($^1/_2$ liter) milk
4 to 5 tablespoons (60 to 70 grams) unsalted butter
10 $^1/_2$ ounces (300 grams) anchovy fillets in oil, drained
1 cup (250 milliliters) extra-virgin olive oil
1 red bell pepper, cut into sticks
1 head Savoy cabbage, cored and cut into wedges
2 carrots, cut into sticks
1 Jerusalem artichoke, cut into sticks

In a pot, cook the garlic in the milk over very low heat so that the cloves don't boil but instead slowly soften and dissolve. The resulting liquid should be creamy. In a pan, melt the butter and sauté the anchovies over very low heat until they dissolve, about 20 minutes. Add the anchovy butter to the garlic mixture and cook for an additional 5 minutes. Stir in the oil, cook for a few minutes to allow the flavors to marry, and serve the sauce warm with the raw vegetables for dipping.

« TERRINA DI PROSCIUTTO E PISTACCHI »
PROSCIUTTO AND PISTACHIO TERRINE

A plain prosciutto terrine can be a little mundane. This one is made more colorful and flavorful through the addition of pistachios! The prosciutto used here is prosciutto cotto, or cooked prosciutto—similar to baked ham.

SERVES 4 TO 6

1 3/4 pounds (800 grams) prosciutto cotto
1 cup (2 sticks) plus 5 tablespoons (300 grams) unsalted butter, softened
1 tablespoon brandy
White pepper to taste
Salt to taste
1/4 cup (25 grams) shelled pistachios, chopped
Toasted bread

Line a loaf pan with plastic wrap and set aside. In a food processor fitted with the metal blade, process the prosciutto. Add 1 stick plus 6 tablespoons (200 grams) of the butter, the brandy, and pepper and process until soft and fluffy. Taste and adjust salt. In a bowl, mix the pistachios with the remaining 7 tablespoons (100 grams) butter. Transfer half the prosciutto mixture into the prepared pan and smooth with a spatula. Arrange the pistachio mixture on top in an even layer. Top with the remaining prosciutto mixture and smooth. Refrigerate until chilled. To serve, unmold onto a platter, peel away the plastic wrap, and serve with toast.

« MARÒ LIGURE »
FAVA BEAN "PÂTÉ"

Despite the fact that I lived in the Liguria region for my entire childhood and young adulthood, I first heard of this dish just a few years ago. I loved it immediately. This is a simple purée of fresh fava beans flavored with thyme, cheese, oil, and garlic.

SERVES 4 TO 6

14 ounces (400 grams) shelled fresh fava beans, boiled until very soft,
    cooking water reserved
Fresh thyme leaves to taste
1/2 clove garlic, peeled
2 to 3 tablespoons grated Parmesan
Salt to taste
1/2 cup (100 milliliters) extra-virgin olive oil
Salami, pecorino cheese, and toasted bread for serving

If you have the patience, remove the skins around the fava beans. Add them to a food processor fitted with the metal blade. Add the thyme leaves, garlic, Parmesan, salt, and oil and process until smooth. With the processor running, slowly add the cooking water through the tube until the mixture is smooth and spreadable. Transfer the pâté to a bowl and serve with salami, pecorino, and toast.

« TERRINA DI FAVE E ASPARAGI »
TERRINE OF FAVA BEANS AND ASPARAGUS

This terrine is wrapped in pancetta, and when you slice it, you'll reveal tender asparagus in a fava filling. I made it for a recent family gathering at my country house and it was a hit. Unfortunately, I only made one terrine and there were twenty of us! My sister was the last to arrive, and although she heard about it, she never got to taste it.

SERVES 4 TO 6

9 ounces (250 grams) asparagus
10 ounces (300 grams) shelled fresh fava beans
2 large eggs
2/3 cup (150 grams) ricotta
1/3 cup (30 grams) grated Parmesan
Salt to taste
4 ounces (120 grams) thinly sliced pancetta

Preheat the oven to 320°F (160°C). Steam the asparagus until tender. Separately, boil the fava beans until soft, about 15 minutes; drain, cool slightly, then remove the skins. In a food processor fitted with the metal blade, puree the fava beans with the eggs, ricotta, and Parmesan. Season lightly with salt (keep in mind that the pancetta wrap will be salty). Line a loaf pan with the pancetta slices, letting them hang over the side. Fill the pan with half of the fava mixture and smooth with a spatula. Arrange the cooked asparagus stalks in a single layer, then top with the remaining fava mixture. Fold the pancetta over the top and bake until the pancetta is crispy, 40 to 50 minutes.

« TERRINA DI PESCI AFFUMICATI »
SMOKED FISH TERRINE

This terrine is easy to make, but it's wonderful. The different colors make it really special.

SERVES 4 TO 6

3/4 cup plus 1 tablespoon (200 grams) heavy cream
Juice of 1 lemon
5 sheets (10 grams) gelatin
10 ounces (300 grams) smoked salmon
Pepper to taste
10 ounces (300 grams) smoked swordfish
2 tablespoons vodka
Minced fresh marjoram, chives, and dill to taste

Combine the cream with the lemon juice and set aside for 10 to 15 minutes to sour. Soak the gelatin in cold water to soften. Meanwhile, combine the smoked salmon and about half of the soured cream in a food processor fitted with a metal blade. Add a generous grinding of pepper and process until smooth. Remove to a bowl and set aside. Clean the bowl and blade of the food processor and process the swordfish with the remaining soured cream and some more pepper until smooth. Remove to a second bowl and set aside. Remove the softened gelatin and transfer to a small pot with the vodka. Place over low heat and simmer gently until the gelatin dissolves.

Add half of the gelatin mixture to the salmon mixture and the remaining gelatin mixture to the swordfish mixture. Stir both to combine thoroughly. Line a loaf pan with plastic wrap. Add the salmon mixture and smooth with a spatula. Sprinkle with the marjoram, chives, and dill in an even layer. Top the herbs with the swordfish mixture and smooth the top. Fold the plastic over the top and refrigerate the terrine until set, at least 4 hours. To serve, unmold to a platter and carefully peel off the plastic wrap.

« PÂTÉ ALLA MELAGRANA »
POMEGRANATE PÂTÉ

At my house, pâté is a must on the Christmas table. Over the years, I've made it many different ways, but this is the festive version that I prefer for the holidays—the pomegranate gelatin gives it a lovely color and unique flavor. Guanciale is Italian cured pork jowl. If you can't locate it, you can substitute pancetta or even bacon.

SERVES 6 TO 8

5 sheets (10 grams) gelatin
Seeds of 1 to 2 pomegranates, plus additional for garnish (optional)
1 yellow onion, sliced
Extra-virgin olive oil for sautéing
4 ounces (120 grams) guanciale, chopped
10 ounces (300 grams) veal loin, chopped
Salt and pepper to taste
9 ounces (250 grams) calf's liver, chopped
1/2 cup (100 milliliters) Marsala wine
1 sprig thyme
1 sprig rosemary
1 bay leaf
1 whole clove
1 cup (1 stick) plus 6 tablespoons (200 grams) unsalted butter

Soak the gelatin in cold water to soften. In a food processor fitted with the metal blade, puree the pomegranate seeds, then transfer them to a fine-mesh strainer or chinois to collect the juice. Transfer the pomegranate juice to a small pot, add the softened gelatin, and heat gently. Meanwhile, line a loaf pan with plastic wrap. When the gelatin has dissolved, pour the pomegranate juice and gelatin mixture into the pan and refrigerate until set. In a large pan, sauté the onion in a small amount of oil until soft. Add the guanciale and the veal loin to the pan and lightly brown. Season to taste with salt and pepper, then add the calf's liver. When the liver has browned, add the Marsala. Add the thyme, rosemary, bay leaf, and the clove and cook, covered, until the meat is cooked through. Remove the thyme, rosemary, bay leaf, and clove and discard. Transfer the meat and any juices to a food processor fitted with the metal blade. Add the butter and process until smooth. Pour the meat mixture over the pomegranate gelatin in the loaf pan, smooth the top with a spatula, cover with the plastic wrap, and refrigerate until set. To serve, unmold the pâté onto a platter and carefully peel away the plastic. Cut into slices. Garnish the pâté with some additional pomegranate seeds if you like.

« CHIPS POLENTA E FUNGHI »
FRIED POLENTA WITH MUSHROOMS

I love breaded and fried mushrooms, but for this dish I bread and fry pieces of polenta instead, then serve them with a porcini mushroom preparation that is very light yet deliciously flavorful. Paired with a glass of red wine, this antipasto gets any dinner off to a great start. Choose the readymade polenta that's sold in a tube—just slice and use.

SERVES 4 TO 6

Mushrooms
1/2 cup (100 milliliters) heavy cream
Juice of 1/2 lemon
7 ounces (200 grams) frozen porcini mushrooms
1 clove garlic, peeled
Extra-virgin olive oil for sautéing
Salt to taste
Minced fresh chives to taste
1 egg white (optional)

Polenta
1 pound (500 grams) readymade polenta
Finely ground corn meal for dredging
Peanut oil for deep-frying

To make the mushrooms, combine the cream and the lemon juice and set aside to sour, 10 to 15 minutes. Meanwhile, sauté the mushrooms and garlic clove in a small amount of oil over medium-high heat until the mushrooms are golden and soft. Remove and discard the garlic, salt the mushrooms, and transfer them to a cutting board. Roughly chop the mushrooms. Add the mushrooms and chives to the soured cream. If you prefer more of a mousse than a sauce, beat the egg white to soft peaks and fold it into the mushroom mixture.

To make the polenta, slice the polenta very thinly, $1/10$ inch (2 millimeters) or less. Dredge the polenta slices in corn meal, and fry them in a generous amount of hot peanut oil until brown and crisp. Drain briefly on paper towels and serve hot with the mushrooms.

« CROCCHETTE DI PATATE E MOZZARELLA »
POTATO AND MOZZARELLA CROQUETTES

I used to buy croquettes like these in the frozen food section of the supermarket. One day, I tried my hand at making them and I realized they're not difficult at all. If you boil the potatoes in advance, they're quick, too. Not only that, but the homemade version tastes much better.

SERVES 4

2 pounds (1 kilogram) potatoes
2 tablespoons (30 grams) unsalted butter
2 large egg yolks
$1/3$ cup (30 grams) grated Parmesan
Salt to taste
1 fresh mozzarella ball (8 ounces/225 grams)
Anchovy fillets in oil, *quanto basta*

1 large egg, lightly beaten
Breadcrumbs for dredging
Vegetable oil for deep-frying

Boil, peel, and mash the potatoes. Mix the potatoes with the butter, egg yolks, and Parmesan until well combined. Season with salt (but remember that the croquettes will have anchovies in the center) and set aside to cool. Once the potato mixture has cooled, cut the mozzarella into cubes. Pull off a small piece of the potato mixture and form it into a ball, placing a mozzarella cube and half of an anchovy fillet in the center. Roll the croquette between your palms to make it slightly oval with tapered ends. Repeat with the remaining potato mixture, mozzarella, and anchovies. Dredge the croquettes first in the beaten egg and then in the breadcrumbs and fry until brown and crisp. Drain briefly on paper towels and serve hot.

« CROCCHETTE GENOVESI »
GENOESE POTATO CROQUETTES

These are classic potato croquettes with a little touch of something extra in the form of Genoa's most famous sauce—pesto—and mozzarella. Take care when frying these to leave them in the oil just until browned—if they fry for too long the filling will begin to leak out and spatter everywhere.

SERVES 4 TO 6

1 $^1/_2$ pounds (700 grams) potatoes
2 large eggs
$^1/_3$ cup (30 grams) grated Parmesan
$^1/_4$ cup plus 2 tablespoons (100 grams) readymade pesto
Salt and pepper to taste
Nutmeg to taste
2 fresh mozzarella balls (8 ounces/225 grams), diced
Unbleached all-purpose flour for dredging
Breadcrumbs for dredging
Vegetable oil for deep-frying

Boil, peel, and mash the potatoes. In a large bowl, mix the potatoes, 1 egg, Parmesan, and pesto with the salt, pepper, and nutmeg until well combined. Wetting your hands occasionally to keep them from sticking, form the dough into a long cylinder and cut it into croquettes. Stuff each croquette with one or more cubes of mozzarella, being sure to enclose the cheese completely in the potato mixture. Lightly beat the remaining egg in a small bowl. Dredge the croquettes first in the flour, then in the beaten egg, and then in the breadcrumbs; fry until just golden. Drain briefly on paper towels and serve hot.

« PILOT DI PATATE »
PIEDMONT POTATO FRITTERS

These potato fritters, a specialty of the Piedmont region, are made with a mixture of salami, potatoes, and grated Parmesan cheese. It's impossible not to like them!

SERVES 4 TO 6

Extra-virgin olive oil for sautéing
2 yellow onions, sliced
5 ounces (150 grams) peeled salami, crumbled
1 ⅓ pounds (600 grams) potatoes
6 large eggs, lightly beaten
2 tablespoons grated Parmesan
Salt and pepper to taste
Vegetable oil for pan-frying

In a sauté pan with a small amount of olive oil, sauté the onions with the salami. Let the mixture cool, then transfer to a large bowl. Peel the potatoes and grate them on the large holes of a four-sided box grater, letting the grated potatoes fall into the same bowl. Add the eggs, mix well to combine, then stir in the grated cheese. Season with salt and pepper. Heat an inch or two of vegetable oil in a pan and drop in a few spoonfuls of the salami mixture. Don't crowd the pan. Cook the fritters until browned, then turn and cook until browned on the other side. Remove cooked fritters to paper towels and repeat with remaining salami mixture. Serve hot.

« CROCCHETTE DI ROSA »
ROSA'S COD CROQUETTES

Raise your hand if you can resist fried food. Anybody? Me neither! Well, these seem fried, but they're actually baked in the oven. They're healthier, they're easy, and they'll help keep your kitchen clean, too. My friend Rosa came up with these for her children. I like to serve them to guests, but when I do I have to fend off my own kids, Matilde, Eleonora, and Diego, who happily eat them as well.

SERVES 4

10 ounces (300 grams) cod fillet
7 ounces (200 grams) shelled shrimp
1 large egg
3 tablespoons grated Parmesan
1 teaspoon grated, peeled fresh ginger
Juice of ½ lemon
Parsley leaves to taste
Salt to taste
Extra-virgin olive oil for making a smooth mixture and for drizzling
Breadcrumbs for dredging

Preheat the oven to 350° F (180° C). Line a baking sheet with parchment paper. Check to make sure there are no bones left in the cod. Place the fish in a food processor fitted with the metal blade along with the shrimp, egg, cheese, ginger, lemon juice, and parsley. Process until ground together, then season with salt and add enough oil to make a smooth mixture that forms a ball when you pinch off a piece and squeeze it in your fist. Take about 1 tablespoon of the cod mixture and form it into a croquette. Repeat with remaining mixture. Dredge the croquettes in the breadcrumbs and arrange on the prepared baking sheet. Drizzle with a little olive oil and bake until crisp, about 20 minutes, turning the croquettes halfway through. Serve hot.

« ALICI FRITTE »
FRIED ANCHOVIES

Oily fish like anchovies are not only relatively inexpensive, but rich in omega-3 fatty acids—and simply delicious when fried. So, allow yourself to indulge in these fried treats every once in a while.

SERVES 4

1/4 cup breadcrumbs, plus more for dredging
7 ounces (200 grams) mild cheese, such as provolone, or 1 to 2
**   tablespoons grated Parmesan**
Leaves of 1 sprig parsley
Salt to taste
10 ounces (300 grams) fresh anchovies, gutted, boned, and butterflied
Unbleached all-purpose flour for dredging
1 large egg, lightly beaten
Vegetable oil for deep-frying

In a food processor fitted with the metal blade, process the breadcrumbs, cheese, parsley leaves, and a pinch of salt. Stuff the anchovies with this mixture, then press the two halves of each anchovy together firmly to close. Dredge the anchovies in the flour, then the egg, then the breadcrumbs. Fry until golden, which should take only a few minutes, and serve immediately.

Note: You can also make fried anchovies with the breadcrumb mixture on the outside. Prepare the breadcrumb mixture, then dredge the anchovies in the egg and then the breadcrumbs, skipping the flour. Press the two halves of each anchovy together firmly and fry.

« PATATE ROMANTICHE »
"ROMANTIC" FRIED POTATOES WITH SAGE

I made these "romantic" potatoes for my husband, Fabio, the first time he appeared on my show.

SERVES 2

1 potato
Sage leaves, *quanto basta*
1 egg white
Vegetable oil for pan-frying
Coarse sea salt

Peel the potato, rinse it to wash off the starch, dry it, and slice it as thinly as possible. (The slices should be somewhat transparent.) Wash the sage leaves and dry thoroughly between paper towels. Brush one slice of potato with a little of the egg white, place a sage leaf on top, and place a second potato slice on top. (In other words, you're making a sandwich with the sage leaf as the filling.) Press together firmly. Repeat with remaining potato slices. Heat enough vegetable oil in a pan to submerge the potato sandwiches completely. Drop in a few, taking care not to crowd the pan, and cook until browned. (If you have enough oil in the pan, you shouldn't need to turn them.) With a slotted spoon, remove to paper towels and repeat with the remaining potato sandwiches. Sprinkle with coarse salt and serve hot.

« LE MIE OLIVE ASCOLANE »
FRIED STUFFED OLIVES, MY WAY

Last year I got the idea to make olives the way they do in Ascoli, where they stuff them with meat, bread them, and fry them. I love them, but I usually buy the frozen ones in the grocery store that are pre-stuffed—all I have to do is fry them. The challenge, besides striking the right balance with the filling, was going to be pitting all those olives one by one. So I bought pitted olives and cut them in half the long way, then I made tiny meatballs and stuffed them between the olive halves. I dredged them in flour, beaten egg, and breadcrumbs, and fried them. Those olives were amazing! Unfortunately, I lost the piece of paper where I'd written the recipe. Then, a year later, I found it in the kids' toy box! Now that I've included the recipe in this book, I know I won't ever misplace it again.

SERVES 6 TO 8

5 ounces (150 grams) frozen mirepoix (minced carrots, onion, and celery)
Extra-virgin olive oil for sautéing
4 ounces (100 grams) ground chicken
4 ounces (100 grams) ground pork
4 ounces (100 grams) ground beef
1 tablespoon tomato paste dissolved in 1 tablespoon water
2 1/2 ounces (70 grams) prosciutto crudo
2 1/2 ounces (70 grams) mortadella
2 ounces (50 grams) Parmesan
3/4 ounce (20 grams) pecorino
2 slices white sandwich bread, crusts removed
1/4 cup (50 milliliters) whole milk
2 large eggs
20 pitted green olives
Unbleached all-purpose flour for dredging
Breadcrumbs for dredging
Vegetable oil for deep-frying

Sauté the mirepoix in a small amount of olive oil to defrost it. Add the ground meats and the dissolved tomato paste, and cook until the meat is cooked through. Transfer the meat mixture to a food processor fitted with the metal blade and process along with the prosciutto, mortadella, Parmesan, pecorino, bread, and milk. Add 1 egg and process to combine. Cut the olives in half the long way. Pinch off a small amount of the meat mixture and stuff it between two halves of an olive. Press together. Repeat with remaining filling and olives. Lightly beat the remaining egg. Dredge the stuffed olives in the flour, then the beaten egg, and then the breadcrumbs. Fry in a generous amount of oil until browned. Remove with a skimmer and serve hot.

« POLPETTE DI FORMAGGIO »
FRIED CHEESE BALLS

These are great either as a cocktail snack or vegetarian entrée.

SERVES 4

1/2 cup (100 grams) ricotta
2 cups (200 grams) grated pecorino (not overly aged)
Minced oregano leaves to taste
Minced mint leaves to taste
3 large eggs
2 tablespoons breadcrumbs, plus more for dredging
Vegetable oil for deep-frying
Salt to taste

In a bowl, combine the ricotta and the pecorino. Mix in the minced herbs. Add 2 eggs and mix again. Sprinkle with 2 tablespoons breadcrumbs, then form the mixture into balls. Lightly beat the remaining egg. Dredge the balls first in the egg and then in the breadcrumbs. Fry until golden brown. Drain briefly on paper towels, season with salt, and serve hot.

« FRITTO DI ASPARAGI E BURRATA »
FRIED ASPARAGUS AND BURRATA

This is a dish for people who really love to eat, and I'm one of them—it's one of my all-time favorites. Burrata—a soft, creamy cheese—is already pretty great in its natural state, but when mixed with anchovies and cream it gets even better. I serve the cheese in an attractive bowl, arrange the fried asparagus and eggs alongside, and let diners serve themselves. It looks very chic, if I do say so myself!

SERVES 2

3 large eggs
6 asparagus stalks

9 ounces (250 grams) burrata
3 anchovy fillets in oil, drained
1/4 cup (50 milliliters) whole milk
1/4 cup (50 milliliters) heavy cream
Breadcrumbs for dredging
Vegetable oil for deep-frying
Salt to taste

Place 2 eggs in a small pot and add water to cover. Bring to a boil, reduce heat to a simmer, and simmer 10 minutes to make hard-boiled eggs. Put the eggs under cold running water until cool, then peel them and set aside. Cook the asparagus in boiling salted water, leaving it fairly al dente. In a blender or food processor fitted with the metal blade, process the burrata and anchovy fillets, adding enough milk to make a creamy mixture. (You may not need all the milk.) Whip the cream to soft peaks and fold it into the cheese mixture.

Cut the hard-boiled eggs in half the long way. Lightly beat the remaining egg. Dredge both the asparagus and the hard-boiled egg halves first in the beaten egg and then in breadcrumbs. Fry in a generous amount of oil until golden and serve alongside the cheese mixture.

« ONION RING E SALVIA FRITTA »
ONION RINGS AND FRIED SAGE

Serving some fried tidbits during cocktail hour is always a winning strategy. The only problem is that they have to be prepared at the last minute so that they're crisp and hot, which means the host is in the kitchen rather than circulating with guests. But it's worth it.

SERVES 4

2 yellow onions
3/4 cup (100 grams) unbleached all-purpose flour, plus more for dredging
1 teaspoon baking powder
Salt to taste

Sparkling water, *quanto basta*
Breadcrumbs for dredging
Vegetable oil for deep-frying
Leaves of 1 bunch sage

Peel the onions and cut them into thick slices, then separate the slices into rings. Whisk together the flour, baking powder, and a little salt. Whisk in enough sparkling water to make a batter that is not too runny. Dredge the onion rings first in the batter, then in the breadcrumbs, and fry in hot oil. Dredge the sage leaves in the batter and fry those as well. Drain briefly on paper towels and serve hot.

« FRITTELLE DELL'ORTO »
VEGETABLE FRITTERS

These are wonderful as an appetizer, but they also work as a side dish. Unlike most fried foods, they are best served at room temperature. I encourage my guests to eat them with their hands.

SERVES 4 TO 6

4 cups (500 grams) unbleached all-purpose flour
1 1/2 teaspoons baking powder
Salt to taste
1 carrot, cut into matchsticks
1 zucchini, cut into matchsticks
Vegetable oil for deep-frying

In a large bowl, sift together the flour and the baking powder. Add salt and whisk in enough water to make a thick, smooth batter. Cover and set aside at room temperature for 45 to 60 minutes. Divide the batter between 2 bowls. Stir the carrot matchsticks into one portion of batter. Stir the zucchini matchsticks into into the other portion. Fry 1-tablespoon portions of the batter and vegetables in hot oil until golden. Transfer to paper towels to drain and sprinkle with a little additional salt.

« FRITTELLE DI SPINACI E STRACCHINO »
SPINACH PANCAKES AND STRACCHINO CHEESE

These pancakes are easy to prepare. Stracchino is a soft cheese that not only adds flavor, but melts when it's spread between the hot pancakes and helps hold them together.

SERVES 2

2 large eggs
3 tablespoons unbleached all-purpose flour
Salt and pepper to taste
3 $1/2$ ounces (100 grams) fresh spinach
1 teaspoon baking powder
$1/4$ cup (50 milliliters) whole milk
Extra-virgin olive oil for cooking the pancakes
9 ounces (250 grams) stracchino cheese

Mix the eggs and flour. Season with salt and pepper and whisk until smooth. Mince the spinach (a food processor is great for this) and add it to the egg mixture, whisking until well combined. Add the baking powder and milk to the batter and whisk until smooth. Heat a skillet and lightly coat it with oil. Drop about $1/3$ of the batter into the skillet to form a round pancake. Cook until bubbles form on the top, then flip and cook until set. Remove to a warm plate. (You can put the cooked pancakes in the oven set on low to keep them warm.) Repeat to make 3 pancakes in all. Place one of the pancakes on a serving platter and spread about $1/2$ of the stracchino on top. Place another pancake on top, and spread with the remaining stracchino. Top the cheese with the final pancake. Press gently with your hands so that some of the cheese comes out the sides. Slice into wedges and serve.

« ROTOLINI DI PORRO E SPECK E TORTELLINI FRITTI »
LEEKS, SPECK, AND FRIED TORTELLINI

The idea of frying fresh (not boiled) tortellini is pure genius. They come out crunchy and delicious, and I find guests often can't figure out what they are. You can use pasta with either a vegetable or meat filling—you want the kind sold in the refrigerator case at your supermarket. I like to serve leek and speck bundles with them. Speck is a cured pork product.

SERVES 4

2 ounces (50 grams) scamorza cheese
1 leek
3 1/2 ounces (100 grams) speck, cut into rectangles
1 egg white
Breadcrumbs for dredging
Vegetable oil for deep-frying
1 package refrigerated (not frozen or dried) readymade tortellini
Salt to taste

Cut the cheese into matchsticks. Make a slit in the leek the long way, open it like a book, and blanch it for a few minutes. Drain the leek and cut it into squares. Wrap each piece of cheese with a piece of speck, and then enclose both in a piece of leek. Roll up the packets and dredge them in the egg white and then in breadcrumbs. Be sure to cover the ends with breadcrumbs so that the cheese doesn't leak out. Fry in hot oil until golden. Fry the tortellini until golden in the same oil. Remove with a slotted spoon, salt lightly, and serve.

« STECCHI DI POLPETTINE »
CHICKEN MEATBALL SKEWERS

These are very light steamed chicken meatballs, made tasty through the addition of green onion and olives. I roll them in creamy cheese and chopped pistachios and serve them on wooden skewers.

SERVES 4

1 pound 5 ounces (600 grams) chicken meat
1 green onion
$^1/_3$ cup (60 grams) taggiasca olives, pitted
1 ounce (30 grams) pecorino
Salt and pepper to taste
1 large egg
14 cup (80 grams) shelled pistachios
Spreadable cheese, *quanto basta*

Cut the chicken into cubes, then place it in a food processor fitted with the metal blade, along with the onion, olives, pecorino, and salt and pepper. Process until finely ground. Add the egg and process again to combine. With wet hands (to keep the mixture from sticking) form the chicken mixture into small meatballs, about twelve in all. Cook the meatballs in a steamer until the chicken is fully cooked, about 15 minutes. Drop the cooked meatballs into ice water for a few seconds to cool them. Meanwhile, chop the pistachios. Stir the spreadable cheese with a spoon to soften it. Drain the cooked meatballs and roll them first in the cheese and then in the pistachios. Thread wooden skewers with 3 meatballs apiece and serve.

« POLPETTE CON FRUTTA SECCA »
VEGETARIAN "MEATBALLS" WITH NUTS

Who says the big-name chefs only make fancy dishes? Bruno Barbieri, one of the three judges on Italian MasterChef, loves a good meatball! He made this meatless version with nuts and a cheese sauce when he appeared on my show.

SERVES 4

1 large or 2 medium (220 grams) potatoes
1 pound (500 grams) fresh spinach
Butter for sautéing
Extra-virgin olive oil for sautéing
Grated Parmesan to taste
1 large egg, separated
Salt and pepper to taste
Chopped hazelnuts and pistachios (keep them separate) or sliced
    almonds for coating
1 cup (250 milliliters) heavy cream
7 ounces (200 grams) sweet Gorgonzola
1 bay leaf

To make the meatballs, boil, peel, and mash the potatoes. Transfer the mashed potatoes to a bowl. Sauté the spinach in butter and oil, then mince the cooked spinach (in a food processor fitted with the metal blade or with a knife), and combine with the mashed potatoes. Add the Parmesan, the yolk of the egg, salt, pepper, and just enough egg white to bind the mixture so that you can form the mixture into small balls. Form balls the size of a walnut. Dredge the balls in the hazelnuts and then the pistachios, or just in the almonds. Brown them in a small amount of oil. To make the cheese sauce, combine the cream and Gorgonzola in a small pot, add the bay leaf, and season with salt and pepper. Heat gently, stirring frequently, until the cheese mixture forms a smooth sauce. Remove and discard the bay leaf. Serve the meatballs on a pool of the cheese sauce.

« RUOTA DI CARNE »
MEAT PINWHEEL

This dish is as interesting as the writer who taught me to make it, Simonetta Agnello Hornby. It reflects her Sicilian background, and it looks beautiful, too.

SERVES 4 TO 6

10 ounces (300 grams) ground veal
10 ounces (300 grams) ground pork
1 large egg
3 tablespoons breadcrumbs

3 tablespoons grated Parmesan
Salt and pepper to taste
Whole milk, *quanto basta*
1 onion
Extra-virgin olive oil for coating and drizzling
Bay leaves for interspersing
Juice of 1 lemon

Preheat the oven to 350° F (180° C). Place the veal and pork in a large bowl. Add the egg, 1 tablespoon breadcrumbs, 1 tablespoon cheese, salt, and pepper and combine, then add enough milk to make a moist mixture. Fill a small bowl with water. Wet your hands with the water and begin to shape the meat mixture into ovals the size and shape of a small egg. Wet your hands in the bowl of water periodically to keep the mixture from sticking until you have made all the meatballs.

Cut the onion into wedges and break into petals. Cradle a meatball in each petal. Lightly oil a round baking dish and sprinkle about 1 tablespoon breadcrumbs on the bottom of the dish. Beginning in the center of the dish, create a spiral by alternating meatballs in onion petals with bay leaves. Start with the larger outer pieces of onion and move down in size so that the smallest ones are on the outside of the spiral. When you've fit all the meatballs into the dish, sprinkle the remaining 1 tablespoon bread-crumbs and 2 tablespoons cheese on top and drizzle with a little oil. Bake until the meatballs are crisp but take care not to burn them, 20 to 30 minutes. Remove from the oven, sprinkle with the lemon juice, and allow to rest 10 minutes before serving.

« POLPETTE E SALAME »
FAVA BALLS AND SALAMI

Salami and fava beans are a perfect combination. When I have an informal gathering, I often serve a big basket of fresh fava beans in the pods and a salami and let people cut off chunks for themselves. Here is a slightly more elegant presentation of those same ingredients. I usually use toothpicks and spear one fava ball and one piece of salami on each one.

SERVES 4

7 ounces (200 grams) shelled fava beans
1 green onion
Salt to taste
1 1/2 ounces (40 grams) pecorino
2 large eggs, separated
1 1/3 cups (300 grams) ricotta
Unbleached all-purpose flour for dredging
Vegetable oil for deep-frying
Salami slices, *quanto basta*

Boil the fava beans and remove the tough skin around each bean. Place the cooked fava beans and the onion in a food processor. Season with salt, and process. Add the pecorino cheese and the yolks of the 2 eggs and process again. Using your hands, mix in the ricotta and form small balls. Dredge the balls in the egg whites and then the flour. Fry the balls in a generous amount of oil, then skewer them on toothpicks with the salami slices.

POLPETTE DI TONNO
TUNA MEATBALLS

Children love tuna meatballs like these.

SERVES 4

1 slice white sandwich bread
1/4 cup (50 milliliters) whole milk
1 (5-ounce/150-gram) can tuna in oil, drained
2 large eggs
Minced parsley to taste
Salt to taste
1/2 cup (50 grams) breadcrumbs
Vegetable oil for deep-frying

Soften the sandwich bread in the milk and crumble it. Combine the tuna with the crumbled bread mixture. Add 1 egg, the parsley, and salt and knead until thoroughly combined. Shape the mixture into small balls. Dredge the balls in the remaining egg, lightly beaten, and then in the breadcrumbs and fry in a generous amount of oil. Taste and sprinkle with salt if needed before serving.

« RICOTTINE AL FORNO »
MINI RICOTTA SOUFFLÉS

These small ricotta soufflés, spiced up with sun-dried tomatoes, get any dinner off on the right foot. A few drops of honey add an unexpected grace note.

SERVES 4 TO 6

4 ounces (about 25 pieces/125 grams) sun-dried tomatoes in oil
1 1/4 cups (250 grams) ricotta
1/2 teaspoon minced chives
1/2 teaspoon thyme leaves
2 ounces (50 grams) Parmesan, grated
3 1/2 ounces (100 grams) soft goat cheese
1 egg white
Salt and pepper to taste
Extra-virgin olive oil for oiling dishes
Honey to taste

Preheat the oven to 350° F (180° C). In a food processor fitted with the metal blade, process about 15 sun-dried tomatoes with the ricotta, chives, thyme, Parmesan, goat cheese, and egg white. Season with salt and pepper and pulse until well combined. Oil small ramekins and transfer the ricotta mixture to the ramekins. Bake until golden brown, about 25 minutes. Mince the remaining sun-dried tomatoes and sprinkle them over the soufflés. Drizzle with a little honey and serve hot.

« BIGNÈ AL GRANA »
CHEESE PUFFS

These little puffs are great for showing off your skills. They have a buttery flavor that makes them irresistible. Serve them with some sparkling wine and you'll impress your guests.

SERVES 4

Extra-virgin olive oil for oiling pan
7 tablespoons (100 grams) unsalted butter
Salt to taste
1 $^1/_4$ cups (150 grams) unbleached all-purpose flour
3 large eggs, lightly beaten
3 $^1/_2$ ounces (100 grams) Parmesan, grated
Grated nutmeg to taste

Preheat the oven to 350° F (180° C). Oil a jelly-roll pan and set aside. Place 1 cup (250 milliliters) water in a pot and bring to a boil. Add the butter and a pinch of salt. Reduce to a low simmer and add the flour, whisking to combine well and eliminate any clumps. Transfer the flour and butter mixture to a bowl and add the eggs, whisking vigorously to keep them from curdling. Whisk in the Parmesan and season with nutmeg. Allow the dough to cool to room temperature, and then shape it into small balls. Place the balls on the prepared pan and bake until golden, 10 to 12 minutes.

« SOUFFLÉ AL FORMAGGIO »
CHEESE SOUFFLÉ

Making a soufflé is considered the test of a true chef, but here's a little secret: It's not that difficult. It's all about the timing. Rule number one: Never open the oven during baking. Rule number two: Serve immediately, because a soufflé deflates in about 30 seconds. That said, you need to get it to the table quickly in order to receive the praise due to you. However, a soufflé tastes delicious even after it falls, so you don't need to worry about dishing it out and eating it immediately.

SERVES 4

3 tablespoons (40 grams) unsalted butter, plus more for buttering dishes
1/4 cup plus 2 tablespoons (50 grams) unbleached all-purpose flour, plus
    more for flouring dishes
3/4 cup plus 1 tablespoon (200 milliliters) whole milk at room
    temperature
Salt to taste
Grated nutmeg to taste
7 ounces (200 grams) Gruyère, grated
3 1/2 ounces (100 grams) Parmesan, grated
3 large eggs, separated
White pepper to taste

Preheat the oven to 320° F (160° C). Butter one large soufflé dish or individual dishes. Dust with flour, shaking out any excess. Set aside. Make a béchamel: Place the butter in a pot and melt over low heat. Add the flour, stirring to combine thoroughly with the butter, then slowly pour in the milk. Cook, stirring constantly, to thicken. Taste and season with salt and nutmeg, then remove from the heat. Immediately stir in both cheeses, the egg yolks, and white pepper. Stir to combine thoroughly (you can use your hands if you like) and set aside to cool. When the mixture has cooled, whip the reserved egg whites to stiff peaks and fold them into the cheese mixture. Pour the mixture into the prepared soufflé dish or dishes and bake for 35 minutes. (Remember not to open the oven door during baking.) Serve as quickly as possible.

« SPUMANTE DI MELA CON BIGNÈ »
SPARKLING WINE WITH CALVADOS AND TUNA PUFFS

This sounds like a complicated dish, but all of it can be made in advance, it doesn't require that much effort, and yields great returns. It's perfect for a romantic evening. Calvados is apple brandy.

SERVES 4

5 ounces (150 grams) robiola cheese
1 (3 1/2-ounce/100-gram) single-serving can tuna in oil, drained

10 readymade prebaked pastry shells
1 red apple
1 ¹/₂ cups (350 milliliters) Calvados
1 vanilla bean
1 cinnamon stick
1 bottle (750 milliliters) sparkling white wine, chilled

For the filling for the puffs, in a food processor fitted with the metal blade, process the robiola with the tuna. If the pastry shells are the closed type, cut off the tops. If they aren't hollow, use a finger to make room for the filling. Fill each shell with some of the tuna mixture, replace the tops, and set aside to rest for at least 1 hour so the filling flavors the pastry and softens it a little.

To make the sparkling wine cocktail, core the apple and cut it into thin slices. Pour the Calvados into a bowl and macerate the apple slices in it, along with the vanilla bean and the cinnamon stick, for 1 hour. Strain the liquid, divide it among 6 champagne flutes, and distribute the sparkling wine among them. Garnish each flute with a slice or two of apple and serve along with the puffs.

« TORTA DI PISELLI »
PEA TART

My young son Diego hardly eats anything! Peas are one of the few things he likes, so I turn myself inside out coming up with recipes using peas. This savory tart includes not just peas, but ricotta and mortadella, an Italian cured sausage. Even Diego is powerless to resist a slice smothered in a lovely golden saffron sauce.

SERVES 4 TO 6

Tart
Extra-virgin olive oil for sautéing
2 shallots, peeled and sliced
2 (14-ounce/800-gram) bags frozen peas
Salt to taste
1 cup (200 grams) ricotta
2 large eggs

1 egg yolk
5 ounces (150 grams) Parmesan, grated
Grated nutmeg to taste
1 package readymade short-crust pastry dough
7 ounces (200 grams) thinly sliced mortadella

Saffron Sauce
2 tablespoons ricotta
Extra-virgin olive oil to thin ricotta
1/8 teaspoon (1/2 envelope) powdered saffron dissolved in 1 tablespoon
    whole milk
Salt to taste

Preheat the oven to 350°F (180°C). Line a tart pan with parchment paper and set aside. In a pan with a little olive oil, sauté the shallots with the peas. Season with salt, add about 1/2 cup (100 milliliters) water, and cook, covered, until the peas are soft, 10 to 12 minutes. Set aside 2 to 3 tablespoons cooked peas for a garnish; transfer the rest to a blender or food processor fitted with the metal blade and process with the ricotta, eggs, egg yolk, Parmesan, and a little nutmeg.

Roll out the pastry dough and fit it into the prepared pan. Pour in half of the pea filling. Arrange the mortadella on top in a single layer. Pour the rest of the filling on top and bake until filling is set, about 40 minutes. For the sauce, combine the ricotta with a little oil to thin. Stir in the saffron milk and season with salt. Glaze the finished tart with the saffron sauce or serve the sauce on the side. Either way, garnish the finished tart with the reserved peas.

« ERBAZZONE »
SAVORY GREENS PIE

This is a classic dish from the Emilia region of Italy. It's a double-crust pie with greens.

SERVES 4

2 leeks, minced
Extra-virgin olive oil for sautéing

5 ounces (150 grams) pancetta, diced
1 pound (500 grams) Swiss chard
9 ounces (250 grams) fresh spinach
2 cloves garlic
Salt to taste
1/2 cup (50 grams) grated Parmesan
2 packages readymade puff pastry dough
Minced parsley to taste

Preheat the oven to 350° F (180° C). In a pan, sauté the leeks in oil with the pancetta. Add the chard, spinach, and garlic, season with salt, then add 1 cup (250 milliliters) water, cover the pan, and braise until the greens are cooked. Remove from the heat and set aside to cool. When the greens are cool, stir in the Parmesan. Roll out one package of dough onto a baking pan. Place the greens and parsley on top. Roll out the second package of dough and place it on top of the greens. Pierce the top crust with a fork, drizzle with a little oil, and bake until golden, about 50 minutes.

« CASATIELLO »
NEAPOLITAN SAVORY PIE

Casatiello is a rustic savory pie from Naples that is usually served at Easter. That's why it almost always includes hard-cooked eggs.

SERVES 6 TO 8

4 3/4 cups (600 grams) unbleached all-purpose flour
Salt and pepper to taste
4 ounces (120 grams) lard, melted, plus more for greasing the pan
1 envelope active dry yeast dissolved in 1 1/2 cups (350 milliliters) warm
    water
7 ounces (200 grams) spicy salami, diced
3 1/2 ounces (100 grams) provolone cheese, diced
1/2 cup (40 grams) grated Parmesan
1/2 cup (40 grams) grated pecorino
6 large eggs, thoroughly washed

CREAMY ARTICHOKE TORTE

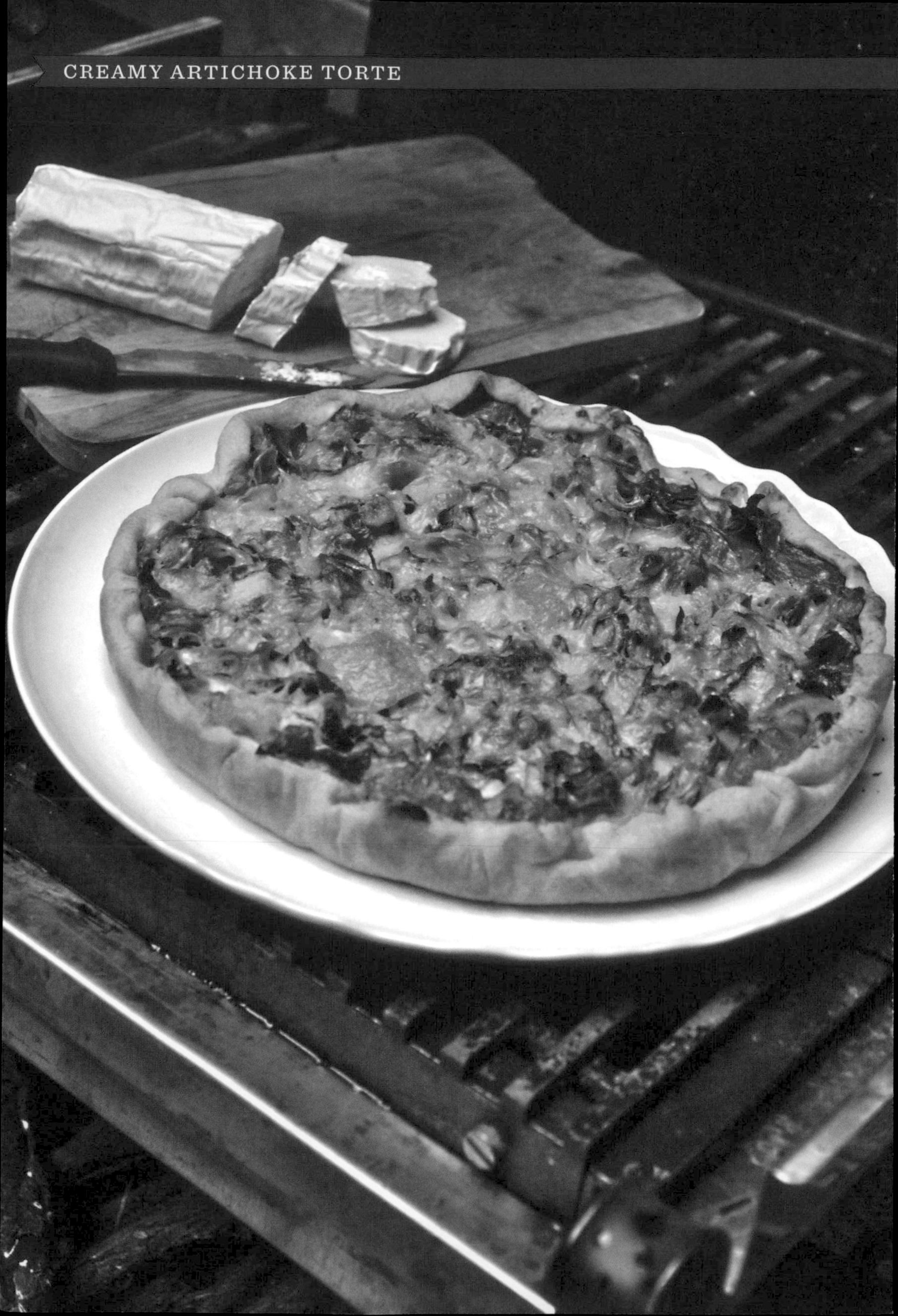

To make the dough, combine the flour with salt and pepper and the lard and stir. Slowly add the dissolved yeast, stirring. The dough should be soft and malleable. If it is too liquid, add a little flour; if it is too hard, add a little additional water. Transfer dough to a clean bowl, cover with plastic wrap, and set aside to rise for 2 hours.

Preheat the oven to 400° F (200° C). Grease a tube pan with lard. Cut off a small portion of the dough. On a lightly floured surface, roll out the remaining dough into a rectangle. In an even layer, arrange the salami and provolone on the dough running the long way. Sprinkle with the grated cheeses. Roll the rectangle into a cylinder and gently place it in the prepared pan. Pinch the ends together as you set it down. Place 5 eggs in their shells at regular intervals around the ring. Press lightly to push them into the dough. Roll the reserved dough into short strips and use the strips to make an X on top of each egg to hold it in place. Pinch the strips to the top of the ring. Lightly beat the remaining egg and brush it on top of the pie. Bake until golden brown, 40 to 45 minutes.

« TORTA SALATA CREMOSA DI CARCIOFI »
CREAMY ARTICHOKE TORTE

This savory torte can't properly be called a "quiche" because it has no eggs, but it docs have plenty of flavor. The secret weapon here is the combination of artichokes and mascarpone cheese. This was part of the buffet we enjoyed in celebration of my daughter Matilde's first communion, and it was a big hit. I actually baked it the night before, and then just before serving I put the goat cheese on top and reheated it. My mother and my sister were crazy about it!

SERVES 6

2 potatoes
1 lemon
6 baby artichokes
Extra-virgin olive oil for sautéing (about 1 tablespoon)
1 clove garlic, peeled
Salt to taste
$1/4$ teaspoon (1 envelope) powdered saffron dissolved in 1 to 2
    tablespoons water

Marjoram leaves to taste
Minced parsley to taste
1 (8-ounce/250-gram) tub mascarpone cheese
1 cup (100 grams) grated Parmesan
1 package readymade short-crust pastry dough
3 ¹/₂ ounces (100 grams) buche de chèvre or another soft-ripened goat cheese

Preheat the oven to 350° F (180° C). Peel the potatoes and dice them. Juice the lemon and add the juice to a bowl full of cold water. Trim the artichokes: Working one at a time, remove any leaves from the stem, and then cut off the stem, leaving an inch or two. Pull off and discard any hard, dark colored leaves. When you have revealed the light green portion of the artichoke, peel any tough skin off the outside of the stem. Cut off the top of the artichoke completely. Cut the artichoke in half the long way and use the tip of a paring knife to dig out the fuzzy part in the center. Slice the cleaned artichoke into thin wedges and drop them into the bowl with the water and lemon juice. Repeat with remaining artichokes. When all the artichokes have been trimmed and sliced, sauté them briefly in a large pan in a small amount of oil along with the potatoes and garlic clove. Salt the artichokes and add the saffron water, marjoram, and parsley and cook, covered, until the artichokes and potatoes are easily pierced with a fork. Transfer the vegetable mixture to a large bowl and add the mascarpone and Parmesan, stirring to combine thoroughly.

Roll out the dough to cover the bottom and an inch or two up the sides of a springform pan and fit the dough into the pan. Pour in the filling and bake until the filling and crust are golden brown, about 30 minutes. Remove the torte from the oven, arrange the goat cheese in a single layer on top (if it is a log, simply slice it; otherwise, break it up into tablespoon-sized pieces and dot it over the top), and return the torte to the oven to melt the goat cheese, about 3 minutes longer.

« PLUM CAKE DI FAGIOLINI »
SAVORY CAKE WITH GREEN BEANS

A "plum cake," despite the name, does not contain fruit. It is a plain cake similar to a pound cake. This is a savory version packed with flavor. It makes a wonderful side dish, or you can serve slices in your bread basket.

SERVES 4 TO 6

9 ounces (250 grams) green beans
2 cups (250 grams) unbleached all-purpose flour
3 large eggs, lightly beaten
Salt to taste
$1/2$ cup (100 milliliters) whole milk
3 tablespoons extra-virgin olive oil
3 $1/2$ ounces (100 grams) blue cheese
$1/2$ cup (50 grams) chopped walnuts
2 teaspoons (8 grams) baking powder
Mixed salad greens for serving
Extra-virgin olive oil for dressing greens
Balsamic vinegar for dressing greens

Preheat the oven to 400° F (200° C). Line a loaf pan with parchment paper and set aside. Chop about $2/3$ of the green beans and reserve the rest whole. Blanch the beans separately in boiling salted water for 5 minutes, drain, and set aside. In a bowl, combine the flour, eggs, salt, milk, and oil and whisk batter until smooth. Stir in the chopped green beans, crumble in the blue cheese, and sprinkle in the walnuts. Pour the batter into the prepared pan, smooth the top, and bake until the top springs back when pressed with a finger, about 35 minutes. Let the cake cool in the pan on a wire rack for 5 minutes, then unmold and allow to cool completely. Before serving, toss the whole green beans with the salad greens. Make a vinaigrette with oil, balsamic vinegar, and a pinch of salt, toss with the salad, and serve with the cake.

« TORTA SALATA INTEGRALE »
WHOLE-GRAIN SAVORY TART

Carrots, spinach, and saffron result in three different colored fillings that make this checkered tart a winner. With so many ingredients, each bite is new and different.

SERVES 4 TO 6

Crust
1/2 envelope active dry yeast dissolved in 1/2 cup (100 milliliters) warm water
1 tablespoon honey
1 cup (130 grams) unbleached all-purpose flour
1 cup (130 grams) whole-wheat flour
2 tablespoons oil
Salt to taste

Orange Filling
2 carrots, boiled and drained
1/4 cup (50 grams) ricotta
3 ounces (80 grams) scamorza cheese, grated
Salt to taste

Green Filling
9 ounces (250 grams) spinach, cooked
1/4 cup (50 grams) ricotta
3 tablespoons grated pecorino
Salt to taste

Yellow Filling
1 onion, boiled and drained
1/4 cup (50 grams) ricotta
1/2 teaspoon (2 envelopes) powdered saffron dissolved in 1 tablespoon whole milk
Salt to taste

To make the crust, pour the yeast mixture and honey into a large bowl. Add both flours, the oil, and a little salt. Knead, first in the bowl and then on a work surface, until you have a smooth, compact ball of dough. Place the dough in a clean bowl, cover with plastic wrap, and set aside to rise for 1 hour.

Meanwhile, make the fillings. For the orange filling, blend the carrots, ricotta, scamorza, and a little salt in a blender or food processor fitted with the metal blade. Do the same for the other two fillings, washing the blender or food processor in between. Taste all three and adjust the salt.

Preheat the oven to 350° F (180° C). Cut off $1/4$ of the dough and set aside. Roll out the remaining dough and fit it into a tart pan. Roll the reserved dough (on the work surface, using your hands) into cylinders and use the cylinders to create a lattice. Fill the diamonds in the lattice with the three fillings, alternating the colors. Bake until the crust is golden, about 25 minutes.

« PIZZA CON IL CORNICIONE »
STUFFED-CRUST PIZZA

I have to thank Caterina Varvello, who talked about this pizza with a stuffed crust so much that I had to try to make one. It's incredible!

SERVES 4

1 batch readymade pizza dough
1 cup (250 milliliters) tomato puree
1 fresh mozzarella ball (8 ounces/225 grams), diced
4 to 5 anchovy fillets in oil, drained
1 cup (200 grams) ricotta
Fresh basil leaves to taste
Extra-virgin olive oil for drizzling
Salt to taste

Preheat a convection oven to 425° F (220° C). Line a pizza pan with parchment paper. Roll out the dough and place it on the prepared pan. Leaving a 2-inch border all around, top the dough with the tomato puree, then scatter the mozzarella over the puree. Place the anchovy fillets on top of the mozzarella. Spread the ricotta around the border. Roll up the border of the pizza, sealing in the ricotta. Add the basil and drizzle with some olive oil. Salt to taste and bake until the crust is browned, 10 to 15 minutes.

« PITTA CHICCULIATA »
CALABRESE STUFFED PIZZA

Pitta is a kind of focaccia from Calabria filled with a delicious combination of tomatoes, tuna, capers, and anchovies.

SERVES 4

Extra-virgin olive oil for oiling the pan and sautéing
1 pound (500 grams) readymade pizza dough
1 clove garlic
1 (28-ounce/1 kilogram) can chopped tomatoes
Fresh basil leaves to taste
1 tablespoon salted capers, soaked and rinsed
Anchovy fillets in oil, drained, to taste
1 (6-ounce/180-gram) can tuna in oil, drained
2 tablespoons pitted black olives
Salt to taste
Unbleached all-purpose flour for the work surface
1 large egg, lightly beaten

Preheat the oven to 400° F (200° C). Lightly oil a pizza pan and set aside. Cover the pizza dough with a dish towel and allow to rise at room temperature for 40 minutes.

Meanwhile, prepare the sauce: Brown the garlic clove in some oil, tilting the pan so that it remains submerged in the oil. Add the tomatoes, basil, capers, anchovy fillets, tuna, and olives. Taste and adjust salt (you may not need any, since the olives and the capers are salty) and cook over medium-low heat until thick, about 30 minutes.

Cut the dough into two balls and, on a lightly floured surface, stretch them by hand or roll out with a rolling pin to form 2 disks the size of the pan. Place one disk of dough on the pan. Spread the sauce on top. Place the second disk over the sauce and pinch all around the edge to seal. Brush the top of the pizza with the beaten egg and cook in the preheated oven until golden, about 30 minutes.

« SFORMATO DI ZUCCHINE CON CAPRINO »
ZUCCHINI AND GOAT CHEESE FLAN

This flan is special. You make a base of zucchini topped with creamy, slightly acidic goat cheese, and you put a crust on top of that. Once it's cooked you flip it over and serve.

SERVES 4 TO 6

Extra-virgin olive oil for sautéing
4 zucchini, sliced into rounds
1 clove garlic
Salt to taste
1/2 cup (100 milliliters) béchamel
2 large eggs
1/4 cup grated Parmesan
2 rounds goat cheese, at room temperature
1 package readymade puff pastry dough

Preheat the oven to 350° F (180° C). Line a loaf pan with parchment paper and set aside. In a small amount of oil over low heat, cook the zucchini with the garlic until soft. Season with salt. Remove and discard the garlic. Transfer the cooked zucchini to a blender or food processor. Add the béchamel, eggs, and Parmesan and process until smooth. Pour the mixture into the prepared pan and smooth the top with a spatula. Bake until set, about 40 minutes. Spread the goat cheese on top of the zucchini. Cut a rectangle of puff pastry dough to fit the top of the loaf pan and place on top of the goat cheese. Bake on the convection setting until the puff pastry is browned, an additional 15 to 20 minutes. Remove the pan to a wire rack to cool for 5 minutes. Invert onto a platter and serve.

« FLAN DI PEPERONI »
PEPPER AND ANCHOVY FLANS

Peppers and anchovies are a magical pairing. These miniature flans are an excellent appetizer, but they can also be served as a side dish.

SERVES 4

Extra-virgin olive oil for oiling ramekins and sautéing
2 red bell peppers, sliced
Salt to taste
2 tablespoons anchovy paste
1 cup (250 milliliters) heavy cream
3 large eggs

Preheat the oven to 350° F (180° C). Oil 4 ramekins and set aside. In a skillet, sauté the peppers with a little oil and a sprinkle of salt. When they're soft and well cooked, puree them in a blender or food processor. Mix 1 tablespoon anchovy paste with $3/4$ cup (175 milliliters) cream. Add the cream mixture to the peppers, then add the eggs. Salt to taste and mix until smooth and thoroughly combined.

Fill the ramekins with the pepper mixture and bake in a bain-marie (meaning with the ramekins sitting in a pan of water so that water comes about halfway up the sides of the ramekins) until set, about 50 minutes. Let the flans cool in the ramekins, then run a butter knife around the edges of the ramekins, invert onto serving dishes, and lift up the ramekins. Make a sauce by whisking the remaining 1 tablespoon anchovy paste with the remaining $1/4$ cup (50 milliliters) cream. Serve with the flans.

« CROSTINI MOZZARELLE E POMODORO »
MOZZARELLA AND TOMATO CROSTINI

Don't be fooled by the name—these are very sophisticated little treats. The bread is a dark rye bread, and the tomatoes come in the form of a light-as-air mousse. You can either buy "party-sized" bread that is already sliced or cut larger slices into small squares.

SERVES 8

4 sheets (8 grams) gelatin
2 green onions
Extra-virgin olive oil for sautéing
3 cups (750 milliliters) tomato puree
Salt to taste
1 (1-pound/500-gram) loaf dark rye bread
1 pound (500 grams) mozzarella, preferably buffalo-milk mozzarella
Fresh basil leaves for garnish

Soak the gelatin sheets in cold water to soften. Mince the onions and sauté in a pan in a little oil, then add the tomato puree, season with salt, and cook over medium-low heat until thickened, 10 to 15 minutes. Remove the gelatin from the soaking water, squeeze out any excess water, and add to the pan. Continue cooking, stirring constantly, until the gelatin has dissolved. Set the mixture aside to cool, giving it an occasional stir. When it has cooled to room temperature, refrigerate it until set, at least 30 minutes.

When the tomato mousse has set, slice the mozzarella and cut the bread into small squares, if necessary. The slices of cheese and bread should be about the same size. Place a slice of mozzarella on each slice of bread. Using two spoons, shape the tomato mousse into quenelles (oval-shaped balls), then top each slice of mozzarella with a quenelle. Garnish with basil leaves and serve.

« BRUSCHETTA DI POMODORO DI CATE »
CATE'S TOMATO BRUSCHETTA

This is the perfect summer antipasti, a recipe from my dear friend Caterina. The fresh tomato sauce used here would be wonderful served over some pasta—and some black olives would be a tasty addition, too!

SERVES 4

3 to 4 (400 grams) very firm, ripe tomatoes
Leaves of 1 bunch basil

1 tablespoon capers
1 clove garlic, peeled
1 pinch dried oregano
Salt to taste
Chile pepper flakes to taste
Extra-virgin olive oil for dressing
Red wine vinegar for dressing
Slices of lightly toasted country bread

Cut a small X in the base of each tomato. Bring a pot of water to a boil and dunk the to-matoes in the boiling water for a few seconds. Remove with a slotted spoon and peel. (If the tomatoes have absorbed a great deal of water, set them in a colander in the sink and allow them to drain for 10 minutes.) In a blender or a food processor fitted with the metal blade, combine the tomatoes, basil leaves, capers, and garlic and process very briefly. You want the tomatoes to be chunky. Transfer the tomato mixture to a bowl and add the oregano, salt, chile pepper flakes, a drizzle of oil, and a little vinegar. Toss to combine. Serve with the toasted bread, allowing guests to help themselves.

« BRUSCHETTE IN PADELLA »
PAN-FRIED BRUSCHETTA

I got the idea for this dish from a movie—the wonderful *Julie & Julia*. The scene that inspired me showed the protagonist chatting with her husband as she fried lovely thick pieces of bread in a skillet until they were crisp and golden. I couldn't get that image out of my head. These pan-fried bruschetta must be served right after you make them.

SERVES 2

7 ounces (200 grams) very ripe cherry or grape tomatoes
Extra-virgin olive oil for drizzling and pan-frying
Salt to taste
Leaves of 1 sprig basil
1 small, soft loaf ciabatta
1 clove garlic

Cut the tomatoes into quarters and place them in a bowl. Drizzle with some oil, season with salt, and tear the basil leaves into the bowl. Cut the bread into slices about 1 inch thick. Peel the garlic, cut it in half, and rub the cut side against the surface of the bread slices. Place a generous amount of oil in a pan and brown the bread slices on one side. Remove the slices, heat additional oil (the bread will have absorbed most of the oil), and return the slices to the pan to brown the other side. When the bread slices are brown and crisp on both sides, remove them to a platter, distribute the tomato mixture on top, and serve immediately.

« CROSTINI ALLE VONGOLE »
CLAM CROSTINI

Clam crostini is a typical dish of the Romagna region. In the Romagna beach town of Riccione, tiny clams are called *poveracce*, or "little paupers," but I think clams are fit for a prince!

SERVES 4 TO 6

3 cloves garlic
Extra-virgin olive oil for sautéing
1 pinch chile pepper flakes
1 package frozen clams
1 baguette

Peel and crush the garlic cloves, then sauté them in oil with the chile pepper flakes, tilting the pan to keep the garlic submerged in the oil. Add the clams (still frozen) to the pan. Turn the heat to low until the clams have defrosted, then turn it to high and allow some of the liquid to evaporate. Meanwhile, cut the baguette into slices about $1/2$ inch to $3/4$ inch thick and toast them in a toaster. When the clams are cooked (follow package instructions, but it shouldn't take long), place the toasted bread on a serving platter or wooden board, top each with a generous spoonful of clams and some of their juices, and serve immediately.

« BISCOTTI FARCITI AL FORMAGGIO »
CHEESE AND POPPY SEED SANDWICHES

If you're looking for a fun little bite to serve with an apéritif, this recipe is for you. Just take some tasty round crackers, such as Ritz, and sandwich a creamy cheese spread between them. You can use almost any soft cheese you like. These are a little like ice cream sandwiches, and rolling them in poppy seeds gives them a touch of class.

SERVES 4 TO 6

3 $1/2$ ounces (about $1/2$ cup/100 grams) robiola cheese
3 $1/2$ ounces (1 small round/100 grams) soft goat cheese
2 tablespoons grated pecorino
7 ounces (2 sleeves/200 grams) round butter crackers, such as Ritz
    crackers
Poppy seeds, *quanto basta* (about $3/4$ cup)

In a small bowl, mix together the robiola, goat cheese, and pecorino until creamy. Arrange half of the crackers flat side up on the work surface. Spread a teaspoon or two of the mixture on each one. Top each with another cracker, flat side down. Press lightly on the crackers to even out the cheese mixture. Clean the edges with your finger or with the back of a spoon. Place the poppy seeds in a soup bowl, shake gently to arrange in an even layer, then roll the cracker sandwiches in the poppy seeds, or dip them in the poppy seeds at regular intervals to make stripes.

« SALATINI ALLE NOCCIOLE »
SAVORY HAZELNUT PASTRIES

These little savory hazelnut bites are perfect for munching while you sip a glass of chilled prosecco. All the ingredients for a perfect evening!

SERVES 4

$1/3$ cup (50 grams) hazelnuts
1 stick plus 6 tablespoons (200 grams) unsalted butter, softened
1 $2/3$ cups (200 grams) unbleached all-purpose flour

2 cups (200 grams) grated Parmesan
2 large eggs, lightly beaten
Salt and pepper to taste

Toast the hazelnuts in a skillet until lightly golden, then rub them in a clean dish tow-el to remove the skins. In a food processor, process the hazelnuts until very finely ground. On a work surface, knead together the butter and the flour and then—work-ing quickly so the butter doesn't melt—incorporate the Parmesan, ground hazelnuts, eggs, and salt and pepper to taste. Form the resulting dough into a ball, wrap in plastic wrap, and refrigerate for 1 hour.

Preheat the oven to 350° F (180° C). Line a jelly-roll pan or cookie sheet with parch-ment and set aside. On a lightly floured work surface, roll out the dough into a thin sheet. Flour the top of the dough lightly as well, if necessary, to keep the rolling pin from sticking. Cut out circles of dough with a cookie cutter or the rim of a juice glass. Transfer the circles to the prepared baking sheet. Gather the scraps and reroll them to use them up. (Don't reroll more than once—you can cut these into diamonds or squares so you won't have any scraps.) Bake the pastries until crisp and brown, about 10 minutes. Let the pastries cool to room temperature on the pan before serving.

« BIGNÈ ALLA CREMA DI PROSCIUTTO »
PASTRY PUFFS WITH PROSCIUTTO CREAM

Readymade pastry shells and puffs are a great convenience, but they can be a little dry. My trick for making them tasty is to fill or stuff them in advance and let them rest for a few hours. That way the pastry softens a little and takes on some of the flavor of the filling.

SERVES 4

5 ounces (150 grams) prosciutto cotto
2 tablespoons ricotta
1 tablespoon mascarpone
2 to 3 drops lemon juice
Salt to taste
12 readymade pastry puffs or pastry shells

In a food processor fitted with the metal blade, mince the prosciutto. Transfer it to a bowl and add the ricotta, mascarpone, lemon juice, and a little salt. Mix to combine thoroughly. If you are using pastry puffs, cut off the tops and set them aside. Fill the puffs or shells, and return the tops to the puffs. Chill the puffs in the refrigerator for at least 2 hours to soften the pastry.

« PANZEROTTI AL RAGÙ »
PANZEROTTI FILLED WITH MEAT SAUCE

In my hometown of Alessandria, in Piedmont, we have pizza, focaccia, and *farinata*, but growing up I had never heard of the savory pastries called *panzerotti*. I discovered them when I went to Milan to attend college, and I made up for lost time! They're not hard to make, especially if you use readymade pizza dough. The only tricky part is to be sure that you seal the ends very tightly before you fry them in oil, or the filling will leak out and you'll end up with sadly empty *panzerotti*.

MAKES 6 PANZEROTTI

Meat Sauce
5 ounces (150 grams) frozen mirepoix (minced carrots, onion, and
    celery)
Extra-virgin olive oil for sautéing
1 clove garlic
10 ounces (300 grams) ground beef
1 cup (250 milliliters) white wine
Salt to taste
1 cup (250 milliliters) tomato puree
1 bay leaf
2 ounces (60 grams) Swiss cheese, grated

Pastry
1 unbaked pizza crust
Flour for work surface
Oil for deep-frying

To make the meat sauce, in a large pan, sauté the mirepoix in oil with the garlic. Add the meat, breaking it up with your hands or a fork, and brown, then add the wine and allow it to evaporate. Season with salt and add the tomato puree and the bay leaf. Turn the heat to medium-low and cook, covered, until thickened, about 30 minutes. Remove from heat and allow to cool. Remove and discard bay leaf.

Meanwhile, set the pizza crust on a lightly floured work surface, lightly flour the top, and roll it a little thinner. Cut out circles of dough using a cookie cutter or the rim of a glass. Knead together any scraps, reroll, and cut additional circles. When the sauce has cooled, stir the Swiss cheese into it. Place a spoonful of this mixture in the center of each dough circle. Fold the dough circles in half to create semi-circles. Seal the edges by pinching firmly. Fry the pastries in abundant hot oil, remove with a skimmer, and drain briefly on paper towels before serving.

« FOCACCE RIPIENE »
STUFFED FOCACCIA

MAKES 2 STUFFED FOCACCIA, ABOUT 6 LARGE SQUARES EACH

Flour for work surface
2 batches readymade focaccia dough or pizza dough
2 fresh mozzarella balls (8 ounces/225 grams), sliced
7 anchovy fillets in oil, drained
4 zucchini blossoms
Coarse sea salt to taste
Extra-virgin olive oil for drizzling
5 slices grilled eggplant in oil
4 cherry tomatoes, halved
Grated Parmesan to taste

Preheat a convection oven to 400° F (200° C). Line two jelly-roll pans with parchment paper and set aside. On a lightly floured surface, roll out one batch of dough to a rectangle, sprinkling the top lightly with flour to keep the rolling pin from sticking. On one half of the rectangle, arrange half of the mozzarella slices, the anchovies, and the zucchini blossoms. Fold over the empty half of the dough and pinch the edges together to seal. Lightly flour the top and gently roll again with the rolling pin to press the two halves together. Sprinkle coarse sea salt on top and drizzle with a generous amount of olive oil. Roll out the other batch of dough and on one half arrange the remaining mozzarella, the eggplant, and the tomatoes, and sprinkle grated Parmesan on top. Fold the empty half over and pinch the edges together to seal. Lightly flour the top and gently roll again with the rolling pin to press the two halves together. Sprinkle coarse sea salt on top and drizzle with a generous amount of olive oil. Transfer the two stuffed focaccia to the prepared pans and bake until golden, about 10 minutes. Cut and serve warm or at room temperature.

« QUICHE Z.Z. »
SQUASH AND GORGONZOLA PIE

One Z in the name of this pie stands for *zucca*, or squash, and the other stands for 'zola, my nickname for delicious Gorgonzola cheese! This is the best dish I've created over the past year. I actually have to give it away to friends when I make it, or I'll eat the whole thing in one sitting.

MAKES 1 PIE, ABOUT 8 SLICES

1 winter squash, such as butternut or acorn squash, about 1 1/2 pounds
    (700 grams)
1 1/4 cups (250 grams) ricotta
10 ounces (300 grams) Gorgonzola cheese, cut into cubes
1/2 cup (50 grams) grated Parmesan
2 large eggs, lightly beaten
Salt to taste
1 batch readymade puff pastry, rolled into a circle

Preheat the oven to 350° F (180° C). Line a tart pan with parchment paper and set aside. Peel and seed the squash and chop the flesh. Boil the squash in salted water until very soft. Drain, transfer to a large bowl, and crush with a fork. Add the ricotta, the Gorgonzola, the Parmesan, and the eggs to the bowl. Stir to combine thoroughly. Season to taste with salt. Arrange the puff pastry in the prepared pan, trimming off

any excess. Crimp the edges and pierce the bottom with a fork in several places. Pour the filling into the crust and bake until the filling is puffy and golden, with a scattering of dark spots, about 40 minutes.

« MELANZANE A BRUSCHETTA »
EGGPLANT BRUSCHETTA

Rather than making bruschetta on a slice of bread, for this dish, I've used the eggplant as the "bread" and topped it with chopped tomatoes.

SERVES 2 TO 4

2 eggplant
1 clove garlic, peeled
Salt to taste
Extra-virgin olive oil for drizzling
4 anchovy fillets in oil, drained and chopped
$1/2$ cup (50 grams) grated Parmesan
7 ounces (200 grams) cherry tomatoes, halved
Fresh basil leaves to taste

Preheat the oven to 350° F (180° C). Cut the eggplant in half the long way and, with the tip of a paring knife, make several cuts through the flesh on the cut side without piercing the skin. Cut the garlic clove in half and rub the cut side against the eggplant, then discard the garlic. Arrange the eggplant halves, cut side up, in a baking dish. Season with salt and drizzle with some olive oil. Sprinkle with the chopped anchovy fillets (or insert pieces of the anchovy fillets into the cuts you made with the paring knife) and the grated Parmesan. Spoon the tomatoes on top and drizzle with additional oil, sprinkle with a little more salt, and place the basil leaves on top of the tomatoes. Bake until the eggplant is soft, 45 to 50 minutes. Serve warm or at room temperature. A tip from my mother: Chop up any leftovers and use as a pasta sauce. Delicious!

« CROSTINI GORGONZOLA NOCI »
CROSTINI WITH GORGONZOLA AND WALNUTS

These crostini are quick and easy, and they pair beautifully with a nice glass of red wine.

SERVES 2 TO 4

1 baguette
3 1/2 ounces (100 grams) sweet Gorgonzola cheese
8 to 10 shelled walnuts, chopped

Preheat a convection oven to 400° F (200° C) or preheat a broiler. Cut the baguette into 1/2-inch slices. Spread each slice with a spoonful of Gorgonzola. Sprinkle some chopped walnuts onto each. Bake in the convection oven or run under the broiler until the cheese melts. Serve immediately.

« MILLEFOGLIE DI PATATE »
POTATOES STACKED WITH SMOKED SCAMORZA

Like many antipasto, this one would also make a good light lunch, especially if you paired it with a nice green salad. It's basically a grilled cheese sandwich with slices of roasted potatoes in place of the bread.

SERVES 4

4 potatoes
Fresh rosemary to taste
Fresh marjoram leaves to taste
Fresh sage leaves to taste
Extra-virgin olive oil for coating potatoes
Salt and pepper to taste
6 ounces (160 grams) smoked scamorza, sliced
3 1/2 ounces (100 grams) thinly sliced prosciutto cotto

Preheat the oven to 475° F (250° C). Line a jelly-roll pan with parchment paper. Peel the potatoes and cut them into thin slices the long way. Arrange them on the prepared pan. Mince the rosemary, marjoram, and sage and mix with some oil. Season with salt and pepper. Pour this mixture over the potato slices. Roast the potatoes until they are easily pierced with the tip of a paring knife, 10 to 15 minutes. Remove the pan from the oven but leave the oven on. Working on the jelly-roll pan, make the stacks. On $1/3$ of the potato slices, alternate slices of scamorza, prosciutto, and potato until you've used up all the potato slices. Return the stacks to the oven to melt the cheese, 4 to 5 minutes, and serve hot.

« FARIFRITTATA CON VERDURE »
CHICKPEA FLOUR PANCAKE WITH VEGETABLES

A *farifrittata* is a pancake made with chickpea flour that's chock-full of vegetables. Not only is it tasty and good for you, but it's gluten-free. Thanks to Francesca Senette for this recipe.

SERVES 4

1 $1/4$ cups (150 grams) chickpea flour (not roasted)
Salt and pepper to taste
$1/2$ teaspoon extra-virgin olive oil, plus more for sautéing vegetables
3 leeks
2 carrots
Fresh basil leaves to taste
Fresh oregano leaves to taste
Chile pepper flakes to taste

Place the chickpea flour in a bowl. Whisking constantly, gradually pour in 1 $1/4$ cups (300 milliliters) water to make a smooth batter. Season with salt and pepper, whisk in the oil, and set aside to rest at room temperature for 2 hours. Meanwhile, slice the leek into rounds and julienne the carrots. Sauté the vegetables in a little oil over low heat until soft. Remove from the heat and stir in basil, oregano, and chile pepper flakes to taste. To make the pancake, stir the vegetables into the batter. Either cook in a pan like a frittata, turning once to brown both sides, or preheat the oven to 350° F (180° C), pour the batter into a parchment-lined baking pan, and bake until firm, about 30 minutes.

« CROSTINI RADICCHIO E SCAMORZA »
CROSTINI WITH RADICCHIO AND SCAMORZA

These crostini are super-easy to prepare. In winter, I accompany them with red wine and a cheese board with a selection of specialty jams.

SERVES 2

Extra-virgin olive oil for sautéing
1 head radicchio, cut into ribbons
1 shallot, minced
Salt and pepper to taste
2 tablespoons red wine vinegar
4 or 5 slices whole-wheat bread
2 ounces (50 grams) smoked scamorza, sliced

Preheat the broiler. In a small amount of oil, sauté the radicchio with the shallot. Season with salt and pepper, then pour in the vinegar, turn the heat to low, and simmer gently, stirring occasionally, for 10 minutes. If the pan seems too dry, add a small amount of water. Meanwhile, arrange the bread slices on a jelly-roll pan. Distribute the radicchio mixture over the bread slices, top with slices of scamorza, and broil for 5 minutes. Serve hot.

« VERDURE CON FONDUTA DI TALEGGIO »
VEGETABLES WITH TALEGGIO FONDUE

This is my favorite kind of appetizer—lots of vegetables dipped in a luxurious and creamy cheese fondue. One suggestion: If you have a fancy leather couch in your living room, serve this at the table rather than letting your guests eat it standing up during cocktail hour. The risk of staining is just too high!

SERVES 4 TO 6

1 zucchini
1 bell pepper

1 carrot
1 small head broccoli
Extra-virgin olive oil for tossing
3 to 4 tablespoons breadcrumbs
Salt to taste
$\frac{1}{4}$ cup (50 milliliters) whole milk
1 egg yolk, lightly beaten
5 ounces (150 grams) taleggio cheese, cut into cubes

Preheat the oven to 375° F (190° C). Line a baking pan with parchment paper and set aside. Cut the zucchini, bell pepper, and carrot into bite-sized pieces. Break down the broccoli crown into small florets and cut the stems into bite-sized pieces. Place all the vegetables in a bowl, drizzle with some olive oil, the breadcrumbs, and salt to taste. Toss to coat. Transfer the vegetables to the prepared pan and roast until golden but still firm, about 15 minutes, turning once or twice. To make the fondue, place the milk in a small pot and warm over low heat. Remove the milk from the heat just before it comes to a boil. Energetically whisk in the egg yolk. Return the pot to low heat and cook, whisking constantly, until the mixture begins to thicken. Remove from heat and add the taleggio, whisking until the cheese has melted. (You may need to return the pot to low heat to melt the cheese completely—just be sure to whisk constantly and remove the pot from the heat as soon as the cheese has melted.) Transfer the cheese mixture to a fondue pot set over the lowest flame possible and serve with the vegetables for dipping.

« PERE RIPIENE »
STUFFED PEARS

An old Italian proverb says, "Don't let the farmer know how good cheese is with pears." The idea was that the farmer might keep those things for himself if he realized what an inspired pairing that is! This is a fancy version of that same delicious duo. Look for small, firm green pears to use in this dish.

SERVES 4

4 small pears
3 ounces (80 grams) stracchino cheese (see note)
3 tablespoons grated pecorino

Salt and pepper to taste
1/3 cup (30 grams) walnuts, finely chopped

Cut off the tops of the pears and reserve. Scoop out the flesh with a melon baller, keeping the pear skins intact. Remove and discard any core and seeds. In a blender or a food processor, process half the pear flesh with both cheeses, a pinch of salt, and a little pepper. Taste and add more pear flesh if you like. (I usually use only half.) Process until smooth. Fill the pear skins with the cheese filling, sprinkle with the nuts, and replace the tops. Refrigerate the pears until just before serving.

Note: If you prefer a stronger-tasting filling, replace the stracchino with an equal amount of Gorgonzola.

« COZZE AL GRATIN »
STUFFED MUSSELS

I can eat an endless number of stuffed mussels! I've also made this using crushed leftover taralli breadsticks in place of the breadcrumbs. It's an interesting twist. You will notice that this recipe does not call for any salt—the shellfish and the cheese are salty enough on their own.

SERVES 4 TO 6

2 pounds (1 kilogram) mussels
2 cloves garlic
Extra-virgin olive oil for cooking the mussels and drizzling
1/2 cup (100 milliliters) white wine
Minced parsley leaves to taste
2 ounces (50 grams) pecorino, grated
2 cups (200 grams) breadcrumbs

Preheat the broiler. Clean the mussels and remove their beards. Place them in a pan with the garlic and a little oil. Turn the heat to medium-high, pour in the wine, cover, and cook until the shells open. Set the mussels aside until cool enough to handle, discarding any with unopened shells. Strain the cooking liquid through a fine-mesh sieve and reserve. When the mussels have cooled, pull off and discard the empty halves of the shells.

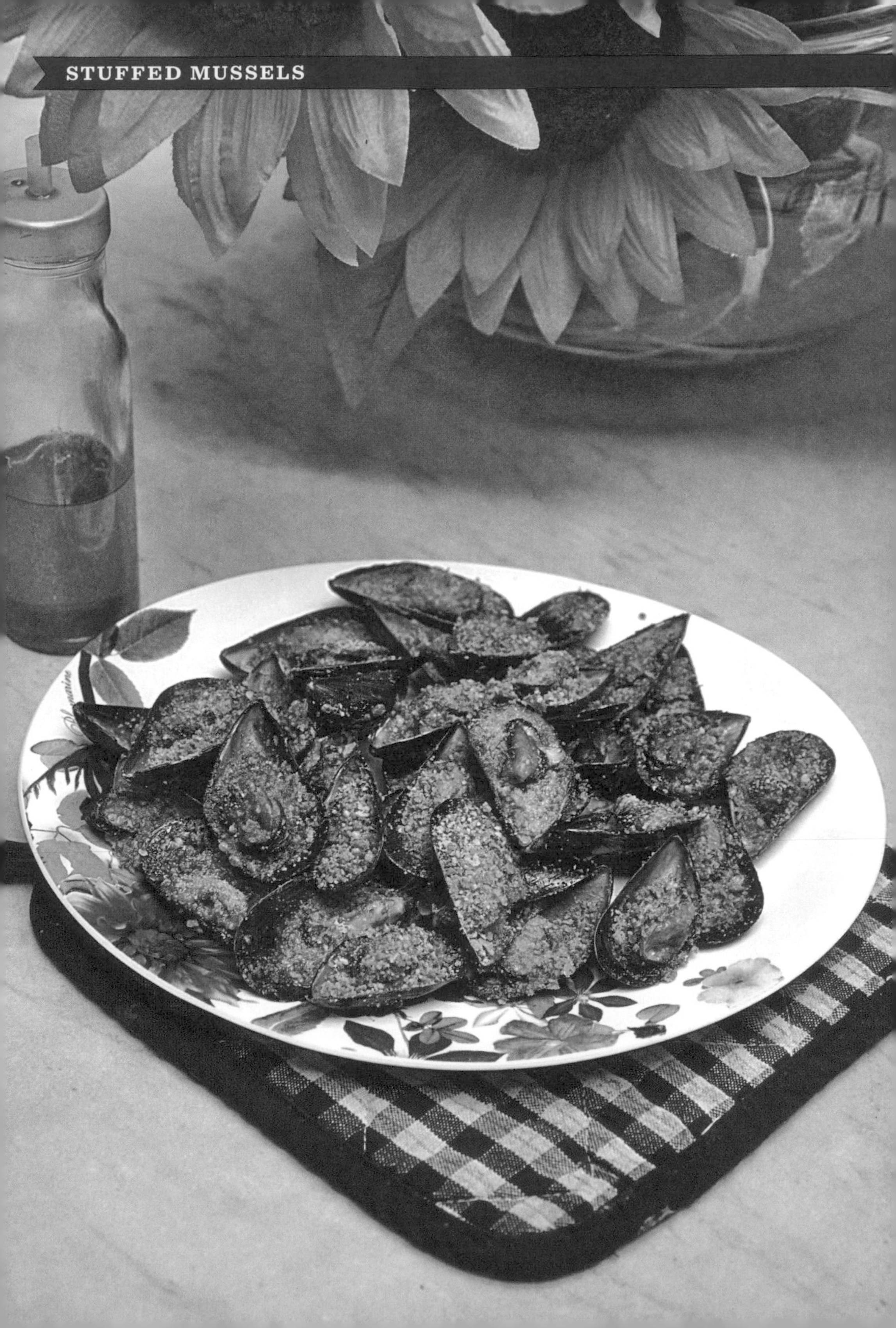

STUFFED MUSSELS

Place the mussels in their half-shells on a jelly-roll pan, open side up. In a small bowl combine the parsley, pecorino, and breadcrumbs. Stir in enough reserved cooking liquid to moisten. Fill the shells with the breadcrumb mixture. You can fill the shells one by one with a spoon, or simply sprinkle the mixture over the mussels and let some of it fall in between them onto the pan. Drizzle with a little oil and broil until the breadcrumbs turn golden brown, which should only take a few minutes. Serve immediately.

« UOVA E SEPPIE IN BIANCO E NERO »
EGGS AND CUTTLEFISH IN CUTTLEFISH INK

Moreno Cedroni, a masterful chef who's especially expert in the cooking of fish, taught me a really neat trick for serving a little package of poached egg with cuttlefish and cuttlefish ink. You seal it up in plastic wrap and boil it!

SERVES 4

Tomato puree, *quanto basta*
Salt and pepper to taste
Vegetable oil for oiling plastic wrap
4 large eggs
1 cuttlefish, cut into strips
1 packet cuttlefish ink

Briefly cook the tomato puree to thicken. Season with salt and pepper and set aside. Line 4 ramekins with plastic wrap, letting several inches of plastic wrap hang over the sides. Oil the plastic wrap, and then crack one of the eggs into each lined ramekin, taking care not to break the yolks. Divide the strips of raw cuttlefish among the ramekins and add a little cuttlefish ink to each. (Reserve some of the ink.) Gently close up each plastic packet and twist it at the top to seal. Bring a pot of water to a boil and lower the plastic packets into it, attaching them to the rim of the pot so that the filled part of the plastic is submerged, but the twisted top of each packet is not. (Just press the plastic against the rim of the pot and it should stick.) While the eggs are poaching, decorate 4 serving plates with the remaining cuttlefish ink and some tomato puree. When the eggs have cooked for 5 minutes, remove the packets from the water, carefully remove the plastic, and place the poached eggs and cuttlefish on the serving plates. Season with salt and pepper and serve.

« ROTOLINI DI TROTA SALMONATA »
TROUT ROLLS

This cold dish is served on a bed of bean sprouts with a refreshing raspberry sauce. I adapted the technique that Moreno Cedroni taught me for making poached eggs: I wrap the trout rolls in plastic so they keep their shape. The technique is his, but Lorenzo Boni shared this recipe with me.

SERVES 4

4 cups (1 liter) white wine
4 cups (1 liter) plus 3 tablespoons white wine vinegar
1 bay leaf
5 to 6 fresh basil leaves
Parsley leaves to taste
$1/4$ clove garlic
1 tablespoon capers
2 salmon trout fillets, skinned
Salt and pepper to taste
3 tablespoons sugar
4 raspberries, lightly crushed
Bean sprouts for garnish

Place the white wine, 1 liter vinegar, and the bay leaf in a pot and bring to a boil. Meanwhile, mince together the basil, parsley, garlic, and capers. Pound the trout fillets lightly so that they are the same thickness. Salt and pepper the fillets, then place them on a work surface skinned side down, sprinkle the minced herb mixture on them, and roll them up. Wrap the rolled trout fillets in plastic wrap and twist the ends (like a hard candy), making sure the packets are tightly sealed. Poke holes in the plastic with a toothpick and lower the trout rolls into the boiling wine mixture. Lower the heat to a simmer and cook until firm, about 10 minutes. When the rolls are cooked, remove them from the cooking liquid with a slotted spoon and allow them to cool in the plastic.

Meanwhile, make the sauce. In a small pan, combine the remaining 3 tablespoons vinegar, the sugar, and the raspberries and simmer until the liquid is slightly reduced, about 3 minutes. Slice the trout, then carefully peel off the plastic. Scatter the bean sprouts on a serving platter. Arrange the trout rolls on the bean sprouts and drizzle the raspberry sauce on top.

« FIORI DI ZUCCA RIPIENI DI PESCE »
ZUCCHINI BLOSSOMS STUFFED WITH FISH

Since I'm married to a Roman man, I know my way around a zucchini blossom. I'd always prepared them stuffed with mozzarella and anchovies and then fried. In this recipe, from Lorenzo Boni, the blossoms are filled with minced fish and then steamed. The results are delicate and delicious.

SERVES 4 TO 6

1 dorade fillet (3 to 6 ounces), skinned
1 salmon fillet (3 to 6 ounces), skinned
Fresh chives to taste, plus minced fresh chives for garnish
Fresh parsley leaves to taste
3 tablespoons heavy cream
Salt and pepper to taste
6 zucchini blossoms
Extra-virgin olive oil for drizzling

In a food processor fitted with the metal blade, grind the dorade and the salmon with chives, parsley, and the cream. Season with salt and pepper. Trim the zucchini blossoms and remove their pistils. Fill them with the fish mixture. Gently fold the blossoms to close and place them in a steamer. Steam until firm, about 10 minutes, drizzle with a little extra-virgin olive oil, and garnish with the minced chives. Serve immediately.

« POLPO IMBOTTIGLIATO »
OCTOPUS IN A PLASTIC BOTTLE

My friend Rosa Prinzivalli taught me this trick for making thinly sliced octopus carpaccio. I kept eating this dish in restaurants, but I couldn't figure out how the chefs made such perfect round slices. It's actually fairly easy to do—you stuff the octopus into an empty plastic water bottle!

SERVES 3 TO 4

1 octopus
2 bay leaves
1 tablespoon black peppercorns
Extra-virgin olive oil for drizzling
Salt to taste
Caper berries for garnish
Parsley leaves for garnish

Bring a large pot of water to a boil. Add the octopus to the pot with the bay leaves and peppercorns and cook until soft, about 1 hour. Let the octopus cool in the cooking water. Cut off the top of a plastic bottle. Stuff the octopus into the bottle using a round meat pounder. Press firmly. With the meat pounder on top, acting as a weight, place the bottle with the octopus in the freezer and freeze until firm but not frozen all the way through, 2 to 3 hours. Using kitchen shears, cut away the bottle and thinly slice the octopus with a very sharp knife. Place the slices on a platter, drizzle with some olive oil, sprinkle with salt, and garnish with caper berries and parsley leaves.

« UOVA RIPIENE PASQUALI »
HARD-BOILED EGGS WITH ANCHOVIES FOR EASTER

Eggs are a must at Easter, of course, but I like them any time of year. These are great as a summertime snack, especially after a trip to the beach, when the fresh air has given everyone an appetite.

SERVES 2 TO 4

4 large eggs
1/2 cup (100 milliliters) extra-virgin olive oil, plus more necessary
Leaves of 1 sprig parsley, plus parsley leaves for garnish
Pepper to taste
1 teaspoon anchovy paste
Cherry tomatoes for garnish

Hard-boil the eggs: Place the eggs in a pot with water to cover, bring to a boil, then lower the heat to a simmer and simmer for 10 minutes. Run the cooked eggs under cold water and peel. Cut each egg in half the long way and remove the yolk. In a blender or a food processor fitted with the metal blade, combine the yolks, oil, parsley leaves, a generous amount of pepper, and the anchovy paste. Process until fluffy. If the mixture looks dry, add a little more oil. Stuff each egg white with a generous spoonful of the yolk mixture and refrigerate until just before serving. Garnish with additional parsley and cherry tomatoes.

« CESTINI DI VERDURE »
VEGETABLE NESTS

Store-bought puff pastry is a wonderful item that can be used to make many marvelous dishes. I love to use the pastry to make little "nests" and then fill them with vegetables and cheese for a pretty appetizer. Thanks for this one go to Lorella Marchetti—a wonderful hair stylist and cook!

SERVES 4

1 package readymade puff pastry dough
1 large egg, lightly beaten
1 eggplant
Extra-virgin olive oil for sautéing
Salt to taste
2 ounces (50 grams) provolone, cut into cubes
1 1/4 cups (250 grams) ricotta
2 ounces (50 grams) Parmesan, grated
Thinly sliced prosciutto cotto, *quanto basta*

Preheat the oven to 400° F (200° C). Put 4 aluminum baking cups upside down on a jelly-roll pan or cookie sheet and set aside. Cut the puff pastry into strips about 1/2 inch wide and 4 inches long and weave them together. Lightly run a rolling pin over the woven strips to make them stick together. Using the upside down baking cups, shape the puff pastry sheets into baskets. Trim off any excess dough, roll it into thin ropes, and use that to make the rims of the baskets, pressing them firmly against the strips. Brush the baskets with the beaten egg and bake until golden, about 10 minutes. Remove from the oven and set aside to cool. Meanwhile, cut the eggplant into dice and sauté in a small amount of oil with some salt until soft. Transfer the eggplant to a bowl and combine with the provolone, ricotta, and Parmesan. Slip the baskets off of the baking cups, turn them over, and line them with the prosciutto slices, then fill the baskets with the eggplant mixture. Place the baskets under the broiler for 5 minutes and serve immediately.

« PEPERONI IN TARTARE CON I CAPPERI »
PEPPER TARTARE WITH CAPERS

Pepper tartare is a wonderful vegetarian dish that pairs beautifully with a fresh buffalo-milk mozzarella for a refreshing summer lunch. This is one of Fabio's all-time favorites.

SERVES 4

1 red bell pepper
Minced garlic to taste
Extra-virgin olive oil for sautéing
3 tablespoons capers with their brine
1 fresh mozzarella ball (8 ounces/225 grams), preferably buffalo-milk
    mozzarella

Cut the pepper into very small dice. Sauté the garlic in a little oil, then add the pepper, capers, and about half the brine from the capers. Cook over medium-low heat until the pepper is soft, about 10 minutes. (Do not salt!) Set the mixture aside to cool. Cut the mozzarella into thick slices, arrange 1 or 2 slices on each serving plate, and cover with the pepper mixture. Serve at room temperature.

« PEPERONCINI RIPIENI »
STUFFED CHERRY PEPPERS

I adore stuffed cherry peppers. Unfortunately, the ones you can buy in a jar at the grocery store are never very good, so I have to make my own. I used to eat this delicious dish all the time at my friend Arianna Torriani's house when I was a kid. Her mother, Eliana, made—and still makes—the best snacks for her friends and family. This recipe is all hers! Be sure not to touch your eyes after handling chile peppers.

MAKES 2 JARS

8 cherry peppers
2 cups (500 milliliters) white wine vinegar, plus more if needed
2 cups (500 milliliters) white wine, plus more if needed
8 anchovy fillets in oil, drained
8 capers
Extra-virgin olive oil for covering the peppers in the jars

Trim the peppers, cut off the stems, and scoop out the white ribs, membrane, and seeds. This is important: If you don't scrape the inside of the peppers clean, they'll be unbearably hot and inedible. Combine the vinegar and the wine in a pot. If the liquid won't cover the peppers, add more of each in equal amounts. Bring to a boil, and boil the peppers for 3 minutes. Remove the peppers with a skimmer and set them on a clean dish towel to cool. When the peppers are cool enough to handle, wrap 1 anchovy fillet around 1 caper and insert it into one of the peppers. Repeat with the remaining anchovies, capers, and peppers. Arrange the stuffed peppers in clean, dry jars (I always run mine through the dishwasher to be sure they are perfectly clean), and add extra-virgin olive oil to cover completely. Leave the jars open for 10 minutes and if the level of the oil has sunk, add more to cover. Seal the jars and store in the refrigerator.

« INVOLTINI RADICCHIO, NOCI, E RICOTTA »
RADICCHIO, WALNUT, AND RICOTTA PACKETS

The first time I made these, I had guests over for dinner. I made a few, just to hear their opinion. Well, they devoured them instantly! I quickly made two more pans of them. Fortunately, they're ready in an instant. Don't be tempted to add more nuts, because they'll be dry. And don't add salt, either.

SERVES 4 TO 6

1 head radicchio
1/2 cup (50 grams) walnuts, plus walnut halves for garnish
1/2 cup (100 grams) ricotta
10 thin slices prosciutto crudo
Extra-virgin olive oil for drizzling

Preheat the oven to 350° F (180° C). Line a jelly-roll pan with parchment paper and set aside. Bring a pot of water to a boil. Carefully detach 10 leaves from the radicchio, boil them for 30 seconds, and drain. Finely chop the walnuts and mix them with the ricotta. Place one radicchio leaf on the work surface. With a paring knife, cut out the thick white rib and discard. Place a slice of prosciutto on top of the leaf. (If the prosciutto slice is much larger than the radicchio leaf, trim to fit.) In the center, place a spoonful of the ricotta mixture. Fold the radicchio leaf envelope-style and place it on the prepared pan. Repeat with remaining leaves, prosciutto slices, and ricotta mixture. Bake for 10 minutes. Serve warm, drizzled with a little olive oil and garnished with a few walnut halves.

FIRST COURSES

« VELLUTATA BIANCO NATALE »
CREAM OF CAULIFLOWER SOUP

Cauliflower can surprise you. Boiled cauliflower is bland, but if you transform it into a creamy soup, it's truly tasty. Serve this soup in small cups with generous dollops of bright orange salmon roe like little piles of precious gems on top.

SERVES 4

1 shallot, thinly sliced
Extra-virgin olive oil for sautéing
5 ounces (130 grams) cauliflower
1 rib celery (optional)
1 tablespoon vegetable broth granules (or the serving size indicated on the package)
Salt to taste
3/4 cup plus 1 tablespoon (200 milliliters) heavy cream
White pepper to taste
1/4 cup salmon roe

In a soup pot, sauté the shallot in a small amount of olive oil until soft. Chop the cauli-flower and the celery, if using, and add them to the pot. Add water to just to cover the cauliflower and stir in the broth granules and a little salt. Simmer until the cauliflow-er is very soft, about 40 minutes. If the cauliflower is cooked but the mixture seems too watery (or tastes bland), remove 1/2 to 1 cup (100 to 250 milliliters) of the liquid and reserve so that you can return some back to the pot if you decide it's needed later. Stir in the cream and simmer for 3 minutes more. Puree the soup with an immersion blender until thick and velvety. To serve, ladle into small cups and top each serving with a generous grinding of pepper and 1 tablespoon salmon roe.

« CAPPUCCINO AI FUNGHI »
MUSHROOM "CAPPUCCINO"

This is a lovely cream of mushroom soup with whipped cream and crispy prosciutto on top. To give your guests a real surprise, serve it in coffee cups. This recipe was provided by Barbara Boncompagni, who has been invaluable to me in my television career.

SERVES 4

1 shallot
Extra-virgin olive oil for sautéing
1 pound (450 grams) white button mushrooms, roughly chopped
1 potato, peeled and cut into cubes
1 tablespoon vegetable broth granules (or the serving size indicated on the package), dissolved in $1/2$ cup (100 milliliters) water
Salt to taste
2 to 3 thin slices prosciutto crudo, cut into strips
$1/2$ cup (100 milliliters) heavy cream
2 tablespoons grated Parmesan
Pepper to taste
Toasted sesame seeds for garnish

In a soup pot, thinly slice the shallot and sauté it with a little oil, then add the mushrooms and cook for a few more minutes. Add the potato and the broth, taste and adjust the salt, and cook over low heat for about 15 minutes. Meanwhile, in a pan with no oil, cook the prosciutto. It should crisp up like bacon. Whip about 2 tablespoons (30 milliliters) of the cream and fold the Parmesan into it. Stir the remaining $1/4$ cup plus 2 tablespoons (90 milliliters) cream into the soup. Blend the soup until smooth (an immersion blender works best) and transfer to small cups. Top each serving with some of the whipped cream, a strip of crispy prosciutto, pepper to taste, and a sprinkling of toasted sesame seeds.

« ZUPPA DI VERZA »
CABBAGE SOUP

It's hard to believe, but I arrived at the tender age of 38 without ever having cooked cabbage. My parents never served it, so I wasn't in the habit of preparing it. I didn't know what I was missing—cabbage is great! In addition to more complex preparations, such as the Milanese classic *cassoeula,* cabbage lends itself to lots of simple and tasty dishes that appeal to children as well as adults. This warm and welcoming soup brightens any winter evening.

SERVES 4

Extra-virgin olive oil for sautéing and drizzling
1 onion, minced
1 carrot, minced
1 celery rib, minced
1 clove garlic, crushed
7 ounces (200 grams) smoked pancetta, cut into cubes
1 (1-pound/500-gram) head Savoy cabbage, cored and cut into ribbons
2 potatoes, peeled and cut into cubes
1/2 of a 15-ounce can (200 to 250 grams) cannellini beans, rinsed and
      drained
Salt to taste
1 cup (200 grams) short-grain Italian rice, such as arborio
Grated Parmesan to taste
Pepper to taste

In a soup pot, sauté the onion, carrot, and celery in a small amount of oil until soft, then add the garlic and pancetta and cook until browned. Add the cabbage, potatoes, and beans plus water to cover. Salt to taste and cook, covered, until vegetables are soft, about 45 minutes. Add the rice. Add more water to the pot if the soup looks too thick, and cook over medium heat until rice is cooked through, an additional 15 minutes. You can prepare the soup in advance and let it sit, but you may need to thin it with a little more water (and be sure to taste and adjust seasoning) before serving. Top each serving with grated Parmesan, extra-virgin olive oil, and pepper and serve hot.

SOLE SOUP

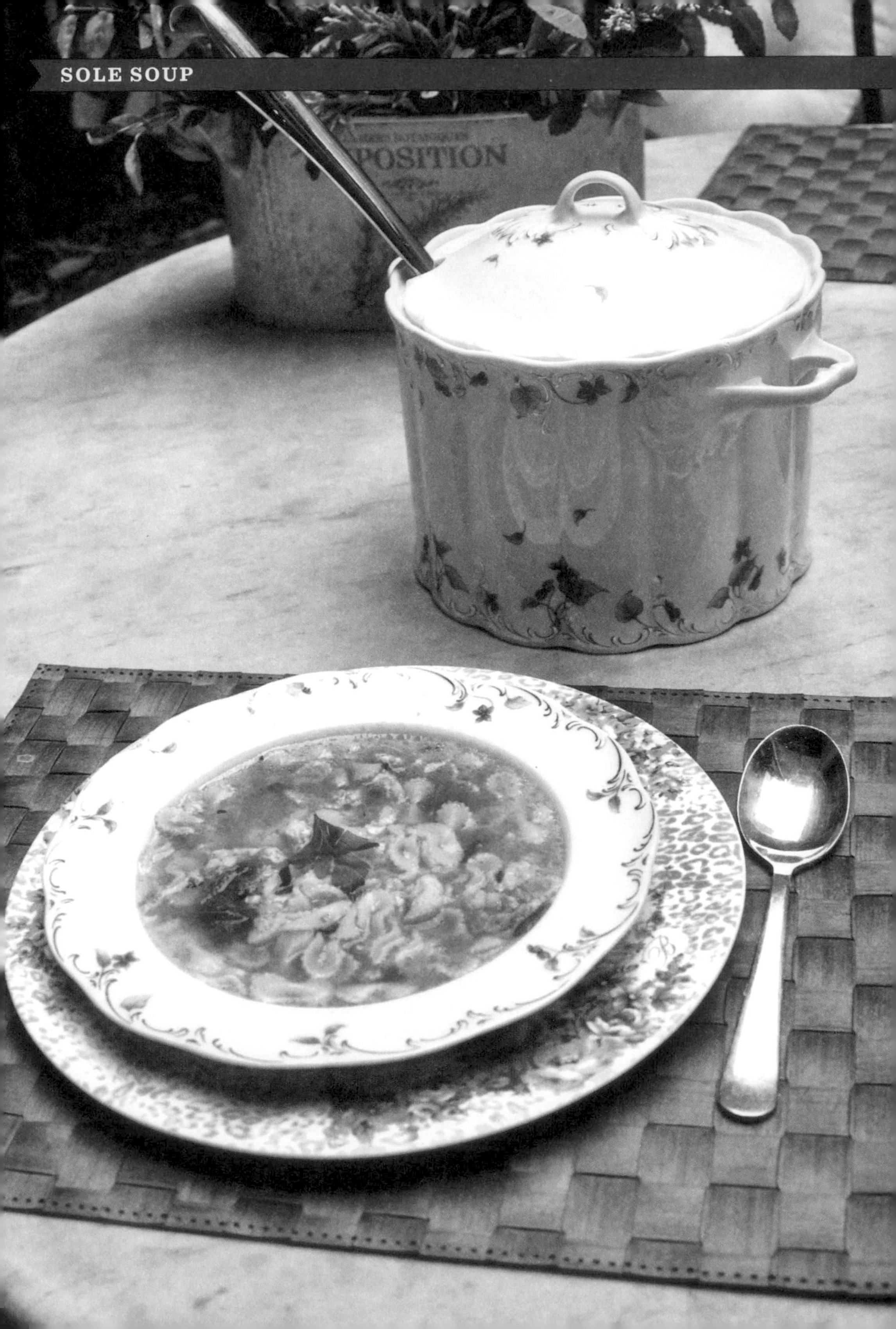

« MINESTRINA DI SOGLIOLA »
SOLE SOUP

This is a traditional dish from the Romagna region. I ate it at Gher, an excellent restaurant near the port in Riccione, and I immediately asked for the recipe. My kids are crazy about this—and they're not the only ones!

SERVES 4

1 clove garlic
Extra-virgin olive oil for sautéing
5 to 6 small tomatoes, diced
4 skinless sole fillets
Salt to taste
1 cup (100 grams) egg farfalline (small bow-tie pasta) or other small
    pasta for soup
Minced fresh parsley leaves to taste
Sliced country bread, toasted, for serving

In a soup pot, sauté the garlic in some oil. As soon as the garlic is soft, add the tomatoes and cook for an additional 2 minutes. Add the sole fillets, season with salt, and cook for 2 minutes more. Add about 2 cups (500 milliliters) water, bring to a boil, and cook the pasta in the soup. When the pasta is cooked, ladle the soup into serving bowls and top with minced parsley. Serve with toasted bread.

« VELLUTATA DI CECI E ARAGOSTA »
CHICKPEA AND LOBSTER SOUP

Chickpeas and lobster are a somewhat unusual and excellent pairing. I always buy frozen lobster, which is much less trouble than fresh.

SERVES 4

1 yellow onion, minced
3 ounces (80 grams) pancetta, diced

2 tablespoons extra-virgin olive oil
2 (15-ounce/500-gram) cans chickpeas, rinsed and drained
1 tablespoon vegetable broth granules (or the serving size indicated on
    the package)
Salt and pepper to taste
1 frozen lobster tail
1 shallot
Unsalted butter to taste
Minced fresh thyme leaves to taste
Minced fresh tarragon leaves to taste
1 cup (250 milliliters) brandy

In a soup pot, sauté the onion and pancetta in the oil. Add the chickpeas. Add cold water to cover and stir in the broth granules and salt and pepper. Bring to a boil, then lower the heat to a simmer and simmer for 15 minutes. Puree the soup until smooth and set aside. Meanwhile, bring another large pot of salted water to a boil. Drop in the lobster tail (still frozen) and boil for 10 minutes. Cut the lobster tail into medallions (with the shell on). Mince the shallot. Melt a generous amount of butter in a large skillet until foamy and sauté the lobster tail and shallot in the butter. Add a generous amount of both thyme and tarragon, then add the brandy to the pan and cook until most of the liquid has evaporated. Season with salt and pepper. To serve, distribute the chickpea soup among individual soup bowls and place the lobster on top. Garnish with additional thyme and tarragon if desired.

« PASTINA E LENTICCHIE »
LENTILS WITH SMALL PASTA

People of all ages love this dish. It's a great choice for kids who are just starting to eat solid foods (Diego gobbles it up), but it has enough flavor and substance for grown-ups, too. Of course, legumes are very healthful, which is important as well!

SERVES 4

2 to 3 green onions, minced
Extra-virgin olive oil for sautéing

1 (15-ounce/500-gram) can lentils, rinsed and drained
1 cup tomato puree or canned crushed tomatoes
Salt to taste
Minced fresh rosemary leaves to taste
2 1/2 to 3 cups (250 to 300 grams) egg farfalline (small bow-tie pasta) or
     other small pasta for soup
Grated Parmesan to taste

In a soup pot, sauté the onions in a little oil until golden. Add the lentils and cook briefly, stirring frequently. Add the tomato puree, season with salt and rosemary, and cook, covered, for 10 minutes. In a separate pot, cook the pasta in boiling salted water. Reserve 1 cup pasta cooking water and drain the pasta, then transfer to the pot with the lentils. Remove the pot from the heat and stir in the pasta cooking water and a generous amount of grated Parmesan. The mixture should be quite thick. Serve hot or allow to cool slightly.

« PASSATELLI IN BRODO »
BREADCRUMB PASTA IN BROTH

This unusual pasta from the Romagna region is a specialty of my dear friend Cristina Pistocchi. She often invites us over for a casual Sunday supper that starts with steaming bowls of broth with passatelli, a lovely way to end any weekend. This isn't complicated, but there are a few tricks to getting it right. Cristina was generous enough to share her method.

SERVES 6 TO 8

1 beef flank steak
1 beef top round steak
2 carrots
1 rib celery
1 tomato
1 small chicken or chicken parts for broth
1/2 cup (50 grams) breadcrumbs, plus more if needed
5 ounces (150 grams) Parmesan, grated

BREADCRUMB PASTA IN BROTH

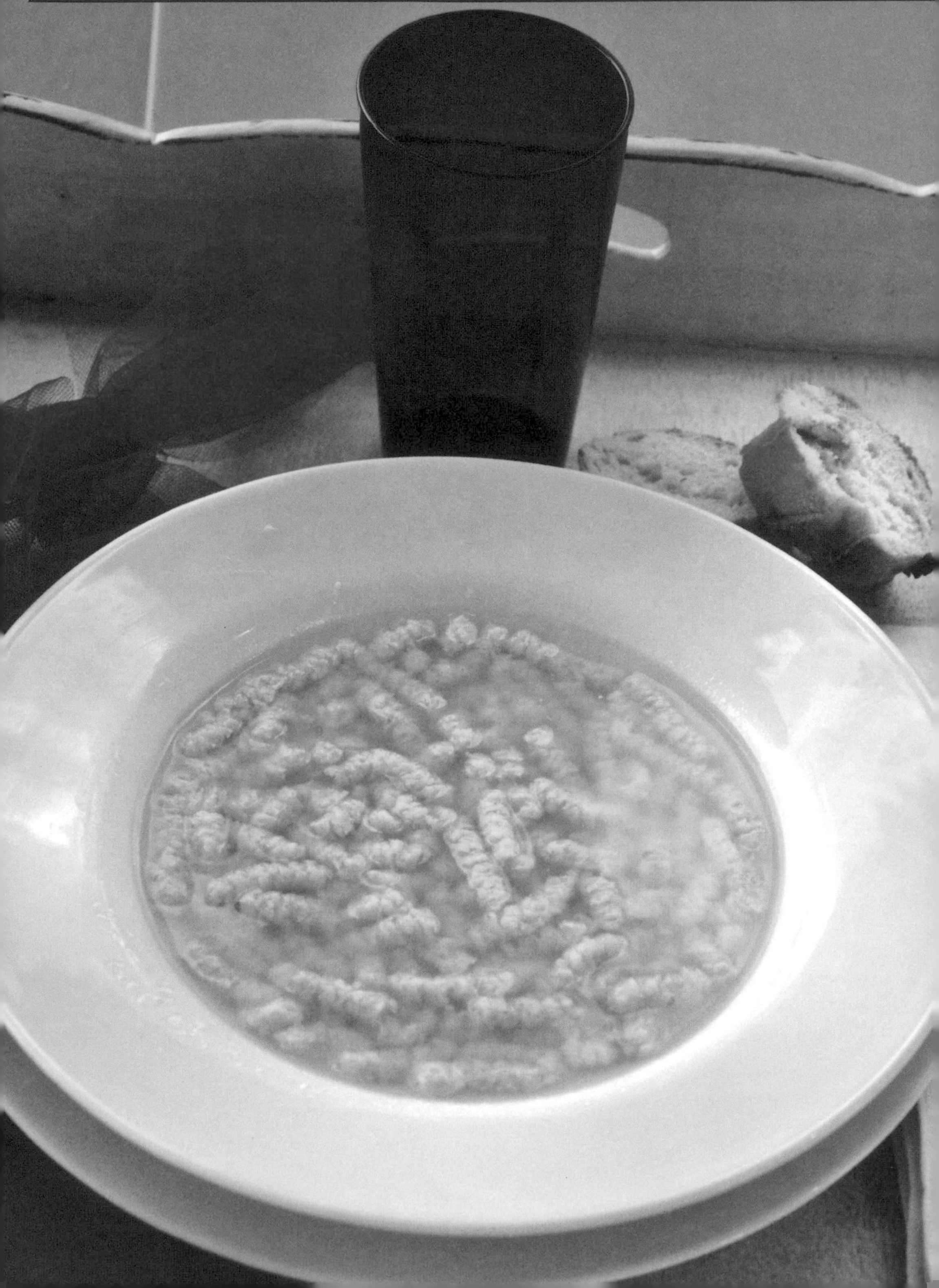

1 tablespoon unbleached all-purpose flour
Grated zest of 1 lemon
Grated nutmeg to taste
Salt to taste
2 large eggs

To make the broth, place the flank and top round steaks, carrots, celery, and tomato in a large pot. Add water to cover, bring to a boil, then lower the heat to a simmer and simmer for 2 hours. Add the chicken or chicken parts and simmer for an additional 30 minutes. Strain the broth through a sieve lined with paper towels or a coffee filter.

When you are ready to make the pasta, place the broth in a soup pot and bring to a boil. Meanwhile, in a bowl combine the breadcrumbs, Parmesan, flour, lemon zest, a pinch of grated nutmeg, and salt to taste. Make a well and add the eggs. Lightly beat the eggs with a fork, and then mix them into the dry ingredients. When you have a crumbly dough, knead it by hand (you may find it easier to knead it in the bowl rather than on a work surface) until smooth. Add additional breadcrumbs if the dough feels too sticky. Cut the dough in half and form into 2 balls, which should be about the size of tennis balls. Place them in a potato ricer fitted with the disk with large holes. Press the dough through the potato ricer to make strings. Cut the strings off with a knife every 3 inches or so, letting them fall directly into the pot of boiling broth. When the pasta rises to the surface of the broth, it is cooked. Transfer to individual soup plates and serve.

« ZUPPA DI VALPELLINE »
VALPELLINE SOUP

I wasn't terribly enthusiastic about this dish when my staff presented me with the recipe, but it elicited quite a strong reaction when I made it on my show. I could hear people murmuring their approval throughout the studio audience. When we were done taping, I really wanted to try it—but there was none left. This is a hearty dish perfect for a cold winter day. It comes from the mountainous Valle d'Aosta region.

SERVES 4 TO 6

Extra-virgin olive oil for oiling the baking dish and sautéing
1 1/2 ounces (40 grams) pancetta, diced
1/2 head Savoy cabbage or green cabbage, cored and cut into ribbons
Fresh rosemary leaves to taste
Fresh sage leaves to taste
1 (1-pound/500-gram) loaf dark rye bread, sliced
Cooking juices from roasted meat or meat extract thinned with water to
    taste
Salt and pepper to taste
7 ounces (200 grams) thinly sliced prosciutto crudo
3 1/2 ounces (100 grams) Fontina cheese, thinly sliced
6 cups (1 1/2 liters) beef broth

Preheat the oven to 350° F (180° C). Oil a baking dish and set aside. Sauté the pancetta in a pan with a little oil. Add the cabbage and some minced rosemary and sage and cook over low heat until the cabbage is very soft—it should be almost melting. Line the bottom of the prepared dish with some of the bread slices. Drizzle some of the cooking juices over the bread and top with some of the cabbage. Season with salt and pepper. Place additional whole leaves of rosemary and sage on top. Spread some of the prosciutto on top in a single layer, and spread some of the cheese slices on top of that in a single layer. Continue to layer the ingredients in this order, ending with the Fontina cheese, until all the ingredients have all been used. Pour the broth over the dish and bake until the top is browned and bubbling and the bread has absorbed a good amount of the broth, about 1 hour. Serve hot.

« MINESTRA DI UGO »
UGO'S LENTIL AND BROCCOLI SOUP

Ugo is my dear friend Ugo Conti, an actor who has appeared in such unforgettable films as *Mediterraneo* and is also an excellent cook. Soups are his specialty.

SERVES 4

1 (15-ounce/500-gram) can lentils, rinsed and drained
Chopped broccoli florets to taste

1/4 yellow onion, chopped
Salt to taste
1/2 package (200 grams) spaghetti or short pasta
Extra-virgin olive oil for drizzling
Grated Parmesan to taste

In a soup pot, combine the lentils, broccoli, and onion. Add water to cover, bring to a boil, then lower the heat to a simmer and simmer for 10 minutes. Season with salt. Break the spaghetti with your hands and let it fall into the pot. (You don't need to break short pasta.) Stir once and cook until the spaghetti is tender, then transfer to soup bowls and top each serving with a drizzle of oil and a generous amount of grated Parmesan. Serve hot.

« MINESTRA DI RISO INTEGRALE E SOGLIOLE »
SOUP WITH BROWN RICE AND SOLE

This soup is very filling but healthful, and it combines flavors in an interesting way. As a native of Piedmont, I had only eaten Jerusalem artichokes in bagna cauda, our region's most famous dish. Tasting them in a soup was a revelation.

SERVES 4

1 tablespoon vegetable broth granules (or the serving size indicated on
     the package)
1/3 cup (80 grams) short-grain brown rice
1/3 cup (80 grams) pearled barley
1/3 cup (80 grams) pearled farro
7 ounces (200 grams) Jerusalem artichokes, sliced
4 baby artichokes, trimmed and cut into wedges
12 ounces (350 grams) skinned sole fillets
Sesame seeds for dredging
Breadcrumbs for dredging
Extra-virgin olive oil for drizzling
Salt to taste

In a soup pot, combine the broth granules and rice with 2 cups (500 milliliters) water and bring to a boil, then lower the heat to a brisk simmer for 10 minutes. Add the barley (and additional water if the liquid no longer covers the grains), simmer for 10 minutes, and then add the farro (and additional water if needed). Cook for 10 minutes, then add the Jerusalem artichokes and baby artichokes and cook for 10 minutes more. The vegetables should be soft, but not falling apart.

Meanwhile, preheat the broiler. Line a jelly-roll pan with parchment paper and set aside. Cut the sole fillets into bite-sized pieces and dredge them in a mixture of equal amounts sesame seeds and breadcrumbs. Arrange the sole pieces on the prepared pan, drizzle with oil, sprinkle with salt, and broil for 5 minutes. Distribute the cooked soup and sole pieces among individual soup bowls. Serve hot.

« SPAGHETTI CON LA MOLLICA »
SPAGHETTI WITH BREADCRUMBS

This is the classic Italian dish to make when you've got nothing in the house and need to get dinner on the table, or when unexpected guests have just shown up at your door. It relies on a few inexpensive ingredients, but it is mighty tasty.

SERVES 2 TO 3

Salt to taste
1/2 package (250 grams) spaghetti
6 ounces (160 grams) bread, crusts removed (stale bread is fine)
2 sun-dried tomatoes in oil
2 cloves garlic
Extra-virgin olive oil for sautéing
2 anchovy fillets in oil, drained
Minced fresh parsley leaves to taste

Bring a large pot of salted water to a boil and cook the spaghetti. In the meantime, in a food processor fitted with the metal blade, grind the bread and the sun-dried tomatoes. In a pan large enough to hold the spaghetti, brown 1 clove garlic in oil, tilting the pan to keep the garlic submerged in the oil. Add the breadcrumb mixture, cook and stir until brown, then remove to a bowl, but don't bother to clean the pan. Add a little more oil to the pan and sauté the remaining clove garlic with the anchovies until the garlic browns and the anchovies dissolve. When the pasta is cooked, drain it in a colander and add it to the pan. Sprinkle with about half the breadcrumb mixture and toss over medium heat. Sprinkle with the remaining breadcrumbs and parsley and serve.

« SPAGHETTI AL PESTO DI AGRUMI »
SPAGHETTI WITH CITRUS PESTO

Filippo La Mantia, a famous native Sicilian chef, is just as sunny and welcoming as the food he cooks. He refuses to use garlic or onion in his cooking, which makes the level of flavor he achieves in this citrus pesto even more amazing.

SERVES 2

1 potato, peeled and cut into small dice
Extra-virgin olive oil for pan-frying, for the pesto, and for drizzling
Salt to taste
$1/3$ package (150 grams) spaghetti
$1/4$ cup tightly packed fresh basil leaves
5 fresh mint leaves
$1/4$ cup tightly packed fresh parsley leaves
1 tablespoon capers
Sections of $1/2$ orange, peel, seeds, and white pith removed
1 tablespoon pistachios
9 cherry tomatoes
Grated Parmesan to taste

In a small pan, fry the potato in about 1 inch oil until browned and crisp. Remove with a slotted spoon or skimmer and drain on paper towels. Meanwhile, bring a large pot of salted water to a boil and cook the pasta. In a food processor fitted with the metal blade or a blender, grind together the basil, mint, parsley, capers, orange sections, pistachios, and 5 cherry tomatoes with a little oil to make a paste. Cut the remaining 4 cherry tomatoes into quarters and set aside for garnish. When the pasta has finished cooking, reserve some of the pasta cooking water. Drain the pasta, and transfer it to a large pan with the orange and herb mixture. Toss over medium heat. If the pan looks dry, add the pasta cooking water, 1 to 2 tablespoons at a time. Sprinkle with grated Parmesan and mix in the fried potato cubes. Divide the pasta among individual serving bowls, top with the reserved quartered tomatoes, and drizzle with a little more olive oil. Serve hot.

« FARFALLE CON CREMA DI GRANA E PETALI DI ZUCCA »
FARFALLE PASTA WITH SQUASH "PETALS" AND GRANA CHEESE

My kids love this dish, but it's not just for children—all my friends like it, too.

SERVES 4

7 ounces (200 grams) winter squash, such as butternut or acorn squash
Coarse sea salt to taste
Minced fresh rosemary leaves to taste
Extra-virgin olive oil for drizzling
2 egg yolks
3/4 cup (70 grams) grated grana or Parmesan cheese, plus more for
**   serving**
3/4 cup plus 1 tablespoon (200 milliliters) heavy cream
Salt and pepper to taste
2/3 package (300 grams) farfalle (bow-tie pasta)

Preheat a convection oven to 400° F (200° C). Line a jelly-roll pan with parchment paper and set aside. Peel and seed the squash, cut the squash into quarters, and chop the flesh into thin slices. Arrange the slices in a single layer on the prepared pan and sprinkle with coarse salt and minced rosemary. Drizzle with some extra-virgin olive oil and bake until the edges of the squash slices begin to brown, about 10 minutes.

To make the sauce, combine the egg yolks, Parmesan, and cream in a small pot and cook, whisking constantly, over low heat until the sauce thickens and looks shiny and smooth. Remove from the heat and season with salt and pepper. Bring a large pot of salted water to a boil and cook the pasta. Drain the pasta, transfer to a bowl, and toss with the prepared sauce. Divide the pasta with the sauce among individual serving dishes. Top each portion with some of the squash petals. Sprinkle with a little additional grated Parmesan and a grinding of black pepper and serve hot.

« SPAGHETTI AGLI AGRETTI O BARBA DEL FRATE »
SPAGHETTI WITH SALTWORT GREENS

I'd heard about saltwort greens—which grow along the shoreline—for years before I finally had a chance to taste them. They're slightly bitter and quite grassy tasting. This recipe calls for boiling them in salted water right along with the pasta, and then topping the dish with a Gorgonzola cream and some ground hazelnuts. It's a fantastic combination.

SERVES 4

Salt to taste
7 ounces (200 grams) saltwort or other wild, bitter greens, roots
trimmed and rinsed well under cold running water
$^2/_3$ package (300 grams) spaghetti
3 $^1/_2$ ounces (100 grams) sweet Gorgonzola cheese, cut into cubes
1 cup (250 milliliters) heavy cream
$^1/_3$ cup (40 grams) hazelnuts, toasted, skinned, and chopped

Bring a large pot of salted water to a boil and cook the saltwort greens and spaghetti. Meanwhile, make the sauce: Combine the Gorgonzola with the cream in a pan big enough to hold the spaghetti. Cook over low heat, whisking frequently, until the cheese has melted. Drain the spaghetti and greens in a colander and add to the pan with the cheese mixture. Cook, tossing energetically, over high heat until the pasta has absorbed the sauce, about 2 minutes. Sprinkle with the chopped hazelnuts and serve immediately.

« ORECCHIETTE AL CAVOLFIORE »
ORECCHIETTE WITH CAULIFLOWER

The fresh orecchiette sold in the refrigerator case at your supermarket are so delicious that they hardly need any sauce at all, except that their cup shape is so well-suited to holding little bits and pieces, it's a shame to eat them plain. This dish is not only a perfect light weekday choice, but it's inexpensive to boot. To avoid a boiled cauliflower smell in your house, use frozen cauliflower florets.

SERVES 4

3 cloves garlic, crushed
3 anchovy fillets in oil, drained
Extra-virgin olive oil for sautéing
1 (1-pound/450-gram) bag frozen cauliflower florets
Salt and pepper to taste
3 tablespoons breadcrumbs
10 ounces (300 grams) fresh orecchiette
2 tablespoons grated Parmesan

In a pan large enough to hold the pasta, brown the garlic with the anchovies in some olive oil, tilting the pan so the garlic remains submerged in the oil. When the garlic is soft and the anchovies have dissolved, add the cauliflower florets (no need to thaw them), season with salt and pepper, cover, and cook until the florets are easily pierced with a fork. (I often crush them with a fork a little to make a kind of chunky puree.)

Meanwhile, in a nonstick pan, toast the breadcrumbs over medium heat. (Keep a close eye on them—they can burn easily.) Bring a large pot of salted water to a boil and cook the pasta. Reserve some of the pasta cooking water, drain the pasta, and add it to the pan with the cauliflower. Toss over medium heat and add some pasta cooking water, 1 to 2 tablespoons at a time, if the pan looks dry. Transfer the pasta to a serving dish. Sprinkle with the toasted breadcrumbs and grated Parmesan and serve immediatcly.

« ORECCHIETTE CON PESTO DI PISTACCHI E ZUCCHINE CHIPS »
ORECCHIETTE WITH PISTACHIO PESTO AND FRIED ZUCCHINI

Adding a special garnish to a pasta or risotto dish is a great way to elevate it above the ordinary. In this case, fried zucchini dress up a dish of orecchiette topped with a mint and pistachio sauce.

SERVES 4

²/₃ cup (80 grams) pistachios
1 clove garlic
Leaves of 1 bunch mint
Leaves of 2 bunches fresh basil
Salt to taste
Extra-virgin olive oil for making the pesto
1 zucchini, cut into very thin rounds
Unbleached all-purpose flour for dredging
Vegetable oil for pan-frying
10 ounces (300 grams) fresh orecchiette
Grated Parmesan cheese to taste

In a food processor fitted with the metal blade or a blender, grind the pistachios with the garlic. Add the mint and basil leaves and a pinch of salt. Continue to grind while drizzling in extra-virgin olive oil in a thin stream until the mixture has the consistency of a paste. Dredge the zucchini rounds in flour and pan-fry them in a generous amount of vegetable oil until golden and crisp. Transfer to paper towels to drain and salt lightly. Meanwhile, bring a large pot of salted water to a boil and cook the pasta. Drain in a colander, then transfer to a large bowl. Add the pesto and a generous amount of grated cheese to the pasta and mix to combine. Divide the pasta among individual pasta bowls, top each serving with the fried zucchini, and serve immediately.

« CONCHIGLIONI DEL BARONE »
PASTA WITH BUTTER AND AMARETTO COOKIE CRUMBS

If you are a fan of Mantua's typical tortellini with a sweet filling, you will love this pasta, which has similar flavors but is much quicker to prepare. Daniele Barone shared this delicious dish with me.

SERVES 2 TO 3

Salt to taste
¹/₂ package (250 grams) conchiglioni pasta (shells)
5 ounces (150 grams) amaretti cookies
5 tablespoons (70 grams) unsalted butter, cut into pieces

1 cup (100 grams) grated Parmesan
Pepper to taste

Bring a large pot of salted water to a boil and cook the pasta. Crumble the amaretti cookies by hand, leaving some larger pieces. In a serving bowl, combine about $2/3$ of the cookie crumbs with the butter. When the pasta is cooked, drain and transfer to the bowl. Toss to combine with the cookie crumbs and melt the butter. Divide among individual serving dishes and top with the remaining cookie crumbs, the grated Parmesan, and a generous amount of pepper. Serve immediately.

« CONCHIGLIE ALLE PATATE »
PASTA WITH POTATOES

This is an inexpensive dish that's rich with flavor. Crunchy little cubes of potato and pasta are a winning combination, and the shape of the conchiglie (shells) is perfect for harboring little surprising bursts of flavor. The breadcrumb topping makes it even better.

SERVES 4

2 cloves garlic, crushed
Extra-virgin olive oil for sautéing and for breadcrumb mixture
2 potatoes, peeled and cut into small dice
Minced fresh rosemary leaves to taste
3 slices bread, crusts removed
Fresh basil leaves to taste
Salt to taste
$2/3$ package (300 grams) conchiglie (shells)
Pepper to taste
Grated pecorino to taste

In a pan, sauté the garlic in some olive oil. Add the potato cubes and rosemary and cook until the potatoes are golden and crisp. Meanwhile, toast the bread. In a food processor fitted with the metal blade, grind the toasted bread with basil leaves to taste and a little oil to make a moist breadcrumb mixture. Bring a large pot of salted water to a boil and cook the pasta. Reserve a little pasta cooking water, then drain the pasta and add it to the pan with the potatoes. Sprinkle with some pepper and pecorino and add a tablespoon or two of the pasta cooking water if the pan looks dry. Transfer to a serving dish, sprinkle the breadcrumb mixture on top, and serve immediately.

« ORECCHIETTE PATATE E RUCOLA »
ORECCHIETTE WITH POTATOES AND ARUGULA

So many people make important contributions behind the scenes to the work that I do. Chefs, writers, the production team, and friends all play a big part. I especially treasure people who offer their personal experiences and expertise. One of those is Francesca Di Maio, who provides me with the tips that I dispense at the end of every show. This recipe is hers, and she's from the Puglia region, so she knows a lot about orecchiette, that area's signature pasta.

SERVES 4

Salt to taste
1 potato, peeled and sliced into rounds
$\frac{1}{2}$ package (250 grams) orecchiette
1 bunch arugula
2 cloves garlic
Extra-virgin olive oil for drizzling
6 cherry tomatoes, halved
Grated Parmesan to taste

Bring a large pot of salted water to a boil. Add the potato slices. When the water returns to a boil, add the orecchiette. When it returns to a boil again, add the arugula. In the meantime, over medium heat, sauté the garlic cloves in olive oil, tilting the pan to keep the garlic submerged. Add the tomatoes and cook, stirring frequently. When the pasta and potatoes are cooked, drain and add to the pan, along with the arugula. Toss over medium heat, then transfer to a serving bowl. Sprinkle with grated Parmesan, drizzle with a little olive oil, and serve immediately.

« SPAGHETTONI CON PESTO TRAPANESE »
SPAGHETTONI WITH TRAPANESE PESTO

A nice plate of pasta is always a pleasure. This may not look like much—just pasta with tomato sauce—but take just one bite and you'll realize it's very special. This sauce can be prepared in advance. It's a beautiful dish, and absolutely delicious—truly perfect in every way.

SERVES 4

1 1/3 pounds (600 grams) ripe tomatoes
3 tablespoons almonds
Leaves of 1 sprig basil
1/2 clove garlic
Coarse salt to taste
1/2 cup (100 milliliters) extra-virgin olive oil, plus more for drizzling
14 ounces (400 grams) fresh spaghetti alla chitarra or other fresh long
     egg noodles
Grated pecorino to taste
Pepper to taste

Cut an X in the base of each tomato. Bring a large pot of water to a boil and boil the tomatoes for 2 minutes. Remove with a slotted spoon and peel. Chop the peeled tomatoes by hand. Meanwhile, in a food processor fitted with the metal blade or a blender, grind the almonds, basil, garlic, a pinch of coarse salt, and the oil. In a serving bowl, combine the chopped peeled tomatoes with the almond mixture. Bring a large pot of salted water to a boil, cook the pasta (fresh pasta is ready very quickly), drain, and add to the bowl with the sauce. Toss to combine. Drizzle with additional oil, sprinkle with a generous amount of grated pecorino, and season with pepper. Serve immediately.

« LINGUINE AL PESTO ALTERNATIVO »
LINGUINE WITH "ALTERNATIVE" PESTO

I love pesto, but I sometimes crave something other than basil. Over the years, I've developed some alternatives—this is one of my most successful riffs on pesto.

SERVES 3 TO 4

Salt to taste
$2/3$ package (300 grams) linguine
$3\,1/2$ ounces (100 grams) arugula
Fresh thyme leaves to taste
Fresh marjoram leaves to taste
2 tablespoons (20 grams) pine nuts
$1/2$ clove garlic
2 tablespoons (20 grams) almonds
$1/4$ cup (50 milliliters) extra-virgin olive oil
8 sun-dried tomatoes in oil, diced
Grated Parmesan to taste

Bring a large pot of salted water to a boil and cook the pasta. Meanwhile, set aside a few of the prettiest arugula leaves to use for the garnish. Blanch the rest of the arugula in a small pot of boiling water and shock it in cold water. Grind the blanched arugula in a food processor with thyme and marjoram to taste. Add the pine nuts, garlic, almonds, the oil, and a pinch of salt and grind again. If the pesto seems dry, thin it with a little of the pasta cooking water. When the pasta is cooked, drain and toss with the pesto in a serving bowl. Sprinkle the sun-dried tomatoes and grated Parmesan on top. Garnish with the reserved arugula leaves and serve immediately.

GARGANELLI PASTA WITH ZUCCHINI, SAFFRON, AND BACON

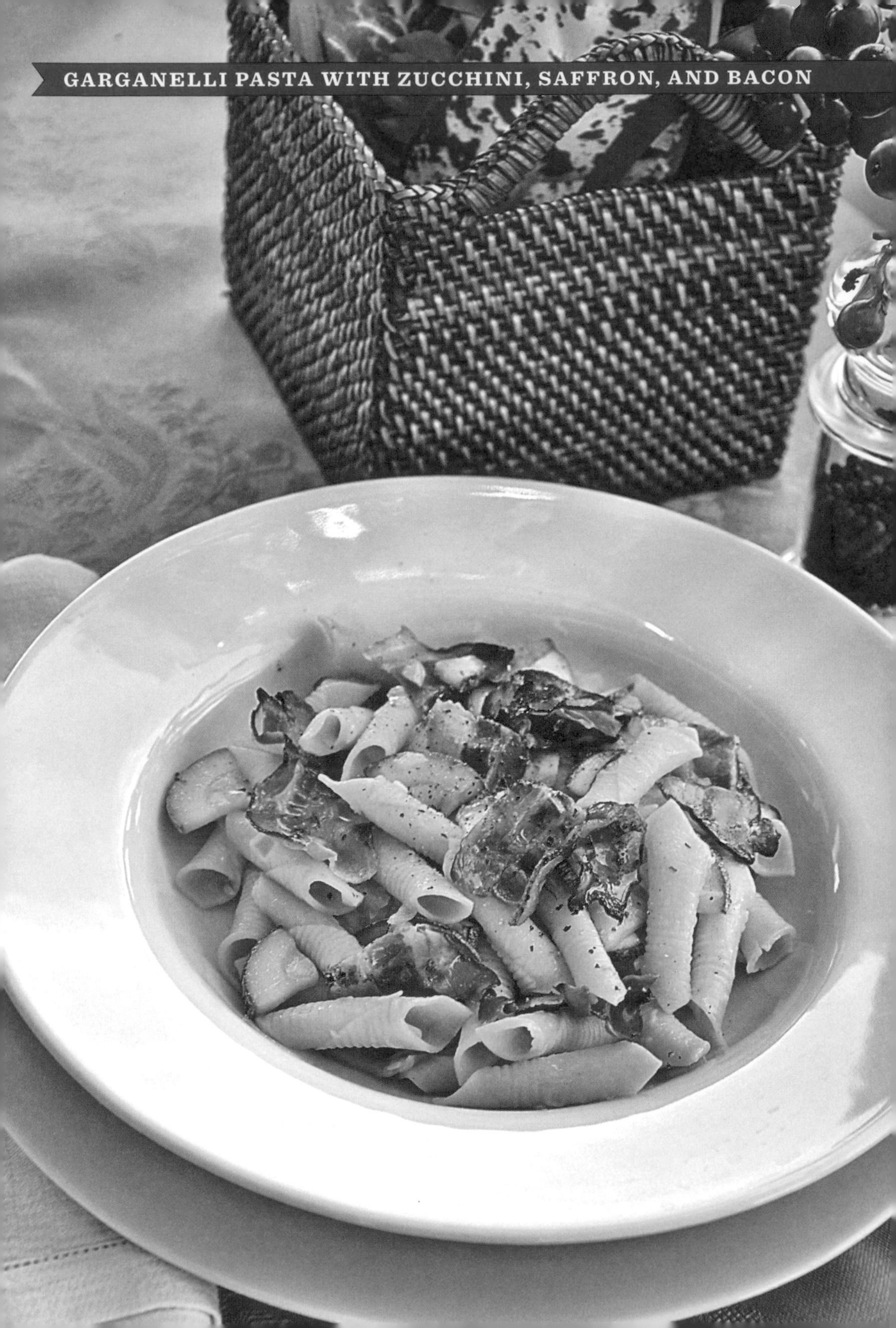

« GARGANELLI CON ZUCCHINE, ZAFFERANO E BACON CROCCANTE »

GARGANELLI PASTA WITH ZUCCHINI, SAFFRON, AND BACON

My kids love bacon, and who am I to deny them? If they could eat whatever they wanted, they'd probably dig in to a big American breakfast of bacon and eggs every morning. This dish is my attempt at a compromise: the delicious taste of bacon along with plenty of healthy zucchini. Garganelli are egg pasta that look like quills.

SERVES 4

$1/2$ yellow onion or 1 shallot, sliced
Extra-virgin olive oil for sautéing
3 zucchini, thinly sliced into rounds
Salt to taste
$1/2$ package (250 grams) garganelli or other egg pasta
4 slices (100 grams) bacon, minced
$1/4$ teaspoon (1 envelope) powdered saffron
Grated Parmesan (optional)
Pepper to taste

In a large pan, sauté the onion in a generous amount of olive oil until transparent. Add the zucchini, season with salt, and cook until the zucchini are soft. Meanwhile, bring a large pot of salted water to a boil and add the pasta. While the pasta is cooking, cook the bacon (no need to add oil) in a skillet until very crispy. Transfer the bacon to paper towels to drain. Reserve 1 cup pasta cooking water and drain the pasta in a colander. Add the pasta to the pan with the zucchini and cook, tossing briskly, over medium heat for 1 minute. Dissolve the saffron powder in the reserved pasta cooking water and add that to the pan as well. Cook, stirring, until the pasta is bright yellow and there is no more liquid in the pan. Stir in the grated Parmesan if using. Transfer to a serving bowl and fold in the bacon. Season with pepper and serve immediately.

« FARFALLE ALLA ZUCCA CON PINOLI E PROSCIUTTO »
FARFALLE PASTA WITH SQUASH, PINE NUTS, AND PROSCIUTTO

This is a classic dish that is always a hit with both children and adults. It looks very pretty, too!

SERVES 3 TO 4

14 ounces (400 grams) winter squash, such as butternut or acorn squash
1 shallot
Extra-virgin olive oil for sautéing
Salt to taste
1 tablespoon vegetable broth granules (or the serving size indicated on
    the package), dissolved in $1/2$ cup (100 milliliters) water
Minced fresh rosemary leaves to taste
$1/2$ cup (80 grams) pine nuts
3 ounces (80 grams) prosciutto cotto, diced
$2/3$ package (300 grams) farfalle (bow-tie pasta)
Shaved Parmesan to taste

Peel and seed the squash and cut it into cubes. Mince the shallot and sauté it in a large pan with some oil, then add the squash. Salt to taste and add the dissolved broth granules. Season with minced rosemary and cook over medium heat, covered, until the squash is soft, 10 to 15 minutes. If the pan is getting too dry, add a little water. Meanwhile, in another pan over medium heat, toast the pine nuts, additional minced rosemary, and the prosciutto, shaking the pan frequently to keep the nuts from burning. Bring a large pot of salted water to a boil and cook the pasta. When the pasta is cooked, drain it in a colander, then add it to the pan with the squash. Sprinkle with the pine nut and prosciutto mixture and toss to combine. Distribute among individual pasta bowls, top with Parmesan shavings, and serve immediately.

« STRASCINATI CON BROCCOLETTI E FONDUTA »
STRASCINATI PASTA WITH BROCCOLI AND MELTED TALEGGIO

This is a simple yet very effective idea: broccoli and strascinati pasta tossed with a rich taleggio sauce. This is the perfect winter dish.

SERVES 4

9 ounces (250 grams) taleggio cheese, cut into cubes
1 tablespoon (20 grams) unsalted butter
$1/2$ cup (150 milliliters) whole milk
1 egg yolk
14 ounces (400 grams) broccoli
Salt to taste
1 package (400 grams) strascinati pasta
Extra-virgin olive oil for drizzling
Grated nutmeg to taste
Pepper to taste
Grated Parmesan to taste

Combine the taleggio, butter, and milk in the top of a double boiler and cook over low heat, whisking constantly, until the butter has melted. Add the egg yolk and cook for 10 minutes more. Remove from the heat and whisk in about $1/2$ cup cold water to cool down the sauce. Separate the broccoli florets and stems and dice the stems. (Discard any fibrous ends.) Bring a large pot of salted water to a boil and add the broccoli. When the water returns to a boil, add the pasta. Meanwhile, place the cheese sauce in a serving bowl. When the pasta and broccoli are cooked, drain and add to the serving bowl. Toss to combine. Top with a drizzle of olive oil, grated nutmeg, pepper, and grated Parmesan and serve immediately.

« FARFALLE FUCSIA DI UGO TOGNAZZI »
UGO TOGNAZZI'S FUCHSIA FARFALLE WITH BEETS

If you want to amaze your guests, prepare this dish. Not only is it a shockingly bright color, but it offers an unusual flavor as well. To top it off, it's got an interesting history: It was one of the dishes that the late actor Ugo Tognazzi used to prepare for his famous dinners. His son Gianmarco Tognazzi, also an actor, came on the show and cooked it with me. You can purchase vacuum-packed cooked beets in the refrigerator case at your grocery store.

SERVES 4 TO 6

1 yellow onion, thinly sliced
2 tablespoons (30 grams) unsalted butter
$1/4$ cup plus 1 tablespoon (75 milliliters) extra-virgin olive oil
1 cup (250 milliliters) white wine
2 cooked beets, diced
Salt and pepper to taste
1 cup (250 milliliters) heavy cream
1 package (400 grams) farfalle (bow-tie pasta)
Juice of $1/2$ lemon
3 tablespoons grated Parmesan
Fresh basil leaves to taste, cut into ribbons

In a pan, sauté the onion in the butter and oil. When it begins to color, add the white wine and allow most of it to evaporate. Add the beets, season with salt and pepper, and cook for 3 minutes more. Transfer the contents of the pan to a food processor fitted with the metal blade or a blender, add the cream, and process until smooth. Bring a large pot of salted water to a boil and cook the farfalle.

In a large pan, heat the beet mixture over low heat for a few minutes. Stir in the lemon juice and Parmesan. When the pasta is cooked, drain it and add it to the pan, tossing to combine with the sauce. Distribute among individual pasta bowls and garnish with the basil ribbons.

« PASTA FREDDA ALLE MELANZANE »
EGGPLANT PASTA SALAD

I find pasta salad is either great or terrible. It needs a little twist in order to fall on the great side of the scale. Fabio still loves pasta salad with canned tuna, mozzarella, and cherry tomatoes, but I refuse to make it—it's been done a million times. This pasta salad is pretty unique. It includes an arugula pesto, chickpeas, and roasted eggplant.

SERVES 4

2 eggplants
Salt to taste
$1/4$ cup plus 2 tablespoons (90 milliliters) extra-virgin olive oil for
    drizzling
$1/2$ package (250 grams) fusilli pasta
1 (15-ounce/500-gram) can chickpeas, rinsed and drained
1 bunch arugula
Juice of 1 lemon
3 tablespoons grated Parmesan

Preheat the oven to 400° F (200° C). Slice the eggplants into rounds and place them on a jelly-roll pan. Salt them, drizzle them with a little olive oil, and bake until they are soft, about 20 minutes. Set aside a few of the prettiest slices of eggplant to use for the garnish.

Meanwhile, bring a large pot of salted water to a boil and add the chickpeas and the pasta. (The canned chickpeas are already cooked, but you want to soften them a bit more.) While the pasta is cooking, in a food processor fitted with the metal blade or a blender, combine the arugula, a pinch of salt, the lemon juice, olive oil, grated Parmesan, and a few drops of the pasta cooking water and process until smooth. Drain the chickpeas and pasta and run cold water over them. Drain briefly again, then transfer to a serving bowl. Drizzle some olive oil over the pasta and chickpeas and toss to combine. Cut all but the reserved eggplant slices into small pieces and add those to the bowl as well, then add the arugula pesto and stir to combine thoroughly. Garnish with the reserved eggplant slices.

« PENNE ALLE CIME DI RAPA E PANCETTA AFFUMICATA »
PENNE WITH BROCCOLI RABE AND SMOKED PANCETTA

Traditionally, broccoli rabe is served with orecchiette pasta, but I think it goes well with penne, too. Try this and see whether you agree!

SERVES 4

Salt to taste
10 ounces (300 grams) broccoli rabe
$2/3$ package (300 grams) penne
3 $1/2$ ounces (100 grams) smoked pancetta, diced
2 cloves garlic
1 yellow onion, diced
Extra-virgin olive oil for sautéing
Chile pepper flakes to taste
Pepper to taste
Grated pecorino for serving

Bring a large pot of salted water to a boil and cook the broccoli rabe. Bring a separate large pot of salted water to a boil and cook the pasta. In a large pan over medium heat, sauté the pancetta, garlic, and onion in oil. Remove and discard the garlic once it is dark brown. Drain the cooked broccoli rabe and add it to the pan, along with some chile pepper flakes. Cook over medium-high heat, stirring frequently, for about 3 minutes. When the pasta is cooked, reserve a little cooking liquid, then drain the pasta and add it to the pan with the broccoli rabe and the pancetta. Add the pasta cooking water, 1 to 2 tablespoons at a time, if the pan seems dry. Season with pepper and serve with a generous amount of grated pecorino on the side.

« PENNE ALLE ERBE FINI »
PENNE WITH MINCED HERBS

This is one of the quickest pasta dishes there is, but it has an intense flavor. The secret is to mince the herbs very finely so that they almost become a paste. Whisking a little of the pasta cooking water into the cheese results in a creamy sauce.

SERVES 2

Salt to taste
$1/2$ package (200 grams) penne
Fresh sage, basil, rosemary, and thyme leaves to taste
1 tablespoon unsalted butter
$1/2$ teaspoon extra-virgin olive oil
2 tablespoons spreadable cheese
Pepper to taste

Bring a large pot of salted water to a boil and cook the pasta. In the meantime, place the herbs in a food processor and very finely mince. Place the butter in a large pan with the oil and melt the butter over low heat. Add the minced herbs and the cheese. Stir in about $1/4$ cup of the pasta cooking water and whisk until smooth. The sauce should be the consistency of sour cream. If not, add 1 to 2 tablespoons more cooking water, whisking until smooth between additions, until it reaches the desired consistency. Season the sauce with salt and pepper, keeping in mind that the pasta cooking water is also salted. When the pasta is cooked, drain in a colander, add to the pan with the cheese mixture, and toss over low heat until combined. Serve immediately.

« PENNETTE CON CREMA DI PISELLI E STRACCHINO »
PENNETTE WITH PEAS AND STRACCHINO CHEESE

Peas and mild, creamy stracchino cheese (which you can purchase in Italian specialty stores) are a winning combination. This dish is irresistible!

SERVES 3 TO 4

Salt to taste
$1/2$ package (250 grams) pennette pasta
$3/4$ cup (100 grams) frozen peas
$1/4$ cup (50 milliliters) whole milk
$1/4$ cup (50 grams) stracchino cheese
Fresh marjoram leaves to taste
Fresh thyme leaves to taste
1 tablespoon unsalted butter
Grated Parmesan to taste

Bring a large pot of salted water to a boil and cook the pasta. In a separate pot, boil the peas in salted water. In a third pot, scald the milk. When the peas are cooked, drain them, reserve about half, and transfer the remaining half to a food processor fitted with the metal blade or a blender. Add the stracchino, the scalded milk, marjoram, and thyme to the food processor and puree. When the pasta is cooked, drain in a colander and transfer to a serving bowl. Add the butter and toss with the pasta to melt, then toss in the pureed pea mixture and the reserved whole peas. Sprinkle with grated Parmesan and serve immediately.

« VERMICELLI AL CIPOLLOTTO DI TROPEA »
VERMICELLI WITH TROPEA ONIONS

This wonderful dish is from Aimo, the chef at the restaurant Aimo e Nadia in Milan. When I invited him to appear on my show, I begged him to teach me to make this specific dish because Fabio adores it. You won't believe that you can make something so delicious out of ten onions and a few other ingredients. Tropea onions are extra-sweet red onions that are usually torpedo-shaped. They are available at farmer's markets and specialty food stores. Though Vidalia onions look different, they are similarly sweet and may be easier to find.

SERVES 4

3 tablespoons extra-virgin olive oil
2 bay leaves
2 cloves garlic, minced
10 Tropea or Vidalia onions, sliced

Vegetable broth (broth made with a bouillon cube is fine), *quanto basta*
Chile pepper flakes, *quanto basta*
Fresh basil leaves to taste
Salt to taste
2/3 package (300 grams) vermicelli pasta
10 cherry tomatoes, diced
Fresh parsley leaves to taste
Grated Parmesan to taste

In a pan large enough to hold the pasta, add the olive oil then the bay leaves and warm over low heat. Add the garlic and onions and cook over low heat, uncovered, for about 15 minutes, adding small amounts of broth to keep the pan from getting dry. When the mixture looks soft and moist like an onion jam, remove from the heat, season with chile pepper flakes, basil (if the basil leaves are large, tear them by hand as you add them to the pan), and salt. Bring a large pot of salted water to a boil and cook the vermicelli. When the pasta is cooked al dente, reserve 2 cups pasta cooking water. Drain the pasta, add it to the pan with the onion mixture, and toss over high heat. If the pan begins to look dry, add some of the reserved pasta cooking water, a little at a time. Add the tomatoes and parsley and toss to combine. Remove the pan from the heat, sprinkle with grated Parmesan, and toss to combine. Serve immediately.

« REGINETTE DI VITTORIO EMANUELE II »
REGINETTE PASTA WITH PORCINI MUSHROOMS

Reportedly this was a favorite dish of the last king of Italy. Apparently he liked it showered with thin shavings of white truffle, but I promise that this more plebeian version is very good as well!

SERVES 4

1 yellow onion, sliced
7 ounces (200 grams) prosciutto cotto, diced
Extra-virgin olive oil for sautéing
7 ounces (200 grams) frozen chopped porcini mushrooms
Salt to taste
1/2 cup (100 milliliters) white wine

2/3 package (300 grams) reginette pasta
3 large eggs
1/2 cup (50 grams) grated Parmesan
Pepper to taste
Minced fresh parsley leaves to taste

In a large pan, sauté the onion and prosciutto in a little oil. Add the mushrooms, season with salt, pour in the wine, and cook until the mushrooms are soft, 10 to 15 minutes. Meanwhile, bring a large pot of salted water to a boil and cook the pasta. When the pasta is cooked, drain in a colander and then transfer to the pan with the mushroom mixture. Cook and stir over medium heat for 2 minutes, then remove from the heat. In a small bowl, beat together the eggs with the grated cheese, then briskly stir the egg mixture into the pasta. Sprinkle with pepper and minced parsley and serve immediately.

« SCIALATIELLI IN SALSA DI CIPOLLE »
SCIALATIELLI PASTA IN ONION SAUCE

Nothing simpler, nothing better! The only "trick" to this pasta is that you have to be patient about stewing the onions. You don't want to brown them. They should basically break down and melt into a puree. Also, while I usually rely on anchovy fillets in oil, here I use the type preserved in salt. They require a little more effort—you have to rinse and bone them—but they also have more flavor, so they really elevate a dish like this one, where the anchovies are one of a small number of ingredients. Scialatielli are long noodles that resemble fat spaghetti.

SERVES 4

1 small onion, thinly sliced
Extra-virgin olive oil for sautéing
5 anchovy fillets in salt, rinsed and boned
1 fresh bay leaf, minced
1/2 cup (100 milliliters) white wine
Salt to taste
1/2 package (250 grams) scialatielli or any other long fresh noodles
Pepper to taste

In a pan, sauté the onion in a generous amount of olive oil. When it becomes transparent, add about $1/2$ cup water, cover, and braise over low heat for 5 minutes. Add the anchovy fillets and the bay leaf to the onions and stir to combine. The anchovies should quickly dissolve into the mixture. Cover and continue to braise. When most of the water has evaporated, add the white wine and let it evaporate at a gentle simmer. Remove the onion sauce from the heat. Bring a large pot of salted water to a boil and cook the pasta. (Fresh pasta cooks quickly.) When the pasta is cooked, drain it in a colander and add it to the pan with the onions, still off the heat. Stir to combine well. Top with a generous grating of pepper and serve immediately.

« MEZZEMANICHE SQUACQUERONE E CRUDO »
MEZZEMANICHE WITH SQUACQUERONE CHEESE AND PROSCIUTTO

I spend every summer on the Adriatic coast in the Romagna region, where one traditional beach food is *piadina*: a flatbread cooked on a griddle and filled with various items, frequently squacquerone—a soft, spreadable cheese—arugula, and prosciutto. Here, I've used those same ingredients in a pasta dish. It brings me right back to those days of sun and salt air! Mezzemaniche are similar to rigatoni.

SERVES 2 TO 3

Salt to taste
$1/2$ package (250 grams) mezzemaniche or other short tubular pasta
2 tablespoons extra-virgin olive oil
Pepper to taste
1 cup (250 grams) squacquerone or another soft, spreadable cheese
1 bunch arugula
2 ounces (50 grams) thinly sliced prosciutto crudo
Shaved Parmesan to taste

Bring a large pot of salted water to a boil and cook the pasta. While the pasta is cooking, in a food processor fitted with the metal blade or a blender, process the olive oil, a pinch of salt and pepper, and the squacquerone cheese until well combined. Reserve a few of the prettier leaves of arugula. Add the remaining arugula and 2 to 3 slices of prosciutto to the processor or blender, reserving the remaining prosciutto slices.

MEZZEMANICHE WITH SQUACQUERONE CHEESE AND PROSCIUTTO

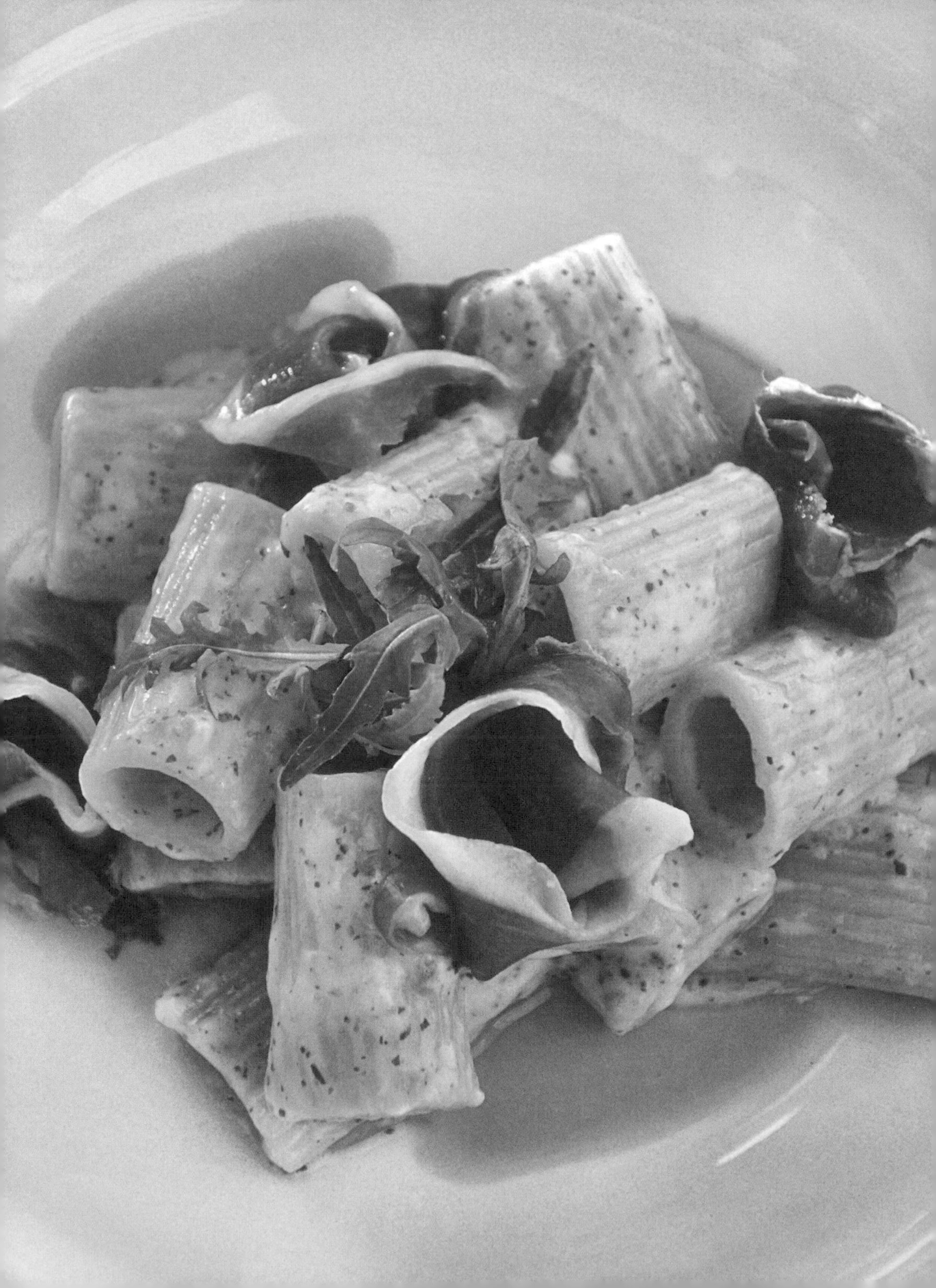

Process into a puree, adding a little of the pasta cooking water if the mixture looks dry. It should have the consistency of sour cream. Cut the reserved prosciutto slices into wide strips. When the pasta is cooked, drain it in a colander and toss it with the arugula and cheese puree in a serving bowl. Garnish with the reserved arugula leaves (tear into pieces if they are large), the prosciutto strips, and the shaved Parmesan and serve immediately.

« PENNONI ITALIANI »
TRICOLOR PENNONI

This tricolor pasta dish displays the colors of the Italian flag. It's pretty to look at and easy to prepare. There's just one thing to watch out for: Don't add the mozzarella with the pan still over the heat, as it will clump up into a single glob. Pennoni are simply larger-sized penne.

SERVES 4

Salt to taste
3/4 package (350 grams) pennoni pasta
1 pound (500 grams) cherry tomatoes
3 cloves garlic
Extra-virgin olive oil for sautéing
1 fresh mozzarella ball (8 ounces/225 grams), diced
Fresh basil leaves to taste

Bring a large pot of salted water to a boil and cook the pasta. Meanwhile, slice the cherry tomatoes in half, transfer them to a bowl, salt to taste, toss, and set aside. Crush the garlic and, in a large pan, sauté it in a generous amount of olive oil, tilting the pan to keep the garlic cloves submerged. Add the tomatoes, stir to combine, lower the heat, and cook, covered, while the pasta is cooking. Stir the tomatoes occasionally, but be gentle—try not to break them up. When the pasta is cooked, drain it in a colander and add it to the pan with the tomatoes. Turn the heat up to medium-high and cook briefly while tossing the pasta with the tomatoes to combine. Transfer the pasta to a serving bowl. Scatter on the diced mozzarella and basil leaves and serve immediately.

« SPAGHETTI ALLA CHITARRA CON PÂTÉ D'OLIVE E POMODORO*
SPAGHETTI ALLA CHITARRA WITH OLIVE PASTE AND TOMATOES

This dish always reminds me of the early years in my relationship with Fabio when we used to prepare romantic dinners for two. We were crazy about spaghetti alla chitarra—fresh egg noodles that are made with an instrument that looks like a guitar—and this is the perfect sauce for them. In those days, I made a dainty portion of pasta. Today our family has grown so large that I need a whole package and sometimes more!

SERVES 4

Salt to taste
9 ounces (250 grams) fresh spaghetti alla chitarra or other fresh long egg
    noodles
1 yellow onion, thinly sliced
Extra-virgin olive oil for sautéing
3 tablespoons olive paste
1 (15-ounce/400-gram) can whole peeled tomatoes
Chile pepper flakes to taste
Fresh basil leaves to taste

Bring a large pot of salted water to a boil and cook the pasta. In a large pan over medium heat, sauté the onion in a small amount of oil. Add the olive paste, tomatoes, a pinch of chile pepper flakes (more if you like it spicy), and a small amount of salt. (Olive paste is quite salty.) When the pasta is cooked, reserve about 1 cup cooking water and drain the pasta in a colander. Add a little cooking water to the pan to moisten the sauce—you probably won't need more than $1/4$ cup. Transfer the pasta to the pan and toss over medium heat until the pasta is coated with the sauce. Tear basil leaves over the pasta and serve immediately.

« CARBONARA MONFERRINA »
CARBONARA FROM MONFERRATO

I'm embarrassed to admit that I heard of this dish, which is from my hometown of Monferrato in Piedmont, for the first time just a few months ago. And now I don't know how I've lived all these years without it. It's a wonderful alternative to the typical Roman carbonara that incorporates asparagus, one of my favorite vegetables.

SERVES 4

Salt to taste
1 bunch asparagus
2 ounces (50 grams) smoked pancetta, diced
2 cloves garlic
Extra-virgin olive oil for sautéing
9 ounces (250 grams) egg fettuccine or other fresh long egg noodles
1 large egg
1 egg yolk
2 tablespoons grated Parmesan
1 tablespoon ricotta
Pepper to taste

Bring a large pot of salted water to a boil for the pasta. Trim the asparagus, keeping the tips and about 2 inches of the stalks. (Reserve the rest for soup or another use.) If the asparagus you are using is particularly thick, cut the tips in half the long way. In a large pan, sauté the pancetta and garlic in a small amount of oil until the garlic begins to brown. Add the asparagus tips and just enough water to come about halfway up the asparagus. Cook over medium-low heat, covered, until the asparagus is tender, about 3 minutes. Add the pasta to the cooking water. (Egg pasta cooks quickly.) In a small bowl, beat the egg, the yolk, the grated Parmesan, and the ricotta until thoroughly combined and creamy. When the asparagus is cooked, remove and discard the garlic cloves. When the pasta is cooked, drain it in a colander and add it to the pan with the asparagus. Toss to combine. Remove the pan from the heat and pour the egg and ricotta mixture over the pasta. Toss to combine, season with pepper, and serve immediately.

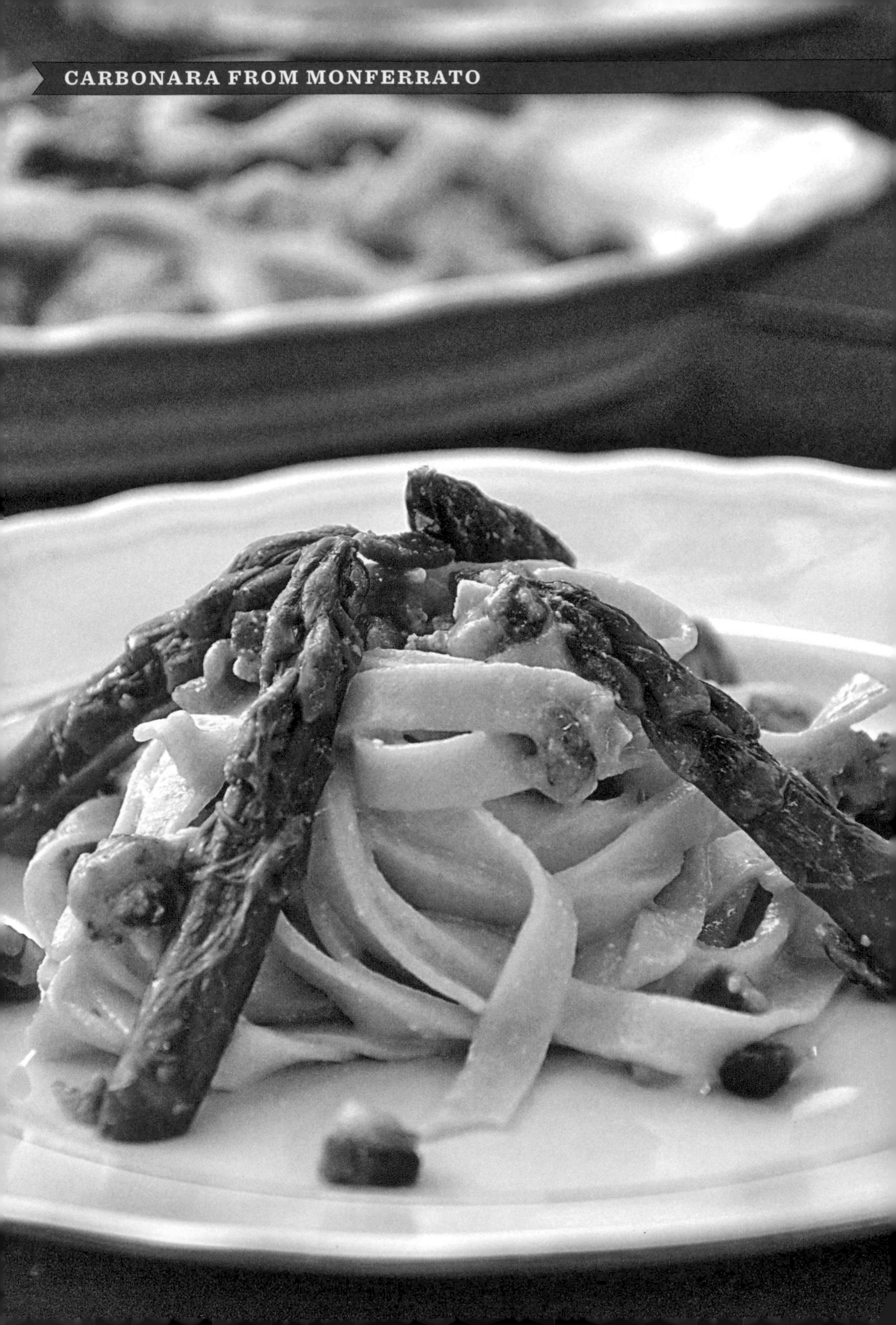
CARBONARA FROM MONFERRATO

« PENNETTE ALLA VODKA ANNI '80 »
EIGHTIES-STYLE PENNETTE ALLA VODKA

Who knows why certain dishes fall in and out of fashion, just like certain clothing styles. Penne in vodka sauce is just as delicious now as it was at the peak of its popularity in the 1980s. Fabio made this dish for me on one of our first dates. He tried to get fancy and burn off the vodka, but he only succeeded in setting off the smoke alarm, which in turn caused a fuse to blow. We ended up eating by candlelight. Now that I'm telling the story, I think maybe he did that on purpose! Pennette are small penne.

SERVES 2 TO 3

1 dried or fresh chile pepper
1/2 cup (100 milliliters) vodka
Salt to taste
1/2 package (250 grams) pennette or other short dried pasta
1 yellow onion, minced
Extra-virgin olive oil for sautéing
3 1/2 ounces (100 grams) pancetta, diced
1 cup (250 milliliters) tomato puree
1/2 cup (150 milliliters) heavy cream
Grated Parmesan to taste

Place the chile pepper in the vodka to infuse it. Bring a large pot of salted water to a boil and cook the pasta. Meanwhile, in a large pan, sauté the minced onion in a small amount of oil and add the pancetta. When the onion is golden brown, remove the chile pepper from the vodka and add the vodka. Add the tomato puree and the cream to the pan, stir to combine, taste and adjust salt, and cook over low heat, stirring occasionally, to reduce the sauce slightly to the consistency of sour cream. When the pasta is cooked, drain it in a colander and add it to the pan with the sauce. Sprinkle with grated Parmesan and serve immediately.

« AVEMARIE DELLA CONTESSA »
THE COUNTESS'S AVEMARIE PASTA WITH SAFFRON AND MARROW

The countess referenced in the recipe title is Marta Marzotto, a lovely woman and fantastic hostess who has dictated fashion and style in Italy for as long as I can remember. She serves this dish when entertaining in chic mountain resorts—Cortina or St. Moritz. Avemarie are a short, tubular pasta. Here they are cooked risotto-style rather than boiled.

SERVES 2 TO 4

1 tablespoon vegetable broth granules (or the serving size indicated on
    the package), dissolved in 3 cups (3/4 liter) water
5 ounces (150 grams) frozen mirepoix (minced carrots, onion, and
    celery), thawed
Extra-virgin olive oil for sautéing
1/2 package (250 grams) avemarie or other short tubular dried pasta
1 cup (250 milliliters) white wine
1/2 teaspoon (2 envelopes) powdered saffron
1/2 cup (100 milliliters) heavy cream
Marrow from 1 marrow bone
Unsalted butter to taste
Grated Parmesan to taste
Salt to taste

Place the broth in a small pot, bring to a boil, then lower the heat to a gentle simmer. Meanwhile, in a food processor, puree the mirepoix until creamy. (Alternatively you can chop equal amounts of fresh carrot, celery, and onion and puree them.) Place a little oil in a large pan and sauté the pureed mirepoix. If necessary, add the vegetable broth in small amounts, 1 to 2 tablespoons at a time, to keep the pan from getting dry. Add the uncooked pasta and stir to coat with the puree. Add the wine, stir, and let it evaporate. Begin adding the broth in small amounts (about 1/4 cup at a time), stirring constantly and allowing it to be absorbed between additions. (You may not use all the broth, or you may run out of broth. If you do, simply add water to the pot, bring it back to a boil, turn it down to a simmer, and proceed.) When the pasta is just slightly under-done, add the saffron and the cream and continue to cook, stirring, until absorbed. In another pan, heat up the marrow for just a few seconds (any longer and it will melt).

Stir the butter and grated Parmesan into the pasta until the butter has melted. Season with salt. Remove the pan from the heat, divide the pasta among individual serving plates, and add a small piece of marrow to each plate. Serve immediately.

« CONCHIGLIE AI FORMAGGI E GRANELLA DI NOCCIOLE »
CONCHIGLIE WITH CHEESE AND HAZELNUTS

A confession: I don't love pasta with cheese. I find it a little bland. But this version, with little crunchy bits of hazelnut, won me over! Caciotta is a mild cheese from central Italy that combines cow's and sheep's milk. If you can find it, use it, but feel free to replace it—and any of the other cheeses called for in the recipe—with what you have on hand. In fact, this recipe is perfect for using up any leftover bits and pieces of cheese hanging around your refrigerator.

SERVES 6

Salt to taste
1 package (500 grams) conchiglie pasta (shells)
1 cup (100 grams) shelled hazelnuts, toasted and skinned
Fresh sage leaves to taste
1/2 cup (150 milliliters) whole milk
9 ounces (250 grams) soft cheese
9 ounces (250 grams) Gorgonzola, cut into cubes
2 ounces (50 grams) Gruyère, cut into cubes
2 ounces (50 grams) caciotta cheese, cut into cubes
2 ounces (50 grams) taleggio cheese, cut into cubes
Pepper to taste
Grated Parmesan to taste

Bring a large pot of salted water to a boil for the pasta. Meanwhile, in a food processor fitted with the metal blade, chop the hazelnuts with a few sage leaves. (The nuts should be left fairly chunky—you don't want to grind them to a powder.) Place a large pan over low heat. Combine the milk and the soft cheese in the pan and whisk until the cheese has melted. Add the Gorgonzola, Gruyère, caciotta, and the taleggio and continue cooking over low heat, whisking frequently, until melted. If the pan looks dry, add a little more milk. When the pasta is cooked, drain it in a colander, add it to the pan with the cheese, and toss briefly to combine. Transfer the pasta to a serving dish or to individual serving plates, top with the hazelnut mixture and season to taste with pepper. Serve immediately with the grated Parmesan on the side.

« MALLOREDDUS ALLA CAMPIDANESE »
SARDINIAN MALLOREDDUS

For years I held my birthday celebrations in Punta Marana in Sardinia. Each year, the menu was the same: malloreddus (Sardinia's famous little dumplings) and porcetto (Sardinia's famous roast suckling pig). Preparing porcetto at home would be all but impossible, but you can find malloreddus in Italian specialty stores and other gourmet stores to make this festive pasta dish.

SERVES 4 TO 6

Salt to taste
1 package (500 grams) malloreddus
Extra-virgin olive oil for sautéing
1 clove garlic
7 ounces (200 grams) sausage
1 (15-ounce/420-milliliter) can tomato puree
1 bay leaf
Fresh basil leaves to taste
**$1/4$ teaspoon (1 envelope) powdered saffron dissolved in 1 tablespoon
     water**
Shaved Sardinian sheep's milk cheese for garnish

Bring a large pot of salted water to a boil and cook the pasta. Meanwhile, place a medium pan over medium heat and add some oil and the garlic. Remove the sausage filling from the casing, crumble it into the pan with your hands, and cook until the sausage has lost its raw red color. Add the tomato puree, a little salt, the bay leaf, basil leaves, and the dissolved saffron and cook, stirring occasionally, until the sausage is cooked through and much of the liquid has evaporated, 15 to 20 minutes. When the pasta is cooked, drain it in a colander and transfer to a serving bowl. Pour the sausage mixture over it and toss to combine. Garnish with the shaved cheese and serve immediately.

« ORECCHIETTE CON BRACIOLE »
ORECCHIETTE WITH STUFFED BRACIOLE

Braciole are wonderful little packets of meat stuffed with pancetta, cheese, garlic, and parsley. This recipe is from Italian tennis star Flavia Pennetta, who is a champion in the kitchen just as she is on the court.

SERVES 4

12 thin slices beef
12 thin slices pancetta
1 clove garlic, minced
Minced fresh parsley leaves to taste
Grated pecorino to taste
Extra-virgin olive oil for sautéing
1 yellow onion, thinly sliced
$1/2$ cup (100 milliliters) white wine
1 (15-ounce/420-milliliter) can tomato puree
Salt to taste
$1/2$ package (250 grams) orecchiette

Place one slice of beef on a work surface and set one slice of pancetta on top. Top the pancetta with a little of the minced garlic (or, if you'd rather, you can skip the garlic here and include a whole clove in the sauce), a little minced parsley, and some grated pecorino. Roll up the package and keep it closed with a toothpick or some kitchen twine. Repeat with the remaining beef, pancetta, garlic, parsley, and most of the cheese (reserve a little for the garnish). Heat a small amount of oil in a large pan over medium heat. Add the onion and then the beef packets in a single layer. Cook until the onion is browned and the packets are browned on all sides. (Use tongs to turn them.) Add the white wine and allow most of the liquid to evaporate. Add the tomato puree, lower the heat to a gentle simmer, and cook about 1 hour.

When the sauce is done, bring a large pot of salted water to a boil and cook the orecchiette. When the pasta is cooked, drain it in a colander and transfer to a serving bowl. Remove the toothpicks or twine from the meat packets and transfer them to the serving bowl with the orecchiette. Pour the tomato and onion sauce in the pan over the pasta and toss to combine. Top with the reserved grated cheese and serve immediately.

« PASTA CON SALSICCIA E FUNGHI »
PASTA WITH SAUSAGE AND MUSHROOMS

If you think the prima ballerina at La Scala is always on a diet and not allowed to eat, you haven't met my friend Marta Romagna. Marta is the prima ballerina at La Scala because she works hard every day rehearsing—which means she can actually eat more than the average person, including hearty dishes like this one. I made this pasta last Christmas thinking it would be good for kids, but all the adults turned up their noses at my fancy purple-potato gnocchi and dished up this buffet item for themselves.

SERVES 4

3 ½ ounces (100 grams) dried porcini mushrooms
1 yellow onion, minced
Extra-virgin olive oil for sautéing
10 ounces (300 grams) sausage
1 (15-ounce/420-milliliter) can tomato puree
Salt and pepper to taste
1 package (400 grams) mezzemaniche or other short, tubular pasta
Grated Parmesan cheese to taste

Place the dried mushrooms in a bowl and add water to cover. Set aside to soak until soft. When the mushrooms are soft, in a large pan, sauté the minced onion in a small amount of oil until transparent. Gently remove the mushrooms from the bowl using your hands (don't pour them out into a strainer, as there may be some grit left in the bottom of the bowl), squeeze them as dry as possible, and add them to the pan with the onion. Continue cooking, stirring frequently, until the onion has browned. Remove the casing from the sausage and crumble the filling into the pan with your hands. Cook until the sausage loses its raw red color, then add the tomato puree. Lower the heat to a simmer. Season with salt and pepper and cook, covered, until the sauce has reduced and the sausage is cooked through, about 20 minutes.

Meanwhile, bring a large pot of salted water to a boil and cook the pasta. When the pasta is ready, drain it in a colander and transfer it to a serving bowl. Pour the sausage mixture over it and toss to combine. Top with grated Parmesan and serve immediately.

« PASTA ALLA GENOVESE »
PASTA WITH WHITE RAGÙ

This dish is a meal all by itself. My sister once even scarfed up leftovers that I'd re-heated! This sauce is called a "white" ragù because it doesn't have any tomatoes. The recipe is from Francesca La Torre.

SERVES 4

1 large yellow onion, thinly sliced
Extra-virgin olive oil for sautéing
1 pound (500 grams) ground beef
1 cup (250 milliliters) white wine
Salt to taste
1 bay leaf
2 potatoes, peeled and cut into small cubes
Vegetable oil for deep-frying
Salt to taste
3/4 package (350 grams) sedanini or other short, tubular dried pasta
Minced fresh parsley leaves to taste
Grated Parmesan to taste

In a medium pan, cook the onion in a small amount of oil until softened. Add the ground beef, breaking it up with a fork. Cook until its raw red color is gone, then add the wine. Season with salt and add the bay leaf. Lower the heat to a simmer, cover the pan, and cook for 10 minutes. Fry the potato cubes in the oil until golden and crisp. Transfer to paper towels to drain and salt lightly. Bring a large pot of salted water to a boil and cook the pasta. When the pasta is cooked, drain it in a colander and transfer to a serving dish. Add the meat mixture and toss to combine. Sprinkle with a generous amount of minced parsley and then the potatoes and grated cheese. Serve immediately.

« STROZZAPRETI AL RAGÙ »
STROZZAPRETI WITH RAGÙ

This recipe is from Martina Colombari, who is a native of Riccione in the Romagna region. She confided in me that she doesn't really like to cook, but she makes a great version of this classic dish. Making the pasta known as strozzapreti (literally "priest-chokers") is fun and easy—the whole family will enjoy rolling the dough between their palms.

SERVES 4 TO 6

Extra-virgin olive oil for sautéing
5 ounces (150 grams) frozen mirepoix (minced carrots, onion, and celery)
8 ounces (250 grams) ground beef
1 cup (250 milliliters) white wine
1 cup (250 milliliters) tomato puree
Salt to taste
4 cups (500 grams) unbleached all-purpose flour, plus more for flouring the pan
1 large egg
Grated Parmesan for serving

In a medium pan, heat some olive oil over medium heat and cook the mirepoix until soft. Add the ground beef, breaking it up with a fork as you do, and brown. Add the wine and allow it to evaporate. Add the tomato puree, season with salt, lower the heat to a gentle simmer, cover, and cook about 20 minutes.

Meanwhile, lightly flour a jelly-roll pan and set aside. Place the flour in a pile on a work surface (or in a large bowl if you are not familiar with making pasta) and create a well in the center. Crack the egg into the well. Beat the egg with a fork, pulling in some of the flour from the walls of the well as you do. When you have incorporated the egg into the flour and have a very dry, crumbly dough, add some water, about 2 tablespoons at a time, kneading between additions, until you have a soft, smooth dough. Roll out the pasta dough with a rolling pin and cut it into thin strips. (You can also use a pasta machine if you prefer.) Make the strozzapreti by holding a strip of pasta vertically between your palms and quickly rubbing your palms together so that the strip curls up and also breaks into small pieces. Place the pieces on the prepared pan in a single layer and repeat with the remaining strands of pasta dough. Bring a large pot of salted water to a boil and cook the pasta. (Fresh pasta does not take long to cook.) When it is cooked, drain it in a colander and transfer to a serving bowl. Top with the meat sauce, toss to combine, and serve with grated Parmesan on the side.

« SPAGHETTI ALLE DUE BOTTARGHE »
SPAGHETTI WITH FISH ROE TWO WAYS

Savory fish roe—caviar, if you like—is enhanced further by being featured here in two forms: fresh roe, and bottarga, cured roe that is grated in small quantities over pasta. Stefania Rocca introduced me to this spectacular dish.

SERVES 2 TO 3

Salt to taste
$1/2$ package (250 grams) spaghetti
2 sacs striped bass roe
1 bay leaf
$1/2$ rib celery
1 sac mullet bottarga, grated
Extra-virgin olive oil for sautéing
Grated zest of $1/2$ orange
Grated zest of $1/2$ lemon
Minced fresh parsley leaves to taste
Toasted and skinned hazelnuts, chopped, to taste

Bring a large pot of salted water to a boil for the pasta. Place the fresh roe sacs in a pot with water to cover, add the bay leaf and celery, bring to a boil, and cook for about 5 minutes. Drain and set aside. Place about $3/4$ of the grated bottarga in a pan with a little oil. Add the citrus zests and place over low heat. Add about $1/4$ cup pasta cooking water to the pan with the bottarga and cook for 2 minutes, stirring frequently. Pierce the sacs of fresh roe and use a fork to transfer the roe gently to the pan with the bottarga. Add some minced parsley to the pan as well. Keep the bottarga mixture over low heat, adding more pasta cooking water if the pan begins to look dry. When the pasta is cooked, drain it in a colander, then add it to the pan with the bottarga and the roe, tossing to combine. Transfer to a serving bowl. Sprinkle on some more minced parsley, the chopped hazelnuts, and the reserved grated bottarga. Serve immediately.

« SPAGHETTI AL PESTO DI TONNO »
SPAGHETTI WITH TUNA

This is a quick, easy, and nutritious pasta dish with a smooth sauce made from anchovies and capers. Add a little chile pepper if you like it hot.

SERVES 2 TO 3

Salt to taste
1/2 package (250 grams) spaghetti
2 (5-ounce/300-gram) cans tuna in olive oil, drained
5 anchovy fillets in oil, drained
2 tablespoons capers, rinsed and drained
Fresh parsley leaves to taste
Extra-virgin olive oil for sautéing and drizzling
2 to 3 cloves garlic
Chile pepper flakes to taste (optional)
3 1/2 ounces (100 grams) cherry tomatoes, quartered

Bring a large pot of salted water to a boil and cook the spaghetti. Meanwhile, in a food processor fitted with the metal blade or a blender, combine the tuna, anchovies, and capers and process. Add about 1/4 cup of the pasta cooking water and some parsley and process again to make a smooth, creamy sauce. In a large pan, heat some olive oil and sauté the garlic and the chile pepper, if using. Add the anchovy and caper sauce and whisk to combine. Cook over low heat until reduced slightly. When the pasta is cooked, reserve some pasta cooking liquid, drain the pasta in a colander, transfer it to the pan with the sauce, and place the pan over medium-high heat. Toss the pasta briskly with the sauce, and add 1 to 2 tablespoons of the reserved cooking liquid if the pan looks dry. Transfer to a serving dish. Top with the quartered tomatoes, drizzle with a little oil, and serve immediately.

« SPAGHETTI TONNO E AGRUMI »
SPAGHETTI WITH TUNA AND CITRUS

Tuna and citrus is always a winning combination. This is the perfect dish to prepare at a beach house!

SERVES 4

Salt to taste
2/3 package (300 grams) spaghetti
1 lime
1 orange
1 pink grapefruit
1 tablespoon Worcestershire sauce
1 clove garlic, crushed
Extra-virgin olive oil for sautéing
7 ounces (200 grams) fresh tuna, diced
Minced fresh parsley leaves to taste
Pepper to taste

Bring a large pot of salted water to a boil for the pasta. Meanwhile, grate the zest from the lime and reserve. Juice the lime, orange, and grapefruit into a bowl. Whisk in the Worcestershire sauce and set aside. In a large pan, sauté the garlic in some oil until golden brown, 2 to 3 minutes. Remove and discard the garlic. Add the diced tuna and the lime zest to the garlic-infused oil in the pan and cook over medium heat until just seared, about 1 minute. Season with salt, add the citrus juices and Worcestershire, and cook for an additional 3 minutes. When the pasta is cooked al dente, drain it in a colander and add to the pan with the tuna. Toss briskly over medium-high heat. Sprinkle with minced parsley, season with pepper, and serve immediately.

« TROFIE CON FAGIOLINI E CALAMARI »
TROFIE PASTA WITH GREEN BEANS AND CALAMARI

The classic dish from Liguria is flour-and-water trofie pasta (a short, twisted pasta with tapered ends that you can buy in Italian specialty stores), potatoes, green beans, and pesto. Here I've replaced the potatoes with tender calamari. Be sure not to overdo it with the pesto—you want just enough to bind the pasta and the other ingredients together without turning the whole dish bright green.

SERVES 4

6 ounces (150 grams) green beans, trimmed
Salt to taste
$2/3$ package (300 grams) trofie pasta
2 cloves garlic, crushed
Extra-virgin olive oil for sautéing
2 squid, cleaned and chopped
1 tablespoon readymade pesto
Fresh basil leaves for garnish

Cut the green beans in half the short way. Bring a large pot of salted water to a boil and add the green beans. Boil for 5 minutes, then add the pasta. Meanwhile, in a large pan, brown the garlic in a little oil, tilting the pan so that the garlic remains submerged in the oil. Remove and discard the garlic and add the chopped squid. Cook just until the squid turns opaque, probably no more than 1 minute, and remove from the heat. When the pasta is cooked, reserve some of the cooking water, drain the pasta in a colander, and add the pasta to the pan with the squid. Remove the pan from the heat, toss to combine, then add the pesto and toss to combine. If the pasta looks dry, add 1 to 2 tablespoons cooking water and toss again. Garnish with basil leaves and serve.

« FARFALLE ALLA CREMA DI SCAMPI »
FARFALLE PASTA IN LANGOUSTINE SAUCE

The challenge when making pasta with shellfish is to create a sauce that truly marries with the pasta. Otherwise, you've just got plain pasta in oil with a few pieces of seafood on top of it. In this recipe, the langoustines are pureed into what is unmistakably a sauce.

SERVES 3 OR 4

Salt to taste
$1/2$ package (250 grams) farfalle (bow-tie pasta)
1 yellow onion, minced
Unsalted butter for sautéing
Extra-virgin olive oil for sautéing
$1/2$ cup (100 milliliters) brandy
6 to 7 ounces (150 to 200 grams) frozen shelled langoustine tails
2 tablespoons tomato puree
Fresh basil leaves to taste
Pepper to taste
3 or 4 frozen whole langoustine tails

Bring a large pot of salted water to a boil and cook the pasta. Meanwhile, in a large pan, cook the onion in a combination of equal parts butter and oil until transparent. Add the brandy and allow most of the liquid to evaporate. Add the frozen langoustine tails. (If they have thawed, add any liquid that they gave off as well.) Add the tomato puree, basil leaves, and a little salt and cook over medium heat until the langoustines are cooked and the sauce is still a little liquid, about 1 minute. Place the cooked langoustines and all the liquid from the pan in a blender and puree, then return it to the pan. (I do this right in the pan with an immersion blender.) Adjust salt and pepper and stir in a little more butter until melted. When the pasta is cooked, use a slotted spoon or skimmer to remove it to a colander to drain, then drop the whole langoustine tails into the water to cook, about 1 minute. Add the pasta to the pan with the sauce and toss to combine. Divide the pasta among individual serving bowls and add 1 whole langoustine tail to each portion. Serve immediately.

« FUSILLI AL TONNO E TARALLI »
FUSILLI WITH TUNA AND TARALLI

There are thousands of recipes in Italy for pasta with fresh tuna. This one is special, however. The sauce includes a little ginger and soy sauce, along with sun-dried tomatoes. The capper is that this uses crumbled taralli—traditional Italian breadsticks—in place of the usual breadcrumbs. You can purchase taralli in Italian specialty stores and some cheese shops.

SERVES 4

Salt to taste
$2/3$ package (300 grams) fusilli
1 lemon
$1/4$ cup plus 2 tablespoons (90 milliliters) extra-virgin olive oil
Thinly sliced fresh ginger, *quanto basta*
9 ounces (250 grams) fresh tuna, diced
Fresh mint leaves (optional)
7 to 8 sun-dried tomatoes in oil, chopped
2 tablespoons soy sauce
Pepper to taste
Crushed taralli for topping

Bring a large pot of salted water to a boil and cook the pasta. Grate the zest of the lemon and juice the lemon. Heat a large pan over medium heat and add 2 tablespoons of the oil. When the oil is hot, add the ginger, tuna, and the lemon zest. Cook until the tuna is seared, 2 to 3 minutes, then remove from the heat and add the mint leaves, if using. In a food processor fitted with the metal blade or a blender, combine the sun-dried tomatoes, soy sauce, 1 tablespoon lemon juice, and remaining $1/4$ cup (50 milliliters) oil. Adjust salt and pepper. When the pasta is cooked, drain it in a colander. Transfer the pasta to a serving bowl, top with the sun-dried tomato mixture and the tuna, and toss to combine. Sprinkle with the crushed taralli and serve immediately.

« ORECCHIETTE CON BROCCOLETTI E SEPPIOLINE »
ORECCHIETTE WITH BROCCOLI AND CUTTLEFISH

Orecchiette with broccoli is really great on its own, but with the addition of tender rings of cuttlefish it becomes outstanding. Thanks to the singer Duilio, who invited me to his birthday party and inspired this dish.

SERVES 6

Salt to taste
1 package (500 grams) orecchiette
1 (10-ounce/300-gram) package frozen broccoli (or 1 small bunch fresh broccoli, chopped)
3 cloves garlic, crushed
Chile pepper flakes to taste
Extra-virgin olive oil for sautéing
6 to 8 small cuttlefish
1 tablespoon tomato paste

Bring a large pot of salted water to a boil and add the orecchiette and broccoli at the same time. Meanwhile, in a large pan, sauté the garlic and chile pepper flakes in a generous amount of oil. (Tilt the pan so that the garlic is submerged in the oil.) Cut the cuttlefish into rings, leaving the tentacles intact. Remove and discard the garlic, add the cuttlefish to the pan, and cook just until opaque, probably no more than 1 minute. Season with salt and remove the pan from the heat. When the pasta and broccoli are cooked, reserve about 1 cup cooking liquid and drain the pasta and broccoli in a colander. Add the tomato paste to the pan with the cuttlefish and stir to combine, then add the pasta and broccoli. Add a small amount of the cooking liquid if the pan looks dry. Toss briefly over medium heat to combine, then serve.

« PASTA FREDDA CON VONGOLE E PESTO »
PASTA SALAD WITH CLAMS AND PESTO

The challenge in making a pasta salad with clams is to make sure that the pasta takes on the flavor of the seafood. Here that's accomplished by collecting the cooking liquid from the clams and adding it to the water used to cook the pasta. A spoonful of pesto brings the whole dish together.

SERVES 4

2 cloves garlic
Extra-virgin olive oil for sautéing and drizzling
9 ounces (250 grams) frozen clams
$1/2$ cup (100 milliliters) white wine
Salt to taste
$1/2$ package (250 grams) penne
1 pound 5 ounces (600 grams) plum tomatoes, diced
1 tablespoon readymade pesto
Fresh basil leaves to taste
Pepper to taste

In a medium pan, sauté the garlic in a small amount of oil, tilting the pan to keep the garlic submerged. Add the clams. Add the white wine and allow most of the liquid to evaporate, about 1 minute. Place a sieve in a bowl and drain the clams, collecting any liquid in the bowl. Add the liquid to a large pot, along with enough salted water to cook the pasta, and bring to a boil. Add the penne to the pot of boiling water, and while they are cooking, place the clams in a serving bowl with the tomatoes and the pesto. Stir to combine. When the pasta is cooked, drain it in a colander, add it to the serving bowl, and toss to combine. Drizzle with a little olive oil, tear basil leaves over the pasta, and season with pepper. Serve at room temperature or chilled.

« SCIALATIELLI CON TRIGLIE E PEPERONI »
SCIALATIELLI PASTA WITH MULLET AND PEPPERS

Fabio gave me the idea for this pasta. He's always helpful—even his criticism is constructive. I was experimenting with a pasta using canned crab and peppers. After he told me (maybe a little too honestly) what he thought of it (not much), he then suggested, "I think mullet would be good." And he was right!

SERVES 6

4 green onions, thinly sliced into rings
1 small bell pepper, cut into small dice
Extra-virgin olive oil for sautéing
7 ounces (200 grams) mullet fillets, skinned and pin bones removed with
    tweezers
Salt to taste
1 package (500 grams) fresh egg noodles of choice
Pepper to taste
Minced fresh parsley to taste

In a large pan over medium-high heat, cook the onions and bell pepper with a generous amount of oil until browned, about 5 minutes. Add the mullet fillets, season with salt, and cook for 5 minutes, stirring to break up the fish flesh. Bring a large pot of salted water to a boil and cook the pasta. (Fresh egg pasta cooks very quickly.) Reserve $1/2$ cup pasta cooking water. Drain the pasta in a colander, then add the pasta and reserved cooking water to the pan with the mullet. Raise the heat to high and toss the pasta in the pan until the cooking liquid has been absorbed and the sauce coats the pasta. Sprinkle with pepper and minced parsley and serve immediately.

Note: If you have leftovers of this pasta, toss the pasta with diced mozzarella and spread evenly in a baking dish (the larger the better as far as I'm concerned—you get more crispy top crust). Sprinkle the top with grated Parmesan, drizzle with a little extra-virgin olive oil, and broil until the top is crisp and browned, about 5 minutes.

« CARBONARA DI MARE »
SEAFOOD CARBONARA

This is another recipe from the excellent Lorenzo Boni. It uses both fresh and smoked tuna.

SERVES 2 TO 3

Salt to taste
$1/2$ package (250 grams) mezzemaniche or other short tubular pasta
1 clove garlic
Extra-virgin olive oil for sautéing
5 ounces (150 grams) fresh tuna, diced
2 to 3 slices smoked tuna, cut into strips
3 egg yolks
3 to 4 tablespoons grated Parmesan
Minced fresh parsley leaves to taste
Pepper to taste

Bring a large pot of salted water to a boil and cook the pasta. Meanwhile, in a large pan, brown the garlic in a small amount of oil. Remove and discard the garlic and add the fresh tuna. Cook over high heat just until seared, about 1 minute, then remove from the heat. Add the smoked tuna to the pan. In a medium bowl, beat the egg yolks with the Parmesan and a generous amount of minced parsley, salt, and pepper. When the pasta is cooked al dente, reserve about $1/4$ cup cooking water, then drain the pasta in a colander. Add the pasta to the pan with the tuna and cook over medium heat, tossing to combine. Remove from the heat and pour the egg mixture over the pasta and enough cooking water to moisten. Toss to combine; the pasta should be coated with the sauce. Serve immediately.

« TAGLIOLINI AL LIMONE »
TAGLIOLINI WITH LEMON

Pasta with lemon is always tasty. When I'm in a hurry, I just put the pasta in a bowl and top it with butter or oil and squeeze half a lemon over the plate. Then I sprinkle on plenty of grated cheese and pepper. I do the same thing with rice sometimes. This dish is a little more sophisticated—and suitable even for a fancy dinner. Tagliolini are thin fresh egg noodles.

SERVES 4

4 tablespoons (50 grams) unsalted butter
1 lemon, zest grated and juiced, plus lemon slices for garnish
Salt and pepper to taste
1/2 package (250 grams) fresh tagliolini or other fresh long egg noodles
3/4 cup (70 grams) grated Parmesan

In a small pan or pot, melt the butter over low heat with the lemon zest. Whisk in the lemon juice, season with salt and pepper, and remove from the heat. Bring a large pot of salted water to a boil and cook the pasta. When the pasta is cooked (fresh pasta cooks quickly), reserve about 1/2 cup cooking water. Drain the pasta in a colander, but don't drain it completely dry. Transfer to a serving bowl. Pour the lemon juice mixture over the pasta and add a little of the cooking water if the pasta looks dry. Toss vigorously to combine. Sprinkle with the grated cheese and continue to toss vigorously—the cheese should melt as it mixes with the hot pasta and combine with the liquid to create a silky sauce. Sprinkle with additional cooking water if the dish looks dry. Top with a little additional pepper, garnish with lemon slices, and serve immediately.

« TAGLIATELLE AI CARCIOFI CROCCANTI »
TAGLIATELLE WITH CRISPY ARTICHOKES

After you've heard the words "fried artichokes," need I say more, or are you already pulling out your pots and pans and writing a shopping list? This is a beautiful-looking dish, but it tastes even better than it looks. Tagliatelle are fresh egg noodles, very similar to fettuccine.

SERVES 4

Juice of 1 lemon
3 baby artichokes
$^1/_2$ cup (100 milliliters) heavy cream
2 egg yolks
1 cup (100 grams) grated Parmesan
Vegetable oil for pan-frying
Unbleached all-purpose flour for dredging
Salt to taste
$^1/_2$ package (250 grams) fresh tagliatelle or other fresh long egg noodles
Pepper to taste

Juice the lemon and add the juice to a bowl full of cold water. Trim the artichokes: Working one at a time, remove any leaves from the stem, and then cut off the stem, leaving an inch or two. Pull off and discard any hard, dark-colored leaves. When you have revealed the light green portion of the artichoke, peel off any tough skin from the outside of the stem. Cut off the top of the artichoke completely. Cut the artichoke in half the long way and use the tip of a paring knife to dig out the fuzzy part in the center. Slice the cleaned artichoke into thin wedges, then into very thin slices, and drop the slices into the bowl with the water and lemon juice. Repeat with the remaining artichokes.

Combine the cream, egg yolks, and grated cheese in a small pot and cook over very low heat, whisking constantly, until thickened to the consistency of sour cream. Remove the cheese sauce from the heat. Heat several inches of vegetable oil in another pan. Remove the artichoke slices from the water and dry them thoroughly with paper towels or a clean dish towel, then dredge them in flour. Fry the artichokes in the pan until golden and crisp—work in batches if you must in order to avoid crowding the pan. Remove to paper towels to drain and salt lightly. Bring a large pot of salted water to a boil and cook the pasta. When the tagliatelle are cooked, reserve a little of the cooking water and drain them in a colander. Transfer the tagliatelle to a large bowl, top with the cheese sauce, and toss to combine. Add a little of the cooking water if the pasta looks dry (you may not need any) and toss to combine. Divide the pasta among individual serving bowls, top each portion with some pepper and crispy artichokes, and serve immediately.

« TAJARIN AL TARTUFO BIANCO »
TAJARIN PASTA WITH WHITE TRUFFLE

Tajarin are egg noodles from the Piedmont region made with plenty of egg yolk as opposed to whole eggs. The result is a rich-tasting pasta with an almost orange color. The traditional topping for tajarin is white truffle, but it's almost impossible to prepare this dish in a quantity that serves more than four people—it dries out too quickly. You probably wouldn't want to anyway, since you'd spend an arm and a leg on white truffle, which is very costly!

SERVES 3 TO 4

1 ⅔ cups (200 grams) unbleached all-purpose flour, plus more for
    flouring the work surface, pasta, and pan
5 egg yolks
1 large egg
Salt to taste
Melted unsalted butter to taste
1 small jar (about 3 ounces/75 grams) white truffle cream
White truffle, *quanto basta*

Flour a jelly-roll pan and set aside. Place the flour in a pile on a work surface (or in a large bowl if you are not familiar with making pasta) and create a well in the center. Place the yolks and the whole egg in the well and add a pinch of salt. Beat the egg with a fork, pulling in some of the flour from the walls of the well as you do. When you have incorporated all of the egg into the flour, knead until you have a soft, smooth dough. Clean the work surface, flour lightly, and roll out the dough into a very thin sheet using a rolling pin. Flour the sheet of dough lightly, roll into a flat cylinder, and slice into very thin noodles (less than 1/10 inch wide). Transfer the noodles to the prepared pan, shaking them gently as you do to separate them. If they won't fit on the pan in a single layer, flour another jelly-roll pan and use that as well.

Bring a large pot of salted water to a boil and cook the pasta. When the pasta is cooked (fresh egg pasta cooks quickly), reserve some of the pasta cooking water, then drain the pasta briefly but not completely in a colander. Transfer the pasta to a bowl. Pour the melted butter and the white truffle cream over the pasta and toss to combine. Add a small amount of cooking water if the pasta looks dry. Divide among individual serving bowls, shave a generous amount of white truffle over each portion, and serve immediately.

« TAGLIATELLE GIALLE CON PLATESSA »
TAGLIATELLE WITH PLAICE AND SAFFRON

My kids love pasta with fish, especially Eleonora, who can eat three plates of this at one sitting. This is really a one-dish meal—throw together a salad and you've got dinner. Plaice is a flat white fish. You can also use sole.

SERVES 6

Salt to taste
1 package (500 grams) fresh tagliatelle or other fresh long egg noodles
1/2 yellow onion, thinly sliced
Extra-virgin olive oil for sautéing
4 plaice fillets, skinned
1 cup (250 milliliters) white wine
1/4 teaspoon (1 envelope) powdered saffron dissolved in 1 tablespoon
     pasta cooking water
12 cherry tomatoes, halved
Minced fresh parsley leaves to taste
Black pepper or chile pepper flakes to taste

Bring a large pot of salted water to a boil and cook the pasta. Meanwhile, in a large pan, brown the onion in a generous amount of oil. Cut the fish fillets into bite-sized pieces and add them to the pan. Cook over medium heat, stirring frequently, until they have broken down, about 2 minutes. Season with salt and add the white wine and diluted saffron. Add the tomatoes and cook for 2 minutes, stirring frequently. When the pasta is cooked (fresh pasta cooks quickly), drain it and add it to the pan with the fish. Toss to combine. Sprinkle with minced parsley and black pepper or chile pepper flakes and serve immediately.

« TAGLIATELLE PANNA ACIDA E CAVIALE »
TAGLIATELLE WITH CAVIAR

This pretty and elegant recipe makes quite an impression on guests. Fabio made this dish for me one year on our anniversary, and he used authentic beluga caviar in place of the less expensive lumpfish caviar. It was incredible, but beluga caviar is so costly

that we ended up in the kitchen, scraping out the pan with pieces of bread just to be sure we didn't waste any! Not a romantic image, but it tasted splendid.

SERVES 4 TO 6

Juice of $1/2$ lemon
1 cup (250 milliliters) heavy cream
Salt to taste
1 tablespoon vegetable broth granules (or the serving size indicated on the package)
1 package (500 grams) fresh tagliatelle or other fresh long egg noodles
1 leek, thinly sliced
Unsalted butter for sautéing
Extra-virgin olive oil for sautéing
1 to 2 jars lumpfish or beluga caviar
Minced fresh chives for garnish

In a small bowl, whisk together the lemon juice and cream. If you have time, do this an hour or so in advance of cooking to sour the cream fully, but if not, that's fine. Bring a large pot of lightly salted water to a boil for the pasta. Stir the broth granules into the boiling water and cook the pasta. In a large pan, sauté the leek in equal amounts butter and oil over low heat until soft. Add about $1/2$ cup pasta cooking water to the pan and braise the leek. When the pasta is cooked, remove with a skimmer and transfer to the pan with the leek. If the pan looks dry, add a little more of the pasta cooking liquid. Remove the pan from the heat and stir in the soured cream. Toss to combine, then sprinkle with the caviar and fold gently, trying not to break the roe. Garnish with minced chives and serve immediately. (Alternately, distribute the tagliatelle among individual serving plates and top each portion with caviar and chives, but you must move very quickly when doing this or the pasta will dry out.)

« TAGLIATELLE AL NERO DI SEPPIA E SUGO DI CERNIA »
TAGLIATELLE WITH CUTTLEFISH INK AND GROUPER

This dish of stark black and white contrast is a showstopper. Always wear gloves when working with cuttlefish ink, though, or you'll have stained hands for days.

SERVES 4

1 $^2/_3$ cups (200 grams) unbleached all-purpose flour
$^3/_4$ cup (100 grams) durum flour for pasta
3 large eggs
Salt to taste
1 packet cuttlefish ink
3 cloves garlic
Extra-virgin olive oil for sautéing
6 grouper fillets
6 cherry tomatoes, halved
White wine to taste

Whisk together the flours, place them in a pile on a work surface (or in a large bowl if you are not familiar with making pasta), and create a well in the center. Add the eggs to the well, along with a pinch of salt and the cuttlefish ink. Beat the eggs and ink with a fork, pulling in some of the flour from the walls of the well as you do. When you have incorporated all the egg into the flour, knead until you have a smooth dough that is uniformly black. Roll the dough through a pasta machine and when it has been rolled through the thinnest setting, cut it into noodles about $^1/_3$ inch wide (usually the second smallest width on the machine). If you don't have a pasta machine, roll out the dough with a rolling pin to form a flat very thin cylinder, and use a knife to cut thin noodles. Bring a large pot of salted water to a boil and cook the pasta. For the sauce, sauté the garlic in oil, tilting the pan so that the garlic cloves remain submerged. Add the fillets and cook, stirring frequently, until they have broken down, about 2 minutes. Add the cherry tomatoes, moisten the pan with a little white wine, and cook, covered, until the liquid has evaporated, 3 to 4 minutes. When the pasta is cooked (fresh pasta cooks quickly), drain it in a colander and then transfer it to the pan with the fish sauce. Briefly toss over medium heat to combine and serve immediately.

« TIMBALLO DI TAGLIATELLE CON POLPETTINE »
TIMBALLO OF TAGLIATELLE WITH SMALL MEATBALLS

This recipe is from my brother, Roberto, who loves to travel to far-flung places. He's driven his motorcycle over the dangerous roads of Africa, Asia, and the Middle East and written well-researched books about those places. So you'd probably expect him to give me a recipe for crocodile or something, right? But no. This is a classic Neapolitan timballo, a nest of noodles with a delicious surprise hidden in the center: meatballs and peas. Maybe traveling so much has made Roberto appreciate the food of his native country even more!

SERVES 6 TO 8

Unsalted butter for baking dish, sautéing, coating pasta, and dotting the
      top
Breadcrumbs for coating baking dish and sprinkling on top
1 stale roll
1/2 cup (150 milliliters) whole milk
4 ounces (120 grams) ground beef
1 large egg, lightly beaten
1/2 cup (50 grams) grated Parmesan, plus more for topping pasta
Salt to taste
Extra-virgin olive oil for browning meatballs
1 pinch meat extract
1 (10-ounce/250- to 300-gram) can of peas, rinsed and drained
1 package (500 grams) fresh tagliatelle or other fresh long egg noodles
1 tablespoon vegetable broth granules (or the serving size indicated on
      the package) dissolved in 1/2 cup (100 milliliters) water
1 fresh mozzarella ball (8 ounces/225 grams), diced

Preheat the oven to 350° F (180° C). Butter a round cake pan (or, if you don't want to invert the timballo, a springform pan set on a jelly-roll pan to catch the filling if it leaks), then sprinkle with breadcrumbs. Tilt the dish to coat all the surfaces with breadcrumbs, then dump out the excess. Soak the roll in the milk until soft. In a bowl, combine the ground beef, softened roll (crumble it with your fingers), egg, grated cheese, and salt to taste. Knead the meat mixture, then create very small meatballs the size of marbles. In a large pan, brown the meatballs in some oil. (Cook in batches, if necessary, to avoid crowding the pan.) In another pan, melt some butter with the meat extract and sauté the peas. Bring a large pot of salted water to a boil and cook the pasta. When the pasta is cooked, drain it and transfer it to a bowl. Add the vegetable broth and a generous amount of butter and grated Parmesan.

Place about 1/3 of the tagliatelle in the prepared pan and make an indentation in the center. Place the meatballs, peas, and mozzarella in the center. Cover with the remaining pasta. Dot the top with butter and sprinkle with some breadcrumbs. Bake until golden brown, about 20 minutes. If you are very brave, you can invert the timballo: First, cut gently around the perimeter of the pan with a butter knife. Then, place a serving platter upside down on top of the pan and flip, then lift away the pan. If you don't want to risk it, just serve slices out of the pan. (If you used a springform pan, just unbuckle the outer ring and remove the timballo.)

« PICI ALLE ERBE »
PICI PASTA WITH HERBS

I first tasted this dish as part of a fabulous meal consisting of ancient dishes. If I recall correctly, it has Etruscan origins. Pici are fresh, thick spaghetti served in a sauce that couldn't be easier—simply blend together a hard-boiled egg and a variety of herbs, pasta cooking water, and pecorino cheese. The result is creamy and delicious and feels thoroughly modern.

SERVES 2 TO 3

1 large egg
Salt to taste
1/2 package (250 grams) fresh pici pasta or other fresh egg noodles
1/4 cup tightly packed parsley leaves
1/4 cup tightly packed basil leaves
1/4 cup marjoram leaves
1/2 clove garlic
3 tablespoons grated pecorino, plus more for serving (optional)
Pepper to taste
1/4 cup (50 milliliters) extra-virgin olive oil

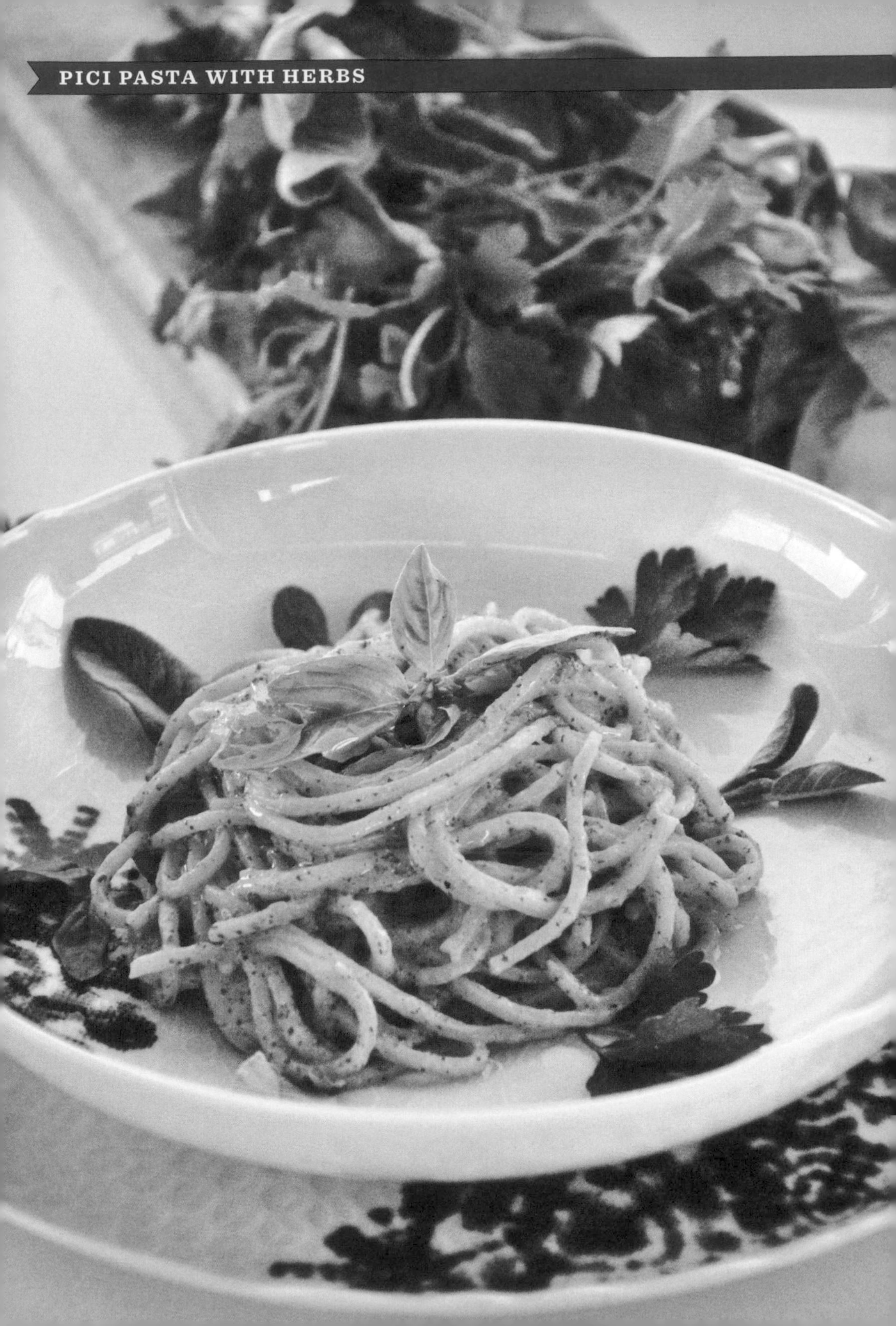

PICI PASTA WITH HERBS

Boil the egg for 10 minutes (counting from the moment the water comes to a boil), then run under cold water and peel. Bring a large pot of salted water to a boil and cook the pasta. Meanwhile, set aside a few whole herb leaves for garnish. For the sauce, place the parsley, basil, marjoram, garlic, and hard-boiled egg in a food processor fitted with the metal blade or a blender. Add the pecorino, pepper to taste, and the oil and process. Add enough of the pasta cooking water to the mixture to make a creamy sauce. When the pasta is cooked (fresh pasta cooks quickly), drain it in a colander, then transfer to a serving bowl and toss with the sauce. Sprinkle with additional grated pecorino if desired. Garnish with the reserved herb leaves and serve immediately.

« PIZZOCCHERI VALTELLINESI »
VALTELLINA-STYLE BUCKWHEAT PASTA

Pizzoccheri buckwheat noodles are a specialty from Valtellina, and they're really tasty and different. This is a winter dish; if you want to eat pizzoccheri in summer, substitute more seasonal vegetables. Casera is a local cheese. Look for it in Italian specialty stores or use the more widely available fontina in its place.

SERVES 4 TO 6

3 1/3 cups (400 grams) buckwheat flour
3/4 cup (100 grams) unbleached all-purpose flour, plus more for work
    surface
Salt to taste
7 ounces (200 grams) Savoy cabbage, chopped
1 large or 2 small potatoes, peeled and diced
Shaved Casera cheese to taste
Grated Parmesan to taste
1 stick plus 3 tablespoons (150 grams) unsalted butter
Fresh sage leaves to taste
1 clove garlic, minced
Pepper to taste

Warm a serving dish in the oven. Whisk together the flours in a large bowl. Add enough room-temperature water to make a soft dough. Knead for 5 minutes. (You can also put the flours in a food processor fitted with the dough blade and, with the processor running, slowly add water through the feed tube until the dough forms a ball.) Place the dough on the work surface, cover with an inverted bowl, and allow to rest for 15 to 30 minutes. Lightly flour the work surface and roll out the dough until it is about $1/10$ inch thick. Lightly flour the sheet of dough and cut it into strips 3 inches wide. Lightly flour the strips and stack them on top of one another, then cut them the short way so you have short noodles that are a little less than $1/4$ inch wide.

Bring a large pot of salted water to a boil. Add the cabbage and potatoes, cook for 5 minutes, then add the pasta. When the pasta is cooked, about 10 minutes later, remove some of the pasta and the vegetables with a skimmer and transfer to a warm serving dish. Sprinkle with a generous amount of both types of cheese. Repeat, making layers of pasta and vegetables alternating with layers of cheese. In a small pan, melt the butter over medium heat and fry the sage leaves and minced garlic until browned and crisp, watching carefully so that they don't burn, about 1 minute. Pour the butter, sage, and garlic over the dish, top with a little pepper (do not toss to combine), and serve immediately.

« CANEDERLI »
DUMPLINGS FROM ALTO ADIGE

I tasted these dumplings for the first time just a few years ago, and I've been a little obsessed with them ever since. These are great on a cold winter day or after a run down the slopes.

SERVES 4

About 5 slices (200 grams) bread
$1/2$ cup (150 milliliters) whole milk
2 large eggs, lightly beaten
Salt and pepper to taste
3 $1/2$ ounces (100 grams) speck
1 yellow onion
Unsalted butter for sautéing
Extra-virgin olive oil for sautéing
Minced fresh parsley leaves to taste
$1/3$ cup (40 grams) unbleached all-purpose flour, plus more for dredging

Grated nutmeg to taste
4 to 6 cups (1 to 1 1/2 liters) beef broth (broth made with bouillon cubes is
    fine) for cooking the dumplings and serving
Grated Parmesan for finishing
Minced fresh chives for finishing

In a large bowl, soak the bread in the milk until it is soft enough to crumble with your hands. Add the eggs and season with salt and pepper. Knead by hand until the mixture is well combined, then set aside to rest. Meanwhile, in a food processor fitted with the metal blade, process the speck with the onion. Sauté the speck mixture in equal amounts butter and oil until golden, then add to the bread mixture. Knead again. Add parsley, the flour, and nutmeg. Knead again. Shape the dough into small dumplings, using your hands as you would for meatballs. Place the broth in a pot and bring to a boil. Dredge the dumplings in flour, then cook them in the broth. Divide the dumplings and broth among individual soup plates. Top with grated Parmesan and minced chives and serve piping hot.

« STRASCINATI ALLA CREMA DI CECI DI LEO »
LEO'S STRASCINATI PASTA WITH CHICKPEA SAUCE

This dish was a childhood favorite of my dear friend Leonardo Gallo, who happens to be the doctor who delivered all three of my babies. The chickpeas here are cooked for a long time so that they basically dissolve into a creamy sauce. If you can't find strascinati pasta in the refrigerator case or freezer at your grocery store or Italian specialty store, use orecchiette—preferably fresh orecchiette—in their place.

SERVES 4

2 cloves garlic
1 (15-ounce/500-gram) can chickpeas, rinsed and drained
1 tablespoon vegetable broth granules (or the serving size indicated on
    the package)
Salt to taste
1 bay leaf
1/2 package (250 grams) strascinati pasta

Grated Parmesan to taste
Extra-virgin olive oil for sautéing and drizzling

In a large pan, sauté the garlic in oil, tilting the pan to keep the garlic cloves submerged. Add the chickpeas, $1/2$ cup water, the vegetable broth granules, salt, and the bay leaf. Lower the heat to a gentle simmer and cook until the chickpeas are very soft, about 30 minutes. As they soften, crush them with a fork. If the chickpeas begin to look dry, add 1 to 2 tablespoons water. In the end, you should have a silky, creamy sauce. Season with salt. Bring a large pot of salted water to a boil and cook the strascinati. Add about $1/4$ cup pasta cooking water to the chickpea sauce in the pan, then drain the pasta and add it to the pan. Toss the pasta and sauce over low heat. Remove the pan from the heat and stir in a generous amount of grated Parmesan. Drizzle with a generous amount of olive oil and serve immediately. (Act quickly, as the sauce is quickly absorbed by the pasta and will turn dry.)

« GNOCCHI ALLA PARIGINA »
GNOCCHI WITH BÉCHAMEL AND GRUYÈRE

My mother used to serve this dish whenever she had a fancy dinner party, and I've always loved it, but my mother had hers prepared by a nearby restaurant, so I never knew how it was made. Finally, I've managed to develop a good recipe for it—and now I'm sharing it with you.

SERVES 4

1 $1/4$ cups (300 milliliters) whole milk
7 tablespoons (100 grams) unsalted butter
Salt to taste
1 $2/3$ cups (200 grams) unbleached all-purpose flour
6 large eggs
$1/2$ cup (50 grams) grated Parmesan
1 cup (250 grams) readymade béchamel
1 cup (100 grams) grated Gruyère

To make the gnocchi dough, place the milk in a small pot with the butter and a little salt. Bring to a boil and, as soon as the first bubbles form, remove from the heat. Whisk to combine. Whisk in the flour gradually until the mixture forms a ball. (You may not need all the flour. Let this mixture cool slightly, stir in the eggs, one at a time, then the grated Parmesan, and allow the dough to cool completely.

Preheat the oven to 350° F (180° C). Bring a large pot of salted water to a boil for cooking the gnocchi. Place the gnocchi dough in a pastry big fitted with a metal tip or a plastic freezer bag with a corner snipped off. Working directly over the pot of boiling water, squeeze the bag and use a knife to cut off pieces of dough at approximately 3/4-inch (2-centimeter) intervals. Wet the knife occasionally to keep it from sticking. As soon as the gnocchi float to the top of the water, remove with a skimmer and transfer to a baking dish. When all the gnocchi are cooked and in the dish, whisk together the béchamel and the Gruyère and pour it over the gnocchi. Bake until the top is nicely browned, 8 to 10 minutes. If after 10 minutes the top is not as browned as you would like, you can put the pan under the broiler for 1 to 2 minutes. Just keep an eye on it so it doesn't burn.

« GNOCCHI AL RAGÙ BIANCO »
GNOCCHI WITH WHITE RAGÙ

I've always loved gnocchi, but I don't think the readymade ones you buy in the grocery store are very good. The best thing to do is to take the time to make your own. Paired with a meat sauce without tomato, they're really special.

SERVES 4 TO 6

5 ounces (150 grams) frozen mirepoix (minced carrots, onion, and celery)
Extra-virgin olive oil for sautéing
Unsalted butter for sautéing
7 ounces (200 grams) ground veal
7 ounces (200 grams) ground chicken
7 ounces (200 grams) ground pork
1/2 cup (100 milliliters) white wine
1/2 cup (100 milliliters) whole milk
1/2 cup (100 milliliters) heavy cream
Minced fresh sage leaves to taste
Minced fresh rosemary leaves to taste

Salt to taste
1 pound (500 grams) starchy potatoes
1 ²/₃ cups (200 grams) unbleached all-purpose flour
Minced fresh parsley leaves to taste
Grated Parmesan to taste

In a large pan, sauté the mirepoix in equal amounts oil and butter. Add the veal, chicken, and pork, breaking them up as you add them to the pan, and cook until just beginning to brown. Add the wine, then the milk, cream, sage, rosemary, and a pinch of salt and cook, covered, over low heat for 30 minutes. Meanwhile, to make the gnocchi, place the potatoes in a pot, cover with water, and boil until easily pierced with a fork. Drain and pass through a potato ricer into a large bowl. (The peel should come off.) Add the flour and some salt and knead by hand until you have a soft dough. Pinch off egg-sized pieces of the dough and roll under your palms on a work surface into ropes, then cut the ropes into little cylinders with a knife. Bring a large pot of salted water to a boil and cook the gnocchi. As soon as the gnocchi rise to the surface, they are done. Remove with a skimmer, place in a serving bowl, and toss with the meat sauce. Sprinkle with minced parsley and grated Parmesan and serve immediately.

« ROTOLO DI GNOCCHI »
GNOCCHI ROLL

As I've already mentioned, I love gnocchi, so when I heard about this dish I just had to try it: It's a roll of gnocchi dough stuffed with prosciutto and cheese and topped with tomato sauce.

SERVES 4

11 ounces (300 grams) potatoes
3/4 cup (100 grams) unbleached all-purpose flour, plus more for the work
    surface
Salt and pepper to taste
3 processed cheese slices
3 1/2 ounces (100 grams) thinly sliced prosciutto cotto
1 clove garlic

1 (28-ounce/1-kilogram) can crushed tomatoes
Minced fresh marjoram leaves to taste
Extra-virgin olive oil for drizzling
Grated Parmesan to taste

To make the gnocchi dough, place the potatoes in a pot, cover with water, and boil until easily pierced with a fork. Drain and pass through a potato ricer into a large bowl. (The peel should come off.) Add the flour and some salt and pepper and knead by hand until you have a soft dough. With a rolling pin, on a lightly floured surface, roll out the dough about 3/4 inch thick. Flour the top of the dough and the rolling pin, if necessary. Place the cheese slices on top in a single layer, just to one side of the center of the dough, then cover the surface of the dough with the prosciutto. Roll up the dough jelly-roll style, wrap tightly in parchment paper, and tie the ends with kitchen twine.

Bring a large pot of water to a boil and cook the rolled dough in it for 25 minutes. Remove the roll and set aside to cool. Meanwhile, to make the tomato sauce, place the garlic and crushed tomatoes in a medium pan, season with salt, and heat over medium heat. Season with marjoram and cook for 10 minutes, stirring frequently. To serve, cut the roll into slices. Arrange the slices on a serving dish and top with the tomato sauce, a drizzle of olive oil, a sprinkling of Parmesan, and additional minced marjoram.

« AGNOLOTTI AI CARCIOFI »
ARTICHOKE AGNOLOTTI

Agnolotti are a must in my home for Christmas. Agnolotti are traditionally filled with a meat mixture, but last year I made them with this creamy artichoke filling. It's fun to get the whole family together to make stuffed pasta for the holidays– and it makes quick work of what is admittedly a tedious task. You can serve these simply, topped with melted butter and a sprinkling of grated cheese, because the filling is so flavorful it really needs nothing more.

SERVES 4 TO 6

6 baby artichokes
1 small yellow onion, thinly sliced

1 clove garlic, minced
2 tablespoons extra-virgin olive oil, plus more for sautéing
Minced fresh parsley leaves
Salt and pepper to taste
2 1/2 cups (300 grams) unbleached all-purpose flour
3 large eggs
2/3 cup (150 grams) ricotta
3/4 cup (75 grams) grated Parmesan, plus more for finishing
Melted butter for drizzling

Trim the artichokes: Working one at a time, remove any leaves from the stem, and then cut off the stem, leaving an inch or two. Pull off and discard any hard, dark-colored leaves. When you have revealed the light green portion of the artichoke, peel off any tough skin from the outside of the stem. Cut off the top of the artichoke completely. Cut the artichoke in half the long way and use the tip of a paring knife to dig out the fuzzy part in the center. Slice the cleaned artichoke into thin wedges. Repeat with the remaining artichokes. In a large pan, sauté the onion and garlic in some oil until the onion begins to brown. Add the artichokes and parsley, season with salt and pepper, and cook over low heat, covered, until the artichokes are very soft. If the artichokes begin to stick to the pan, add small amounts of water. Set the artichoke mixture aside to cool.

Meanwhile, prepare the pasta. Place the flour in a pile on a work surface (or in a large bowl if you are not familiar with making pasta) and create a well in the center. Add the eggs, a pinch of salt, and the olive oil to the well. Beat the egg with a fork, pulling in some of the flour from the walls of the well as you do. When you have incorporated all the egg into the flour, knead until you have a soft, smooth dough, about 10 minutes. Wrap the dough in plastic wrap and set aside to rest for 30 minutes. Roll the dough into thin strips using a pasta machine.

Transfer the cooled artichokes to a food processor fitted with the metal blade or a blender, add the ricotta and 1/2 cup (50 grams) grated Parmesan, and process until smooth. Place one strip of pasta on a clean work surface. Dot the right side of the strip of pasta with small amounts of the filling, about 1 heaping teaspoon each, leaving a little space in between and a border on the right side. Fold the left half of the strip of pasta over the filling, press firmly with your fingertips around the filling to seal the two halves together, and then cut with a pastry wheel between the spoonfuls of filling to make individual pieces of pasta. Bring a large pot of salted water to a boil and cook the pasta. Remove with a skimmer (dumping the pot into a colander will cause some of the pasta packets to break open). Transfer to a serving bowl, top with a generous amount of melted butter and grated Parmesan, and serve immediately.

Note: Making agnolotti is definitely a project, and if you have even one piece of pasta left over, you won't want to waste it! But you can actually make this dish with stuffed pasta that you buy at the supermarket if you prefer—just boil 1 package (500 grams) vegetable ravioli and toss with a tablespoon or two of melted butter, then proceed as follows: Preheat a convection oven to 400°F (200°C). In a bowl, combine the cooked ravioli, $3/4$ cup (200 milliliters) béchamel, 5 ounces (150 grams) diced mozzarella (about 1 heaping cup), and 3 ounces (80 grams) prosciutto cotto cut into strips. Pour the whole thing into a baking dish and sprinkle $1/4$ cup (25 grams) grated Parmesan on top. Bake for 10 minutes, and then broil for a few minutes to brown the top.

« CAPPELLETTI IN BRODO »
CAPPELLETTI IN BROTH

I'm not going to lie—this dish isn't easy, but this is the classic dish of the Romagna region, which is famous for fantastic egg pasta. A few years ago, I decided to give it a try and make cappelletti for twenty people. I worked nonstop for two days. Then, on December 25th, my sister, Cristina, who's an anchorwoman, found out she'd have to leave early and fly to Rome to do the news that evening. I didn't want her to miss out, so I served the cappelletti a little too al dente. Actually, they were hard. All my work was in vain due to a silly error in timing! Cappelletti means "little hats," because they look like tri-corner hats when they are finished.

SERVES 6

1 sirloin steak
Extra-virgin olive oil for sautéing
Salt to taste
1 slice mortadella
4 large eggs
1 1/2 cups (150 grams) grated Parmesan
1 tablespoon soft cheese, such as cream cheese
1 tablespoon ricotta

2 $1/2$ cups (300 grams) unbleached all-purpose flour
Durum flour for pasta for rolling dough
Capon broth, *quanto basta*

For the filling, in a pan cook the steak in a small amount of oil with a little salt until browned, about 5 minutes. Cut the steak into pieces and place it in a food processor fitted with the metal blade with the mortadella and process. Add 1 egg, the grated Parmesan, soft cheese, and ricotta and process again until combined. The filling should be soft and dense. Incorporate additional grated Parmesan or soft cheese if necessary.

To make the pasta, place the all-purpose flour in a pile on a work surface (or in a large bowl if you are not familiar with making pasta) and create a well in the center. Place the remaining 3 eggs in the well. Add a pinch of salt and beat the eggs with a fork, pulling in some of the flour from the walls of the well as you do. When you have incorporated all of the eggs into the flour, knead until you have a soft, smooth dough, about 10 minutes. Form the dough into a ball, cover with a clean dish towel, and set aside to rest for 10 minutes. Roll out the dough using a pasta machine or a rolling pin, flouring it with durum flour to keep it from sticking. Cut the dough into 2-by-2-inch squares. Place a small amount of the filling on one square. Fold the square in half into a triangle. Bring the two corners of the base together and pinch to seal. Set aside and repeat with remaining pasta and filling. Bring the broth to a boil in a large pot and boil the cappelletti in the broth. (Fresh pasta cooks quickly; when they float to the top they are done.) Serve immediately.

« TORTELLI DI ZUCCA »
SQUASH TORTELLI

Sadly, I never get to make this dish, because Fabio hates squash. He's only eaten this tasty stuffed pasta from Mantua one time in his life, when he was trying everything to get me to go out with him and I kept saying no. Those were the days! In any case, this is another recipe from the Tognazzi family, and I think Simona Izzo for it. Mostarda is not mustard, but a cooked fruit preparation similar to chutney. Look for it in Italian specialty stores.

SERVES 4

1 (1 1/4-pound/600-gram) winter squash, such as butternut or acorn
    squash
3 1/2 ounces (100 grams) amaretti cookies, plus *quanto basta* for finishing
1 piece pear mostarda
1 cup (100 grams) grated Parmesan, plus more for finishing
Grated nutmeg to taste
Zest of 1 lemon
Salt and pepper to taste
3 1/4 cups (400 grams) unbleached all-purpose flour
3 large eggs
Unsalted butter for finishing
Fresh sage leaves for finishing

Preheat the oven to 350° F (180° C). Seed the squash and cut it into thick wedges with the peel still on. Place it on a foil-lined jelly-roll pan and bake until very soft, about 1 hour. Remove and discard the peel (which should come away easily) and puree with a food mill, a food processor fitted with the metal blade, or simply by crushing it with a fork. In a food processor, mince the amaretti with the mostarda and add the mixture to the squash. Sprinkle with the Parmesan, nutmeg, lemon zest, salt, and pepper. Set the filling aside to rest for a couple of hours—this is not entirely necessary, but it improves the flavor.

Meanwhile, prepare the pasta. Place the flour in a pile on a work surface (or in a large bowl if you are not familiar with making pasta) and create a well in the center. Place the 3 eggs in the well. Add a pinch of salt and beat the eggs with a fork, pulling in some of the flour from the walls of the well as you do. When you have incorporated all of the eggs into the flour, knead until you have a soft, smooth dough, about 10 minutes. Roll out the dough using a pasta machine or a rolling pin. Cut out circles of pasta with the rim of a drinking glass. Place a small amount of filling in the center of each circle and fold in half to form a half-moon shape. Press the edges together to seal. Bring a large pot of salted water to a boil for the pasta. In a large pan, brown the butter with a generous amount of sage. When the pasta is cooked (fresh pasta cooks quickly), remove from the pot with a skimmer and transfer to the pan with the browned butter. Toss to combine. Divide among individual serving plates and top each portion with a generous amount of grated Parmesan and additional amaretti cookies that you have crushed by hand into large pieces. Serve immediately.

« LASAGNE VEGETARIANE »
VEGETARIAN LASAGNA

I've been working on this recipe for years, making little improvements here and there. The robiola and mozzarella combination is excellent, and a little pesto makes the whole thing smell and taste terrific. If your supermarket doesn't carry fresh lasagna noodles, it may carry sheets of fresh pasta dough already rolled out. Simply cut these into broad noodles and cook them for this dish. You'll need about $1/2$ pound (225 grams) noodles; the pasta sheets usually come in 1-pound (450-gram) packages.

SERVES 4 TO 6

2 leeks, thinly sliced
Extra-virgin olive oil for sautéing
1 red bell pepper, diced
1 eggplant, diced
2 zucchini, diced
Salt to taste
1 pound (400 grams) robiola cheese
Grated Parmesan, *quanto basta*
1 cup (150 milliliters) whole milk
8 ounces (225 grams) fresh lasagna noodles
1 fresh mozzarella ball (8 ounces/225 grams), sliced
Pesto, *quanto basta*

Preheat the oven to 350° F (180° C). In a large pan, brown the leeks in a small amount of oil. Add the bell pepper and the eggplant and cook over medium heat, stirring occasionally, for 10 minutes. Add the zucchini and some salt and cook, covered, until the vegetables are soft but not falling apart. In a small bowl, whisk together the robiola, grated Parmesan, and milk. Season with salt. The result should be smooth and creamy; adjust with more milk or cheese if necessary. Spread a little of the robiola mixture on the bottom of a baking dish. Build layers in this order in a baking dish from the bottom up: pasta, cheese mixture, vegetables, mozzarella, grated Parmesan, and pesto. Repeat until you have used up the ingredients. (The number of layers will depend on the size of your baking dish.) Bake in the preheated oven until the noodles are soft and the top is browned, about 20 minutes. Allow to settle for about 10 minutes before serving.

« LASAGNE AI CARCIOFI »
ARTICHOKE LASAGNA

As you've probably figured out by now, artichokes are one of my favorite vegetables. I like them sautéed, fried, even raw. They're great on their own, and they make everything else a little better—including lasagna. Here they're combined with smoked prosciutto cotto. This can be a little hard to track down, so feel free substitute any other pork product that you like.

SERVES 4

6 baby artichokes
2 cloves garlic, minced
Extra-virgin olive oil for sautéing
Salt to taste
Minced fresh parsley leaves to taste
2 3/4 cups (700 grams) readymade béchamel
1 cup (250 milliters) whole milk
1 package (200 grams) oven-ready lasagna noodles
5 ounces (150 grams) thinly sliced smoked prosciutto cotto
Grated Parmesan to taste

Preheat the oven to 350° F to 400° F (180° C to 200° C). Trim the artichokes: Working one at a time, remove any leaves from the stem, and then cut off the stem, leaving an inch or two. Pull off and discard any hard, dark-colored leaves. When you have revealed the light green portion of the artichoke, peel off any tough skin from the outside of the stem. Cut off the top of the artichoke completely. Cut the artichoke in half the long way and use the tip of a paring knife to dig out the fuzzy part in the center. Slice the cleaned artichoke into thin wedges and then cut those into thin slices. Repeat with the remaining artichokes. In a large pan, sauté the artichokes and garlic in a small amount of oil with salt and parsley. Cook over medium heat until the artichokes are soft. Add small amounts of water to the pan, 1 to 2 tablespoons at a time, if the artichokes begin to stick. In a small bowl, whisk together the béchamel and milk. Spread some of the béchamel mixture on the bottom of a baking dish. Build layers in a baking dish in this order from the bottom up: pasta, béchamel, artichokes, prosciutto, grated Parmesan. Repeat until you have used up the ingredients. (The number of layers will depend on the size of your baking dish.) Sprinkle a generous amount of grated Parmesan on top. Bake in the preheated oven until the noodles are soft and the top is browned and crusty, about 20 minutes. Allow to settle for about 10 minutes before serving.

« LASAGNE AI BROCCOLI »
BROCCOLI LASAGNA

Here's a way to get even children to beg for more broccoli: cook it soft, combine it with cheese and prosciutto, and bake it into a lasagna!

SERVES 4

Salt to taste
1 large or 2 small heads broccoli
Unsalted butter for sautéing
Extra-virgin olive oil for sautéing
1 clove garlic
1 cup (250 milliliters) readymade béchamel
2 cups (500 milliliters) whole milk
1 package (250 grams) oven-ready lasagna noodles
7 ounces (100 grams) thinly sliced prosciutto cotto
1 cup (100 grams) grated Parmesan
Pepper to taste

Preheat the oven to 350° F (180° C). Bring a large pot of salted water to a boil. Break up the broccoli into florets, boil them until they can be pierced with a knife but still offer some resistance, and drain. In a pan, sauté the broccoli in equal amounts butter and oil with the garlic clove until they are lightly colored and have taken on the flavor of the garlic. Remove and discard the garlic. In a bowl, combine the béchamel and 1 cup milk and set aside. Build layers in a baking dish in this order from the bottom up: $1/2$ of the pasta, $1/3$ of the broccoli, $1/3$ of the thinned béchamel, pepper to taste, $1/2$ of the prosciutto, $1/3$ of the grated Parmesan. Make a second layer with the same ingredients, and then a third layer with the remaining broccoli, thinned béchamel, and Parmesan. Slowly pour the milk into corners of the dish until the pan is filled with a fair amount of liquid. You may not have to use all the milk. Bake until the noodles are soft and the top is browned and crusty, about 30 minutes. Allow to settle for about 10 minutes before serving.

« LASAGNE CON CREMA DI GORGONZOLA »
GORGONZOLA LASAGNA

The Gorgonzola sauce in this lasagna is very rich, so I interspersed some cubes of neutral potato among the layers to balance out the flavor. Those crunchy walnuts are great, too!

SERVES 4

Salt to taste
1 potato, peeled and cut into very small dice
7 ounces (200 grams) sweet Gorgonzola
1 $1/2$ cups plus 2 tablespoons (400 grams) heavy cream
Whole milk for the sauce
Oven-ready lasagna noodles to cover the surface area of your pan 4 times
Grated Parmesan to taste
$1/3$ cup (30 grams) walnuts, roughly chopped
2 ounces (50 grams) sharp Gorgonzola, cut into cubes
Unsalted butter for dotting the top

Preheat the oven to 350° F (180° C). Bring a small pot of salted water to a boil and cook the potato cubes until soft. Meanwhile, in another small pot, combine the sweet Gorgonzola with the cream and enough milk to create a sauce and cook over low heat, whisking frequently, until the cheese has melted. Spread a little of the Gorgonzola sauce on the bottom of the pan. Cover with a single layer of noodles. Top with about $1/4$ of the remaining Gorgonzola sauce, $1/4$ of the potatoes, and $1/4$ of the grated Parmesan. Repeat three more layers in the same order, from the bottom up: noodles, Gorgonzola sauce, potatoes, Parmesan. Sprinkle the top with the walnuts and the cubes of sharp Gorgonzola. Dot with a generous amount of butter and bake until the noodles are soft and the top is browned and crusty, about 20 minutes. Allow to settle for about 10 minutes before serving.

« LASAGNE FUMÉE »
LASAGNA WITH SMOKED SCAMORZA AND RICOTTA

The smoked scamorza used in this lasagna makes it really special—more of an adult treat than the standard version.

SERVES 4

1 yellow onion, sliced
Extra-virgin olive oil for sautéing
2 1/2 cups (600 milliliters) tomato puree
Fresh basil leaves to taste
Salt to taste
Sugar to taste
5 ounces (150 grams) smoked scamorza
2 cups (400 grams) ricotta
3/4 cup (80 grams) grated Parmesan
1 package (250 grams) oven-ready lasagna noodles

In a medium pan, brown the onion in a small amount of oil, then add the tomato puree and basil leaves. Season with salt, add a pinch of sugar, and cook at a gentle simmer, covered, for 30 minutes. Preheat the oven to 400° F (200° C). Meanwhile, grate the scamorza on the largest holes of a four-sided box grater. Remove 1 tablespoon grated scamorza and set aside. In a medium bowl, combine the ricotta and all but 1 table-spoon of the Parmesan. When the tomato sauce is cooked, spread about 1/4 cup on the bottom of a baking pan and set aside another 1/4 cup. Combine the remaining tomato sauce with the ricotta and Parmesan mixture and set aside 2 tablespoons. In the pan, build layers in this order from the bottom up: pasta, ricotta and tomato mixture, grated scamorza. Repeat until you have used up the ingredients. (The number of layers will depend on the size of your baking dish.) Spread the reserved tomato sauce and tomato and ricotta mixture over the top, then sprinkle with the reserved Parmesan and scamorza. Bake until the noodles are soft and the top is browned and crusty, about 30 minutes. Allow to settle for about 10 minutes before serving.

« LASAGNE AL PESTO, FAGIOLINI E PATATE »
PESTO, GREEN BEAN, AND POTATO LASAGNA

Pesto lasagna is so delicious, and even better with green beans and potatoes. You'll be amazed at how good something so easy can be. Just be sure to use a readymade pesto that's not too oily. Even if you stir in the oil, as the lasagna cooks it will separate out again and leave the top of the dish looking greasy.

SERVES 4 TO 6

Salt to taste
9 ounces (250 grams) green beans, trimmed
3 potatoes, peeled
2 cups ($\frac{1}{2}$ liter) readymade béchamel
1 (10-ounce/300-gram) jar readymade pesto
$\frac{1}{2}$ cup (100 milliliters) whole milk
1 package (250 grams) oven-ready lasagna noodles
Grated Parmesan to taste
Fresh basil leaves for garnish

Preheat the oven to 350° F (180° C). Bring a pot of salted water to a boil and cook the green beans and potatoes. Drain in a colander, then cut the potatoes into small dice and chop the beans into bite-sized pieces. Salt both and set aside. Combine the béchamel and the pesto and add enough of the milk to make a sauce the consistency of sour cream. Spread a little of this mixture on the bottom of a baking pan. In the pan, build layers in this order from the bottom up: pasta (arranged in a single layer, overlapping slightly if necessary), the pesto mixture, and then the potatoes, green beans, and Parmesan. (The number of layers will depend on the size of your baking dish.) End with the pesto mixture, potatoes, green beans, and a generous amount of Parmesan on top. Slowly pour milk into the corners of the dish until the pan is filled with a fair amount of liquid. You may not have to use all the milk. Bake until the noodles are soft and the top is browned and crusty, about 20 minutes. If after 20 minutes the top is not browning to your liking, set under a broiler for a few minutes, watching closely to guard against burning. Allow the lasagna to settle for about 10 minutes before serving. Garnish with basil leaves just before serving.

« LASAGNETTE DI GAMBERONI »
SHRIMP LASAGNA

This elegant baked pasta dish is perfect when you have a few cooked lasagna noodles left over. Just don't stack the noodles when cutting them or leave them uncovered as you work—they'll stick together and you'll never get them apart.

SERVES 4

12 large shrimp, shelled and deveined but tails attached
Cooked lasagna noodles, cut into 12 squares
1 tablespoon vegetable broth or fish broth granules (or the serving size
    indicated on the package) dissolved in $1/4$ cup plus 2 tablespoons (90
    milliliters) warm water
$1/2$ cup (50 grams) grated Parmesan or pecorino
Pepper to taste
Minced fresh parsley leaves to taste
Extra-virgin olive oil for drizzling

Preheat a convection oven to 350° F to 400° F (180° C to 200° C). Place a shrimp on one square of pasta, roll it up with the tail sticking out, and place it in a baking pan seam-side down so the roll stays closed. Repeat with the remaining shrimp and pasta, wedging the shrimp together in the pan. Pour the broth over the shrimp, sprinkle on the cheese, season with pepper, sprinkle with parsley, and drizzle with a little olive oil. Bake until the surface is browned, about 10 minutes. Serve immediately.

« LASAGNE AL SALMONE »
SALMON LASAGNA

I adore the combination of robiola cheese and smoked salmon. This dish is made in an 8-by-8-inch baking pan. You could double the recipe if you want to make a larger amount, but I love all the crispy edges you get with a smaller pan.

SERVES 4

1 shallot, thinly sliced
Unsalted butter for sautéing
14 ounces (400 grams) salmon fillet, skinned
Salt and pepper to taste
3 1/2 ounces (100 grams) smoked salmon, chopped
10 ounces (300 grams) robiola cheese
1/2 cup (100 milliliters) whole milk
6 oven-ready lasagna noodles
3/4 cup (75 grams) grated Parmesan
Breadcrumbs for sprinkling on top
Extra-virgin olive oil for drizzling

Preheat the oven to 350° F (180° C). In a medium pan, cook the shallot in some butter until it begins to color. Add the fresh salmon fillet, season with salt and pepper, and cook, breaking it up with a wooden spoon, until it is cooked through and in pieces. In a food processor fitted with the metal blade, combine the smoked salmon and the robiola. Process while drizzling milk through the feed tube until you have a very loose and creamy mixture. (You will not need all the milk.)

Spread a little of the robiola mixture on the bottom of an 8-by-8-inch (20-by-20-centimeter) baking dish. Layer 2 noodles on top, overlapping slightly if necessary, and cover with additional robiola mixture, half the salmon fillet, and about 1/4 cup (25 grams) grated Parmesan. Layer 2 noodles on top, some more of the robiola mixture, the remaining salmon fillet, and another 1/4 cup Parmesan. Top with the remaining 2 noodles, the remaining robiola mixture, the remaining 1/4 cup Parmesan, the breadcrumbs, and a drizzle of olive oil, and season with pepper. Slowly pour the remaining milk into the corners of the dish until the pan is filled with a fair amount of liquid. You may not have to use all the milk, or you may need a little extra. Cover with aluminum foil and bake for 15 minutes, then remove the foil and bake until the noodles are soft and the top is browned, 5 to 10 minutes. Allow to settle for about 10 minutes before serving.

« ROTOLINI AROMATICI »
PASTA PINWHEELS WITH HERBS

This is a pretty alternative to lasagna or cannelloni.

SERVES 6 TO 8

20 fresh basil leaves
Leaves of 1 sprig fresh thyme
2 tablespoons extra-virgin olive oil
2 1/2 cups (500 grams) ricotta
1 cup (100 grams) grated Parmesan, plus more for sprinkling on top
1 large egg
Salt to taste
Grated nutmeg to taste
1 pound 5 ounces (600 grams) fresh egg lasagna noodles or dried noodles
	that have been cooked and drained
1 2/3 cups (400 grams) readymade béchamel
1/2 cup (100 milliliters) whole milk

Preheat the oven to 350° F (180° C). In a food processor fitted with the metal blade, process the basil and thyme leaves with the oil. Transfer to a bowl and combine with the ricotta, Parmesan, egg, a pinch of salt, and a little nutmeg. Spread some of this mixture on one of the noodles, roll it up jelly-roll style, and then cut it into 1 1/2-inch slices. Repeat with the remaining noodles and filling. Thin the béchamel with some milk (you may not need all of it) until it is a pourable consistency. Pour about 1/2 of the thinned béchamel into a baking pan large enough to hold the pinwheels on their sides in a single layer. Arrange the pinwheels in the pan (they should be pressed up against each other) and pour the remaining thinned béchamel over them. Sprinkle additional Parmesan on top, cover with aluminum foil, and bake for 10 minutes. Remove the foil and bake until nicely browned, about an additional 15 minutes. Serve right from the baking dish at the table.

« ORECCHIETTE GRATINATE AL CAPRINO E MELANZANE »
BAKED ORECCHIETTE WITH GOAT CHEESE AND EGGPLANT

Goat cheese and eggplant are a perfect combination. You won't believe how easy this is, and baked pasta is always a handy option when you're serving a crowd, because you can make it in advance.

SERVES 6

2 eggplants
5 ounces (150 grams) goat cheese
Salt to taste
Extra-virgin olive oil for eggplant paste and for drizzling
1 package (500 grams) orecchiette
3 tablespoons pitted taggiasca olives
Fresh basil leaves to taste
10 ounces (300 grams) cherry tomatoes, halved
Grated Parmesan to taste

Preheat the oven to 350° F (180° C). Cut the eggplants in half the long way and pierce the flesh in several places with the tip of a paring knife. Wrap each of the eggplant halves in aluminum foil and bake until very soft, 40 to 50 minutes. Peel the eggplants and place the flesh in a food processor fitted with the metal blade with the goat cheese and salt to taste. With the processor running, drizzle olive oil through the feed tube until the mixture is a smooth paste.

Bring a large pot of salted water to a boil and cook the orecchiette. Drain in a colander and transfer to a bowl. Add the eggplant paste and 2 tablespoons olives. Tear in some basil leaves. Reserve a few tomatoes and add the rest. Toss to combine. Transfer the eggplant and pasta mixture to a baking dish. Preheat the broiler. Sprinkle the reserved tomatoes and the remaining 1 tablespoon olives on top. Then sprinkle with additional basil and a generous amount of grated Parmesan. Drizzle a little extra oil over the pasta and broil until the surface is browned and crunchy, about 5 minutes. Serve immediately.

« FUSILLI GRATINATI CON ASPARAGI E CRESCENZA »
BAKED FUSILLI WITH ASPARAGUS AND CRESCENZA CHEESE

Asparagus was born to be served with creamy soft cheeses, such as crescenza (available in Italian specialty stores and gourmet cheese shops). This is quick and easy, and it's also not too filling.

SERVES 4

Salt to taste
8 ounces (250 grams) asparagus
1/2 package (250 grams) fusilli
7 ounces (200 grams) crescenza cheese
1/4 cup (50 milliliters) whole milk
Extra-virgin olive oil for moistening pasta
Grated Parmesan to taste
Unsalted butter for dotting the top

Bring a large pot of salted water to a boil. Cook the asparagus in the boiling water until tender, then remove with a slotted spoon or skimmer. Cook the pasta in the same water. Whisk together the crescenza and the milk. The mixture should be the consistency of sour cream or a little thicker—thin with additional milk if necessary. Cut the asparagus stalks into 1-inch pieces, leaving the tips whole (and keeping them separate). Preheat the broiler. When the pasta is cooked, drain it in a colander, transfer it to a bowl, and toss the pasta with the asparagus stalks and just enough oil to coat lightly. Transfer the pasta and asparagus to a baking dish and pour the cheese sauce over it. Scatter the asparagus tips on top, sprinkle with a generous amount of grated Parmesan, and dot the top with butter. Broil until the surface is browned and crunchy, about 5 minutes. Serve immediately.

« PASTICCIO DI GNOCCHI AL FORNO »
BAKED GNOCCHI

Gnocchi with tomato sauce are already delicious, and this dish heightens their appeal by running them under a broiler to create a crunchy top. Thanks to Caterina Balivo for this recipe!

SERVES 4 TO 6

1 yellow onion, minced
Extra-virgin olive oil for sautéing
2 cups (500 milliliters) tomato puree
Salt to taste
1 1/4 pounds (600 grams) starchy potatoes
1 egg yolk
1 2/3 cups (200 grams) unbleached all-purpose flour
4 slices provolone cheese
3 ounces (80 grams) smoked scamorza, grated
Grated Parmesan to taste
Fresh basil leaves to taste

Preheat the oven to 400° F (200° C). To make the sauce, sauté the onion in a small amount of oil until golden. Add the tomato puree, season with salt, and cook over medium heat, covered, until thickened, 15 to 20 minutes. Meanwhile, to make the gnocchi, place the potatoes in a pot, cover with water, and boil until easily pierced with a fork. Drain and pass through a potato ricer into a large bowl. (The peel should come off.) Add the egg yolk, flour, and a pinch of salt and knead by hand until you have a soft dough. Pinch off egg-sized pieces of the dough and roll under your palms on a work surface into ropes, then cut the ropes into little cylinders with a knife. Bring a large pot of salted water to a boil and cook the gnocchi. As soon as the gnocchi rise to the surface, they are done. Remove with a skimmer, place in a baking dish, and toss with the tomato sauce. Arrange the provolone slices on top in a single layer, sprinkle with the grated scamorza, then the grated Parmesan, and scatter with fresh basil leaves. Bake until browned, about 20 minutes. Serve immediately.

« NIDI DI SPAGHETTI AL GRATIN »
BAKED SPAGHETTI NESTS

Famous makeup artist Lola Attomanelli, who does the makeup for the dancers on Striscia La Notizia, a news spoof program, gave me the idea for this recipe. Spaghettoni are extra-thick spaghetti, and burrata is similar to mozzarella, but with a very creamy liquid center.

SERVES 4

Extra-virgin olive oil for oiling the pan and sautéing
2 cloves garlic, crushed
2 1/4 cups (600 grams) crushed tomatoes
Fresh basil leaves to taste
Chile pepper flakes to taste
Salt to taste
1/2 cup (80 grams) pitted taggiasca olives
2 tablespoons (40 grams) capers, rinsed and drained
1 package (400 grams) spaghettoni
1 ball fresh burrata
Breadcrumbs for topping
Grated Parmesan to taste

Preheat the broiler. Oil a baking pan and set aside. In a large pan, sauté the garlic in olive oil until browned. Remove and discard the garlic. Add the crushed tomatoes, basil leaves, chile pepper flakes, and salt. Roughly chop the olives and capers and add to the pan. Cook, covered, over low heat until somewhat thickened, about 10 minutes. Meanwhile, bring a large pot of salted water to a boil for cooking the pasta. When the pasta is cooked but still al dente—you need to be able to bend a strand, but it shouldn't be soft—drain the pasta in a colander. Off the heat, add the pasta to the pan with the sauce and toss to combine. Using a ladle and a large serving fork, twist about 1/4 of the pasta into a nest and place the nest in the prepared baking dish. Repeat with remaining pasta. Place the burrata in a bowl and cut it open. Spoon the liquid from inside the burrata over the top of each nest. Chop the firm outside of the burrata into cubes and sprinkle those over the nests. Sprinkle with breadcrumbs and grated Parmesan. Broil until browned and crisp, about 5 minutes.

« ZUCCOTTO DI ZITI »
ZITI ZUCCOTTO

This is quite an impressive-looking "architectural" dish, suitable for Christmas or another celebration when you want to wow your guests.

SERVES 6

Unsalted butter for greasing baking pan
$1/4$ cup plus 1 tablespoon (30 grams) breadcrumbs
Salt to taste
7 ounces (200 grams) broccoli
1 shallot, minced
$1/4$ cup (50 milliliters) extra-virgin olive oil
2 ounces (50 grams) pancetta, diced
Pepper to taste
$3/4$ package (350 grams) ziti
1 large egg
1 cup (250 grams) readymade béchamel
1 fresh mozzarella ball (8 ounces/225 grams), diced
$1/4$ cup plus 2 tablespoons (40 grams) grated Parmesan

Preheat the oven to 350° F (180° C). Butter a dome-shaped pan or a round cake pan with 8-inch sides. Line the bottom of the pan with a circle of parchment paper (cut to fit). Sprinkle 3 tablespoons breadcrumbs onto the sides of the pan and dump out any excess. Bring a small pot of salted water to a boil. Break the broccoli up into florets and cook them in the salted water until soft. Drain and set aside. In a large pan, sauté the minced shallot in 3 tablespoons olive oil with the pancetta, then add the broccoli. Season to taste with salt and pepper and cook over low heat, stirring occasionally, to combine flavors.

Bring a large pot of salted water to a boil for cooking the pasta. Add 1 tablespoon oil to the pot, then cook the ziti until very al dente. Drain in a colander and run cold water over them. In a large bowl, beat the egg with 2 tablespoons water and a pinch of salt. Transfer the drained ziti to the bowl and toss to combine with the egg mixture. Use your hands to lift out the ziti one at a time from the bowl—leaving behind any excess egg—and arrange the pasta to form a spiral in the bottom of the baking pan, beginning at the center and working outward. You will have some ziti left over. Reserve 8 whole ziti, then break up the others and combine them with the béchamel, mozzarella, broccoli mixture, and 1/4 cup (25 grams) grated Parmesan. Pour this mixture into the pan on top of the ziti spiral. Arrange the reserved whole pieces of pasta in a spiral on top like a lid. Combine the remaining 2 tablespoons Parmesan with the remaining 2 tablespoons breadcrumbs and sprinkle over the surface.

Bake the zuccotto until set and golden, about 40 minutes. Remove from the oven and allow to rest in the pan for 10 minutes. To unmold, run a butter knife around the border of the pan, then place an inverted platter on top of the pan and flip the pan and platter together. Carefully lift away the pan and serve immediately.

« RISOTTO ALLE ERBE »
HERB RISOTTO

This is a simple risotto, but it's so good! The recipe is from Francesco Gotti. There are three special techniques here that really distinguish this risotto from the everyday kind: grinding the raw legumes, the delicious basil sauce, and the addition of ricotta. I wanted to do it justice, so on my program I made it in a gold pot from the professional kitchenware manufacturer Baldassare Agnelli. During filming, as I was sautéing the onion, my friend Francesca and I blurted out at the same time, "Now the onion really is golden brown!"

SERVES 4

1 pound (500 grams) fresh peas in their pods
1 pound 5 ounces (600 grams) fresh fava beans in their pods
5 ounces (150 grams) asparagus tips
1 carrot
1 rib celery
2 yellow onions
Salt to taste
1/4 cup (50 milliliters) extra-virgin olive oil plus more for sautéing
2 cups (400 grams) Italian rice for risotto, such as arborio, carnaroli, or vialone nano

1 cup (250 milliliters) white wine
Leaves of 1 sprig basil
$1/2$ teaspoon coarse salt
1 cup (200 grams) sheep's milk ricotta
4 tablespoons (50 grams) unsalted butter, cut into pieces
1 tablespoon mascarpone
Grated Parmesan to taste

Shell the peas and fava beans, reserving the pods. Place the shelled peas and beans in a food processor fitted with the metal blade. Add the asparagus tips and process until very fine. To make the broth, combine the carrot, celery, 1 yellow onion, a handful of fava bean and pea pods (rinsed thoroughly), and a little salt in a large pot. Add cold water to cover (you'll want 5 to 6 cups broth/$1\,1/4$ to $1\,1/2$ liters in the end), bring to a boil, and then lower the heat to a simmer and simmer until the vegetables have given up all their flavor, 1 to $1\,1/2$ hours. Strain the broth, place it in a pot (you can use the same pot—just rinse it out), bring to a boil, then lower the heat to a simmer and leave at a simmer. Mince the remaining yellow onion. In a large pan, sauté the minced onion in a small amount of oil until golden. Add the rice to the pan and toast, stirring, until the rice becomes translucent. Add the wine and cook, stirring, until it is mostly absorbed. (When you draw a wooden spoon across the diameter of the pan, very little liquid should run into the space.) Add the minced pea, bean, and asparagus mixture to the pan. Stir to combine and add salt to taste. Add about 1 cup (200 milliliters) broth. Simmer, stirring constantly, until the broth is almost absorbed. Continue adding hot broth, about $1/2$ cup (100 milliliters) at a time, stirring constantly and allowing each addition to evaporate almost completely (use the spoon test above, but don't let the pan get so dry that the rice sticks) before adding the next, until the rice is tender but still slightly firm to the bite and the mixture is creamy. (As the rice gets more cooked, add smaller and smaller amounts of liquid.) In a food processor fitted with the metal blade or a blender, process the basil leaves with the coarse salt and $1/4$ cup (50 milliliters) oil. In a small bowl, whisk the ricotta with a pinch of salt until creamy. When the risotto is cooked, remove the pan from the heat and stir in the basil sauce, butter, mascarpone, and grated Parmesan to taste. Stir briskly for several minutes. Divide the risotto among individual serving plates. Top each portion with $1/4$ of the ricotta and serve immediately.

RED RISOTTO WITH RICOTTA QUENELLES

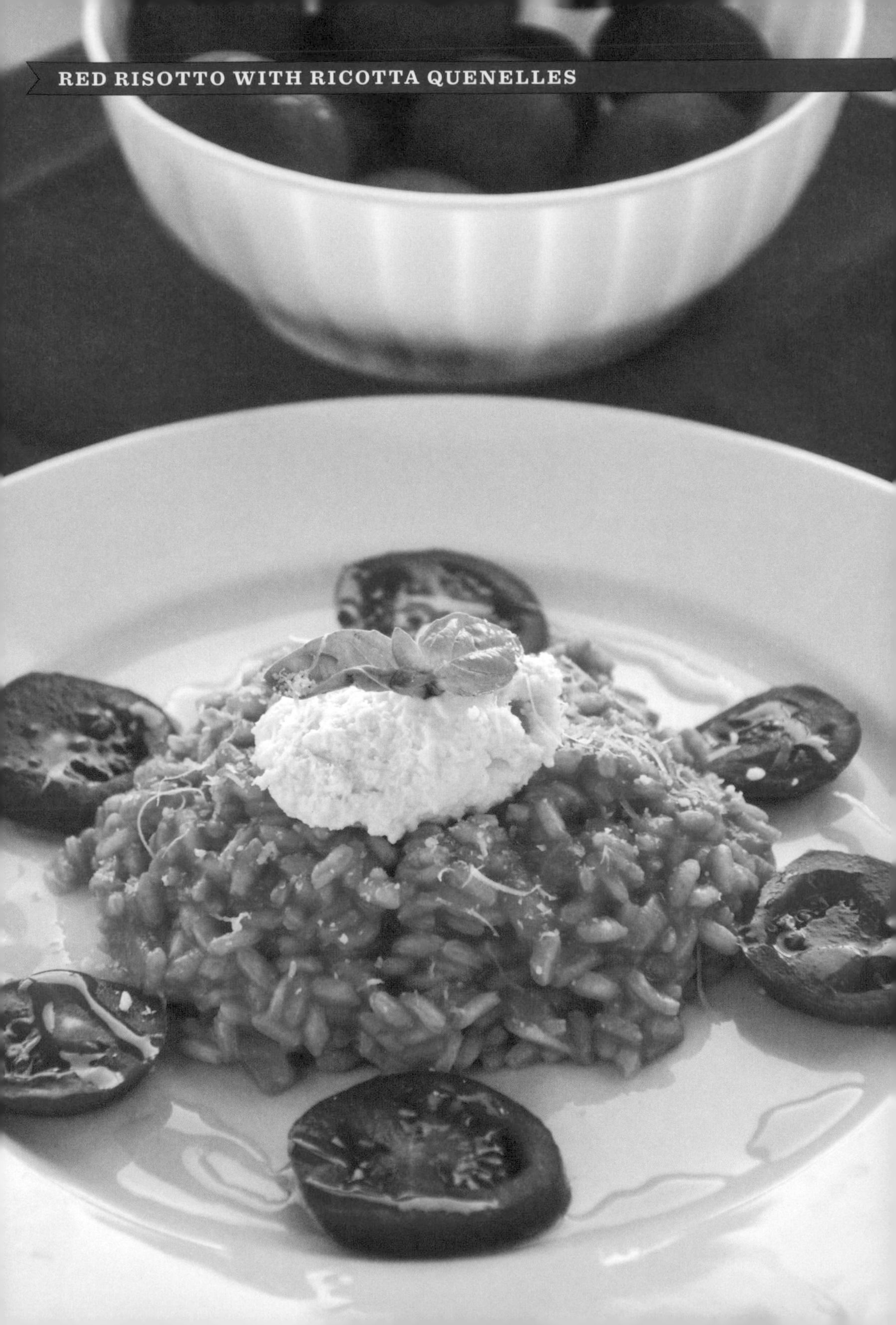

« RISOTTO ROSSO CON QUENELLE DI RICOTTA »
RED RISOTTO WITH RICOTTA QUENELLES

Risotto with tomato sauce is seriously delicious, but maybe a little too plain—in both its appearance and taste—to serve when you're having company. My brother-in-law Giorgio Gori, who loves to cook for his family, makes an incredible version of this dish and is my go-to expert on the subject. But it was my idea to render it a little more sophisticated and refined by adding a quenelle—which is a French word for an oval-shaped ball—of ricotta and grated Parmesan as a garnish. When you mix in the cheese and it blends with the sauce, the dish gets an extra hit of creaminess.

SERVES 3 TO 4

1 tablespoon vegetable broth granules (or the serving size indicated on
    the package)
$1/2$ yellow onion
1 clove garlic, peeled
Extra-virgin olive oil for sautéing (about 1 tablespoon)
1 $1/2$ cups (300 grams) Italian rice for risotto, such as arborio, carnaroli,
    or vialone nano
1 cup (250 milliliters) white wine
2 cups (500 milliliters) strained tomatoes
Salt to taste
Basil leaves to taste
2 tablespoons (30 grams) unsalted butter
$1/2$ cup plus 2 tablespoons (65 grams) grated Parmesan
$1/3$ cup (100 grams) cow's milk, sheep's milk, or goat's milk ricotta

Combine the broth granules and 5 to 6 cups water (1 $1/4$ to 1 $1/2$ liters) in a small pot. Bring to a boil, then lower the heat to a simmer and let it simmer. Mince the onion and sauté it in a large pan with the garlic clove in a little oil. Add the rice to the pan and toast, stirring, until the rice becomes translucent. Add the wine and cook, stirring, until it is mostly absorbed. (When you draw a wooden spoon across the diameter of the pan, very little liquid should run into the space.) Add the strained tomatoes, salt to taste, and basil leaves to taste (tear them into small pieces as you drop them in) to the pan with the rice. Then add about 1 cup broth. Simmer, stirring constantly, until the broth is almost absorbed. Continue adding hot broth, about $1/2$ cup at a time, stirring constantly and allowing each addition to evaporate almost completely (use the spoon test above, but don't let the pan get so dry that the rice sticks) before adding the next, until the rice is tender but still slightly firm to the bite and the mixture is creamy. (As the rice gets more cooked, add smaller and smaller amounts of liquid.) If you are running low on broth and the rice is not yet cooked, add water to the pot and bring it back to a boil. When the rice is almost cooked, make the quenelle mixture: In a small bowl, combine 2 tablespoons Parmesan and the ricotta and mix to combine thoroughly. When the risotto is cooked, remove the pan from the heat and stir in the butter and the remaining $1/2$ cup (50 grams) grated Parmesan. Divide the risotto among individual serving plates. Form quenelles using two spoons to shape the cheese mixture, and top each risotto portion with a quenelle. Serve immediately.

« RISOTTO AGLI SPINACI »
SPINACH RISOTTO

I firmly believe that the true test of a great dish is that it appeals to everyone in every situation, from a humble home-cooked dinner to a fancy party. I ate this risotto at just such a party one night, and since then I've made it for my kids in my own kitchen, and they gobble it up.

SERVES 4 TO 5

5 to 6 cups (1 $1/4$ to 1 $1/2$ liters) beef or vegetable broth
1 yellow onion, thinly sliced
Unsalted butter for sautéing
9 ounces (250 grams) fresh spinach leaves, rinsed and cut into ribbons
Salt to taste
1 cup (250 milliliters) whole milk
2 cups (400 grams) Italian rice for risotto, such as arborio, carnaroli, or
     vialone nano
1 cup (100 grams) grated Parmesan

Place the broth in a pot. Bring to a boil, then lower the heat to a simmer and let it simmer. In a large pan, sauté the onion in butter until golden. Add the spinach and cook until wilted (this should take 1 minute or less). Season with salt. Remove about $1/4$ of the spinach mixture from the pan, squeeze out as much water as possible, and puree in a blender with the milk. Set aside.

Meanwhile, add the rice to the spinach mixture in the pan and toast, stirring, until the rice becomes translucent. Then add about 1 cup (250 milliliters) broth. Simmer, stirring constantly, until the broth is almost absorbed. (When you draw a wooden spoon across the diameter of the pan, very little liquid should run into the space.) Continue adding hot broth, about 1/2 cup (100 milliliters) at a time, stirring constantly and allowing each addition to evaporate almost completely (use the spoon test above, but don't let the pan get so dry that the rice sticks) before adding the next, until rice is tender but still slightly firm to the bite and mixture is creamy. (As the rice gets more cooked, add smaller and smaller amounts of liquid.) If you are running low on broth and the rice is not yet cooked, add water to the pot and bring it back to a boil. When the risotto is cooked, remove from the heat and stir in the spinach and milk mixture and grated Parmesan. Stir briskly for a few minutes, then divide the risotto among individual serving plates and serve immediately.

« RISOTTO ASPARAGI E BURRATA »
ASPARAGUS AND BURRATA RISOTTO

Traditionally, when a risotto is cooked some butter is stirred briskly into it to make a silky sauce. This recipe improves upon that step by using burrata liquid. The results are incredible. Burrata has a liquid center and a more firm exterior. This recipe uses only the liquid center—reserve the firm exterior and use it as you would mozzarella.

SERVES 2

Salt to taste
7 ounces (200 grams) asparagus
1/2 teaspoon beef broth granules
1 shallot, sliced
Unsalted butter for sautéing
Extra-virgin olive oil for sautéing
**1 cup (200 grams) Italian rice for risotto, such as arborio, carnaroli, or
    vialone nano**

Creamy interior of 1 ball fresh burrata
Grated Parmesan to taste
Pepper to taste

Bring a large pot of salted water to a boil and cook the asparagus. When the asparagus are tender, remove them with a slotted spoon and dissolve the broth granules in the cooking water. Lower the heat to a simmer and keep the broth at a simmer.

In a large pan, sauté the shallot in equal amounts butter and oil. Chop the asparagus stems—reserve the tips—and add the chopped stems to the pan. Add the rice to the pan and toast, stirring, until the rice becomes translucent. Then add about 1 cup (250 milliliters) broth. Simmer, stirring constantly, until the broth is almost absorbed. (When you draw a wooden spoon across the diameter of the pan, very little liquid should run into the space.) Continue adding hot broth, about $1/2$ cup (100 milliliters) at a time, stirring constantly and allowing each addition to evaporate almost completely (use the spoon test above, but don't let the pan get so dry that the rice sticks) before adding the next, until the rice is tender but still slightly firm to the bite and the mixture is creamy. (As the rice gets more cooked, add smaller and smaller amounts of liquid.) If you are running low on broth and the rice is not yet cooked, add water to the pot and bring it back to a boil. When the risotto is almost cooked, stir in the asparagus tips and finish cooking.

When the rice is cooked, remove the pan from the heat and stir in the burrata liquid and a generous amount of Parmesan. Stir briskly for a few minutes, then divide the risotto among individual serving plates, sprinkle each portion with some pepper, and serve immediately with additional grated Parmesan on the side.

« RISOTTO ALLA TREVIGIANA »
RISOTTO WITH TREVISO RADICCHIO

Risotto with radicchio was the first dish I ever learned to cook. My mother taught me the secret of risotto—the gradual process of stirring in liquid to help the rice release its starch. I was 16 at the time. I think I made this dish for every boyfriend I ever had back then! Over the years, I've improved the recipe a little, and now I add goat cheese when I make it.

SERVES 2 TO 3

5 to 6 cups (1 $^1/_4$ to 1 $^1/_2$ liters) beef broth made with bouillon cubes or
    granules
1 yellow onion, minced
Extra-virgin olive oil for sautéing
1 head radicchio, preferably curly Treviso radicchio, cut into ribbons
1 cup to 1 $^1/_4$ cups (200 to 250 grams) Italian rice for risotto, such as
    arborio, carnaroli, or vialone nano
$^1/_2$ cup (100 milliliters) red wine
1 small button goat cheese
Grated Parmesan to taste
$^1/_2$ cup (100 milliliters) whole milk
Salt to taste

Place the broth in a pot. Bring to a boil, then lower the heat to a simmer and leave at a
simmer. In a large pan, sauté the onion in oil until golden. Add the radicchio to the pan
and cook until wilted. Add the rice to the pan and toast, stirring, until the rice becomes
translucent. Add the wine and simmer, stirring constantly, until most of the liquid has
evaporated. (When you draw a wooden spoon across the diameter of the pan, very little
liquid should run into the space.) Then add about 1 cup (250 milliliters) broth. Simmer, stirring constantly, until broth is almost absorbed. Continue adding hot broth,
about $^1/_2$ cup (100 milliliters) at a time, stirring constantly and allowing each addition
to evaporate almost completely (use the spoon test above, but don't let the pan get so
dry that the rice sticks) before adding the next, until the rice is tender but still slightly
firm to the bite and the mixture is creamy. (As the rice gets more cooked, add smaller
and smaller amounts of liquid.) If you are running low on broth and the rice is not yet
cooked, add water to the pot and bring it back to a boil. When the rice is cooked, remove
the pan from the heat and stir in the goat cheese and Parmesan. If the dish looks dry,
stir in some or all of the milk. Stir briskly for a few minutes, then taste and adjust salt.
Divide the risotto among individual serving plates and serve immediately.

« RISOTTO GIALLO AI PORRI CROCCANTI »
SAFFRON RISOTTO WITH CRISPY LEEKS

A simple change like using leeks in place of onions really has an impact on this wonderful risotto, but what makes it extra-special are the fried rings of a leek that add a little crunchy element. I always make extra and eat them like potato chips as I'm cooking the risotto—chef's privileges!

SERVES 4

4 leeks, white and green parts sliced
Unbleached all-purpose flour for dredging
Vegetable oil for deep-frying
5 to 6 cups (1 $^1/_4$ to 1 $^1/_2$ liters) beef or vegetable broth made with
    bouillon cubes or granules
Extra-virgin olive oil for sautéing
1 $^1/_2$ cups (300 grams) Italian rice for risotto, such as arborio, carnaroli,
    or vialone nano
1 cup (250 milliliters) white wine
$^1/_2$ teaspoon (2 envelopes) powdered saffron
$^1/_2$ cup (100 milliliters) whole milk
$^1/_2$ cup (50 grams) grated Parmesan
Salt to taste

Separate the slices of the green part of the leeks into rings. Dredge in flour and deep-fry in a generous amount of vegetable oil until golden brown and crisp. Do not allow to burn. Remove to paper towels to drain. Place the broth in a pot. Bring to a boil, then lower the heat to a simmer and leave at a simmer.

In a large pan, sauté the white parts of the leeks in olive oil. Add the rice to the pan and toast, stirring, until the rice becomes translucent. Add the wine and simmer, stirring constantly, until most of the liquid has evaporated. (When you draw a wooden spoon across the diameter of the pan, very little liquid should run into the space.) Then add about 1 cup (250 milliliters) broth. Simmer, stirring constantly, until the broth is almost absorbed. Continue adding hot broth, about $^1/_2$ cup (100 milliliters) at a time, stirring constantly and allowing each addition to evaporate almost completely (use the spoon test above, but don't let the pan get so dry that the rice sticks) before adding the next, until the rice is tender but still slightly firm to the bite and the mixture is creamy. (As the rice gets more cooked, add smaller and smaller amounts of liquid.) If you are running low on broth and the rice is not yet cooked, add water to the pot and bring it back to a boil. When the rice is almost cooked, stir in the saffron.

When the rice is cooked, remove the pan from the heat and stir in the milk and Parmesan. Taste and adjust the salt. Stir briskly for a few minutes, then divide the risotto among individual serving plates, top with some of the crispy leek rings, and serve immediately.

« RISOTTO DI MARE NASCOSTO »
HIDDEN FISH RISOTTO

Risotto is delicious, and it's always a big hit at a party. The only thing to keep in mind when planning a menu is that you'll need to be in the kitchen, stirring continuously, which will keep you away from your guests. I think it's worth it, especially for a fantastic risotto like this one. This risotto tastes intensely of the sea, but it doesn't have any actual pieces of fish in it—the flavor is all from the broth. It is served plain—not even a little fresh parsley on top—to highlight that flavor. Thanks to chef Stefano Bartolini for sharing the recipe.

SERVES 4

2 yellow onions
1 carrot
1 rib celery
1 whole gurnard
3 mullet
1 baby octopus or cuttlefish
5 mantis shrimp
3 shrimp heads
3 cups (750 milliliters) tomato puree
Extra-virgin olive oil for sautéing
2 cups (400 grams) Italian rice for risotto, such as arborio, carnaroli, or vialone nano

HIDDEN FISH RISOTTO

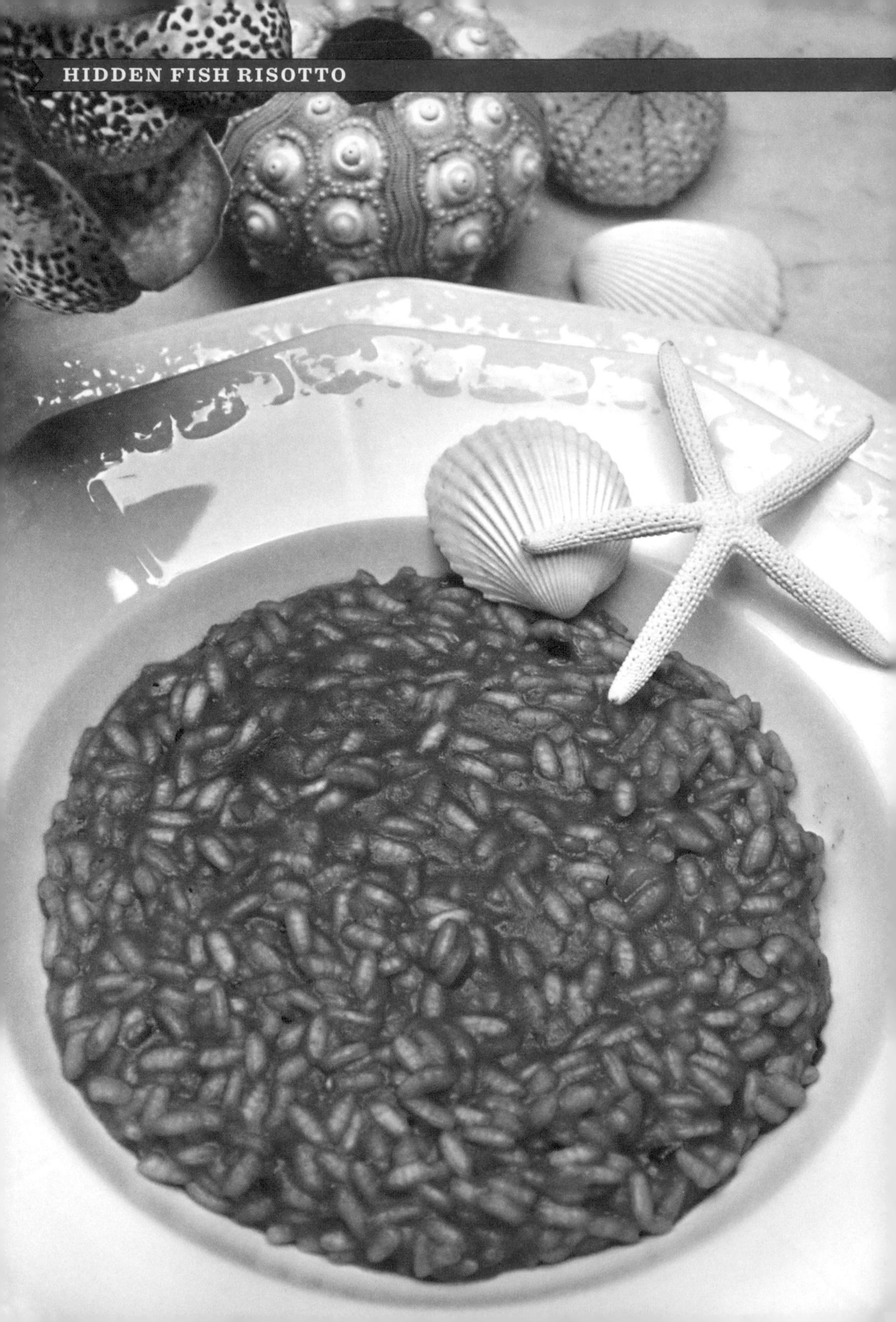

Salt to taste
1 pinch chile pepper flakes

In a large pot, combine 1 yellow onion, the carrot, celery, gurnard, mullet, baby octopus, mantis shrimp, shrimp heads, and tomato puree. Add 2 quarts (2 liters) water. Bring to a boil, then lower the heat to a simmer and cook until all the seafood has given up its flavor, about 2 hours. Do not salt. Strain the broth through a fine-mesh sieve—strain it twice if necessary to be sure that it contains no bones, scales, or fins. Discard the solids. Rinse out the pot, return the broth to the pot, and bring to a simmer.

Slice the remaining yellow onion and, in a large pan, sauté in oil until golden. Add the rice to the pan and toast, stirring, until the rice becomes translucent. Season the rice with salt and the chile pepper flakes. Add about 1 cup (250 milliliters) broth. Simmer, stirring constantly, until the broth is almost absorbed. (When you draw a wooden spoon across the diameter of the pan, very little liquid should run into the space.) Continue adding hot broth, about 1/2 cup (100 milliliters) at a time, stirring constantly and allowing each addition to evaporate almost completely (use the spoon test above, but don't let the pan get so dry that the rice sticks) before adding the next, until the rice is tender but still slightly firm to the bite and mixture is creamy. (As the rice gets more cooked, add smaller and smaller amounts of liquid.) If you are running low on broth and the rice is not yet cooked, add water to the pot and bring it back to a boil. When the rice is cooked, remove the pan from the heat and stir in one last portion of broth. (This risotto should be a little soupier than the usual risotto.) Divide the risotto among individual serving plates and serve immediately with no garnish.

« RISOTTO AI PORRI E MERLUZZO CROCCANTE »
RISOTTO WITH LEEKS AND CRISPY COD

You can serve this as a filling first course or as a one-dish meal. The cod is incorporated into the risotto and also served on top of it.

SERVES 4

5 to 6 cups (1 1/4 to 1 1/2 liters) vegetable broth made with bouillon cubes or granules

2 leeks, thinly sliced
Extra-virgin olive oil for sautéing and pan-frying
4 cod fillets
1 1/4 cups (250 grams) Italian rice for risotto, such as arborio, carnaroli,
    or vialone nano
1/2 cup (100 milliliters) white wine
Breadcrumbs for dredging
Salt to taste
1/2 cup (100 milliliters) whole milk

Place the broth in a pot. Bring to a boil, then lower the heat to a simmer and leave at a simmer. In a large pan, sauté the leeks in olive oil. Add 2 cod fillets and cook, breaking them up with a spoon, until cooked through and broken down. Add the rice to the pan and toast, stirring, until the rice becomes translucent. Add the wine and simmer, stirring constantly, until most of the liquid has evaporated. (When you draw a wooden spoon across the diameter of the pan, very little liquid should run into the space.) Then add about 1 cup (250 milliliters) broth. Simmer, stirring constantly, until the broth is almost absorbed. Continue adding hot broth, about 1/2 cup (100 milliliters) at a time, stirring constantly and allowing each addition to evaporate almost completely (use the spoon test above, but don't let the pan get so dry that the rice sticks) before adding the next, until the rice is tender but still slightly firm to the bite and the mixture is creamy. (As the rice gets more cooked, add smaller and smaller amounts of liquid.) If you are running low on broth and the rice is not yet cooked, add water to the pot and bring it back to a boil.

When the rice is almost cooked, cut the remaining 2 cod fillets in half, dredge in breadcrumbs, and pan-fry in olive oil in another pan. When the rice is fully cooked, remove the pan from the heat. Taste and adjust the salt. Add the milk to the rice and stir briskly for a few minutes, then divide the risotto among individual serving plates. Top each portion with a piece of pan-fried cod and serve immediately.

« RISO E LENTICCHIE »
RICE AND LENTILS

In Italy, lentils are traditionally eaten on New Year's Eve, but I think they should be consumed year-round. They're good for you and they taste great. This dish is from my friend Rosa Prinzivalli. If you have leftovers or make this dish in advance and reheat it, you may need to thin it with a little more broth.

SERVES 4

1 yellow onion, sliced
Extra-virgin olive oil for sautéing and drizzling
2 cups (500 milliliters) tomato puree
3 cups (700 milliliters) beef broth
Salt to taste
1 cup (200 grams) short-grain Italian rice
1 (8-ounce/225-gram) can lentils, rinsed and drained
Minced fresh parsley leaves to taste
Grated Parmesan to taste
Pepper to taste

In a pot, sauté the onion in a small amount of oil. Add the tomato puree and the broth, season with salt, and bring to a boil. Add the rice, lower the heat to a simmer, cover, and cook for 10 minutes, stirring occasionally to keep the rice from sticking. Add the lentils and parsley and cook until the rice is cooked through, about 5 minutes more. Distribute among individual soup plates, top each portion with grated Parmesan, season with pepper, drizzle with olive oil, and serve hot.

« BOMBA DI RISO CON RAGÙ DI QUAGLIA »
RICE BOMBE WITH QUAIL SAUCE

This recipe comes from Lorenzo Boni. When he made this on my show, he garnished it with hard-boiled quail eggs that he shaped into cubes using ice cube trays. So cute!

SERVES 4

Unsalted butter for greasing pan, sautéing, for rice, and dotting the top
Breadcrumbs for coating pan and sprinkling on top
Salt to taste
2 yellow onions
2 1/2 cups (500 grams) short-grain Italian rice
Extra-virgin olive oil for sautéing and for rice
2 quail, broken down and still on the bone
Fresh sage leaves to taste
Juniper berries of 3 sprigs, lightly crushed
Grated nutmeg to taste
1/2 cup (100 milliliters) white wine
1/4 cup dried mushrooms, rinsed and chopped
2 tablespoons tomato paste
1 teaspoon vegetable broth granules
2 drops truffle oil
3 large eggs
1/2 cup (250 milliliters) whole milk
1 1/3 cups (130 grams) grated Parmesan

Preheat the oven to 375° F (190° C). Butter a domed pan, sprinkle with breadcrumbs to coat the sides, and then dump out the excess. Set aside. Bring a large pot of salted water to a boil. Cut 1 onion in half and add to the boiling water, then add the rice and cook it as you would pasta, stirring occasionally. Meanwhile, mince the remaining yellow onion and, in a large pan, sauté it in equal amounts oil and butter, then add the quail pieces, sage, juniper berries, salt, and nutmeg. Add the wine, dried mushrooms, tomato paste, broth granules, and enough water to cover the quail about halfway. Cook, covered, over low heat until the quail is falling off the bone, 20 to 30 minutes. Remove from the heat and allow to cool slightly. With your hands, remove the quail meat from the bone and shred it back into the pot. Drizzle with the truffle oil. In a small bowl, beat the eggs, milk, and some nutmeg.

When the rice is cooked al dente—soft on the outside but still brittle at its core—drain and transfer to a large bowl. Remove and discard the onion. Stir in a generous amount of butter, the Parmesan, a drizzle of olive oil, and the egg mixture. Add about $3/4$ of the rice mixture to the prepared pan, pressing it against the sides and leaving the center empty. Fill the center with the quail mixture. Top with the remaining rice mixture, pressing it across the top over the quail mixture like a lid. Sprinkle with additional breadcrumbs and dot generously with butter. Bake until golden brown and set, about 20 minutes. Let the bombe sit for 10 minutes in the pan, then invert a platter over it and turn over the platter and the pan together. Carefully lift off the pan and serve.

« POMODORI CON IL RISO »
RICE-STUFFED TOMATOES

This is one of Fabio's recipes, and he's made it countless times. It always starts the same way: He comes home and heads to the kitchen, then comes back out and announces, "I've decided to make the tomatoes with the rice." He usually starts cooking too late, so we're all salivating in front of the oven, analyzing the rice and hoping that it's done. When that miracle finally happens, we face another challenge: Tomatoes straight out of the oven are the same temperature as lava coming out of a volcano. When they finally cool, usually some time around eleven P.M., they are delicious!

SERVES 4

4 tomatoes
Salt to taste
$3/4$ cup to 1 cup (150 to 200 grams) short-grain Italian rice
1 clove garlic, crushed
Minced fresh parsley leaves to taste
Minced fresh basil leaves to taste
Pepper to taste
Extra-virgin olive oil for drizzling over tomatoes, adding to rice stuffing,
    and coating potatoes

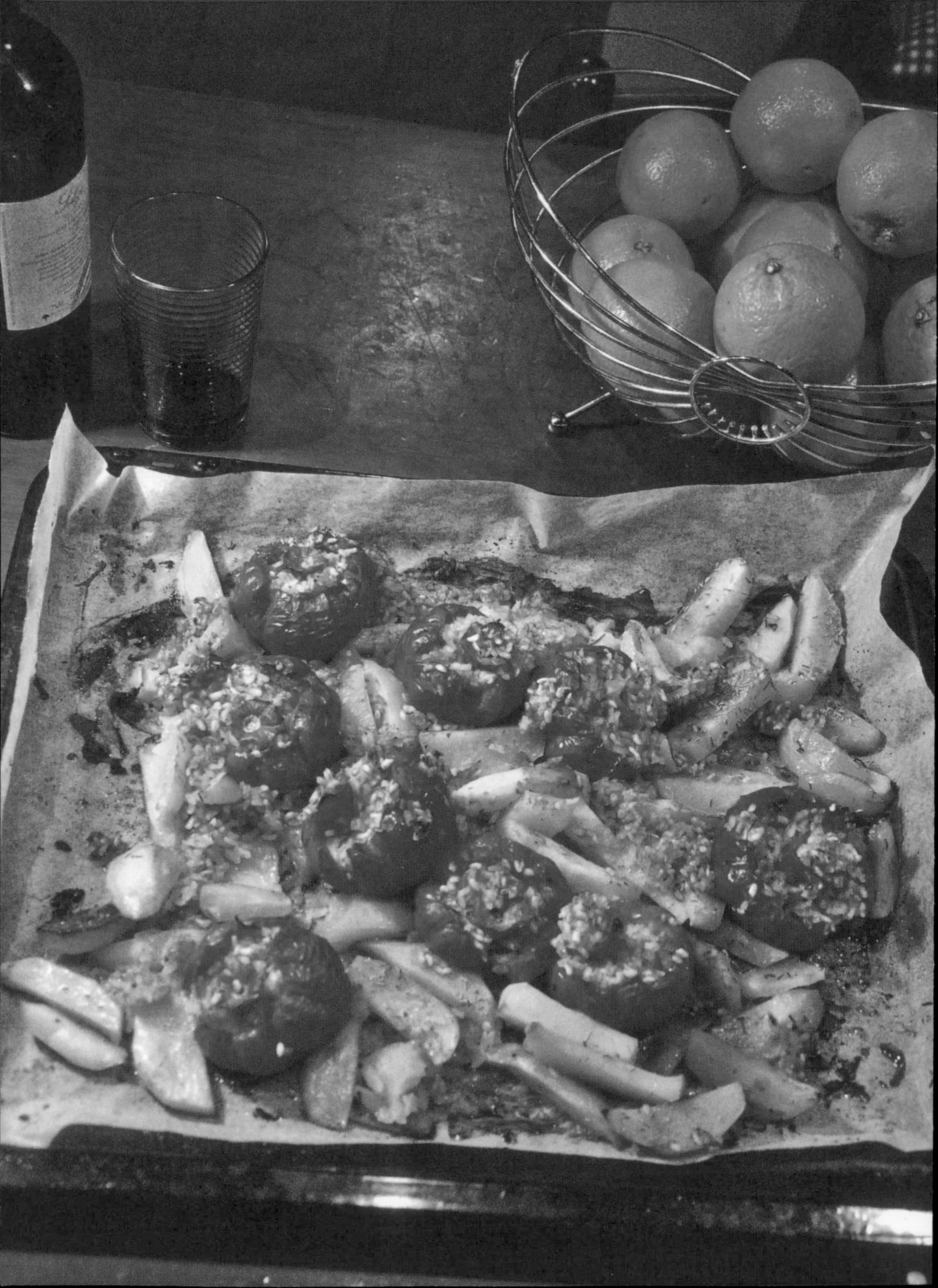

3 potatoes, peeled and cut into wedges
Minced fresh rosemary leaves to taste

Preheat the oven to 350° F (180° C). Cut the tops off the tomatoes and reserve. With the tip of a paring knife, hollow out the tomatoes, saving the pulp in a bowl. Salt the tomatoes. Process the tomato pulp in a blender, transfer to a bowl, and mix it with the rice and garlic and season with parsley, basil, salt, and pepper. Drizzle with a little olive oil. Set the tomato pulp mixture aside to rest for about 30 minutes, then remove and discard the garlic.

Fill the tomatoes part way with the tomato pulp mixture, but leave a little room at the top for the rice to expand. (You probably won't use all the rice mixture.) Place the tomatoes on a parchment-lined jelly-roll pan. In a bowl, toss the potatoes with a little olive oil, minced rosemary, and salt. Scatter the potatoes around the tomatoes, then spoon any remaining rice and tomato mixture over the potatoes. Bake until the rice is tender, about 30 minutes. If the tomatoes look dry and the rice isn't cooked, drizzle with a little water, cover the pan with aluminum foil, and return to the oven. When the rice is cooked, remove the stuffed tomatoes from the oven and allow to cool to room temperature before serving.

« GNOCCHETTI DI RISO GRATINATI »
RICE FLOUR GNOCCHI

These gnocchetti (which just means "small gnocchi") are a little unusual. They're made with rice flour, so they're perfect for people who are gluten intolerant. They're served on a bed of zucchini with pancetta and primo sale, a very mild soft white sheep's cheese similar to farmer's cheese. This is one of the many excellent recipes that Lorenzo Boni has shared with me over the years.

SERVES 4

1 yellow onion, minced
Extra-virgin olive oil for sautéing and drizzling
2 zucchini, thinly sliced
1/4 teaspoon beef broth granules

1 tablespoon unsalted butter
Fresh basil leaves to taste
1 pound (500 grams) potatoes
1 cup to 1 $^1/_4$ cups (150 to 200 grams) rice flour
Salt to taste
1 large egg
3 $^1/_2$ ounces (100 grams) pancetta, diced
3 $^1/_2$ ounces (100 grams) primo sale cheese, crumbled
Diced tomatoes, *quanto basta*
Grated Parmesan to taste

Preheat the oven to 400° F (200° C). Sauté the onion in some olive oil. Add the zucchini and water just to cover, stir in the beef broth granules, and cook over medium heat until soft. When the zucchini are cooked, puree them with the butter and basil in a food processor or a blender (if you have an immersion blender, use it right in the pan). Spread the zucchini mixture in the bottom of a baking pan.

Meanwhile, to make the gnocchi, place the potatoes in a pot, cover with water, and boil until easily pierced with a fork. Drain and pass through a potato ricer into a large bowl. (The peel should come off.) Gradually add the flour (you may not need all of it—stop adding it as soon as the dough is no longer sticky), some salt, and the egg. Knead by hand to form a soft dough. Pinch off egg-sized pieces of dough and roll under your palms on a work surface into ropes, then cut the ropes into little cylinders (about $^1/_2$ inch long) with a knife. Bring a large pot of salted water to a boil and cook the gnocchi. As soon as the gnocchi rise to the surface, they are done. Remove with a skimmer and arrange on top of the zucchini mixture. Sprinkle with the pancetta, primo sale, and tomatoes. Sprinkle with the Parmesan last, then drizzle with a little olive oil. Bake until browned on top, 8 to 10 minutes. Serve right from the pan at the table.

« GNOCCHI DI TREVIGIANA »
RADICCHIO DUMPLINGS

I love radicchio. I love its deep purple color and its bitter taste. If you love it as much as I do, you're going to love this recipe, too.

SERVES 4

1 head radicchio, preferably curly Treviso radicchio, coarsely chopped
$1/2$ yellow onion, minced
Extra-virgin olive oil for sautéing
Salt to taste
$1/2$ cup (100 grams) ricotta
$1/2$ cup (50 grams) grated Parmesan
1 egg yolk
$1/4$ cup plus 2 tablespoons (50 grams) unbleached all-purpose flour, plus
    more for the work surface
Unsalted butter for finishing
2 ounces (50 grams) smoked scamorza, grated

In a pan, sauté the radicchio and the onion in a small amount of oil until wilted. Season with salt. Transfer the radicchio mixture to a bowl. Add the ricotta, Parmesan, egg yolk, and flour. Knead by hand until the mixture clumps together. If it's too loose, add small amounts of flour. Set the dough aside to rest for an hour or so.

Bring a large pot of salted water to a boil. Generously flour a work surface. Pinch off a piece of the dough and roll it into a ball on the floured work surface so that it is coated with flour. Repeat with the remaining dough. Place a generous amount of butter, cut into pieces, in a serving dish. When you have used up all the dough, gently drop the balls into the boiling water using a skimmer or slotted spoon. When the dumplings rise to the surface, they're cooked. Remove them with a skimmer or slotted spoon and transfer to the serving dish. Toss with the butter to melt. Sprinkle with the grated scamorza, toss again, and serve immediately.

« GNOCCHI DI RICOTTA CON BURRO E TIMO »
RICOTTA GNOCCHI WITH BUTTER AND THYME

The first time I made this, I messed it up completely—I bought myrtle rather than thyme, and it didn't taste of anything at all. These gnocchi aren't as soft as potato gnocchi, they're a little more compact. That's what makes them so delicious!

SERVES 4

Salt to taste
1 cup (200 grams) ricotta
1 1/4 cups (150 grams) unbleached all-purpose flour
1 large egg
Pepper to taste
4 tablespoons (50 grams) unsalted butter
Minced fresh thyme or sage leaves to taste
Grated Parmesan to taste

Bring a large pot of salted water to a boil. In a bowl, combine the ricotta and flour. Add the egg. Season with salt and pepper and knead by hand until you have a smooth compact dough. If it's sticky, add a little more flour. Pinch off an egg-sized piece of dough and roll it under your palms on a work surface into a rope. Use a knife to cut it into small cylinders. Repeat with the remaining dough. Cook the gnocchi in the boiling water. Meanwhile, in a large pan melt the butter with the thyme leaves over medium heat. When the gnocchi rise to the surface, they are done. With a skimmer, remove them from the pot and transfer them to the pan. Cook, stirring occasionally, until lightly browned. Season with pepper, sprinkle with grated Parmesan, and serve.

« GNOCCHI DI ZUCCA CON CREMA DELICATA DI GORGONZOLA »
SQUASH GNOCCHI WITH GORGONZOLA

No one can resist these little orange gnocchi—least of all me! If you're not a fan of Gorgonzola, you can dress them in melted butter, sage, and grated Parmesan.

SERVES 4 TO 6

1 (1-pound/500-gram) winter squash, such as butternut or acorn squash
4 tablespoons (50 grams) unsalted butter
Salt to taste
2 cups (250 grams) unbleached all-purpose flour
7 ounces (200 grams) sweet Gorgonzola
1/2 cup (100 milliliters) whole milk
Grated Parmesan to taste
Pepper to taste

Preheat the oven to 400° F (200° C). Seed the squash and cut it into thick wedges with the peel still on. Place it on a jelly-roll pan, cover with foil, and bake until very soft, 40 to 50 minutes. Remove and discard the peel (which should come away easily) and, in a food processor fitted with the metal blade or a blender, puree the hot squash with the butter. Bring a large pot of salted water to a boil. Transfer the pureed squash to a bowl, season with salt, and gradually add the flour, mixing first with a spoon and then by hand. Add just enough flour to create a soft dough that is not too sticky (you may not use all the flour, or you may need a little more). Finish kneading on a work surface. Pinch off an egg-sized piece of dough and roll it under your palms on a work surface into a rope about 1/2 inch wide. Cut the rope into cylinders with a knife, then press each one against the back of the tines of a fork. Repeat with the remaining dough. Cook the gnocchi in the large pot of boiling water. Meanwhile, place the Gorgonzola and milk in a small pot and cook, whisking, over low heat until the cheese has melted. When the gnocchi rise to the surface, they are done. Remove them with a skimmer and place them in a serving dish. Toss with the Gorgonzola sauce, grated Parmesan, and some pepper. Serve immediately.

« GNOCCHI ALLA ROMANA AI FUNGHI »
SEMOLINA GNOCCHI WITH MUSHROOMS

Just recently my friend Loredana Guelpa threw a very elegant dinner party, and I was lucky enough to be invited. As a first course, she served these semolina gnocchi with a porcini mushroom sauce.

SERVES 4

3/4 ounce (20 grams) dried mushrooms
2 cloves garlic, minced
Extra-virgin olive oil for sautéing
8 ounces (250 grams) frozen sliced porcini mushrooms, thawed
Salt to taste
3/4 cup (150 to 170 grams) readymade béchamel
1 quart (1 liter) whole milk
7 tablespoons (100 grams) unsalted butter
2 cups (250 grams) semolina flour
2 egg yolks
1 cup (100 grams) grated Parmesan, plus more for sprinkling

Place the dried mushrooms in a bowl and add water to cover. Set aside to soak until soft. When the mushrooms are soft, in a large pan, sauté the garlic in a small amount of oil until it begins to color. Gently remove the mushrooms from the bowl using your hands (don't pour them out into a strainer, as there may be some grit left in the bottom of the bowl), squeeze them as dry as possible, chop them, and add them to the pan with the garlic. Add the thawed porcini mushrooms to the pan. Season with salt and cook until the mushrooms are quite soft. Stir the mushroom sauce into the béchamel and set aside.

In a small pot, heat the milk over low heat, then whisk in the butter, some salt, and the semolina flour and cook, stirring constantly, until the mixture forms a paste. Remove from the heat, add the egg yolks, and beat energetically with a wooden spoon. Stir in the grated Parmesan. Either oil a work surface or line it with a piece of parchment paper. Spread the semolina mixture to a thickness of about 1/2 inch (1 centimeter). Let the mixture cool completely. Preheat the broiler. With a pastry cutter or an over-turned drinking glass, cut circles out of the cooled semolina. Spread about half the mushroom and béchamel sauce in a baking pan. Top with the gnocchi, which should overlap slightly, like shingles on a roof. Pour the rest of the mushroom and béchamel sauce over them, sprinkle with grated Parmesan, and broil until dotted with dark spots, 5 to 10 minutes.

« POLENTA AI DUE SUGHI »
POLENTA WITH TWO SAUCES

In Piedmont, where I'm from, our mothers feed us polenta practically from the day we're born. This dish offers polenta prepared two ways: in a mushroom and tomato sauce and baked lasagna-style with plenty of cheese.

SERVES 4 TO 6

5 ounces (150 grams) frozen mirepoix (minced carrots, onion, and celery)
Extra-virgin olive oil for sautéing
2 cloves garlic, minced
10 ounces (300 grams) frozen mushrooms
Salt and pepper to taste
1 tablespoon tomato paste
Minced fresh rosemary leaves to taste
1 package instant polenta
4 tablespoons (50 grams) unsalted butter, plus more for stirring into the
    polenta
3 1/2 ounces (100 grams) Fontina cheese, sliced
3 1/2 ounces (100 grams) sweet Gorgonzola, sliced
1 cup (100 grams) grated Parmesan

In a pan, cook the mirepoix in a small amount of oil until browned. Add the garlic and mushrooms, season with salt and pepper, then add the tomato paste, water just to cover, and rosemary and cook over medium heat, covered, for 15 minutes. Meanwhile, cook the polenta in salted water according to package instructions. When the polenta is cooked, add a generous amount of butter, stirring until it has melted. Place about half the polenta in a serving dish and cover with the mushroom sauce. Preheat the broiler. Butter a baking dish with 2 tablespoons butter. Spread about half the remaining polenta in the bottom of the dish. Top with the fontina. Spread with the remaining polenta and top that with the Gorgonzola and Parmesan. Dot with the remaining 2 tablespoons butter. (If you prefer, you can create more layers—just make them thinner.) Broil until the top is browned, about 5 minutes. Serve both types of polenta together.

« INSALATA DI ORZO E FARRO CON PESTO E MOZZARELLA »
BARLEY AND FARRO SALAD WITH PESTO AND MOZZARELLA

Fabio likes traditional rice salad, but I'm not a fan of room-temperature rice. I do like salads like this one, however, that use other grains. Farro is a kind of wheat; you can find whole farro in Italian specialty stores and other gourmet shops.

SERVES 4

1 cup (200 grams) pearled barley
1 cup (200 grams) pearled farro
3 tablespoons pesto
1/2 cup (80 grams) pine nuts, lightly toasted
1 fresh mozzarella ball (8 ounces/225 grams), diced
10 cherry tomatoes, halved
Pitted taggiasca olives to taste
Extra-virgin olive oil for dressing
Salt to taste

Boil the barley and the farro according to package instructions. Drain and run under cold water. Drain again and transfer to a large bowl. Toss the grains with the pesto, pine nuts, mozzarella, cherry tomatoes, and olives. Dress with enough olive oil to keep the grains moist and salt to taste. Toss and serve at room temperature.

« ORZOTTO AGLI SPINACI »
RISOTTO-STYLE BARLEY WITH SPINACH

This is neither a barley soup nor a risotto—though I enjoy both of those—but something in between the two. It also has the advantage of being a healthy first course that you can prepare in advance.

SERVES 4

1 yellow onion, minced
$1/2$ (10-ounce) package (7 to 8 cubes) frozen spinach
1 $1/4$ cups (250 grams) quick-cooking pearled barley
1 tablespoon vegetable broth granules (or the serving size indicated on
    the package)
Salt to taste
Extra-virgin olive oil for drizzling
Grated Parmesan for serving

Off the heat, place the onion, spinach, and barley in a large pot and add water to cover. Bring to a boil, then lower the heat to a simmer. Stir in the broth granules, season with salt, and cook until almost all the liquid has evaporated and the dish has the consistency of a porridge or thick soup, about 15 minutes. Divide among individual serving plates, drizzle with a little olive oil, sprinkle with grated Parmesan, and serve.

« FARRO AI DUE POMODORI »
FARRO WITH FRESH AND DRIED TOMATOES

If you are unfamiliar with farro, it is worth exploring. Farro can be ground to make a nutty flour (often used in pasta and bread), but in whole-grain form, it is a highly digestible, healthful, and delicious alternative to rice and other grains. It is a good addition to soups, and also a terrific base for all kinds of vegetable salads.

SERVES 4

Salt to taste
1 1/4 cups (250 grams) pearled farro
3 tablespoons (30 grams) pine nuts, toasted
14 ounces (400 grams) cherry tomatoes, halved
1/4 cup tightly packed fresh basil leaves
1/4 cup tightly packed fresh mint leaves
6 sun-dried tomatoes in oil
5 anchovy fillets in oil, drained
Extra-virgin olive oil for dressing
3 1/2 ounces (100 grams) feta cheese, cut into cubes

Bring a large pot of lightly salted water to a boil and cook the farro as you would pasta, stirring occasionally. When the farro is tender, drain it, transfer to a bowl, and stir in the pine nuts and cherry tomatoes. In a food processor fitted with the metal blade or a blender, process the basil, mint, sun-dried tomatoes, anchovy fillets, and a drizzle of olive oil to make a smooth dressing. Pour the dressing over the farro and toss to combine. Sprinkle with the feta and serve.

« LASAGNE DI PANE »
BREAD "LASAGNA"

A group of nuns in a convent gave me this recipe. That might sound funny, but nuns are known for their waste-not-want-not ability to transform humble ingredients into wonderful food, and this dish is no exception. It uses leftover bread, and it makes a nice alternative to regular old lasagna.

SERVES 4 TO 6

1 clove garlic, crushed
1 yellow onion, minced
Extra-virgin olive oil for sautéing
4 cups (1 liter) tomato puree
Salt to taste
Sugar to taste
Fresh basil leaves to taste
7 to 8 thick slices country-style bread, crusts removed

2 cups ($^1/_2$ liter) beef broth (broth made with a bouillon cube or broth
    granules is fine)
2 fresh mozzarella balls (8 ounces/225 grams), diced
1 cup (100 grams) grated Parmesan

Preheat a convection oven to 350° F (180° C). In a large pan, sauté the garlic and onion in a small amount of oil until golden. Add the tomato puree and season with salt,
sugar, and basil leaves. Cook, covered, until thick, 15 to 30 minutes. Spread a small
amount of the tomato sauce on the bottom of a baking pan. Place $^1/_2$ the bread in a single layer (cut slices to fit if needed) in the pan. Pour about 1 cup (250 milliliters) broth
over the bread. Spread about $^1/_2$ of the remaining tomato sauce on top, and sprinkle
with about $^1/_2$ the mozzarella and about $^1/_2$ the Parmesan. Make a second layer in
the same order from the bottom up: bread slices, broth, tomato sauce, mozzarella, and
Parmesan. Bake until the lasagna is nicely browned and the bread has absorbed the
liquid, about 20 minutes. Allow to sit for 10 to 15 minutes before serving.

« PISAREI E FASÒ »
BREADCRUMB DUMPLINGS AND BEANS

One Sunday, my kids and I spent the whole day practicing making *pisarei* (little dumplings made of a breadcrumb dough that look like curled-up orecchiette), because I
was supposed to prepare them on my show the next day. I got pretty good at shap-
ing these dumplings, which hails from the Piacenza area, but Matilde and Eleonora
turned out to be very talented! And that night, we ate so many of these dumplings we
could hardly believe it. If you can't locate borlotti or cranberry beans, use pinto beans
in their place.

SERVES 4

1 yellow onion, minced
Extra-virgin olive oil for sautéing
4 ounces (125 grams) pancetta, diced
1 (15-ounce/500-gram) can borlotti or cranberry beans, rinsed and
    drained
1 $^1/_4$ cups to 1 $^1/_2$ cups (300 to 350 milliliters) tomato puree
Salt to taste

Sugar to taste
1/4 cup breadcrumbs
1/4 cup plus 2 tablespoons unbleached all-purpose flour
Grated Parmesan to taste

In a medium pot, sauté the onion in some oil until transparent. Add the pancetta and sauté until browned. Add the beans, sauté for a few minutes, stirring frequently, then add the tomato puree. Season with salt and a pinch of sugar and cook, covered, until the sauce has thickened, 15 to 20 minutes. Meanwhile, bring a large pot of salted water to a boil. In a bowl, combine the breadcrumbs and flour. Season the mixture with salt and begin adding warm tap water, a few tablespoons at a time, kneading by hand between additions, until you have a soft and elastic dough. Pinch off an egg-sized piece of dough and roll it on a work surface under your palms into a rope about 1/2 inch wide. Cut the rope into 1/2-inch pieces. Take one piece of dough and press it hard against the work surface with a finger. At the same time, drag and roll the dough. It should get thinner and curl up on itself at the same time. (Your first few attempts may look flat, but after a little practice you'll get the hang of it.) Repeat with the remaining dough. When the *pisarei* are all formed, cook them in the boiling water. With a skimmer, remove them to a serving dish. Top with the bean sauce and a generous amount of grated Parmesan and serve.

« GNOCCHI DI PANE »
BREAD GNOCCHI

When I have stale bread sitting around, I reach for this recipe. Actually, I'm often tempted to let bread get stale so that I can make these gnocchi—that's how much I like them.

SERVES 4

1 loaf (400 grams) stale country-style bread
2 cups (500 milliliters) whole milk
3 1/2 ounces (100 grams) Prague ham or prosciutto cotto, minced
2 large eggs
3 1/2 ounces (100 grams) soft, mild cheese, such as provolone, grated
1 tablespoon minced fresh parsley leaves

1 ²/₃ cups (200 grams) unbleached all-purpose flour, plus more for
 flouring your hands
Salt and pepper to taste
Unsalted butter for serving
Fresh sage leaves to taste
1 clove garlic, crushed
¹/₄ teaspoon extra-virgin olive oil
Grated Parmesan for serving

Cut the bread into cubes, place it in a bowl, and pour the milk over it. Set aside, tossing it occasionally, until the bread has absorbed the milk, 15 to 30 minutes. Squeeze
the bread and crumble it into a clean bowl. Add the ham, eggs, grated soft cheese, and
parsley. Mix by hand to combine. Begin adding small amounts of the flour (you may
not need all of it), kneading to combine between additions, until you have a smooth
dough that is no longer sticky. Season with salt and pepper and knead by hand a little
more. With floured hands, pinch off an egg-sized piece of dough and roll it on a work
surface under your palms to form a rope. Cut the rope into little cylinders, and then
roll each cylinder lightly against the work surface to form it into an oval. Repeat with
remaining dough.

Bring a large pot of salted water to a boil. In a large pan, melt a generous amount of
butter and add the sage leaves, garlic, and olive oil. Brown the sage leaves and garlic in
the pan. Cook the gnocchi in the boiling water and when they rise to the surface, remove them from the pot with a skimmer and add them to the pan with the melted butter and sage. Toss over medium heat to combine and serve with a generous amount of
grated Parmesan on the side.

‹‹ LASAGNE DI CRÊPES ››
CRÊPE LASAGNA

My mother-in-law, Laura, is the master of this dish. She's been making it for years
without a written recipe. I really wanted to figure out how she does it, so I enlisted my
sister-in-law Fabiana Perrone to figure out the precise amounts. The finished dish is
very pretty—the round crêpes are stacked in a round pan, so it comes out looking like
a layer cake.

SERVES 6

5 ounces (150 grams) frozen mirepoix (minced carrots, onion, and celery)
Extra-virgin olive oil for sautéing
1 pound (500 grams) ground beef and pork
1 sausage, casing removed
1 (15-ounce/420-milliliter) can tomato puree
Salt to taste
7 eggs
1 1/4 cups (150 grams) unbleached all-purpose flour
Whole milk, *quanto basta*
1 tablespoon beef broth granules, dissolved in 2 tablespoons water
Unsalted butter for cooking crêpes
1 cup (250 milliliters) readymade béchamel
Grated Parmesan to taste

Preheat the oven to 350° F (180° C). In a large pan, brown the mirepoix in some oil, then add the ground beef and pork and the sausage. Crumble with a fork and cook until the meat loses its raw red color. Add the tomato puree. Season with salt and cook over medium heat until quite thick, about 15 minutes.

Meanwhile, make the crêpes. In a bowl, combine the eggs and flour and enough milk to make a batter the consistency of heavy cream. Whisk until smooth. Whisk in the dissolved broth granules. Heat a pan—a crêpe pan if you have one—and melt some butter in the pan. Pour in enough batter to coat the pan thinly (about 1/4 cup/50 milliliters, but it will depend on the size of the pan) and quickly tilt the pan in all directions so that the batter forms a circle. Cook until the underside is set, then flip the crêpe and cook the other side. Repeat with the remaining batter, adding butter to the pan between crêpes if necessary. You can stack the crêpes as you finish them. When the tomato sauce is cooked, stir in the béchamel. Spread a little of the sauce in the bottom of a round pan the same size as the crêpes or a little larger. (A springform pan is great for this.) Create alternating layers of crêpe, tomato sauce, and grated Parmesan, in that order, from the bottom up. Bake until the lasagna is browned on top, about 30 minutes. Cut into wedges and serve.

« MILLEFOGLIE DI PATATE E POMODORI »
POTATO AND TOMATO CASSEROLE

This is hearty enough to serve as a one-dish meal rather than a first course. It is also a great choice for vegetarians. My friend Roberta Noè, a sports journalist, provided this recipe. She's an expert cook. Black Venus rice is a short-grain rice from Italy. It will take a little longer to cook than white rice would.

SERVES 4

Salt to taste
1 1/4 cups (250 grams) black Venus rice
Extra-virgin olive oil for oiling pan, drizzling, and for sauce
4 tomatoes, thinly sliced and lightly salted
4 potatoes, peeled and thinly sliced
Chopped sun-dried tomatoes in oil, *quanto basta*
Grated Parmesan, *quanto basta*
2 red onions, thinly sliced into rings
2 tablespoons turbinado sugar
2 tablespoons balsamic vinegar

Bring a large pot of salted water to a boil. Cook the rice as you would pasta, stirring occasionally, until tender. Drain and set aside. Preheat the oven to 350° F (180° C). Lightly oil a baking pan. Arrange about 1/4 of the sliced fresh tomatoes, about 1/3 of the potato slices, a scattering of sun-dried tomatoes, and grated Parmesan in the pan. Repeat the layers in the same order two more times. Top with the remaining fresh tomato slices, drizzle with a little additional olive oil, and bake for 30 minutes. Remove the casserole from the oven, scrape off and discard any burned bits in the top layer of tomatoes, which will be very dark, and return the pan to the oven until the potatoes are soft enough to pierce easily with a fork and the top of the casserole has browned.

Meanwhile, make the sauce. In a pan, sauté the onions in a small amount of oil until soft. Add a little water if the pan looks dry and the onions are sticking. When the onions are very soft and any added water has evaporated, add the sugar and balsamic vinegar and cook until caramelized. When the casserole is fully cooked, remove it from the oven and allow it to set for about 10 minutes. Cut the casserole into squares. Drizzle a little olive oil on each square and serve with the onion sauce and some rice.

« COUSCOUS DI PESCE »
SEAFOOD COUSCOUS

You may be surprised to see couscous in an Italian cookbook, but couscous—especially with seafood—is a traditional dish of Sicily, which has a long and rich Arab culinary tradition. This is a bit of a project, but well worth the effort. For this dish you want precooked or instant couscous, which is by far the more commonly available type.

SERVES 6 TO 8

12 ounces (350 grams) jumbo shrimp
1 yellow onion
3 tablespoons frozen mirepoix (minced carrots, onion, and celery)
Extra-virgin olive oil for sautéing
3 cups (³/₄ liter) white wine
Minced fresh parsley leaves to taste
2 cloves garlic, minced
2 pounds (1 kilogram) clams, purged of sand and rinsed in several
    changes of water
1 pound (500 grams) mussels, cleaned and beards removed
5 grape tomatoes or cherry tomatoes, halved
10 to 11 ounces (300 grams) turbot fillets, skinned and chopped
10 to 11 ounces (300 grams) squid, bodies cut into rings
1 (17.6-ounce/500-gram) package precooked fine couscous (about 3 cups)
Salt to taste

Reserve one shrimp in the shell for garnish. Shell and devein the remaining shrimp and remove heads if still attached. Place the shrimp shells and heads in a pot with ¹/₂ yellow onion (left whole), the mirepoix, and a small amount of oil and cook over medium heat for 1 minute, pressing the shrimp shells and heads against the side of the pot with a wooden spoon to release their juices. Add 1 cup (250 milliliters) white wine, allow the liquid to evaporate, and then pour in about 3 cups (³/₄ liter) water. Add some parsley, bring to a boil, then lower the heat and simmer for about 15 minutes. Meanwhile, in a large pan sauté the garlic in some oil. Add the clams and mussels, pour in 1 cup (250 milliliters) white wine, and cook, covered, until all the shells have opened. Set aside to cool.

Chop the remaining $1/2$ onion. In another pan, sauté the chopped onion in some oil until soft, then add the tomatoes and the turbot. Cook for about 3 minutes, then add the remaining 1 cup (250 milliliters) wine, the shelled shrimp, the shrimp still in its shell, and the squid. Season with salt and cook for 1 additional minute. Strain the juices left in the pan where the clams and mussels were cooked and the broth made with the shrimp shells, combining the two. (You may want to use cheesecloth or a coffee filter to catch all the grit.) Discard the solids. Place the couscous in a large, deep pan. (A wok is perfect.) Off the heat, stir in 2 cups (500 milliliters) of the strained liquid. Set aside to let the couscous rehydrate (follow package instructions). Shell most of the clams and mussels, leaving a few in their shells. When the couscous is tender, fluff it with a fork and add the shelled clams and mussels, the turbot and shrimp, and the remaining strained liquid. Place over medium heat and cook, stirring, until heated through. Sprinkle with some additional parsley, garnish with the reserved shrimp, clams, and mussels still in their shells, and serve immediately.

« TIMBALLINI SICILIANI »
SICILIAN TIMBALES

These little timbales with a hearty meat preparation in the center and a light cauliflower sauce on the outside are a lovely alternative to the usual baked pasta. Cutting into a timbale and seeing the center is an almost mystical experience!

SERVES 4

$1/2$ yellow onion, minced
Extra-virgin olive oil for sautéing and oiling the ramekins
7 ounces (200 grams) ground pork
Red wine to taste
$1/2$ cup (150 grams) crushed tomatoes
Salt to taste
1 head green cauliflower
$1/2$ cup (150 milliliters) broth
Pepper to taste
2 tablespoons ricotta

$1/_2$ cup (50 grams) grated Parmesan
Juice and zest of $1/_2$ lemon
14 ounces (400 grams) readymade bread dough (thawed if frozen)

Preheat the oven to 425° F (220° C). Sauté the onion in a pan with a little oil, then add the pork and cook just until it loses its raw color. Add some wine and allow it to evaporate over high heat. Add the crushed tomatoes, season with salt, and turn the heat to low. Cook, covered, over low heat for 30 minutes. Meanwhile, bring a large pot of salted water to a boil and boil the cauliflower for 20 minutes. Drain and transfer to a food processor fitted with the metal blade or a blender with the broth and process smooth. Season with salt and pepper. When the pork mixture is cooked, let it cool, then stir in the ricotta, grated Parmesan, lemon juice, and a little of the grated lemon zest. Roll out the bread dough and cut it into large circles using the rim of a bowl. Oil 4 ramekins or other individual-sized baking pans (disposable aluminum pans are fine) and line them with the dough circles, letting the dough hang over the sides a few inches. Fill with the pork mixture, then fold the overhanging dough up over the top. Twist it and pinch it together in the middle (like a dumpling) to seal. Pierce the tops in a few places with a toothpick and bake until golden, 25 to 30 minutes. Remove the timbales from the oven and allow them to cool. When you are ready to serve the timbales, reheat the cauliflower sauce and unmold the timbales. Serve each timbale on a bed of cauliflower sauce.

« FRITTATA DI SOPHIA »
SOPHIA LOREN'S FRITTATA

This delicious frittata made with pasta is typical of Southern Italy in its clever use of leftovers. The first time I suggested it, my director, Mario Giordano (who, like me, is from Piedmont in Northern Italy), was horrified! But I think it's a great dish, because the pasta gets crunchy as if it had gone under the broiler, while the eggs, prosciutto, and cheese make it irresistible. Besides, this is Sophia Loren's recipe! At least, that's the rumor...

SERVES 2 TO 3

4 large eggs
Salt and pepper to taste
$1/_2$ cup (50 grams) grated Parmesan cheese

1 fresh mozzarella ball (8 ounces/225 grams), diced

4 slices prosciutto cotto, diced

3 $1/2$ ounces (100 grams) leftover cooked spaghetti in tomato sauce or
    ragù

Extra-virgin olive oil for browning (about 2 tablespoons)

In a medium bowl, beat the eggs. Season with salt and pepper and stir in the grated Parmesan. Stir in the mozzarella and prosciutto, then add the spaghetti and mix carefully to combine. In a pan, heat enough oil to coat the bottom of the pan thinly until very hot, then add the egg mixture. Turn the heat to low, cover the pan, and cook until the bottom of the frittata is nicely browned. Using the cover, flip the frittata. (Simply invert the pan over the cover, return the pan to the stove, then slide the frittata into the pan. Use a fork or spatula to turn the edges under and tuck any stray strands of pasta underneath.) Cover and cook again until the other side is nicely browned. Transfer to a serving platter and serve warm but not piping hot.

ENTRÉES

« TORTA VERDE ALLA LIGURE »
LIGURIAN VEGETABLE PIE

In Ospedaletti, a seaside town in the Liguria region, every café and bakery serves this savory tart made with zucchini and rice. It's very delicate and flavorful. I tried to make it so many times, re-creating it from memory, but with no luck. Finally, Silvana, a cook who happens to be from Ospedaletti, gave me the perfect recipe.

MAKES 1 DOUBLE-CRUST PIE, ABOUT 8 SLICES

1/2 yellow onion, thinly sliced
Extra-virgin olive oil for sautéing
14 ounces (400 grams) light green zucchini, sliced into rounds
Salt to taste
1/3 cup (60 grams) short-grain Italian rice
3/4 cup (75 grams) grated Parmesan
3 large eggs
2 readymade puff pastry dough circles

Preheat the oven to 350° F (180° C). In a medium pan, sauté the onion in some oil, then add the zucchini, season with salt, and cook for 5 minutes over medium heat. Meanwhile, bring a large pot of salted water to a boil and cook the rice as you would pasta, stirring occasionally, but only for 5 minutes. Drain the rice and transfer to a bowl. Add the zucchini mixture and the grated Parmesan. Lightly beat 2 eggs and add to the bowl. Mix to combine. Line a pie or tart pan with one circle of puff pastry dough and pierce in several places with a fork. Pour in the rice mixture and top with the remaining puff pastry dough. Pinch around the border to seal. Lightly beat the third egg and brush it over the surface of the pie. Bake for 30 minutes and then, if your oven has this option, bake so that it is heated only from the bottom for another 5 minutes. Serve warm or at room temperature.

« SFOGLIETTE DI SPINACI E ZUCCA »
SPINACH AND SQUASH PIES

Spinach, squash, and melted cheese tucked into a delicious flaky puff pastry crust—that's one way to get children to eat their vegetables!

SERVES 4

8 ounces (250 grams) fresh spinach
1 shallot, minced
Extra-virgin olive oil for sautéing
Salt to taste
1 leek, sliced into rounds
Unsalted butter for sautéing
5 ounces (150 grams) peeled and seeded winter squash, such as butternut
    or acorn squash, diced
Ground cumin to taste
$1/2$ cup (50 grams) grated Parmesan
1 package readymade puff pastry dough
2 ounces (25 to 30 grams) Gruyère, grated
1 large egg, lightly beaten

Preheat the oven to 425° F (220° C). In a pan, sauté the spinach and shallot in a small amount of oil. Season with salt. In a separate pan, sauté the leek in a little butter and oil until transparent. Add the squash, season with salt, and add the cumin plus water to cover. Cook over medium heat, covered, until the squash is soft. Combine the cooked spinach with the Parmesan. Use the rim of an overturned glass or a pastry cutter to cut out 8 circles of puff pastry dough. Place 4 of the circles on a jelly-roll pan. Top each with about $1/4$ of the spinach mixture, then $1/4$ of the grated Gruyère, and finally $1/4$ of the squash, centering the vegetables and cheese and leaving an empty border around the perimeter of the pastry. Brush the borders of the circles with the egg wash and top each circle with another (empty) circle of dough. Brush the tops with the egg wash as well and bake for 20 minutes.

« PIZZA DI SCAROLA »
ESCAROLE PIZZA

This recipe is from Caterina Varvello, my friend and a colleague on my show. If you are looking for something to whip up and serve with cocktails or an entree for a spur-of-the-moment dinner, this is perfect.

SERVES 4

Extra-virgin olive oil for oiling pan and sautéing
Salt to taste
2 heads escarole
1 clove garlic
4 anchovy fillets in oil
Pine nuts to taste
3 tablespoons pitted black olives
1 batch readymade pizza dough

Preheat the oven to 350°F (180°C). Oil a pizza pan and set aside. (Or, if you have a pizza stone, skip this step.) Bring a large pot of salted water to a boil and cook the escarole. When it has wilted (escarole cooks relatively quickly), drain it well, squeeze out as much water as possible, and chop roughly. In a pan sauté the garlic and anchovies in a small amount of oil, tilting the pan to make sure they remain submerged in the oil. Once the garlic clove is soft, remove and discard it. Add the chopped escarole, pine nuts, and olives to the pan. Cook for a few minutes, stirring frequently. Taste and add salt if necessary. Roll out the pizza dough, place on the prepared pan, if using, distribute the escarole mixture on top, and bake in the preheated oven until the crust is golden, about 20 minutes. Serve immediately.

ESCAROLE PIZZA

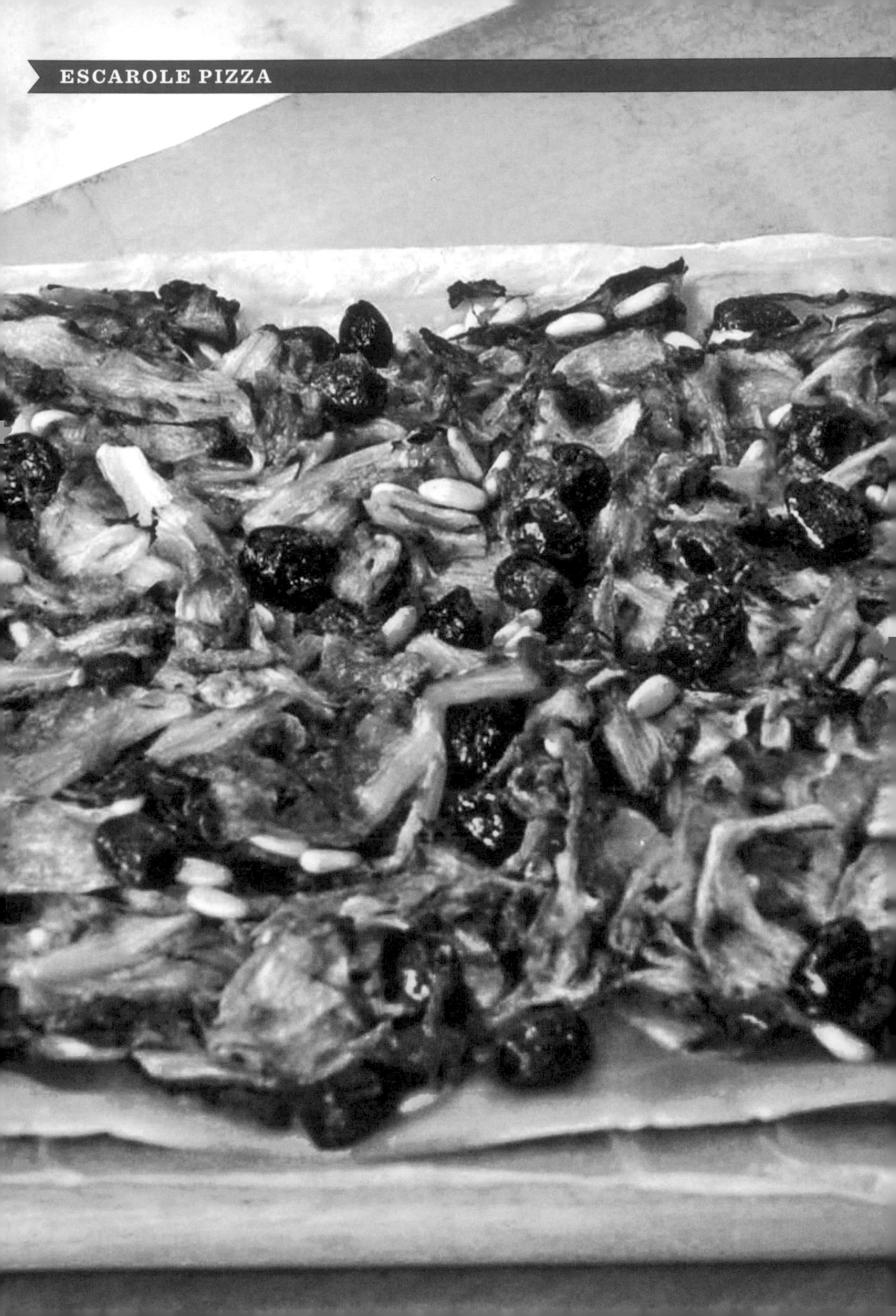

« PIZZA GORGONZOLA E FICHI »
GORGONZOLA AND FIG PIZZA

This pizza couldn't be easier to make, and it tastes of late summer. Enjoy it with a glass of wine while you look through the photos from your summer vacation!

SERVES 4

1 pound (500 grams) readymade pizza dough
5 ounces (150 grams) Gorgonzola, diced
4 to 5 fresh figs, thinly sliced
Fresh rosemary leaves to taste
Extra-virgin olive oil for drizzling

Set the pizza dough at room temperature, cover with a dish towel, and allow to rise for 40 minutes. Preheat the oven to 425° F (220° C). Line a jelly-roll pan with parchment paper. Roll out the dough and place it in the pan. Scatter the Gorgonzola and figs on the dough. Scatter on the rosemary, drizzle with a little oil, and bake until golden, 10 to 15 minutes. Serve hot or at room temperature.

« PASTICCIO DI PATATE E CARCIOFI »
POTATO AND ARTICHOKE CASSEROLE

This is a great vegetarian one-dish meal. As an added bonus, it's very easy to prepare.

SERVES 4

Juice of 1 lemon
4 baby artichokes
2 potatoes, peeled
2 green onions
3 1/2 ounces (100 grams) scamorza cheese
Salt to taste
Extra-virgin olive oil for coating
2 tablespoons breadcrumbs

2 tablespoons grated pecorino
Pepper to taste

Preheat the oven to 400° F (200° C). Line a baking dish with parchment paper. Add the lemon juice to a bowl full of cold water. Trim the artichokes: Working one at a time, remove any leaves from the stem, and then cut off the stem, leaving an inch or two. Pull off and discard any hard, dark-colored leaves. When you have revealed the light green portion of the artichoke, peel off any tough skin from the outside of the stem. Cut off the top of the artichoke completely. Cut the artichoke in half the long way and use the tip of a paring knife to dig out the fuzzy part in the center. Slice the cleaned artichoke into thin wedges and drop them into the bowl with the water and lemon juice. Repeat with remaining artichokes. Thinly slice the potatoes into rounds, slice the onions into rings, and cut the scamorza into cubes. Place the vegetables in a bowl and add some salt, enough olive oil to coat the vegetables, breadcrumbs, and pecorino. Toss to combine, then add the scamorza and toss again. Spread vegetable mixture in the prepared pan, season with pepper, and bake for 30 minutes.

« POLPETTE DI FAGIOLI »
VEGETARIAN BEAN "MEATBALLS"

Every once in a while I like to make "meatballs" that have no meat at all, like these, which are made with beans. Serve them in a tasty tomato sauce and no one will be the wiser. If you can't find borlotti or cranberry beans, use canned pinto beans.

SERVES 4

$1/2$ (15-ounce/200-gram) can borlotti or cranberry beans, rinsed and
    drained
2 egg yolks
$1/2$ **cup (50 grams) grated Parmesan**
$1/3$ **cup (40 grams) whole-wheat flour**
Scant $1/2$ cup (40 grams) breadcrumbs, plus more for dredging
Paprika to taste
Salt to taste
1 clove garlic

1 (28-ounce/1-kilogram) can crushed tomatoes
Rosemary leaves to taste
Extra-virgin olive oil for frying the meatballs
2 large eggs, lightly beaten

Place the beans, egg yolks, grated Parmesan, flour, breadcrumbs, paprika, and a pinch of salt in a food processor or blender and process until smooth. Transfer to a bowl. Meanwhile, to make the sauce, place the garlic, crushed tomatoes, rosemary, and a little salt in a pot and simmer, covered, for 10 minutes. Meanwhile, heat oil in a pan for frying the meatballs. Shape the bean mixture into meatballs. Dredge the meatballs in the beaten eggs and then in breadcrumbs and brown in the oil. Once the meatballs are browned, add them to the pot with the sauce and cook for 3 minutes more. Serve hot.

« INVOLTINI DI VERZA »
STUFFED CABBAGE

This recipe is great for using up leftovers. In the stuffing, you can use whatever you have in the refrigerator: cooked pork, chicken, beef, or a combination. Even a humdrum bit of leftover meat tastes great when wrapped in cabbage and cooked in tomato sauce. A side dish of plain rice is perfect for soaking up any extra sauce.

SERVES 4

Salt to taste
1 head Savoy cabbage
10 to 11 ounces (300 grams) leftover cooked meat or poultry
3 1/2 ounces (100 grams) prosciutto crudo
Leaves of 1 sprig parsley
1 large egg, lightly beaten
1/2 cup (40 grams) grated Parmesan
1 yellow onion, sliced
Extra-virgin olive oil for sautéing
1 cup (250 milliliters) tomato puree
1 cup (250 milliliters) white wine
1 cup (250 milliliters) broth or water

Bring a large pot of salted water to a boil. Detach the cabbage leaves and boil them for 3 minutes. Drain and set aside. In a food processor fitted with the metal blade or a blender, process the meat with the prosciutto and parsley leaves. Transfer to a bowl and knead in the egg and grated Parmesan. You should be able to roll the mixture between your palms to make small meatballs. Cut each cabbage leaf in two, discarding their hard central ribs. Place a small ball of the meat mixture on each $1/2$ cabbage leaf, fold the leaves, and secure them with toothpicks. In a large pan, sauté the onion in a small amount of oil until translucent, then add the cabbage packets. (If they don't fit in a single layer, stack them.) In a small bowl, whisk together the tomato puree, wine, and broth or water and pour the liquid into the pan. Cook over low heat, covered, until the sauce has thickened, 15 to 20 minutes. Remove the stuffed cabbage packets to a serving platter and pour the tomato sauce over them. Serve immediately.

« SPEZZATINO ESTIVO »
SUMMER STEW

The secret to a stew—whether made in the summer or in the winter—is to put all the ingredients into the pot raw and then cook them over low heat. You probably won't want a steaming hot stew in the middle of summer, so serve this at room temperature or slightly warmer with lots of fresh basil leaves—it's very refreshing.

SERVES 4 TO 6

2 pounds (1 kilogram) veal rump roast
Unbleached all-purpose flour for dredging meat
2 cups (500 milliliters) vegetable broth made with a bouillon cube, chilled
1 red onion, thinly sliced
3 tablespoons pitted green olives
1 bay leaf
Salt to taste
$1/4$ cup cherry tomatoes, halved
Fresh basil leaves to taste

Pepper to taste
Extra-virgin olive oil for drizzling

Cut the rump roast into cubes, dredge in flour, and place in a pot. Add the chilled broth, onion, olives, bay leaf, and a little salt. Cover and cook over low heat for 45 minutes, stirring occasionally. Add the cherry tomatoes and cook for an additional 15 minutes. If the pot looks dry, add a small amount of additional broth. Serve warm garnished with basil leaves. Sprinkle with pepper and drizzle with some oil just before serving.

« VIGNAROLA »
SPRING VEGETABLE STEW

A good *vignarola* depends on fresh vegetables. I know shelling fresh peas and fava beans is a pain, and trimming artichokes is no picnic either, but the results are well worth the effort.

SERVES 4

3 baby artichokes
4 green onions
5 to 7 ounces (150 to 200 grams) pancetta, diced
Extra-virgin olive oil for sautéing
10 to 11 ounces (300 grams) shelled fava beans, tough skins removed
10 to 11 ounces (300 grams) shelled fresh peas
Salt to taste
1 tablespoon beef or vegetable broth granules (or the serving size
indicated on the package
Fresh basil leaves to taste
1 fresh mozzarella ball (8 ounces/225 grams), preferably buffalo-milk
mozzarella, sliced

Trim the artichokes: Working one at a time, remove any leaves from the stem, and then cut off the stem, leaving an inch or two. Pull off and discard any hard, dark-colored leaves. When you have revealed the light green portion of the artichoke, peel off any tough skin from the outside of the stem. Cut off the top of the artichoke completely. Cut the artichoke in half the long way and use the tip of a paring knife to dig out the fuzzy part in the center. Slice the cleaned artichoke into wedges. Repeat with the remaining artichokes.

Slice the onions into rings. In a pot, sauté the pancetta in a small amount of oil. Add the onions and, once they have begun to color, add the fava beans, peas, and artichokes. Pour in 1/2 cup (100 milliliter) water, season with salt, stir in the broth granules and basil leaves and cook, covered, over low heat until the vegetables are soft and the liquid is flavorful, 25 to 30 minutes. Let the stew cool to room temperature before serving. Accompany with mozzarella slices.

« SPEZZATINO ALLA ZUCCA »
WINTER SQUASH STEW

This stew is slightly sweet and very comforting in winter. I always serve it with roasted potatoes.

SERVES 4 TO 6

1/4 cup plus 1 tablespoon (35 grams) unbleached all-purpose flour
Grated nutmeg to taste
Salt and pepper to taste
1 pound and 5 ounces (600 grams) pork shoulder, cut into chunks
Unsalted butter for sautéing
Extra-virgin olive oil for sautéing
1/2 cup (100 milliliters) dry Marsala
1 clove garlic
Fresh sage leaves to taste
Fresh rosemary leaves to taste
1 1/4 cups (300 milliliters) beef broth made with broth granules
14 ounces (400 grams) peeled and seeded winter squash, such as
    butternut or acorn, cut into chunks

Combine the flour with a small amount of nutmeg and some salt and pepper. Dredge the pork shoulder chunks in the flour mixture. Melt some butter in a pot along with some oil and brown the meat over medium-high heat. When the meat is browned, add the Marsala and allow most of it to evaporate. Add the garlic, sage, rosemary, and broth and cook, covered, over low heat for 30 minutes. Add the squash, adjust salt, and cook over low heat for an additional 30 minutes. Serve warm.

« FRITTATA DI GAMBI DI CARCIOFO »
ARTICHOKE FRITTATA

Often the meaty stalks of artichokes are discarded, but they're delicious in their own right. Here's a recipe that makes clever use of them. This serves four as an appetizer, or makes a nice light dinner for two when paired with a salad. If you are not confident about flipping the frittata, simply run the pan under the broiler for a few minutes to set the top.

SERVES 2 TO 4

4 to 6 artichoke stems
Salt to taste
1 yellow onion, sliced
1 clove garlic
Extra-virgin olive oil for sautéing
4 large eggs
1/2 cup to 2/3 cup (50 to 60 grams) grated Parmesan

If the artichoke stems are very fibrous, peel them. Bring a small pot of salted water to a boil and boil the artichoke stems for 2 minutes. In a medium pan (cast-iron is ideal), sauté the onion and the garlic clove in a small amount of oil. Drain the artichoke stems, cut them into small dice, add them to the onion in the pan, and cook until lightly browned. Taste and add salt if necessary. Discard the garlic. In a bowl, beat the eggs, then stir in the artichoke mixture and the Parmesan. Add a little more oil to the same pan and heat it over medium heat. Pour in the egg mixture and then use a heatproof spatula to push in the edges as they cook, tilting the pan so that the indents are then filled in with uncooked egg. When the bottom is set and only the center of the frittata remains wet, let it cook undisturbed until the underside is nicely browned, about 3 minutes, then flip the frittata and cook the other side until it is nicely browned, about 3 additional minutes. Serve hot or at room temperature.

« QUICHE DI ASPARAGI »
ASPARAGUS QUICHE

This savory pie replaces the usual ricotta with cream and egg yolks, resulting in a rich and satisfying vegetarian entrée. You can substitute almost any vegetable for the asparagus if you prefer.

SERVES 6

2 bunches asparagus
1 shallot
Extra-virgin olive oil for sautéing (about 1 tablespoon)
Salt to taste
3 egg yolks
1 1/4 cups (300 milliliters) heavy cream
3 tablespoons grated Parmesan
Pepper to taste
1 package readymade puff pastry

Preheat the oven to 350° F (180° C). Cook the asparagus in boiling water briefly, just until tender. Cut off and reserve the tips and chop the stems. Mince the shallot and sauté it in a pan in a small amount of oil until golden. Add the cooked asparagus stems. Season to taste with salt and cook until the asparagus has been flavored with the onion but is still firm, about 5 minutes. In a bowl, beat the egg yolks with the cream, grated Parmesan, and season with additional salt and pepper to taste. Stir in the shallot and asparagus mixture.

Place a piece of parchment paper on a work surface. On top of the parchment, roll out the puff pastry to cover the bottom and sides of a round baking dish. Transfer the crust to the baking dish with the parchment on the bottom. Pierce the pastry with a fork in several places, then pour in the egg mixture. Arrange the asparagus tips in an attractive pattern or randomly on top and bake until the filling is set and dark brown in spots, about 40 minutes.

ASPARAGUS QUICHE

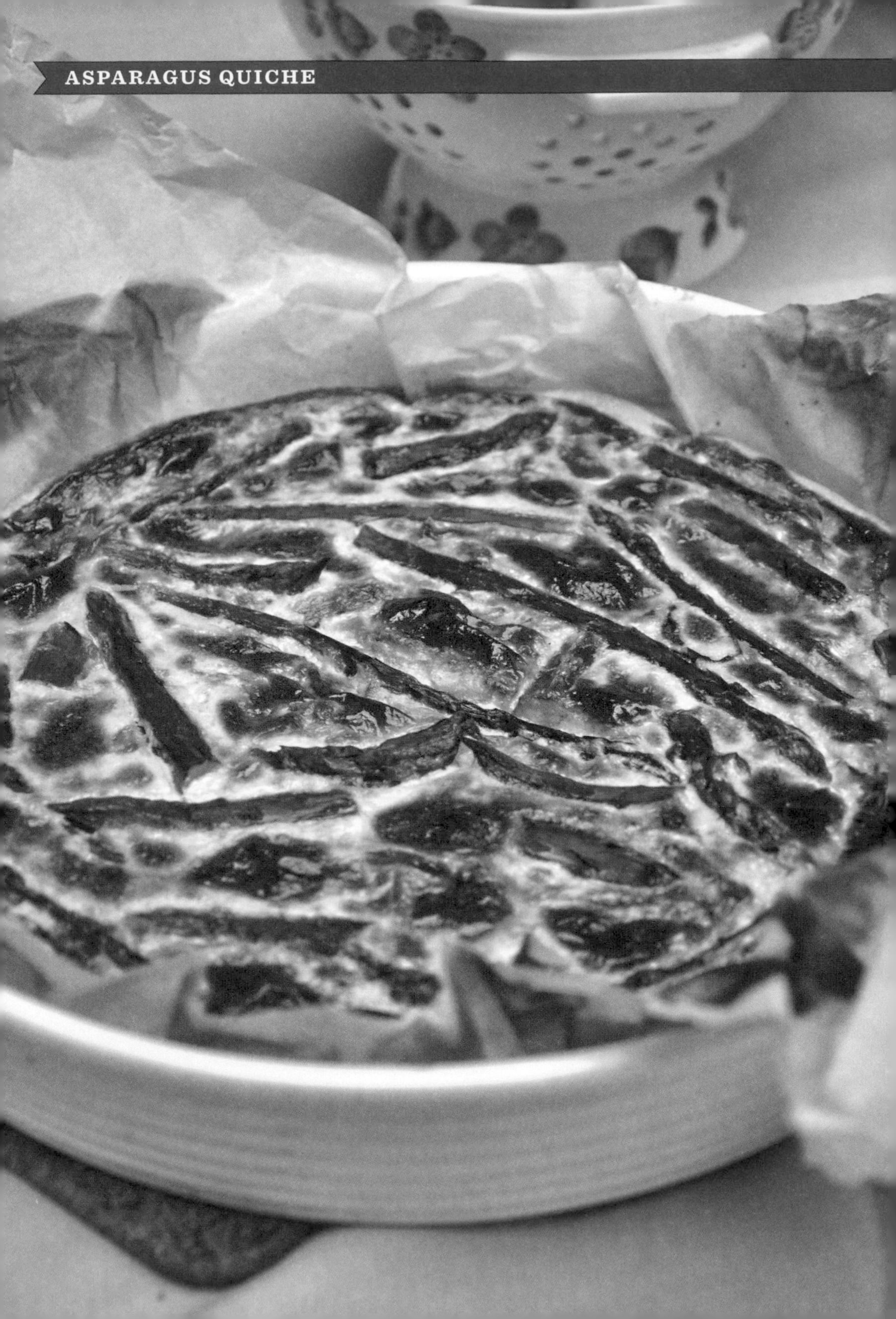

« COCOTTE DI ASPARAGI E UOVA »
BAKED EGGS AND ASPARAGUS

The only trick here is getting the timing right—cook the eggs too long and you've got hard-boiled eggs, and undercook them and they'll be unappealingly liquid. My suggestion is to test this dish out before you serve it to guests. That way, you'll get to know your oven's true temperature. These baked eggs can be served as an elegant appetizer, or you can pair them with toasted slices of country-style bread and a mixed green salad and offer them as an entree. Traditionally, these are made in little cast-iron crocks.

SERVES 4

Salt to taste
8 stalks asparagus
Unsalted butter for sautéing
Grated Parmesan to taste
4 large eggs
4 processed cheese slices, chopped
Truffle oil to taste

Preheat the oven to 400°F (200°C). Bring a pot of salted water to a boil and very briefly cook the asparagus so that the stalks are still fairly crisp. Cut the asparagus into slices, leaving the tips whole. In a pan, melt some butter and sauté the asparagus until browned. Divide the asparagus among individual ovenproof serving dishes, preferably cast-iron crocks. Sprinkle with grated Parmesan and break 1 egg into each of the dishes. Season with salt and top with the processed cheese. Bake for 8 minutes, then raise the oven temperature to 475° F (250° C) and turn it to the convection setting. Bake until the yolks are still soft, the whites are firm, and the cheese has melted, about an additional 5 minutes. Drizzle each crock with a few drops of truffle oil and serve.

« UOVA IN PURGATORIO »
EGGS IN PURGATORY

Eleonora is the one who loves eggs in our house. She'd eat them every day if we'd let her. I don't know why this dish of eggs in tomato sauce is called eggs in purgatory, because Eleonora thinks they're the stuff of paradise!

SERVES 4

1/2 yellow onion, minced
1 clove garlic, minced
Extra-virgin olive oil for sautéing
2 cups (500 milliliters) tomato puree
Salt to taste
Sugar to taste
4 large eggs
Minced fresh basil or parsley leaves to taste
Grated Parmesan to taste (optional)

In a pan, sauté the onion and garlic in a small amount of oil. Add the tomato puree and a little salt and sugar. Cook, covered, over low heat until thickened, about 10 minutes. Break the eggs right into the pan, taking care not to break the yolks. Raise the heat to medium and cook, covered, until the whites are cooked and the yolks are still soft, about 3 minutes more. Garnish with basil or parsley and sprinkle with Parmesan if using. Serve hot.

« FAVE, PISELLI, E UOVA IN CAMICIA »
FAVA BEANS AND PEAS WITH POACHED EGGS

Peas and fava beans are a match made in heaven. My friend Rosa Prinzivalli provided me with this typical Sicilian recipe. If poached eggs are too fussy for you, serve this with fried eggs or no eggs at all. It will still be great. Fabio likes to eat a few slices of fresh mozzarella with this dish, though come to think of it, he likes to eat a few slices of fresh mozzarella with every dish.

SERVES 4

1 small yellow onion, thinly sliced into rings
Extra-virgin olive oil for sautéing
1 pound 5 ounces (600 grams) fresh or frozen shelled fava beans, tough
    skins removed if fresh
1 pound (500 grams) fresh or frozen shelled peas
Salt to taste
1 tablespoon beef broth granules (or the serving size indicated on the
    package)
1 tablespoon white wine vinegar
4 large eggs

In a pan, sauté the onion in a small amount of oil. If using fresh fava beans and peas, add the fava beans and peas. If using frozen fava beans and peas, add the fava beans, cook for 10 minutes, then add the peas. Add 1/2 cup (100 milliliters) water, some salt, and the broth granules. Braise until the vegetables are soft, about 20 minutes. When the vegetables are cooked, poach the eggs: Bring a small pot of water to a gentle simmer and add the vinegar and a pinch of salt. Break 1 egg into a small bowl, then gently tip it into the pot with the water. As the egg white cooks, continuously push it in toward the yolk with a spoon. Poach for 3 minutes. Place about 2 tablespoons of the cooked vegetables on an individual plate. With a slotted spoon or skimmer, gently transfer the poached egg to the plate. Repeat with remaining eggs and vegetables and serve immediately.

« POLENTA CON UOVA DI QUAGLIA »
POLENTA WITH QUAIL EGGS

Little disks of polenta topped with diminutive quail eggs couldn't be more fun! These are a great appetizer for four or a quick dinner for two. It's easy to make a larger portion, too. Readymade polenta is even faster to prepare than instant polenta—it comes in a tube, sort of like store-bought cookie dough. Simply slice, peel off the plastic wrapper, heat, and serve.

SERVES 2 TO 4

7 ounces (200 grams) or about 1/5 tube readymade polenta, sliced into
    disks

Unsalted butter for dotting and browning
1 tablespoon grated Parmesan
Extra-virgin olive oil for sautéing
4 quail eggs
Salt to taste
Fresh sage leaves to taste

Preheat the broiler. Line a jelly-roll pan with parchment paper and place the polenta disks on it in a single layer. Dot the disks with butter, sprinkle with the Parmesan, and broil until browned and crisp, about 3 minutes. Meanwhile, lightly coat a pan with olive oil, place over medium-low heat, and fry the eggs. Salt lightly and cook until the whites are set, about 1 minute. In a separate pan, melt some butter and brown the sage leaves in the butter. Remove the polenta disks from the oven and transfer to individual serving dishes. Top each disk with 1 quail egg, salt if needed, pour the butter and sage leaves over the polenta and eggs, and serve immediately.

« ORTO GRATINATO »
BROILED MUSHROOMS, TOMATOES, AND ZUCCHINI WITH BREADCRUMBS

Sometimes the biggest challenge when putting together a menu is to create balance. I like to serve this as a side dish to accompany a heavier entree, or double or triple it and serve it as a vegetarian entree on its own. Leftovers are delicious, so I like to make a big batch. If you're lucky enough to have access to fresh porcini mushrooms, you can use them in place of the white button mushrooms.

SERVES 2

Salt to taste
1 zucchini, sliced into 1 1/2-inch (4-centimeter) thick rounds
3 small tomatoes, seeded and hollowed out
3 white button mushrooms, stems removed and discarded
3 to 4 slices sandwich bread
Fresh thyme leaves to taste
Fresh basil leaves to taste

Pepper to taste
Fresh parsley leaves to taste
Grated Parmesan to taste
2 to 3 tablespoons white wine
Extra-virgin olive oil for drizzling

Preheat the broiler. Bring a pot of salted water to a boil and boil the zucchini just until slightly tender, about 1 minute. Drain. Hollow out each piece of zucchini. Place the zucchini, tomatoes, and mushroom caps (upside down) on a jelly-roll pan. In a food processor fitted with the metal blade, combine the bread, thyme, basil, pepper, and parsley. Add the Parmesan and 2 tablespoons white wine and process to combine. If the mixture seems dry, add the remaining 1 tablespoon wine. Salt the vegetables lightly, then sprinkle the breadcrumbs over the vegetables, filling the hollowed out zucchini and tomatoes and the mushroom caps. Drizzle with some olive oil, salt again, and broil until golden and crisp, 3 to 4 minutes. Serve hot or at room temperature.

« DOPPIETTA DI MELANZANE »
INDIVIDUAL SERVING EGGPLANT PARMIGIANA

I think we can all agree that eggplant parmigiana is one of the best foods in the world. This is a single-serving version that's as good at room temperature as it is straight out of the oven. Perfect for the summer!

SERVES 2

2 tomatoes
Salt to taste
1 eggplant
Extra-virgin olive oil for brushing eggplant and drizzling
4 ounces (100 grams) caciotta cheese, cut into 6 slices
Grated Parmesan to taste
Fresh basil leaves to taste

Preheat the oven to 350°F (180°C). Line a jelly-roll pan with parchment paper. Slice each tomato into three or more slices. Salt lightly and set aside. Thinly slice the eggplant into six slices and arrange the slices on the prepared pan. Brush both sides of the slices with oil and season with salt. Bake the eggplant slices until they are browned, turning them once, about 30 minutes. Set the eggplant aside to cool. When you are ready to serve the dish, preheat the oven to 350° F (180° C). On a jelly-roll pan, build two towers, in this order from the bottom up: 1 eggplant slice, 1 caciotta slice, a sprinkling of grated Parmesan, 1 tomato slice, basil leaves. Create two more layers for each tower in the same order. Drizzle the tops with a little additional oil and sprinkle with additional Parmesan. Bake just until the cheese melts. Garnish with basil and serve hot or at room temperature.

« BURGER DI CECI »
CHICKPEA VEGGIE BURGERS

It took several tries to come up with a recipe for a veggie burger that I really like. The problem with making burgers out of chickpeas is that they can be dry and heavy. A couple of my attempts had the same dense weight as the sand castles we used to build on the beach! Not very tasty. But these are soft and flavorful. In fact, they're so good that I eat them cold, straight out of the fridge, if I have any left over. Serve these with lettuce, tomato, and buns. You can also top them with slices of cheese to make veggie cheeseburgers.

SERVES 4

1 (15-ounce/500-gram) can chickpeas, rinsed and drained
2 slices sandwich bread
1 shallot
2 teaspoons mustard
2 large eggs
Leaves of 1 bunch parsley
1 pinch ground ginger
Salt to taste
Extra-virgin olive oil for cooking

Place the chickpeas, bread, shallot, mustard, eggs, parsley, ginger, and salt in a food processor fitted with the metal blade and process until almost smooth—the consistency should still be a little bit chunky. Form the mixture into burgers and cook the burgers in a hot grill pan or griddle with a small film of oil until crisp and golden, about 3 minutes per side.

« SPEZZATINO AL LIMONE CARAMELLATO »
CARAMELIZED LEMON CHICKEN

Lemon wedges—rind and all—make this dish especially pretty. Since you are using the rind, be sure to seek out organic, unwaxed fruit.

SERVES 4 TO 6

3 chicken drumsticks
6 boneless skinless chicken thighs, chopped
Salt and pepper to taste
Minced fresh thyme, rosemary, and sage leaves to taste
Extra-virgin olive oil for coating chicken and sautéing
1 lemon, cut into wedges
3 cloves garlic
1 cup (250 milliliters) dry white wine

Season the chicken with salt and pepper, rub it with about 1 tablespoon olive oil, and sprinkle with the minced herbs. Heat a small amount of oil in a pot and sauté the chicken, lemon wedges, and garlic until the chicken begins to brown. Add the wine, lower the heat to a simmer, and cook, covered, until the lemon is caramelized and the chicken is cooked through, about 45 minutes. Check the pan occasionally during cooking and add a little hot water if the chicken looks dry. Serve immediately.

« POLLO ALLA BIRRA CON GINEPRO E ALLORO »
BEER-BRAISED CHICKEN

Chicken is the queen of home cooking. Of course, it can be a little tiresome at times, because chicken doesn't have a lot of flavor on its own. You have to find something to perk it up—either an ingredient or a cooking technique or both. A can of beer does the trick nicely!

SERVES 4 TO 6

6 skinless chicken drumsticks
3 skinless chicken thighs
2 tablespoons unbleached all-purpose flour
Salt and pepper to taste
1 tablespoon juniper berries
4 bay leaves
2 cans beer

In a heavy pot with high sides, arrange the chicken pieces in a single layer. Sprinkle the flour over them, season with salt and pepper, and add the bay leaves and juniper berries. Pour in the beer, which should cover the chicken completely. If it doesn't, add a little water. Bring to a boil, turn the heat down to a brisk simmer, and cook, covered, over medium heat for 30 minutes. After 30 minutes, remove the lid and cook, uncovered, over medium heat until the chicken is tender, about 1 hour longer. As the liquid evaporates, turn the chicken pieces occasionally to keep them moist. If the liquid seems to be evaporating too quickly, cover the pot again. Serve hot or warm.

« POLLO IN CROSTA ALLE OLIVE »
CHICKEN WITH OLIVES IN PUFF PASTRY

Baking chicken in a puff pastry crust takes it from the everyday to truly elegant. Be sure to cook your puff pastry dough until it is nicely browned. Thanks to journalist and gourmet cook Emanuela Sandali for this recipe.

SERVES 4

CHICKEN SKEWERS WITH FRIGGITELLI PEPPERS

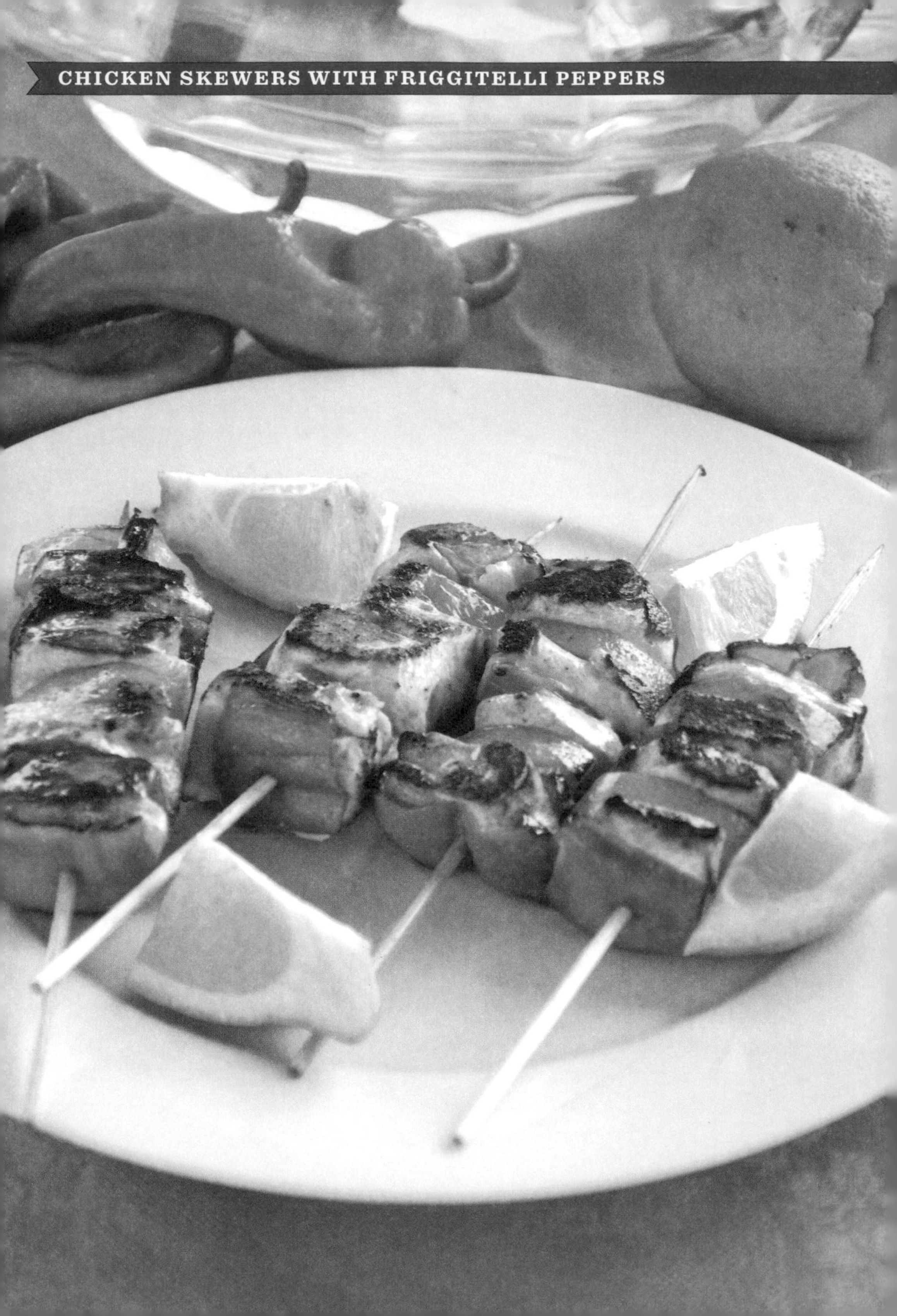

1 yellow onion, thinly sliced
1/3 cup (60 grams) pitted green olives, chopped
1/3 cup (60 grams) pitted black olives, chopped
Extra-virgin olive oil for sautéing
1 boned chicken, cut up, or 4 boneless chicken drumsticks and 4 boneless
    chicken thighs
Unbleached all-purpose flour for dredging chicken, *quanto basta*
Salt to taste
1/4 cup slivered almonds
1/4 cup pine nuts
2 to 3 tablespoons heavy cream
2 packages puff pastry

In a large pot or Dutch oven, sauté the onion and the olives in a small amount of olive oil. Dredge the chicken in flour, season with salt, and add to the pan. Cook, turning occasionally with tongs, until the chicken is nicely browned and cooked through, about 40 minutes. Add the almonds and pine nuts and cook for a few minutes longer to toast the nuts. Remove the chicken from the pot and set aside to cool. When the pot is no longer piping hot, deglaze the pot with the cream, scraping up any browned bits, and pour the liquid over the chicken. Preheat the oven to 350° F (180° C). Line a soufflé dish with one of the packages of puff pastry, leaving the parchment paper underneath (between the pastry and the dish). Arrange the chicken and any liquid on top. Cover with the second batch of puff pastry and pinch the edges together to seal. Bake until the crust is golden brown, about 40 minutes. If the top seems to be browning too quickly, cover with aluminum foil. Serve hot.

« SPIEDINI DI POLLO E FRIGGITELLI »
CHICKEN SKEWERS WITH FRIGGITELLI PEPPERS

These light chicken skewers taste as good as they look. Friggitelli peppers are mild long thin frying peppers.

SERVES 4

2 lemons
Extra-virgin olive oil for marinade and drizzling

Salt and pepper to taste

1 pound 6 ounces (650 grams) boneless skinless chicken breast, cut into
    large cubes

12 friggitelli peppers

Soak 4 wooden skewers in hot water for about 30 minutes. Meanwhile, combine the juice and grated zest of 1 lemon with a small amount of oil, salt, and pepper and marinate the chicken in this mixture while you prepare the rest of the dish. Chop the remaining lemon, leaving a bit of peel on each piece. Cut the frying peppers into chunks. Thread the soaked wooden skewers with alternating pieces of chicken, lemon, and frying pepper. Discard the marinade.

Heat a large pan over high heat. When the pan is hot, brush it with a small amount of oil, add the skewers to the pan, and cook, turning occasionally, until all items are browned and the chicken is cooked through, 8 to 10 minutes. (Cook in batches if necessary.) Serve hot or at room temperature.

« POLLO ALLE MELE »
CHICKEN WITH APPLES

This is one of the few dishes that my mother has ever copied from me. Of course, she's made it her own. She cooks the apples along with the chicken rather than separately. They break down and become more like applesauce that way, but I have to admit that they taste wonderful. I use reinette apples, but if you can't find them, substitute baking apples of your choice.

SERVES 4

Extra-virgin olive oil for sautéing

5 ounces (150 grams) frozen mirepoix (minced carrots, onion, and celery)

4 chicken drumsticks and 2 chicken thighs, or 1 whole chicken cut up

Salt to taste

1/2 cup (150 milliliters) apple juice

1 cup (250 milliliters) vegetable broth (broth made with a bouillon cube
    is fine)

Bay leaves to taste
Juniper berries to taste
2 reinette apples or other baking apples
Unsalted butter for sautéing
Fresh rosemary leaves to taste

Place a small amount of oil in a large pot or Dutch oven and sauté the mirepoix for 2 to 3 minutes. Add the chicken pieces and brown on all sides, turning with tongs. Season with salt, deglaze the pot with the apple juice and the broth, and add bay leaves and juniper berries. Bring to a boil, then lower the heat to a simmer and cook, covered, for 30 minutes. Meanwhile, cut the unpeeled apples into slices and seed them. In a pan, sauté the apples in a generous amount of butter with salt, bay leaf, and rosemary just until browned and remove from the heat. (Do not let the apples break down.) When the chicken is cooked, raise the heat to high and cook, uncovered, until the liquid has reduced to coat the chicken. Serve the chicken hot with the apples on the side.

« POLLO ALLE OLIVE »
CHICKEN WITH OLIVES

Looking for a way to liven up a plain old chicken cutlet? Just add olives, capers, and wine. It's not an oversight that there's no salt listed here—the olives and capers are salty enough.

SERVES 4

Extra-virgin olive oil for sautéing
14 ounces (400 grams) chicken cutlets or boneless skinless chicken
    breast pounded thin, cut into strips
Unbleached all-purpose flour for dredging
1/4 cup pitted green olives
1 tablespoon capers, rinsed and drained
1/2 cup white wine
Whole milk for deglazing pan and making sauce
Fresh basil leaves to taste

Heat a small amount of oil in a pan. Dredge the chicken strips in flour and brown them in the pan, turning once. Meanwhile, in a food processor fitted with the metal blade or a blender, puree the olives and capers into a paste. When the chicken is browned, deglaze the pan with the wine and add the olive and caper paste. Cover and cook for about 5 minutes over medium-low heat. Uncover the pan, remove the chicken to a serving platter, and deglaze the pan with a small amount of milk, whisking to combine it with the cooking juices. Cook until the sauce is reduced slightly, then pour the sauce over the chicken. Garnish with fresh basil leaves and serve immediately.

« POLLO IN CARPIONE »
MARINATED FRIED CHICKEN

Carpione is a marinade from Alessandria, my home town. When I was little, all summer long our refrigerator held a glass dish of slices of chicken in this refreshing vinegar-based sauce. You can also sauce vegetables—most commonly zucchini—with *carpione*, but to me nothing beats lightly breaded and fried chicken. This delicious sauce deserves to be better known! I use red Tropea onions in this sauce because I think they look so pretty, but other types of onions will taste just as good. Make this dish ahead—not only is it convenient to do so, but the sauce keeps the chicken moist and the flavor actually improves as it sits. It will keep for several days.

SERVES 6

14 ounces (400 grams) boneless skinless chicken breast
Vegetable oil for deep-frying
2 large eggs, lightly beaten
1 cup (100 grams) breadcrumbs
Salt to taste
Extra-virgin olive oil for sautéing
10 ounces (300 grams) red onions, thinly sliced
Bay leaves to taste
1 1/2 cups plus 2 tablespoons (400 milliliters) white wine
1 1/4 cups (300 milliliters) apple cider vinegar
Fresh sage leaves to taste
Whole black peppercorns to taste

Slice the chicken into smaller pieces. Heat a generous amount of vegetable oil in a pan. Dredge the chicken slices first in the eggs and then in the breadcrumbs and fry until golden brown and crisp. Cook in batches if necessary to keep from crowding the pan. Transfer the fried chicken to paper towels to drain and salt lightly.

When the chicken has all been cooked, in another pan heat a small amount of olive oil over low heat and sauté the onions with bay leaves until transparent. Do not let them brown. Add the wine and vinegar, a generous amount of sage, a little salt, and a few peppercorns. Simmer for 1 minute, then remove from the heat. Remove the onion and herb mixture from the marinade with a slotted spoon, reserving the cooking liquid. In a glass storage container, alternate layers of the onion mixture with layers of the fried chicken until you have used up both. Pour the reserved cooking liquid over the top. Allow the chicken to cool completely, then seal tightly with a lid or cover securely with plastic wrap and refrigerate. Serve cold.

« POLLO MEDIOEVALE »
MEDIEVAL CHICKEN

I don't know how authentic this dish is, but it's delicious. Almond milk lends an unusual flavor—most grocery stores now carry almond milk alongside soy milk and other lactose-free options.

SERVES 4 TO 6

2 ounces (60 grams) fatback
1 yellow onion
1 ¹/₂ pounds (700 grams) boneless skinless chicken thighs, chopped
Salt to taste
1 cup unsweetened almond milk
Pepper to taste
Juice of ¹/₂ lemon

In a food processor fitted with the metal blade or a blender, puree the fatback with the onion. Place the mixture in a large pot or Dutch oven over medium heat and melt the fatback. When the fatback has melted, add the chicken pieces, season with salt, and brown the chicken on all sides, turning with tongs. Add the almond milk and scrape up any browned bits of chicken from the bottom of the pan. Season with pepper. Cook, stirring occasionally, until the chicken is cooked through, 5 to 10 minutes. Stir in lemon juice and serve immediately.

« LA COSCETTA DI FIORE »
FIORELLO'S CHICKEN THIGHS

The Italian comedian, singer, and actor Fiorello tweeted about this dish one day, and I contacted him immediately and demanded that he give me the recipe! It's similar to a breaded chicken cutlet, but made with dark meat. So, I guess he's a comedian, singer, actor, and cook!

SERVES 4

Extra-virgin olive oil for broiling
4 boneless skinless chicken thighs
2 egg whites
Breadcrumbs for dredging
Salt to taste
Cherry tomatoes, halved, for garnish
Fresh basil leaves for garnish

Preheat the broiler and lightly oil a broiler pan. Pound the chicken thighs until thin. Dredge them in the egg whites and then in breadcrumbs. Season with salt. Arrange the chicken on the prepared pan. Broil until the chicken is cooked through and the coating is browned and crispy. Garnish with cherry tomatoes and basil leaves and serve immediately.

« PETTO DI POLLO FARCITO »
STUFFED CHICKEN BREAST

This chicken breast is rolled up and baked, and when you slice it, the cheese filling melts in the most inviting way. When chicken is rolled up this way, it takes a little longer to cook, so be sure to give this enough time in the pan. My friend Cristina Pistocchi—who generously gave me this recipe—says you're better off cooking it five minutes too long than taking it out five minutes too soon.

SERVES 4

1 boneless skinless chicken breast
Salt to taste
3 1/2 ounces (100 grams) thinly sliced prosciutto cotto
3 processed cheese slices
Rosemary sprigs to taste
Unbleached all-purpose flour for dredging
Extra-virgin olive oil for browning
White wine to taste

Butterfly the chicken breast without separating the 2 halves so that it looks like an open book. (If you do separate the 2 halves accidentally, or if you find it easier to work with 2 pieces, just place them on the work surface so that they overlap slightly.) Season lightly with salt and arrange the prosciutto cotto in a single layer on top. Arrange the cheese slices on top of the prosciutto, overlapping slightly if necessary to make them fit. Roll up the chicken breast tightly, truss with kitchen twine, and tuck fresh rosemary sprigs between the twine and the meat. Dredge the rolled chicken in flour, salt the outside, and heat a small amount of oil over high heat in a pot large enough to hold the chicken. Brown on all sides, then add some white wine and allow most of it to evaporate. Lower the heat to medium and cook, covered, until the chicken is cooked through, 20 to 30 minutes. Remove from the heat and allow to let set until cooled slightly, about 20 minutes, then slice and serve.

« CAPPONE RIPIENO »
STUFFED CAPON

Stuffed capon is delicious and festive—perfect for a big occasion such as Christmas. However, capon can dry out very easily. I like to cook it in broth—that way it can be kept warm for guests for up to two hours. Serves this with mostarda, which is similar to chutney.

SERVES 6 TO 8

1 1/2 yellow onions
1 tablespoon unsalted butter
1 thick slice (100 grams) country-style bread
Whole milk, *quanto basta*, about 1 cup (250 milliliters)
3 1/2 ounces (100 grams) sausage
3 1/2 ounces (100 grams) thinly sliced prosciutto crudo, chopped
2 egg yolks
1/2 cup (50 grams) grated Parmesan
1 tablespoon pistachios
1 capon, cleaned, liver reserved and minced
3 whole cloves
1 rib celery
1 carrot
1 teaspoon coarse salt
Salt to taste
Mostarda for garnish
Rosemary sprigs for garnish

To make the stuffing, thinly slice 1/2 onion and sauté it in the butter in a pan. Soften the bread in milk and then crumble it into a medium bowl. Add the sautéed onion. Remove the casing from the sausages and, with your hands, knead the sausage meat with the bread and the cooked onion. Add the prosciutto, egg yolks, Parmesan, pistachios, and liver and mix until well combined. Stuff the capon, truss the capon's legs with kitchen twine, and sew it closed. Stick the cloves into the remaining onion. In a pot large enough to hold the capon, combine the onion with the cloves, celery, carrot, and enough water to cover the capon. Add the coarse salt and bring to a boil. Gently lower the stuffed capon into the pot, turn the heat down to a simmer, and cook for about 2 hours.

When the capon is cooked, carve it and arrange the pieces on a serving platter with high sides. Taste and adjust salt. Remove the stuffing from the capon carcass, cut it into slices, and place the sliced stuffing on top of the capon meat. Strain the broth from the pot and pour about 1 cup broth over the capon and stuffing. Garnish with mostarda and rosemary sprigs and serve.

« PAPERO ALLA MELAGRANA »
DUCK WITH POMEGRANATE

I've always been interested in historical recipes. The idea of grand banquets and ancient cooking methods, life at court—it all fascinates me, and I read everything about it that I can get my hands on. Caterina de' Medici brought this recipe from Florence to France in the mid-1500s when she married Henry II. It was so popular that it inspired what is today a famous French dish, duck à l'orange.

SERVES 6

1 to 2 pomegranates, seeds removed
1 duck, about 1 3/4 pounds (800 grams), cut up
Extra-virgin olive oil for sautéing
Unsalted butter for sautéing
Salt to taste
1 shallot, sliced
1 cup (250 milliliters) cognac
Leaves of 1 sprig fresh sage
2 tablespoons sugar

In a food processor fitted with the metal blade or a blender, mince the pomegranate seeds, then strain them through a fine-mesh sieve, pressing with the back of a spoon to extract the juice. Reserve both the juice and solids. In a large pot or Dutch oven, brown the duck pieces in equal amounts oil and butter. Season with salt and add the shallot. Add the cognac and allow most of the liquid to evaporate. Add the pomegranate juice, sage, and sugar and cook, covered, over medium heat until the duck is cooked through, about 30 minutes. Transfer the duck to a platter and pour the cooking liquid on top. Scatter with the pomegranate seeds and serve hot.

ENTRÉES

« FILLETTO AL SALE CON SALSA AL PEPE VERDE »
BEEF FILLET WITH GREEN PEPPERCORN SAUCE

This is an excellent choice for those who are watching their weight. The beef is cooked without any butter or oil, and the sauce is made with a yogurt base. That doesn't mean it's not flavorful, however. I got this recipe from Loredana Noto, my faithful breakfast companion.

SERVES 4 TO 6

3 1/3 pounds (1 1/2 kilograms) coarse salt
Sage to taste
Fresh rosemary leaves to taste
Bay leaves to taste
1 beef fillet, about 1 1/2 pounds (700 grams)
1 small container (about 2/3 cup) plain yogurt
1 tablespoon mustard
Salt to taste
1 tablespoon green peppercorns in brine, rinsed and drained, plus more
    for garnish

Preheat the oven to 350° F (180° C). Line a baking pan with high sides that will just hold the fillet without too much extra room (the sides should be a little taller than the fillet) with parchment paper. Scatter some of the coarse salt in a thin layer on the parchment. Scatter with the rosemary and bay leaves and place the fillet on top. Add the remaining coarse salt on and around the fillet to hide it completely. Sprinkle with a few drops of water and bake for about 45 minutes.

Meanwhile, make the sauce: In a small bowl, whisk together the yogurt, mustard, salt to taste, and peppercorns. When the fillet is cooked, remove it from the pan and wipe off the salt with a paper towel or a clean dish towel. Thinly slice the beef and serve with a small amount of the sauce and a few whole peppercorns for garnish.

« TAGLIATA AI FUNGHI PORCINI »
SLICED STEAK WITH PORCINI MUSHROOMS

Steak and porcini mushrooms are costly ingredients, but everybody loves them, including me. Be sure to let the steak sit for about fifteen minutes before you slice it.

SERVES 4

Extra-virgin olive oil for sautéing and brushing
1 clove garlic, crushed
6 small fresh porcini mushrooms, sliced
Salt to taste
Fresh thyme leaves to taste, plus thyme sprigs for garnish
1 pound (500 grams) entrecôte or other high-quality steak
Coarse salt to taste

Heat a small amount of oil in a pan and sauté the garlic, then add the mushrooms. Season with salt and thyme leaves and cook, covered, over low heat until the mushrooms are soft, about 10 minutes. Heat a cast-iron skillet and, when it's very hot, brush it with a small amount of oil and scatter on some coarse salt. Cook the steak in the hot skillet for about 4 minutes on each side. (To get a nice brown crust, turn the steak only once and otherwise do not move it.) Remove the steak from the heat, wrap it in aluminum foil, and set aside to rest for 15 minutes. Slice the steak thinly and arrange it on a warm serving platter. Spread the cooked mushrooms on top and garnish with some sprigs of thyme. Serve immediately.

« FILLETTO IN SALSA DI VINO »
BEEF WITH WINE SAUCE

Fast, tasty, and always impressive—a little honey adds extra interest to this delicious dish.

SERVES 4

4 slices country-style bread
Extra-virgin olive oil for toasting bread and sautéing
4 filet mignon medallions
$1/4$ cup plus 2 tablespoons (50 grams) unbleached all-purpose flour
2 cups (500 milliliters) red wine
2 tablespoons acacia honey
1 bay leaf
Salt to taste

Brush the bread slices with a small amount of oil and toast them in a cast-iron skillet. Remove to a plate. Dredge the filet mignon in the flour, add a small amount of oil to the same cast-iron skillet, and cook the steaks in the skillet, about 2 minutes per side. Remove the steaks from the heat and wrap them in aluminum foil. Add the wine and honey to the same skillet and deglaze the pan, scraping up any browned bits. Add the bay leaf and cook until the sauce is reduced and silky. Return the steaks to the pan for 30 seconds to reheat. Place the toasted bread slices on individual serving plates. Top each slice with a medallion, and pour the sauce over the meat. Serve immediately.

« FILLETTO AL PEPE ROSA »
FILET WITH PINK PEPPERCORNS

This is a little nod to the 1980s, when filet mignon with peppercorns was all the rage. I like pink peppercorns for their subtle flavor and pretty appearance.

SERVES 2

2 thick filet mignon medallions
1 clove garlic
Extra-virgin olive oil for sautéing
2 sprigs rosemary
Salt to taste
1/2 cup (150 milliliters) heavy cream
1 tablespoon pink peppercorns in brine

Tie the medallions with kitchen twine. In a pan large enough to hold the medallions, sauté the garlic in a small amount of oil until browned, then remove and discard. Place the rosemary sprigs in the pan and set the steak on top of them. Cook the steak, about 2 minutes per side. Season with salt and remove from the pan. To the same pan, add the cream, 1 tablespoon peppercorns, and a little of their brine (taste and judge the level of saltiness—you may not want to use all of the brine) and deglaze the pan. Cook over low heat, stirring, for 2 minutes. If the medallions have cooled too much for your liking, return them to the pan and cook about 1 minute per side to reheat. Remove the twine from the medallions and serve them with the sauce, either poured over the steaks or passed on the side.

« TOURNEDOS CON CRUMBLE DI FUNGHI »
TOURNEDOS WITH MUSHROOM CRUMBLE

This dish relies on the dependable combination of steak and mushrooms, but in this case, the mushrooms are dried porcinis that are used to make a crust and crumbly topping.

SERVES 2

2 filet mignon medallions, about 7 ounces (200 grams) each
1/2 ounce (15 grams) dried porcini mushrooms
1 slice country-style bread
1 ounce (30 grams) Parmesan
Fresh thyme leaves to taste
Extra-virgin olive oil for moistening and sautéing
Salt to taste

Preheat the oven to 350° F (180° C). Tie the medallions with kitchen twine. In a food processor or a blender, process the dried mushrooms, bread, Parmesan, thyme leaves, and enough oil to make a moist mixture. Heat a griddle and sear the medallions, about 2 minutes per side. Season with salt and remove from the heat to rest. When the medallions have rested, remove the twine and transfer them to a jelly-roll pan or baking dish. Press most of the porcini mushroom mixture onto the meat to make a crust, reserving a small amount. Sprinkle the reserved mushroom mixture on top without pressing it into the steaks. Bake for 15 minutes.

« MANZO ALL'OLIO DI ROVATO »
ROVATO-STYLE BEEF

This wonderful recipe for a dish from Rovato, near Brescia, was given to me by my colleague Monica Gasparini. Serve this as part of a luncheon buffet—it is prepared and sliced in advance and reheated just before serving.

SERVES 6

1 1/3 pounds (600 grams) beef shoulder
2 cups (500 milliliters) extra-virgin olive oil
2 cloves garlic
2 anchovies
1/2 rib celery
1/2 carrot
1 small yellow onion
1/2 cup breadcrumbs
1/4 cup grated Parmesan
1/4 cup minced fresh parsley leaves

Truss the beef with kitchen twine and set it in a large pot. Pour the olive oil into the pot, then add water to cover. Add the garlic, anchovies, celery, carrot, and onion and cook, covered, over low heat until the liquid is reduced by half and the meat is very tender, at least 2 hours. Remove the pot from the heat and allow the meat to cool in the liquid.

When the meat is cool enough to handle, remove the meat from the liquid, remove the twine, slice the meat, and arrange the slices in a baking dish. Strain the cooking liquid into a bowl and combine it with the breadcrumbs, Parmesan, and parsley. Cover the baking dish and bowl with plastic wrap and refrigerate until ready to bake. About 45 minutes before you wish to serve the beef, preheat the oven to 350° F (180° C). Pour the breadcrumb mixture over the meat and bake until warmed through, about 10 minutes. Serve warm.

« BRASATO AL BAROLO »
BEEF STEW BRAISED IN BAROLO

This is the Piedmont region's most famous dish, and since I'm from Piedmont originally, this recipe is my mother's. She has a real talent for cooking meat, but I will say that in addition to a good recipe like this one, you need a good piece of meat—it should be marbled with a nice amount of fat.

SERVES 6

1 yellow onion, chopped
1 to 2 carrots, chopped
1 to 2 ribs celery, chopped
1 quart (1 liter) Barolo wine
1 clove garlic
2 bay leaves
1 teaspoon peppercorns
1 teaspoon juniper berries
2 to 3 whole cloves
2 $^2/_3$ pounds (1 $^1/_4$ kilograms) beef shoulder
Unsalted butter for sautéing

Extra-virgin olive oil for sautéing
Salt to taste

In a nonreactive dish large enough to hold the beef shoulder, combine the onion, carrots, celery, Barolo, garlic, bay leaves, peppercorns, juniper berries, and cloves. Place the beef in the mixture and marinate, refrigerated, for 12 hours. Remove the meat from the marinade. Strain the marinade, reserving both the liquid and solids. In a large pot, heat equal amounts butter and oil and brown the beef shoulder, about 5 minutes per side. Add the solids strained out of the marinade, season with salt, and cook for about 15 minutes. Then add the liquid from the marinade and cook, covered, over low heat until the meat is extremely tender, at least 2 hours. Remove the meat from the pot and slice. Arrange the slices on a serving platter. Remove the bay leaves from the pot and discard. In a blender (or with an immersion blender if you have one), puree the liquid and other items in the pot. Pour the puree over the sliced meat and serve immediately.

« GULASH TRIESTINO »
TRIESTE GOULASH

Trieste sits in the northeastern corner of Italy, near Croatia and Slovenia, and its traditional dishes, including this goulash, are Eastern European in flavor. This dish is terrific on a cold night.

SERVES 6

1 1/2 pounds (700 grams) onions, thinly sliced
Extra-virgin olive oil for sautéing
1 3/4 pounds (800 grams) beef, cut into chunks
1 teaspoon sweet paprika
1 tablespoon spicy paprika
3 tablespoons tomato paste
Rosemary leaves to taste
Marjoram leaves to taste
Thyme leaves to taste
Salt to taste

In a large pot, sauté the onions in a small amount of oil over low heat until golden. When the onion is golden, add the beef and brown, turning occasionally to cook on all sides. Dissolve both types of paprika in 1 cup water and add that to the pot. Dissolve the tomato paste in 1 to 2 tablespoons warm water and add that as well. Add the rosemary, marjoram, and thyme. Season with salt and cook, covered, over low heat until the beef is very tender, about 1 1/2 hours. Serve warm.

« CARPACCIO DELL'HARRY'S BAR »
HARRY'S BAR CARPACCIO

The venerable Harry's Bar in Venice is famous for its beef carpaccio, which Giuseppe Cipriani created for his friend Amalia Nani Mocenigo, who couldn't eat cooked meat. With its little dots of sauce, it looks like a Kandinsky painting!

SERVES 4

14 ounces (400 grams) beef carpaccio
Salt to taste
3/4 cup plus 1 tablespoon (200 milliliters) mayonnaise
3 tablespoons Worcestershire sauce
Juice of 1/2 lemon
About 3 tablespoons whole milk
White pepper to taste

Divide the carpaccio into 4 equal portions and arrange it attractively on individual serving plates. Salt lightly. In a small bowl, whisk together the mayonnaise, Worcestershire sauce, and lemon juice, then gradually whisk in enough milk to make a sauce the consistency of sour cream. Season with salt and white pepper. Taste and adjust the Worcestershire sauce or lemon juice if necessary to achieve a balanced flavor. Use a spoon to drip small amounts of the sauce over the portions of beef in a decorative manner. Serve immediately.

« INVOLTINI DI BRESAOLA UN PO' SPECIALI »
SPECIAL STUFFED BRESAOLA ROLLS

When Lorenzo Boni, our production chef, suggested that I make bresaola rolls, I made a face. Thin slices of bresaola rolled around cheese are just so common, I thought. But I was wrong. With this very quick recipe, you can make a sophisticated and original dish. All you need is a bed of sliced mushrooms, a few drops of truffle oil (use a light hand, as always), and the ability to give them a quick turn in a pan so that they get crispy on the outside while remaining soft on the inside.

SERVES 4

7 ounces (200 grams) white mushrooms
1 tablespoon extra-virgin olive oil for sautéing
1 clove garlic, minced
Minced parsley to taste
Salt to taste
7 ounces (1 scant cup/200 grams) cream cheese
2 drops truffle oil
3 1/2 ounces (100 grams) bresaola slices

Slice the mushrooms and sauté them in a pan with the oil. Add the garlic and season with parsley and a sprinkling of salt. Don't overcook the mushrooms—you want them to remain firm. Place the cream cheese in a small bowl and add the truffle oil. (It bears repeating that this is a case in which more is *not* better.) Stir to combine. Place a spoonful of the cream cheese mixture on each slice of bresaola and fold up envelope-style. (There's no need for toothpicks.) On a cast-iron grill pan or in a nonstick pan, briefly brown the packets on both sides. Place the mushrooms on a platter, top with the bresaola packets, and serve immediately.

SPECIAL STUFFED BRESAOLA ROLLS

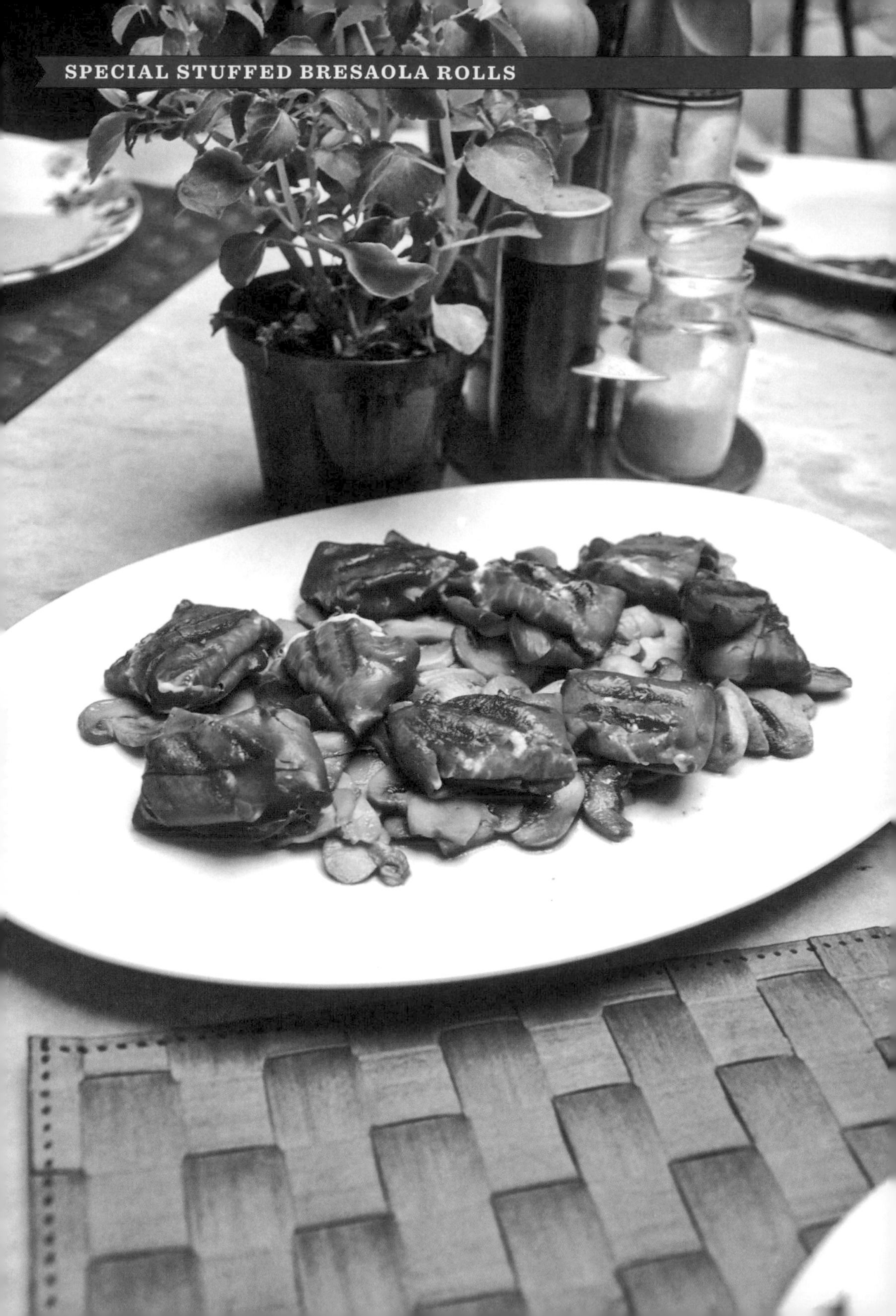

« LENTICCHIE CON POLPETTINE »
LENTILS WITH MEATBALLS

This dish was suggested by Barbara Boncompagni, a priceless advisor on my show. My whole family, including little Diego, just loves lentil soup. This dish goes one better by hiding little marble-sized meatballs in it.

SERVES 4

1/2 yellow onion, sliced
Extra-virgin olive oil for sautéing
1 (15-ounce/500-gram) can lentils, rinsed and drained
1 tablespoon vegetable broth granules (or the serving size indicated on
      the package)
Fresh rosemary leaves to taste
Tomato paste to taste
Salt to taste
9 ounces (250 grams) sausage
3 1/2 ounces (100 grams) brie, rind removed
Unbleached all-purpose flour for dredging

In a pot, sauté the onion in a small amount of oil until browned. Add the lentils, water to cover, the broth granules, rosemary, tomato paste, and salt. Cook until thick, 15 to 20 minutes. While the soup is cooking, remove the sausage from the casing and, in a food processor fitted with the metal blade or a blender, combine the sausage meat with the brie. Form the sausage mixture into small balls the size of marbles or quail eggs, dredge them in flour, and sauté them in another pan in a small amount of oil until browned. When the soup is ready, divide it among soup bowls and top with the meatballs. Serve hot.

« POLPETTINE IN FOGLIA DI LIMONE »
MEATBALLS BAKED IN LEMON LEAVES

No two ways about it: Meatballs are delicious. They're not the most elegant dish, however. I bake these in lemon leaves, which makes them extra-pretty. Find unwaxed fresh lemon leaves at the florist or farmer's market.

SERVES 4 TO 6

14 ounces (400 grams) ground veal
1 cup (100 grams) grated Parmesan
1 large egg
Salt to taste
3 tablespoons breadcrumbs
Grated zest of 1 lemon
Fresh lemon leaves for wrapping meatballs

Preheat the oven to 350° F (180° C). In a bowl, combine the veal, Parmesan, egg, and salt and knead by hand until combined. Add the breadcrumbs and lemon zest and knead them into the mixture. Pinch off a piece of the mixture and shape it into a small cylinder. Repeat with the remaining mixture. Wrap each meatball in a lemon leaf, then secure with a toothpick. Arrange the meatballs in the leaves on a jelly-roll pan and bake for 20 minutes. Serve hot.

« POLPETTE CON FONDUTA DI PORRI »
MEATBALLS WITH LEEK SAUCE

This is another more high-class meatball recipe. These can be served as part of a dinner party, or even at a buffet if you have the patience to make little bite-sized meatballs for a large group.

SERVES 4

2 leeks, sliced
Extra-virgin olive oil for sautéing

Beef broth (broth made with a bouillon cube is fine) for braising and
 thinning sauce
Salt to taste
1 slice country-style bread
1 ½ cups (250 milliliters) whole milk
9 ounces (250 grams) ground beef
1 large egg
½ cup (50 grams) grated Parmesan
Minced fresh basil leaves to taste, for meatballs and garnishing
Unbleached all-purpose flour for dredging

Sauté the leeks over low heat in a small amount of olive oil until transparent. Add a little broth, season with salt, and braise, covered, until the leeks are soft and falling apart, adding more broth as needed. Meanwhile, make the meatballs. In a large bowl, soak the bread in ½ cup (100 milliliters) milk and then crumble it. Add the ground beef and knead by hand. Add the egg, Parmesan, salt, and some basil and knead to combine. Form the mixture into small meatballs, dredge the meatballs in flour, and transfer them to a pan. Add a small amount of oil to the pan and brown the meatballs over medium heat, turning them to cook on all sides. When the leeks are cooked, transfer them to a blender and puree. Add the remaining 1 cup (250 milliliters) milk and enough broth to make a silky sauce. Place a generous spoonful of leek sauce on each individual plate and arrange meatballs on top of it. Garnish with additional minced basil and serve.

« POLPETTONE »
MEATLOAF

This is Matilde's favorite. I incorporate tomato sauce into my meatloaf mixture to keep it moist. I like to make the meatloaf in a ring pan, then I fill the center with lots of carrots and peas sautéed in butter.

SERVES 4 TO 6

Unsalted butter for greasing pan and sautéing
Breadcrumbs for coating pan
7 ounces (200 grams) frozen chopped carrots

7 ounces (200 grams) frozen peas
1 yellow onion, minced
Extra-virgin olive oil for sautéing
1 cup (250 milliliters) tomato puree
Salt to taste
Sugar to taste
Fresh basil leaves to taste
3 to 4 slices bread
14 ounces (400 grams) ground beef
1/2 cup (50 grams) grated Parmesan
1 large egg
Grated nutmeg to taste

Preheat the oven to 350° F (180° C). Butter a ring pan, dust with breadcrumbs (shaking off and discarding the excess), and set aside. Boil the carrots and peas until soft, then drain and reserve. Meanwhile, sauté the onion in a small amount of oil, then add the tomato puree, salt, sugar, and basil and cook, covered, over medium heat until thickened, 10 to 15 minutes. Soften the bread in the sauce and crumble it, then transfer the mixture to a large bowl. When the tomato sauce is cool enough to touch with your hands, add the beef and knead by hand to combine. Add the Parmesan, egg, and nutmeg and knead by hand until well combined. Transfer the mixture to the prepared pan and press it down by hand so that the top is even. Bake until cooked through, 20 to 30 minutes. Place a platter upside down over the pan, then invert and lift off the pan. Sauté the cooked carrots and peas in a small amount of butter, then transfer the vegetables to the center of the meatloaf. (Transfer any peas and carrots that don't fit into a serving bowl.) Serve immediately.

« POLPETTONE ALLE ERBE »
HERBED MEATLOAF

Since Matilde loves meatloaf so much, I've tried dozens of versions, but she's a harsh critic and doesn't approve of all of them. This is one that got high marks from her, thanks to the crunchy topping.

SERVES 6

Fresh mint, parsley, thyme, marjoram, and rosemary leaves to taste
4 sun-dried tomatoes
Zest of 1 lemon
6 slices sandwich bread
1 1/2 pounds (700 grams) ground pork
Whole milk, *quanto basta*
1 large egg
Salt to taste
1/2 cup (50 grams) grated pecorino
Extra-virgin olive oil for drizzling

Preheat the oven to 350° F (180° C). In a food processor fitted with the metal blade, mince the herbs and the sun-dried tomatoes with the lemon zest and 3 slices of the bread. In a bowl, knead the pork with a handful of the herb mixture, reserving the rest. Soften the remaining 3 slices of bread in milk and crumble into the meat mixture. Add the egg, salt, and pecorino and knead by hand until well combined. Shape into a meatloaf and set in a baking pan. Sprinkle with the reserved herb mixture, drizzle with a little olive oil, and bake for 40 minutes. Allow to cool for about 10 minutes before slicing.

« CARNE A PIZZETTA »
PIZZA-STYLE MEATLOAF

This is an alternative to a classic meatloaf. Kids love it because it combines two of their favorites!

SERVES 4

3 slices (250 grams) bread
Whole milk, *quanto basta*, about 1/2 cup (100 milliliters)
10 ounces (300 grams) ground beef
2 large eggs
Salt to taste
1 teaspoon dried oregano
1/2 cup (50 grams) grated Parmesan

7 ounces (200 grams) cherry tomatoes, halved, or 1 cup (250 milliliters)
 tomato puree
1 fresh mozzarella ball, 8 ounces (225 grams), diced
1/4 cup (50 milliliters) pitted green olives, minced

Preheat a convection oven to 350° F (180° C). Line a rectangular baking pan with parchment paper and set aside. In a large bowl, soak the bread in the milk, then crumble it with your hands and knead together with the ground beef. Add the eggs, salt, oregano, and Parmesan to the bowl and knead by hand to combine. Press the meat mixture into a single, even layer in the prepared baking pan (as if it were pizza dough). Sprinkle with the cherry tomatoes or spread on the tomato puree. Bake for about 15 minutes. Remove the pan from the oven and sprinkle with the mozzarella and olives, then return to the oven and bake for an additional 10 minutes. Allow to cool slightly before serving.

« COTOLETTE ALLA PALERMITANA »
PALERMO-STYLE CUTLETS

I like to serve generous portions of appetizers and first courses like pasta or risotto, and when it's time for the entrée, my guests often wave the white flag and tell me they can't take any more food! So, I've learned to make lighter entrées like this one. You can leave out the garlic if you prefer.

SERVES 4

Leaves of 1 sprig parsley
1 small clove garlic
1 cup (100 grams) breadcrumbs
1/2 cup (50 grams) grated mild pecorino
Salt to taste
1 pound (500 grams) beef or veal cutlets
Extra-virgin olive oil for drizzling

Preheat the broiler. If your broiler has a temperature setting, set it to 350° F to 400° F (180° C to 200° C). Line a jelly-roll pan with parchment paper. Mince the parsley and garlic and mix with the breadcrumbs and pecorino. Salt and knead by hand until well combined. Press this mixture against both sides of the cutlets and transfer the cutlets to the prepared pan. Broil, turning once if necessary and keeping a close eye on the cutlets to guard against the breadcrumbs burning, until the meat is cooked through, about 5 minutes per side (but it will depend on how hot your broiler is and how far from the flame your pan sits).

« BIS DI FILLETTI »
NUT-CRUSTED PORK AND VEAL FILLETS

Serving two different types of meat always makes a big impression. I use two different types of nut crusts on them as well.

SERVES 2

$^2/_3$ cup (60 grams) hazelnuts
2 slices sandwich bread
$^1/_2$ cup (60 grams) pistachios
Extra-virgin olive oil for searing and drizzling
2 veal tenderloin medallions
2 pork tenderloin medallions
Salt to taste
Pepper to taste

Preheat the oven to 200° F (100° C). In a food processor fitted with the metal blade, grind the hazelnuts with 1 slice bread. Set aside. Wipe out the work bowl and grind the pistachios with the remaining 1 slice bread. Keep the two mixtures separate. Heat a small amount of olive oil in a pan and sear first the veal medallions and then the pork medallions, turning once with tongs to brown both sides. Salt the meat and place it on a jelly-roll pan. Spoon the pistachio mixture on top of the pork medallions and the hazelnut mixture on top of the veal medallions. Drizzle with a little oil, season with pepper, and bake until the veal is cooked through but still pink and tender, then remove the veal and return the pan to the oven until the pork is fully cooked, about 10 minutes total. Serve hot.

« VALDOSTANE »
VEAL SCALOPPINI WITH PROSCIUTTO AND FONTINA CHEESE

In my opinion, these are best made open-face so that the cheese melts on top.

SERVES 4

Unsalted butter for sautéing
Extra-virgin olive oil for sautéing
Sage leaves to taste
4 veal scaloppini
Unbleached all-purpose flour for dredging
4 thin slices prosciutto cotto
4 thin slices Fontina cheese
Salt and pepper to taste

Heat equal amounts butter and oil in a pan with the sage leaves. Dredge the scaloppini in the flour, then place them in the pan and leave them undisturbed until they are browned underneath. Turn the scaloppini and place 1 slice prosciutto (folded so that it is smaller than the meat and doesn't overhang) and 1 slice fontina (also folded, if necessary, not to overhang) on top of each. Season with salt, turn the heat down to low, and cook, covered, until the cheese has melted and the meat is cooked through, about 1 minute more. Season with pepper and serve immediately.

« COTOLETTE ALLA MARESCIALLA »
VEAL CUTLETS WITH PROSCIUTTO COTTO AND PROVOLONE

This recipe is from my friend Giusi Battaglia, and it's been handed down in her family for generations.

SERVES 2

3 potatoes, boiled, with peel
Salt to taste
Minced parsley leaves to taste
Grated Parmesan, *quanto basta*

2 veal top round scaloppini
2 slices smoked provolone cheese
2 slices prosciutto cotto
Extra-virgin olive oil for pan-frying
2 large eggs, lightly beaten
Breadcrumbs for dredging

Mash the potatoes through a potato ricer into a large bowl. (The peel should come off.) Season the potatoes with salt, and the parsley and Parmesan, and mix to combine. Spread the potato mixture on top of the veal scaloppini. Place 1 slice provolone and 1 slice prosciutto on top of each. Heat a generous amount of oil in a pan. Holding the prosciutto and cheese against the meat, dredge in the egg and then breadcrumbs. Pan-fry for 1 minute with the prosciutto-side down, then turn with tongs and pan-fry until cooked through, about 3 minutes more. Serve hot.

« PICCATINE DI VITELLO »
VEAL PICCATA

Everyone loves this Milanese classic.

SERVES 4

1 pound (500 grams) veal top round, cut into slices
Unsalted butter for sautéing
Extra-virgin olive oil for sautéing
1 clove garlic
Unbleached all-purpose flour for dredging
Salt and pepper
$1/2$ cup (100 milliliters) white wine
$1/4$ cup (50 milliliters) broth
Juice of $1/2$ lemon
Minced fresh parsley leaves

With a paring knife or scissors, make a few small cuts in the sides of the veal slices to prevent them from curling. Combine butter, oil, and the garlic in a pan over medium heat. Dredge the veal in flour, then add it to the pan. Season with salt and pepper, then add the wine and broth and cook, covered, until the meat has cooked through. Add the lemon juice and parsley, then with tongs, remove the meat to a serving platter. Place the pan over high heat and, whisking constantly, reduce the sauce until silky. Pour the sauce over the meat and serve.

« STINCO DI VITELLO »
VEAL SHANK

Veal shank has to cook long and slowly, but it doesn't take much effort. Just find a good book to read while you're waiting and check the oven every twenty pages or so! If you make this dish for a festive dinner party, continue the theme by featuring pomegranates in the centerpiece as well.

SERVES 6 TO 8

1 whole veal shank, about 4 pounds (2 kilograms)
1 (1-pound/500-gram) jar sweet and sour cipollini onions
Salt and pepper to taste
3 tablespoons (40 grams) unsalted butter, cut into pieces
Rosemary sprigs to taste, plus more for garnish
Bay leaves to taste
Sage sprigs to taste
2 cups (500 milliliters) white wine, plus more if needed
2 pomegranates, seeds removed

Preheat the oven to 350° F (180° C). Set the shank in a baking pan with the onions and season with salt and pepper. Dot with the butter. Add the rosemary, bay leaves, and sage, and then pour 1 cup (250 milliliters) wine over the shank. Cover with aluminum foil and roast for 1 hour 30 minutes. Remove the foil and add the pomegranate seeds, reserving a few clusters for garnish. Return to the oven and roast, turning the shank occasionally, until the meat is tender and falling off the bone, about an additional 1 hour 30 minutes. If the pan looks dry, add a little more wine.

When the shank is cooked, transfer it to a serving platter. Remove and discard the rosemary, bay leaf, and sage. Use a slotted spoon to transfer the onions to the serving platter. (Don't worry if some have stuck to the bottom of the pan—just leave them.) Place the baking pan on the stovetop over medium heat and deglaze with about 1 cup (250 milliliters) wine, scraping up any browned bits stuck to the bottom. Reduce the liquid slightly, then pour over the veal shank. Garnish with the reserved pomegranate seeds and a few sprigs fresh rosemary and serve immediately.

« INVOLTINI DI MAIALE AL CANNONAU »
STUFFED PORK ROLLS COOKED IN CANNONAU WINE

These pork rolls stay tender in a sauce made with Sardinia's famous Cannonau wine.

SERVES 4

8 slices sandwich bread
1 cup (250 milliliters) whole milk
5 ounces (150 grams) fatback, minced
1 large egg
1 teaspoon garlic powder
Minced parsley leaves to taste
Salt to taste
14 ounces (400 grams) pork loin, thinly sliced
Unbleached all-purpose flour for dredging
Extra-virgin olive oil for sautéing
1 cup (250 milliliters) Cannonau wine

In a medium bowl, soak the bread in the milk until soft. Add the fatback, egg, garlic powder, and parsley and knead by hand to combine. Season with salt. Set the slices of pork loin on a work surface. Pinch off small pieces of the bread mixture and place 1 piece on each slice of pork. Roll up the pork slices and close them with toothpicks or tie them with kitchen twine. Dredge the rolls in flour. Heat a small amount of oil in a pan large enough to hold the rolls in a single layer and brown them in the pan. Add the wine, lower the heat to medium-low, and cook until the meat is cooked through but still tender and the wine has reduced to create a silky sauce. Serve immediately.

« CARRÉ DI MAIALE ALL'ARANCIA CON SPECK E FRUTTA SECCA »
PORK RIB ROAST WITH ORANGE, SPECK, AND DRIED FRUIT

All the credit for this delicious and beautiful dish of pork wrapped in speck, glazed, and served with dried fruit goes to Annamaria Alvaro, the mother of Paolo Quilici, one of the creators of my show.

SERVES 6

2 cups (500 milliliters) white wine
2 cups (500 milliliters) red wine vinegar
1 yellow onion
1 rib celery, roughly chopped
1 tablespoon juniper berries
1 orange
1 pork rib roast, about 1 1/2 pounds (1 1/4 kilograms)
Salt and pepper to taste
4 ounces (120 grams) speck, sliced
Extra-virgin olive oil for drizzling
2 tablespoons (30 grams) unsalted butter
1/4 cup (40 grams) turbinado sugar
4 prunes, minced

For the marinade, in a pot, combine the wine, vinegar, 2 cups (500 milliliters) water, onion, celery, juniper berries, and the zest of 1/2 orange. Bring to a boil and simmer for 10 minutes. Let the wine mixture cool, then place the rib roast in a nonreactive container with high sides and pour it over the roast. Cover and refrigerate in the marinade for about 5 hours. When you are ready to cook the pork, preheat the oven to 350° F (180° C). Remove the pork from the marinade. Season the pork with salt and pepper and wrap it in the speck slices, arranging them between the bones. Truss with kitchen twine and place in a baking pan. Strain the marinade, reserving both the liquid and the solids. Add the solids from the marinade to the pan with the pork. Drizzle with a little oil and roast the pork for 1 hour 15 minutes, basting frequently with its juices. If the meat begins to look too dark, cover the pan with aluminum foil. Meanwhile, zest the remaining 1/2 orange in thin strips and, in a small bowl, collect the orange pulp (removing and discarding any seeds and white fibrous membrane).

When the meat is cooked, keep it warm and strain the juices from the pan and reserve. In a small pot, cook the butter and sugar until lightly caramelized, then add the prunes, the orange zest, and the orange pulp and bring to a boil. Season with salt and reduce to a syrupy sauce. Carve the rib roast and serve hot topped with the dried fruit sauce.

« TIELLA DI MAIALE »
PORK CASSEROLE WITH PORCINI MUSHROOMS

Feeding a hungry crowd? This is the perfect choice: layers of meat, potatoes, tomato sauce, and mushrooms.

SERVES 6

3 tablespoons extra-virgin olive oil, plus more for oiling pan and
    drizzling
1 1/3 pounds (600 grams) potatoes, peeled and sliced into rounds
1 clove garlic
Chile pepper flakes, *quanto basta*
1 (15-ounce/420-milliliter) can tomato puree
Salt to taste
1 cup (100 grams) grated Parmesan
15 to 18 thin slices boneless pork loin
10 ounces (300 grams) fresh porcini mushrooms, sliced
Minced fresh rosemary leaves to taste
Pepper to taste
Breadcrumbs for topping

Preheat the oven to 350° F (180° C). Lightly oil a baking pan and set aside. Parboil the potatoes for 2 to 3 minutes, then drain and reserve. In a pan, heat 3 tablespoons olive oil and brown the garlic and the chile flakes, then add the tomato puree. Season with salt and cook over low heat for about 15 minutes. In the prepared pan, arrange about $1/4$ of the potatoes, top with $1/4$ of the Parmesan, $1/3$ of the pork, $1/3$ of the to-mato sauce, and then $1/3$ of the mushrooms. Sprinkle with some rosemary and season with salt and pepper. Repeat the layers in the same order two more times. Top with the remaining potatoes, the remaining Parmesan, breadcrumbs, a drizzle of oil, and a sprinkling of rosemary. Pour 1 cup water over the dish and bake until the pork is cooked through and the top is nicely browned, about 45 minutes. Allow to sit 10 min-utes before serving.

« TASCHE DI LONZA »
STUFFED PORK LOIN

Pork and sauerkraut is a match made in heaven. I like to switch things up by serving this with ice-cold beer rather than wine. Ask your butcher to cut the pork loin into slices and then cut a pocket in each slice.

SERVES 4

$1/2$ yellow onion, chopped
6 anchovy fillets in oil, chopped
Extra-virgin olive oil for sautéing
1 small head green cabbage, about 10 ounces (300 grams), chopped, or 1
    (32-ounce/1 kilogram) jar prepared sauerkraut, rinsed and drained
Salt to taste
1 cup (250 milliliters) white wine
1 $1/3$ pounds (600 grams) pork loin, cut into 1-inch slices, 1 deep pocket
    cut into each slice
3 $1/2$ ounces (100 grams) smoked scamorza, sliced
2 tablespoons unbleached all-purpose flour
1 tablespoon sesame seeds
Pepper to taste
Minced fresh rosemary leaves

In a pan, sauté the onion and anchovies in a small amount of oil. Add the cabbage or sauerkraut, salt (if you're using the prepared sauerkraut, it probably doesn't need any additional salt), and about $1/2$ cup (250 milliliters) wine and cook, covered, over medium heat until soft, 15 to 20 minutes for the fresh cabbage and less for the sauerkraut. Stuff each pork loin slice with a piece of the scamorza and a spoonful of the cabbage or sauerkraut mixture. Close up the pockets with toothpicks. Dredge each pork slice in the flour and brown in a small amount of oil in a large pan. Sprinkle with the sesame seeds. Turn the pork once and, when both sides are browned, add the remaining $1/2$ cup (100 milliliters) wine, salt lightly, and season with pepper and a sprinkling of rosemary. Cook, covered, over medium-low heat until most of the liquid has evaporated and the meat is cooked through, 7 to 8 minutes. Serve immediately.

« COSTOLETTE DI AGNELLO ALLE NOCCIOLE »
LAMB CHOPS WITH HAZELNUTS

Who would have guessed that illusionist Marco Berry is an excellent cook? Without any magic tricks, he made these excellent lamb chops in 2 minutes.

SERVES 4

$2/3$ cup (100 grams) hazelnuts, toasted, skinned, and roughly ground
1 cup (100 grams) breadcrumbs
Vegetable oil for pan-frying
6 lamb chops
2 large eggs, lightly beaten
Salt to taste

Combine the ground hazelnuts and the breadcrumbs. Heat a generous amount of vegetable oil in a pan over medium-low heat. When the oil is hot, dredge the lamb chops first in the egg and then in the breadcrumb mixture and fry in the oil until browned on both sides. Keep the temperature low, as the hazelnuts will burn at high heat. Salt and serve hot.

« SALSICCE VESTITE DI PEPERONI »
SAUSAGES WRAPPED IN PEPPERS

This is a hearty entrée that can also be served (in smaller portions, obviously) as an appetizer. Peppers and sausage are one of the all-time great pairings!

SERVES 4

2 bell peppers
2 slices country-style bread
Parsley leaves to taste
Parmesan to taste
Extra-virgin olive oil for moistening topping and sautéing
14 ounces (400 grams) sausages, roughly chopped
1/2 cup (100 milliliters) white wine
Minced fresh rosemary leaves to taste
Salt to taste

Preheat a convection oven to 400° F (200° C). Place the bell peppers in a pan (don't oil the peppers or the pan) and roast them, turning occasionally, until they are dark on all sides, about 20 minutes. Set aside to cool. When the peppers are cool enough to handle, peel them and cut them into strips. In a food processor fitted with the metal blade, grind the bread, parsley, and Parmesan to make a topping. Drizzle with a little oil and process to combine. Brown the sausages in a pan in a small amount of oil, then add the wine and cook until the wine has evaporated and the sausages are cooked through. Wrap the sausages in the pepper strips and arrange them on a parchment-lined baking pan. Sprinkle with the breadcrumb mixture, rosemary, and a pinch of salt and bake until the topping is golden and crisp, about 10 minutes. Serve hot.

« SALSICCIA E FAGIOLI »
SAUSAGES AND BEANS

This stew is a snap to make. It literally couldn't be faster or easier. Aside from the sausages, you probably have all the ingredients on hand.

SERVES 4

1 clove garlic
1 yellow onion, diced
Extra-virgin olive oil for sautéing
14 ounces (400 grams) sausages, roughly chopped
1 cup (250 milliliters) tomato puree
1 cup (250 milliliters) red wine
1 (15-ounce/500-gram) can borlotti beans, rinsed and drained
Salt to taste
Minced fresh rosemary leaves to taste
Ground cayenne pepper to taste

In a pot, sauté the garlic and the onion in a small amount of oil, tilting the pot to keep them submerged in the oil. Add the sausages and brown them lightly, then add the tomato puree. Stir in the wine and the beans and season with salt, rosemary, and cayenne pepper. Cook at a simmer, stirring occasionally, for 20 minutes. Serve hot.

« SALSICCIA E UVA »
SAUSAGES AND GRAPES

The sweet-and-sour sauce counterbalances the heaviness of the meat. Sometimes I cut the sausages into bite-sized pieces and thread the pieces on toothpicks with a grape atop each one. It's perfect as an appetizer with cocktails.

SERVES 4

10 ounces (300 grams) sausage, roughly chopped
Extra-virgin olive oil for sautéing

Salt to taste
1/2 cup (100 milliliters) apple cider vinegar
Minced fresh rosemary leaves to taste
2 to 4 ounces (60 to 100 grams) seedless green grapes, halved if large

Sauté the sausages in a small amount of oil in a pan until browned, about 4 minutes. Season with salt and add the vinegar and rosemary. Cover and cook over medium heat for 4 additional minutes. Add the grapes to the pan and cook over high heat until the grapes have softened and the sausages are cooked through, an additional 4 to 5 minutes. Serve immediately.

Note: Leftover sausages and grapes don't really go with pasta, but they're delicious over rice. Boil some short-grain rice in abundant salted water (cooking it as if it were pasta), then drain and toss it in a pan over medium heat with the leftover sausages and grapes.

« CICERCHIE CON SALSICCE »
CICERCHIE BEANS WITH SAUSAGE

Cicerchie are irregularly shaped beans that taste something like chickpeas. I'll admit, I'd never even heard of them until Daniele Baroni mentioned this dish to me and insisted that I make it on the show. Serve this with toasted pieces of crusty bread.

SERVES 4 TO 6

2 cups (400 grams) dried cicerchie beans
3 1/2 ounces (100 grams) frozen mirepoix (minced carrots, onion, and
    celery)
Extra-virgin olive oil for sautéing and drizzling
14 ounces (400 grams) sausages
2 tomatoes, chopped
1 tablespoon tomato paste
Minced fresh rosemary leaves to taste
Salt to taste

Soak the cicerchie beans overnight in cold water to cover. Bring a pot of unsalted water to a boil. Drain the beans and boil until soft, about 2 hours. When the beans are ready, cook the mirepoix in a pot in a small amount of oil. Remove the casings from the sausages and break them into the pot by hand. Add the tomatoes and the cooked cicerchie. Cook, stirring frequently, for about 3 minutes. Add the tomato paste and rosemary, season with salt, and cook until warmed through, about 10 minutes more. Transfer to a serving bowl, drizzle with a little additional oil, and serve immediately.

« PADELLATA DI COTECHINO E LENTICCHIE »
COTECHINO SAUSAGE AND LENTILS

Cotechino is a fresh pork sausage from Modena that is very flavorful. You can find it in Italian specialty stores. Eating this traditional dish on New Year's Day is supposed to help you grow rich in the coming year—it's always worth a try! This can be made in advance, though you may need to add a little more broth and/or water to the lentils when you reheat them.

SERVES 4 TO 6

1 yellow onion, diced
Extra-virgin olive oil for sautéing
2 (15-ounce/500-gram) cans lentils, rinsed and drained
1 heaping tablespoon tomato paste
$1/2$ cup (100 milliliters) vegetable broth (broth made with a bouillon cube
    is fine)
Salt to taste
Minced fresh rosemary leaves
1 cotechino sausage, cooked according to package instructions

In a pot, sauté the onion in a small amount of oil. Add the lentils, tomato paste, broth, $1/2$ cup water, salt, and rosemary. Cook, covered, over low heat until the liquid has reduced so that the dish is moist but not brothy. Remove the casing from the cotechino and cut it into $1/2$-inch slices. Add the cotechino slices to the pot with the lentils and heat through.

Note: If you have leftover cotechino, use it to make pasta. To serve 4, you'll need 3 small zucchini, 1 leek, and about $^2/_3$ of a package of "straw and hay" pasta, which consists of spinach noodles and egg noodles combined. Cut the cotechino into dice. Slice the leek and the zucchini and sauté them in a pan with a generous amount of olive oil and a little salt. Add the diced cotechino. Cook the pasta in boiling salted water (fresh pasta cooks quickly) and add about $^1/_2$ cup pasta cooking water to the pan with the cotechino. Cook for a minute or so, then drain the pasta and add that to the pan as well. Toss energetically over high heat for no more than 1 minute, then transfer to a serving bowl. Garnish with basil leaves and serve immediately.

« COTECHINO IN CROSTA CON SALSA DI MELE »
COTECHINO SAUSAGE EN CROÛTE WITH A SAUCE OF APPLES

Here's a new twist on an old tradition. This isn't wrapped in a crisp crust, but instead is like a sausage baked inside a loaf of bread. I had to try the recipe three times before I got it just right. I like to serve this as part of a New Year's Eve buffet.

SERVES 4

1 cotechino sausage, cooked according to package instructions
Unbleached all-purpose flour for work surface
9 to 11 ounces (250 to 300 grams) readymade bread dough (thawed if
    frozen)
$^1/_4$ cup tightly packed baby spinach leaves
1 egg yolk
4 to 5 (500 grams) apples, peeled, cored, and diced
1 tablespoon sugar
Juice of $^1/_2$ lemon
$^1/_2$ cinnamon stick
2 tablespoons (30 grams) unsalted butter, cut into pieces
Salt to taste

Preheat the oven to 400°F (200°C). Remove the casing from the cotechino. On a lightly floured work surface, roll out the bread dough into a rough rectangle. Arrange the spinach on top of the dough and set the cotechino in the center. Wrap the cotechino

COTECHINO SAUSAGE EN CROUTE WITH A SAUCE OF APPLES

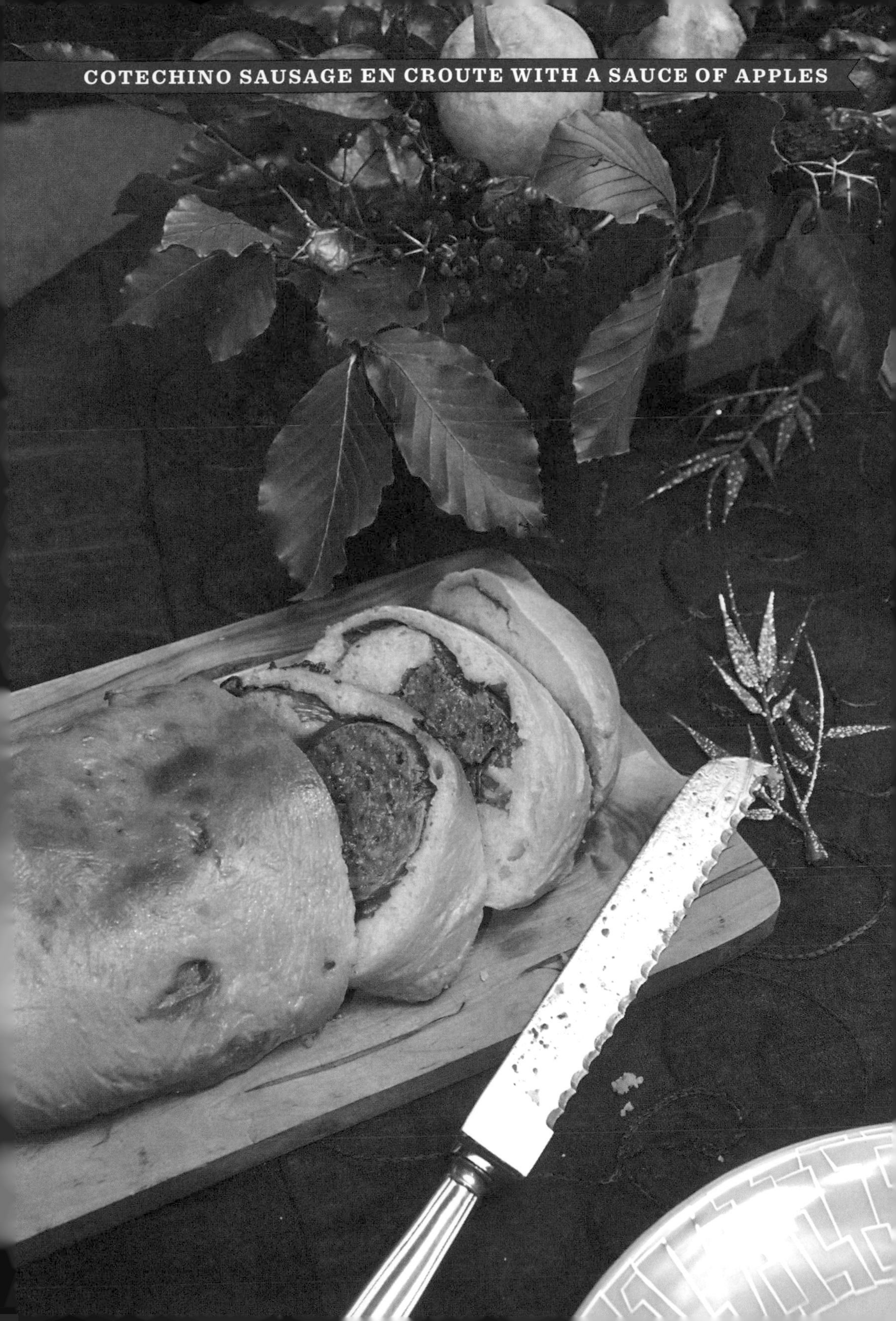

in the dough, pinching the edges together and sealing the ends. Place the loaf on a parchment-lined jelly-roll pan. Beat the egg yolk with about 1 tablespoon water and brush the outside of the loaf with it. Bake until the dough is golden, about 30 minutes.

To prepare the sauce, combine the apples, sugar, lemon juice, and cinnamon stick in a pot. Add $1/2$ cup water and simmer for 15 minutes. Remove from heat and whisk in the butter until melted. Remove and discard the cinnamon stick. To serve, slice the cotechino bread and pass the sauce on the side.

« FILLETTI DI PLATESSA CROCCANTI »
CRISPY FISH FILLETS

This recipe uses fillets of plaice, a mild white fish, but flounder is easier to find in the United States and makes a fine substitute. Be sure to use quick-cooking polenta and not the long-cooking kind.

SERVES 4

1 cup (200 grams) quick-cooking polenta
Minced leaves of 1 sprig rosemary
$1/4$ teaspoon minced garlic
1 tablespoon grated Parmesan
Salt to taste
Extra-virgin olive oil for pan-frying
14 ounces (400 grams) frozen plaice or other thin fish fillets, such as
     flounder, thawed
1 large egg, lightly beaten
Lettuce for garnish

In a wide shallow bowl, such as a soup plate, mix together the quick-cooking polenta, rosemary, garlic, Parmesan, and a little salt. Heat a generous amount of oil in a pan over medium heat. Dredge the fish fillets first in the egg and then in the polenta mixture, pressing the coating into the fish by hand. Fry the fish in the oil until crisp and browned, turning once. Remove to paper towels to drain briefly, then serve the fish fillets on a bed of lettuce.

« ORATA NASCOSTA »
"HIDDEN" DORADE

This super-practical dish is main course and side dish in one—the fish is "hidden" under a vegetable crust. You can use any type of medium-thick fish fillet you like for this—sea bass is also nice. Thanks to my dear friend Rosa Prinzivalli for her useful suggestions. Pachino tomatoes are a variety of very large cherry tomato—use them if you can find them.

SERVES 4 TO 6

Extra-virgin olive oil for oiling pan and drizzling
6 dorade fillets or other medium-thick fish fillets, skin removed
2 potatoes, peeled and sliced into thin rounds
Salt to taste
2 zucchini, sliced into thin rounds
5 pachino or plum tomatoes, halved
1/4 cup (25 grams) breadcrumbs
1/4 cup (25 grams) grated Parmesan
Fresh basil leaves for garnish

Preheat a convection oven to 350° F (180° C). Line a baking dish with parchment paper, then oil the parchment. Use fish bone tweezers to remove any bones left in the fillets. Arrange the fillets in a single layer in the baking dish. Arrange the potato slices around the fish, overlapping them slightly like shingles. Lightly salt the fish and then arrange the zucchini slices on top of the fish in rows, overlapping them slightly like shingles. Scatter the tomatoes around the fish. Salt the vegetables and then sprinkle with breadcrumbs and Parmesan. Drizzle a little additional oil over the fish and vegetables and bake until the vegetables are tender and the fish is cooked through, 15 to 20 minutes. Garnish with basil leaves and serve.

« FILLETTO DI ORATA IN CROSTA DI ZUCCHINE »
DORADE FILLET IN ZUCCHINI CRUST

Zucchini makes a wonderful crust on all kinds of fish. Feel free to substitute other types of fish if you can't find dorade, which is a type of sea bream.

SERVES 2

2 dorade fillets or other medium-thick fish fillets
Extra-virgin olive oil for brushing fillets and drizzling
Salt to taste
1 zucchini
$\frac{1}{2}$ shallot, thinly sliced
Minced fresh thyme or rosemary leaves to taste
Pepper to taste

Preheat a convection oven to 400° F (200° C). Line a baking pan with parchment paper. Set the fillets skin-side down in the pan. Brush the fillets with oil and season with salt. Grate the zucchini on the large holes of a four-sided box grater. In a small bowl, toss the zucchini with the shallot and thyme or rosemary. Season with salt and pepper. Cover the fillets entirely with the zucchini mixture. Drizzle with a little olive oil and bake until the fish is cooked through and the zucchini is soft, about 25 minutes. Run under the broiler to brown the top, about 2 minutes, and serve immediately.

« ORATA AL CARTOCCIO »
DORADE IN FOIL

Cooking in foil is a wonderful technique to use with fish, as it is very forgiving. Not to mention that the pan hardly gets dirty. My mother taught me how to do this, but as clever as she is in the kitchen, even she doesn't have a way around the one inconvenient task involved: filleting the fish once it's cooked.

MAKES 1 WHOLE FISH, 2 TO 4 SERVINGS

1 dorade or other delicate white-fleshed fish, gutted and scaled, about 1/2
    pound (250 grams)
1 clove garlic, sliced
1 tablespoon capers, rinsed and drained
1 tablespoon pitted black olives
1 slice lemon
1 sprig rosemary
1/2 red onion, sliced into rings
1 teaspoon green peppercorns in brine, rinsed and drained
Salt to taste
Extra-virgin olive oil for drizzling
1/2 cup (100 milliters) white wine

Preheat the oven to 350° F (180° C). Place a large rectangle of aluminum foil on a jelly-roll pan or other baking pan. In the center of the foil, place a slightly smaller piece of parchment paper. Fold up the perimeter of the foil. Place the fish in the center of the parchment. Place about 1/2 of the garlic inside the fish and the other half on top. Do the same with the capers and olives. Cut the lemon slice in half and place 1/2 inside the fish and the other 1/2 on top. Sprinkle with the rosemary, onion, peppercorns, salt, a drizzle of oil, and the wine. Close up the foil, twisting the ends like a candy wrapper. Be sure that the top of the foil is tented over the fish and not touching it. Bake for about 25 minutes. Open the foil at the table, fillet the fish, and serve immediately.

« CARTOCCIO DI ORATA E SALMONE »
DORADE AND SALMON IN FOIL WITH VEGETABLES

Your guests are guaranteed to ooh and aah with pleasure when they open these packets and get a whiff of delicate fish and vegetables. Another delightful recipe from Lorenzo Boni.

SERVES 4

1 zucchini, cut into julienne
1 leek, cut into julienne
1 carrot, cut into julienne

1 clove garlic, minced

14 ounces (400 grams) salmon fillet, cut into 8 strips

14 ounces (400 grams) dorade fillet or other medium-thick white fish
    fillet, cut into 8 strips

Salt and pepper to taste

8 fresh basil leaves

8 cherry tomatoes, halved

Extra-virgin olive oil for drizzling

Preheat the oven to 400° F to 425° F (200° C to 220° C). Tear off 4 large sheets of alumi-num foil. In the center of each piece of foil, place a slightly smaller piece of parchment paper. In a small bowl, toss the zucchini, leek, carrot, and garlic to combine. Place $1/8$ of the zucchini mixture on each piece of parchment. Top each portion with 2 pieces of the salmon and 2 pieces of the dorade in a single layer (alternate slices for the prettiest effect). Distribute the remaining zucchini mixture on top of the fish. Season with salt and pepper and add 2 basil leaves on top of each. Place 4 tomato halves in a row on top of each portion. Salt again and drizzle some oil on each. Fold the foil and crimp togeth-er the edges to seal each packet well. Bake until the packets puff up with steam, 15 to 20 minutes. Bring the packets to the table still closed and allow guests to open their own.

« INVOLTINI DI ENRICA »
ENRICA'S DORADE ROLLS

Easiest dish in the world: Just coat fish fillets in some breadcrumbs. Your family will gobble them up just as fast as you can make them. Matilde, Eleonora, and their friend Elisa are the record holders in my house. Fabio doesn't even get a chance to eat any. Enrica has given me many good ideas like this one over the years. If you can find fish labeled "for carpaccio" in your grocery store, buy it and use it in this recipe. Other-wise, pound the fillets yourself, or just use thicker fillets and bake them a little longer.

SERVES 2 TO 3

$1/4$ cup (50 milliliters) extra-virgin olive oil, plus more for oiling pan and
    drizzling

$1/2$ cup (50 grams) breadcrumbs

1 tablespoon capers, rinsed and drained
2 tablespoons grated Parmesan
Leaves of 1 sprig parsley
10 ounces (300 grams) dorade fillet or other white fish fillet, sliced or
    pounded very thin

Preheat a convection oven to 350° F (180° C). Lightly oil a baking pan and set aside. In a food processor fitted with the metal blade or a blender, process the breadcrumbs with the capers, Parmesan, parsley, and 1/4 cup (50 milliliters) oil. If the mixture looks dry, add a little more oil. Place the fillet on a work surface. Cut into smaller portions if necessary. Spread a portion of the breadcrumb mixture in a thin layer on top of each piece of fillet. Roll up each piece jelly-roll style and place in the prepared pan seam-side down. (Fit them in snugly and you shouldn't need toothpicks to keep them closed.) Sprinkle any remaining breadcrumb mixture on top and drizzle with a little additional oil. Bake until the fish is opaque and the breadcrumbs are golden, about 5 minutes (but a little longer if your fillets are thicker). Serve immediately.

« ORATA IN CROSTA »
DORADE EN CROÛTE

I have so much fun making this dish and crafting the gills, tail, eyes, and scales of the fish with dough. My children are harsh critics, though, and always make fun of my artistic skills. Nobody complains about the taste, however. Serve with a simple green salad.

SERVES 4

Leaves of 1 bunch parsley
1 shallot
1/2 bulb fennel
1 tablespoon breadcrumbs
2 packages readymade short-crust pastry dough
Salt and pepper to taste
4 dorade fillets
1 large egg

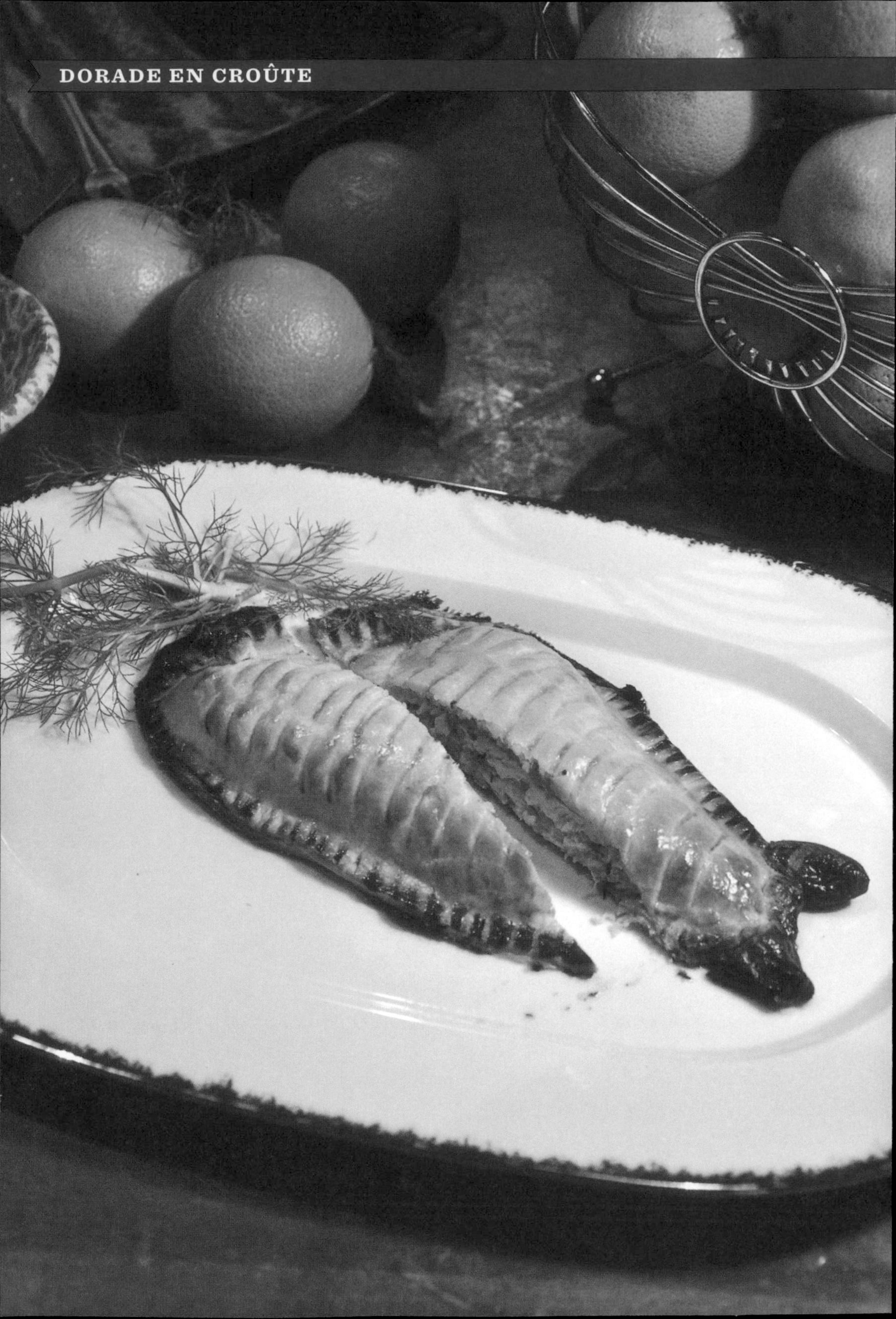
DORADE EN CROÛTE

Preheat the oven to 350° F (180° C). Mince the parsley, shallot, and fennel together and combine with the breadcrumbs in a bowl. Divide each sheet of pastry dough into 2 equal pieces so that you have 4 sheets total. Lightly salt and pepper the fillets and run your hands over them to check for any bones. Tweeze out and discard any that you find. Arrange 2 fillets on 2 of the pieces of pastry dough, skin down. Cover each one with the breadcrumb mixture. Place the remaining 2 fillets on top of the bread-crumb mixture, skin up. Place the remaining 2 pieces of pastry dough on top of the fillets and press the edges together by hand. Trim away any excess dough with a knife (reserve a little to make the eyes) to form the outline of 2 fish. Press all around the edge of the pastry dough with a fork to create a decorative edge. Use a spoon to make the scales. Roll a little of the excess dough into 2 eyes, moisten them, and press them into place. Lightly beat the egg with 2 tablespoons water and brush the outside of the pastry dough all over with the egg wash. Bake until the pastry is golden brown, 25 to 30 minutes. Serve hot.

« BRANZINO ARROTOLATO CON SALSA DI PEPERONE »
SEA BASS IN BELL PEPPER SAUCE

Guaranteed to impress, this dish looks so much more complicated than it is. Substitute any kind of fish fillet for the sea bass, but I do like the way its delicate flavor plays off of the pepper sauce. If you can find fish labeled as "for carpaccio" in your grocery store, buy it and use it in this recipe. Otherwise, thinly slice or pound the fillets yourself.

SERVES 4

1 bell pepper
Extra-virgin olive oil for sauce
Salt to taste
1 1/3 pounds (600 grams) sea bass fillet or other white fish fillet, sliced or
    pounded very thin
Breadcrumbs for coating
Grated Parmesan to taste
3 bay leaves

Preheat the oven to 400°F (200°C). Line a baking dish with parchment paper and set aside. Roast the bell pepper until it is dark on all sides, about 20 minutes. Set aside to cool. Lower the oven temperature to 350° F (180° C). When the pepper is cool enough to handle, peel it and chop it roughly. Place the pepper in a food processor fitted with the metal blade or a blender with a drizzle of olive oil and some salt. Process until smooth.

Meanwhile, cut the fish into smaller portions if necessary. Combine the breadcrumbs and grated Parmesan and press the mixture against the fish on both sides. Roll up the fish and place the rolls in the prepared baking dish, seam side down. (Fit them in the dish snugly and you won't need toothpicks to keep them closed.) Intersperse the bay leaves between the rolls and bake until the fish is opaque, 4 to 5 minutes. Remove and discard the bay leaves and serve the fish immediately with the pepper sauce.

« BOCCONCINI DI PESCE SPADA E MOZZARELLA »
SWORDFISH AND MOZZARELLA BITES

This finger food entrée is perfect for a buffet. If you prefer, use tuna in place of the swordfish. To guard against overcooking the swordfish, toss the cubes of fish in a pan over high heat, then place them in an oven that has been heated and then turned off to finish them. It's most energy efficient to prepare this dish when you've been baking or roasting something else and the oven is still warm.

SERVES 6

7 ounces (200 grams) swordfish in 2 thick slices
Extra-virgin olive oil for sautéing
Coarse salt to taste
2 fresh mozzarella balls, 8 ounces (225 grams)
Fresh basil leaves to taste

If necessary, preheat the oven to 350° F (175° C), then turn it off. Cut the swordfish into cubes. Coat a pan with a small amount of oil and scatter some coarse salt in the pan. Cook the fish pieces over high heat for 2 minutes, turning with tongs, so that they are browned on the outside but not cooked through. Cut the mozzarella into cubes the same size as the swordfish pieces. Thread 1 piece of swordfish and 1 piece of mozzarella on toothpicks. Place the toothpicks in a baking pan and put the pan in the warm oven. Allow to rest in the oven until the swordfish is cooked through and the mozzarella has softened without melting, about 5 minutes (or longer if you want to keep the bites warm). Garnish each toothpick with a small basil leaf or part of a large basil leaf and serve immediately.

« INVOLTINI DI PESCE SPADA E SCAMORZA »
SWORDFISH AND SCAMORZA ROLLS

I first tasted these delicious swordfish rolls in Capri during the second honeymoon that Fabio and I took after being married for a dozen years. It was a romantic time away from our kids, filled with sun, sea, and candlelight dinners. Every time I make these rolls, I feel like I'm back in Capri. But then one of my kids gets into some mischief and I'm brought back to reality!

SERVES 4

12 ounces (350 grams) swordfish, sliced very thinly
3 1/2 to 5 ounces (100 to 150 grams) smoked scamorza, cut into small
    rectangles
Extra-virgin olive oil for drizzling and sautéing
Breadcrumbs for dusting
6 bay leaves
Salt to taste

Cut the slices of swordfish into 3-inch squares. Place a rectangle of scamorza on each. Roll up the squares and close them with toothpicks. Drizzle a little oil over the rolls and dust them lightly with breadcrumbs. Lightly oil a nonstick pan and heat it over medium heat. Add the swordfish rolls and bay leaves and cook the rolls, turning them with tongs, until the fish is opaque and lightly browned. Season and serve immediately.

« PESCE SPADA CHE SI CREDE UN OSSOBUCO »
SWORDFISH COOKED OSSO BUCO–STYLE

Serve these swordfish steaks—which look exactly like ossobuco veal shanks—to your guests and watch the expressions on their faces as they bite into them. The very creative chef Francesco Gotti taught me to make these.

SERVES 2

1 small potato
Salt to taste
1 1/2 cloves garlic
1/4 cup frozen mirepoix (minced carrots, onion, and celery)
Extra-virgin olive oil for sautéing
Unsalted butter for sautéing and finishing
2 thick slices swordfish steak
Unbleached all-purpose flour for dredging
1/2 cup (100 milliliters) white wine
1/2 cup (100 milliliters) tomato puree
1 tablespoon minced parsley
Grated zest of 1/2 lemon

Peel the potato, cut it in half, and scoop out the center of each half to create the "bone" of the ossobuco. Bring a small pot of salted water to a boil and boil the potato until tender. Drain and set aside. Mince 1 clove garlic. In a large pan, sauté the mirepoix and the minced garlic in oil and butter. Dredge the swordfish in flour and add to the pan. Brown both sides, salt, then add the wine to the pan and allow it to evaporate. Remove 2 tablespoons of the mirepoix from the pan and set aside. Add the tomato puree to the pan and cook until reduced into a sauce. Meanwhile, place the reserved mirepoix in the hollowed out potato halves. Remove the swordfish from the pan and cut out a circle in each slice. Insert the potato "bones" with the mirepoix "marrow." For the gremolata, mince the parsley, remaining 1/2 clove garlic, and lemon zest together. Return the swordfish to the pan, dot with a little additional butter, and heat through. Sprinkle with the gremolata and serve immediately.

« TONNO IN ONDA »
TUNA WITH OLIVES AND PESTO

Luca Telese, the host of the show *In Onda*, provided this recipe. It's his son's favorite.

SERVES 2

2 pieces of tuna, about 7 ounces (200 grams) each
Extra-virgin olive oil for sautéing
Salt to taste
3 tablespoons (50 grams) readymade pesto
3 tablespoons breadcrumbs, lightly toasted
1 tablespoon pitted green olives, minced
Fresh basil leaves for garnish

Sauté the tuna in a small amount of oil. Turn to brown on both sides and season lightly with salt. Transfer the cooked tuna to individual plates. Spread the pesto on top of the tuna. Sprinkle with the breadcrumbs and then the minced olives. Garnish with fresh basil leaves and serve immediately.

« POLPETTINE DI MIGUEL »
MIGUEL'S TUNA MEATBALLS

Miguel is the sous chef on my show. He's as good at making desserts as he is at preparing savory dishes like these tuna meatballs. You can also make these in a smaller size and serve them as an appetizer.

SERVES 4

1 baguette (even better if slightly stale)
1 clove garlic
Extra-virgin olive oil for brushing on bread
1 (5-ounce/150-gram) can tuna in oil, drained
2/3 cup (150 grams) ricotta
Parsley leaves to taste

Salt and pepper to taste
2 large eggs, lightly beaten
Vegetable oil for pan-frying

Cut the baguette into slices. Rub the garlic clove against the bread. Arrange the bread on a pan, brush with olive oil, and toast until crisp. (A toaster oven is ideal for this.) Place the toasted bread in a food processor fitted with the metal blade and process until fine. Remove the breadcrumbs and set aside. (No need to clean out the work bowl.) Add the tuna, ricotta, parsley, and some salt and pepper to the food processor and process until smooth. Transfer to a bowl and gradually stir in the breadcrumbs until the mixture clumps together to form balls when you roll it between your palms. Form the mixture into balls. Heat a generous amount of vegetable oil in a pan. Dredge the tuna balls first in the egg and then in the remaining breadcrumb mixture and fry until browned. Serve immediately.

« TEGAME DI ACCIUGHE »
ANCHOVY AND POTATO CASSEROLE

Potatoes, onions, anchovies, and tomatoes are the taste of summer at the beach. This can be served either room temperature or cold—perfect after you've spent a morning playing in the waves.

SERVES 4 TO 6

Extra-virgin olive oil for oiling pan
2 pounds (1 kilogram potatoes), peeled and thinly sliced
1 yellow onion, sliced
Salt to taste
Fresh oregano leaves to taste
10 ounces (300 grams) fresh anchovies, gutted and boned
2 to 3 tomatoes, sliced
Minced parsley leaves to taste
1 clove garlic, minced
1/2 cup (100 milliliters) white wine

Preheat the oven to 350° F (180° C). Lightly oil a baking pan and set aside. Bring a pot of salted water to a boil and parboil the potato slices. In the prepared pan, create layers in this order from the bottom up: onion, salt, potatoes, oregano, anchovies, tomatoes, additional salt. Sprinkle with the parsley and garlic. Gently pour in the wine and $1/2$ cup (100 milliliters) water and bake for 30 minutes. Serve warm or cold.

« FRITTATA DI ALICI »
ANCHOVY FRITTATA

You need only a few minutes to prepare this rustic frittata, unless, of course, you gut and bone the fish yourself. If you are not confident about flipping the frittata, simply run the pan under the broiler for a few minutes to set the top.

SERVES 4

Extra-virgin olive oil for sautéing
12 ounces (350 grams) fresh anchovies, gutted and boned
1 clove garlic, minced
Minced parsley leaves to taste
5 large eggs
Salt to taste
1 tablespoon readymade pesto

Heat a small amount of olive oil in a pan and sauté the anchovies and garlic. Add the parsley to the pan. Beat the eggs with a little salt and the pesto, then pour the egg mixture into the pan and use a heatproof spatula to push in the edges as they cook, tilting the pan so that the indents are then filled in with uncooked egg. When the bottom is set and only the center of the frittata remains wet, let it cook over low heat undisturbed until the underside is nicely browned, about 3 minutes. Flip the frittata and cook the other side until it is nicely browned, about 3 minutes more. Serve hot or at room temperature.

« TORTINO DI ALICI »
ANCHOVY TART

Here is yet another dish that can be prepared in advance and served at room temperature. Be sure to slice the potatoes very thin so that they will be finished cooking along with the rest of the ingredients.

$1/4$ cup plus 2 tablespoons extra-virgin olive oil, plus more for oiling pan
Salt to taste
1 pound (500 grams) potatoes, peeled and thinly sliced
Leaves of 1 sprig parsley
Fresh mint leaves to taste (optional)
$1/2$ clove garlic
1 cup (100 grams) breadcrumbs
1 tablespoon capers, rinsed and drained
Pepper to taste
1 pound (500 grams) fresh anchovy fillets
3 tablespoons grated Parmesan

Preheat the oven to 350° F (180° C). Oil a baking pan and set aside. Bring a pot of salted water to a boil and cook the potatoes for 5 minutes, then drain. Mince together the parsley, mint, if using, garlic, breadcrumbs, and capers. (You can do this in a food processor fitted with the metal blade.) Stir in the olive oil and season with salt and pepper. Arrange a layer of potatoes in the bottom of the prepared pan. Top with some of the breadcrumb mixture. Arrange a layer of anchovies on top of that and cover again with some of the breadcrumbs. Continue alternating layers of potatoes and anchovies with the breadcrumb mixture in between until you have finished the ingredients. Top with the Parmesan. Pour a small amount of water in at the edge of the baking pan. Bake until the top is browned and crisp and the potatoes are baked through, about 15 minutes. Serve hot or at room temperature.

« QUICHE MOZZARELLA E ALICI »
MOZZARELLA AND ANCHOVY QUICHE

Mild mozzarella and sharply flavored anchovies are a perfect match. A layer of bread-crumbs on top of the crust stops the cheese from getting it overly wet and soggy.

MAKES 1 PIE, ABOUT 8 SLICES

1 package puff pastry
1/4 cup (50 milliliters) breadcrumbs
14 ounces (400 grams) mozzarella, sliced
Anchovy fillets in olive oil or salt, *quanto basta,* rinsed and boned
1 large egg
1/4 cup (50 milliliters) whole milk

Preheat the oven to 350° F (180° C). Roll out the puff pastry and line a tart pan with it, leaving the parchment paper underneath (between the pastry and the dish). Pierce with a fork. Sprinkle with the breadcrumbs. Top with the mozzarella and the ancho-vies. Beat the egg with the milk and pour over the anchovies. Bake until set, about 35 minutes. If the top begins to brown too much before the filling is set, cover with alu-minum foil. Serve hot or at room temperature.

« SARDE A BECCAFICO INFILZATE »
SKEWERS OF SICILIAN FRIED SARDINE BALLS

Bet you can't eat just one of these—they're as irresistible as potato chips. Don't make these too far in advance, since they should be warm when you serve them.

SERVES 4 TO 6

12 ounces (350 grams) sardines, gutted and boned
3 tablespoons breadcrumbs, plus more if necessary
2 tablespoons grated mild pecorino
1 tablespoon raisins
Salt to taste

1 tablespoon pine nuts
2 large eggs, lightly beaten
Vegetable oil for deep frying
Bay leaves for garnish

Mince the sardines and place them in a bowl with the breadcrumbs, pecorino, raisins, a little salt, and the pine nuts. Add the eggs and stir to combine. If the mixture is too loose to form into balls, gradually add breadcrumbs in small amounts until it's firm enough. Shape the mixture into balls the size of ping-pong balls. Heat enough oil in a pan to cover the balls, then deep-fry them. Transfer to paper towels to drain. Thread 2 balls onto a skewer with a bay leaf in between them. Repeat with remaining fried balls. Serve warm.

« GAMBERONI IN CROSTA DI BASILICO »
SHRIMP IN A BASIL CRUST

A light dish like this one is wonderful as one course in a multi-course dinner party. Of course, you can also serve this as a heartier dish for two. The scent of the basil is fantastic.

SERVES 4 TO 6

1 roll (preferably stale)
$1/4$ cup tightly packed basil leaves
1 egg white
7 jumbo shrimp, shelled and deveined, heads and tails intact
Extra-virgin olive oil for drizzling and sauce
$3/4$ cup (170 grams) nonfat yogurt
1 tablespoon capers, minced
4 to 5 cherry tomatoes, minced
Salt to taste

Preheat a convection oven to 350° F (180° C). Line a jelly-roll pan with parchment paper and set aside. Mince the roll and the basil together. (A food processor fitted with the metal blade is ideal for this.) Lightly beat the egg white. Dredge the shrimp in the egg white and then in the breadcrumb mixture, pressing to help it adhere. Place the shrimp on the prepared pan, drizzle with a little olive oil, and bake until opaque, about 10 minutes. While the shrimp are baking, combine the yogurt, capers, tomatoes, salt, and a small amount of olive oil. Serve the shrimp hot with the sauce on the side.

« CAPESANTE GRATINATE CON CREMA DI CARCIOFI »
SCALLOPS WITH ARTICHOKE PUREE

I love scallops, but I'm the only one in my family who does. The first time I made this dish, I ate three portions. Afraid I wouldn't be able to stop myself from polishing off the whole lot of them, I brought the rest upstairs to our neighbors, Matteo and Giulia. They immediately popped the cork on a bottle of champagne, the perfect accompaniment. It is nearly impossible to find scallops in the shells in the United States, but you can purchase empty scallop shells to use for serving these and reuse them for other scallop dishes as well. You can also use ramekins.

SERVES 6

1 clove garlic
Leaves of 1 sprig parsley
Salt to taste
6 baby artichokes
Extra-virgin olive oil for pan and drizzling
6 scallops and 6 scallop shells
Breadcrumbs for topping
Grated Parmesan to taste

Preheat the broiler to 350° F (180° C). Place the garlic and parsley in a pot with about 1 inch (3 centimeters) water and some salt. Trim the artichokes: Working one at a time, remove any leaves from the stem, and then cut off the stem, leaving an inch or two. Pull off and discard any hard, dark-colored leaves. When you have revealed the light green portion of the artichoke, peel off any tough skin from the outside of the stem. Cut off the top of the artichoke completely. Cut the artichoke in half the long way and use the tip of a paring knife to dig out the fuzzy part in the center. Slice the cleaned artichoke into 4 wedges and drop them into the pot. Repeat with the remaining artichokes. Bring to a boil and then lower the heat to a simmer until the artichokes are very tender, about 20 minutes.

Transfer the artichokes and the rest of the contents of the pot to a food processor fitted with the metal blade and process until smooth. Brush a pan lightly with oil, heat over medium heat, and sear the scallops, about 2 minutes per side. Salt and set aside. Place a heaping tablespoon of the artichoke mixture in each of the scallop shells. Top with the browned scallops, one per shell. Sprinkle with the breadcrumbs and grated Parmesan and drizzle with some oil. Broil in the preheated oven until the breadcrumbs and Parmesan are browned. Serve hot.

« CAPESANTE CON CREMA DI ZUCCA »
SCALLOPS WITH SQUASH PUREE

Shellfish and creamy vegetable purees are a winning combination. If you can find scallops with the creamy pink roe still attached, buy them and use the roe as directed here. If not, the dish will still taste delicious.

SERVES 5

2 shallots, minced
2 bay leaves
3 tablespoons extra-virgin olive oil, plus more for searing
1 to 2 winter squash, such as butternut or acorn squash (about 2 $3/4$
    pounds/1 $1/3$ kilograms total), seeded, peeled, and diced
1 tablespoon vegetable broth granules (or the serving size indicated on
    the package)
Salt and pepper to taste
5 scallops, preferably with their roe
5 slices smoked pancetta or bacon

In a pot, sauté the shallots and 1 bay leaf in 3 tablespoons olive oil over very low heat for 5 minutes. Add the squash and cook, stirring occasionally, for 10 minutes. Add warm water to cover the squash by $1/2$ inch (2 centimeters) and the broth granules. Season with salt and pepper and simmer for 25 minutes. Add the scallop roe, if using, and cook for an additional 5 minutes, then remove from the heat, remove and discard the bay leaf, and puree the squash mixture. (An immersion blender is ideal.) Roll each scallop in a pancetta slice. Brush a pan with oil, place over high heat, add the remaining bay leaf to the pan, and sear the scallops in the pan, about 2 minutes per side. Transfer the squash puree to individual serving plates and top each portion with a pancetta-wrapped scallop. Serve hot.

« CALAMARI BONI »
LORENZO BONI'S CALAMARI WITH POTATOES AND MORTADELLA

Lorenzo Boni, the head chef for my television program, taught me this recipe. The mortadella in the stuffing is what makes these special.

SERVES 2 TO 4

1 potato
2 cloves garlic, sliced
Extra-virgin olive oil for sautéing
1 (15-ounce/420-milliliter) can tomato puree
Fresh basil leaves to taste, plus minced basil leaves for garnish
Salt to taste
2 slices sandwich bread, crusts removed
Whole milk, *quanto basta*
2 ounces (50 grams) mortadella
4 calamari
2 tablespoons grated Parmesan
1 large egg
Minced parsley leaves to taste
Unsalted butter for sauce
Minced fresh thyme leaves to taste

Bring a pot of water to a boil. Boil the potato until soft and then push it through a potato ricer (the peel will come off). In a large pan, sauté the garlic in a moderate amount of oil. Add the tomato puree and some basil leaves, tearing them if they are large. Season with salt and bring to a simmer. In a bowl, soak the bread in the milk until soft and then crumble. Mince the mortadella and the calamari tentacles together and add them to the bowl with the crumbled bread, Parmesan, egg, potato, and parsley. Knead by hand and then stuff the calamari bodies with this mixture. (Don't overstuff.) Close the calamari with toothpicks, if necessary, and then cook them in the tomato sauce for 25 minutes.

To serve, divide the calamari and tomato sauce among individual serving plates. In a small pan, melt some butter and add the thyme and minced basil. Cook very briefly, just until the butter is flavored with the herbs, and pour some butter sauce over each portion. Serve immediately.

« MOSCARDINI CON POMODORINI SECCHI »
BABY OCTOPUS WITH SUN-DRIED TOMATOES

This dish is a tasty and more interesting alternative to humdrum stewed baby octopus. Taggiasca olives are small black olives grown in the Liguria region. If you leave the pits in while they cook, they'll provide more flavor to the finished dish—just be sure to warn your guests!

SERVES 4

4 pounds (2 kilograms) baby octopus
3 shallots
Extra-virgin olive oil for sautéing (about 1 tablespoon)
2 whole cloves garlic, peeled
3 ounces (about 18 pieces/80 grams) sun-dried tomato halves
1 tablespoon tomato paste
2 tablespoons taggiasca olives
Minced parsley to taste
Salt to taste

Bring a pot of water to a boil and boil the baby octopus until tender, about 50 minutes. Meanwhile, thinly slice the shallots and sauté them in the olive oil with the garlic in another pot large enough to hold the octopus. Add the sun-dried tomatoes, tomato paste, and the olives and cook over low heat until most of the liquid has evaporated.

Remove the cooked octopus with a slotted spoon, reserving the cooking liquid. Drain the octopus in a colander and transfer it to the pot with the tomato mixture. Add enough of the reserved cooking water to make a soupy mixture. Sprinkle with parsley and cook, covered, for 15 minutes more. Taste and adjust salt (you may not need any if the olives are salty). Serve warm but not piping hot.

« POLPO TENERISSIMO CON CIPOLLE »
TENDER OCTOPUS WITH ONIONS

Octopus is only good if it's truly tender. This is a surefire way to make that happen. Thanks to Piera Oberti for this recipe. I like to pair this with mashed potatoes.

SERVES 4

2 small octopus
1 to 2 yellow onions, minced
Extra-virgin olive oil for drizzling
Fresh thyme leaves for garnish

Place the onion in a large pot. Add the octopus (no water or oil or anything else) and cook, covered, over very low heat, turning occasionally, for 2 hours. The octopus and the onions should release plenty of liquid, which will then evaporate, and the onions will melt and be very soft. Chop the octopus and, on a serving platter, mix the octopus pieces with the onions. Drizzle with a little oil, garnish with thyme, and serve.

« POLPO E CECI »
OCTOPUS AND CHICKPEAS

My friend Francesca always has great ideas, and this is one of them—combine octopus with chickpeas rather than the more common potatoes. If you have last-minute guests and need to stretch this to go a little further, stir in some halved cherry tomatoes as well.

SERVES 4 TO 6

1 octopus, about 2 pounds (1 kilogram)
Salt to taste
$1/2$ (15-ounce/500-gram) can chickpeas, rinsed and drained
1 bay leaf
4 green onions, thinly sliced
Minced fresh parsley to taste
Extra-virgin olive oil for dressing
Lemon juice for dressing
Pepper to taste

Bring a pot of unsalted water to a boil and add the octopus. Cook until it is easily pierced with a fork, about 1 $1/2$ hours. Let the octopus cool in the cooking water. Meanwhile, bring another pot of salted water to a boil and cook the chickpeas with the bay leaf for 10 minutes. Drain (remove and discard bay leaf) and transfer to a serving bowl. When the octopus is cool enough to handle, chop the tentacles and transfer to the serving bowl with the chickpeas. Add the onions and parsley. Dress with olive oil and lemon juice and season with salt and pepper. Serve warm or at room temperature.

« CALAMARI RIPIENI DI PATATE »
POTATO-STUFFED CALAMARI

Enjoy this light version of stuffed calamari outside on a patio on a summer night.

SERVES 4

10 ounces (300 grams) potatoes
1 $1/2$ pounds (700 grams) calamari
$1/4$ cup (50 milliliters) pitted black olives
1 clove garlic, crushed
Extra-virgin olive oil for sautéing
Minced parsley leaves to taste
Salt to taste
Grated zest of 1 lemon (optional)

Pepper to taste
1 cup (250 milliliters) white wine
$1/4$ cup diced cherry tomatoes (optional)

Bring a pot of water to a boil. Boil the potatoes until tender, then peel and crush them through a potato ricer (or peel then crush with a fork). Cut off the tentacles of the calamari and mince them. Mince the olives. In a pan, sauté the crushed garlic in a small amount of oil, then add the minced tentacles, olives, and parsley and cook until the tentacles are opaque, about 2 minutes. Transfer to a bowl and combine with the potatoes. Season with salt. Stir in lemon zest, if using. Stuff the calamari bodies with this mixture, but don't overstuff. Close the calamari with toothpicks if necessary. In a pan large enough to hold the stuffed calamari in a single layer, sauté them in a small amount of olive oil until golden, about 2 minutes. Season with salt and pepper, pour over the wine, and cook, covered, over medium-low heat for 15 minutes. After 10 minutes, add the diced cherry tomatoes if using. Garnish with parsley and serve hot.

« CODA DI ROSPO AL LIMONE E POMODORINI SECCHI »
MONKFISH WITH LEMON AND SUN-DRIED TOMATOES

The sharp flavors of lemon and sun-dried tomatoes really wake up mild monkfish.

SERVES 4

2 pounds (1 kilogram) monkfish
Extra-virgin olive oil for sautéing
1 lemon, quartered
1 clove garlic, crushed
Salt to taste
3 ounces (80 grams) sun-dried tomatoes in oil, drained and minced
1 bay leaf
1 cup (250 milliliters) white wine
$1/4$ cup fresh thyme leaves, minced

Truss the monkfish with kitchen twine to look like a pork loin. Heat a small amount of oil in a pot large enough to hold the monkfish. Sauté the monkfish, lemon quarters, and garlic. Season with salt. Add the sun-dried tomatoes, bay leaf, and wine and cook, covered, over medium heat for 15 minutes. Garnish with minced thyme and serve.

« SEPPIOLINE UNA TIRA L'ALTRA »
BAKED CUTTLEFISH

These are irresistible, and there's no reason to hold back—they're baked in the oven rather than fried. Serve these with a salad of mâche dressed simply with olive oil and salt.

SERVES 4

1 pound (500 grams) cuttlefish
1 clove garlic, crushed
Juice of 1/2 lemon
Extra-virgin olive oil for marinade
Chile pepper flakes to taste
Minced fresh oregano leaves to taste
Breadcrumbs for coating
Salt to taste

Preheat a convection oven to 400° F (200° C). Line a baking pan with parchment paper and set aside. Place the cuttlefish in a nonreactive bowl and toss with the garlic, lemon juice, and enough oil to coat and marinate in the refrigerator. In another bowl, combine the chile pepper flakes, oregano, and enough breadcrumbs to coat the cuttlefish. Season with salt and set aside. When the oven has reached the desired temperature, remove the cuttlefish from the marinade (use your hands and let them drain slightly as you lift them) and toss them with the breadcrumb mixture. Place on the prepared pan and bake until crisp, 8 to 10 minutes. Serve hot.

« VONGOLINE IN ZUPPETTA »
CLAMS WITH TOMATO AND GARLIC

Clams are a hurried cook's best friend. Serve this rustic dish as an appetizer or a main course, and encourage diners to eat with their hands. Be sure to serve lots of crusty bread for soaking up the delicious sauce.

SERVES 4

1 clove garlic
Extra-virgin olive oil for sautéing
4 cherry tomatoes, halved
1 pound (500 grams) cockles or other small clams, purged of sand and
    rinsed in several changes of water
1 cup (250 milliliters) white wine

In a large pan, sauté the garlic in a small amount of oil, tipping the pan so that it remains submerged. Add the tomatoes and clams to the pan. Add the wine, cover, and cook over high heat until the shells are open, about 5 minutes. Turn the heat to low, uncover the pan, and crush the tomatoes with a fork to release their liquid. Cook for an additional 1 minute, then serve.

« BACCALÀ IN GRATIN CON BROCCOLI PICCANTI »
BAKED SALT COD WITH SPICY BROCCOLI

Salt cod and broccoli are both robust enough in flavor to stand up to chile pepper. Adjust the amount to suit your audience, but if you have some real pepper-heads coming to dine, feel free to spice fairly heavily. You can substitute fresh cod for the salt cod—just skip the soaking process.

SERVES 4

1 3/4 pounds (800 grams) salt cod, soaked in several changes of water
    overnight or longer
2 bay leaves

CLAMS WITH TOMATO AND GARLIC

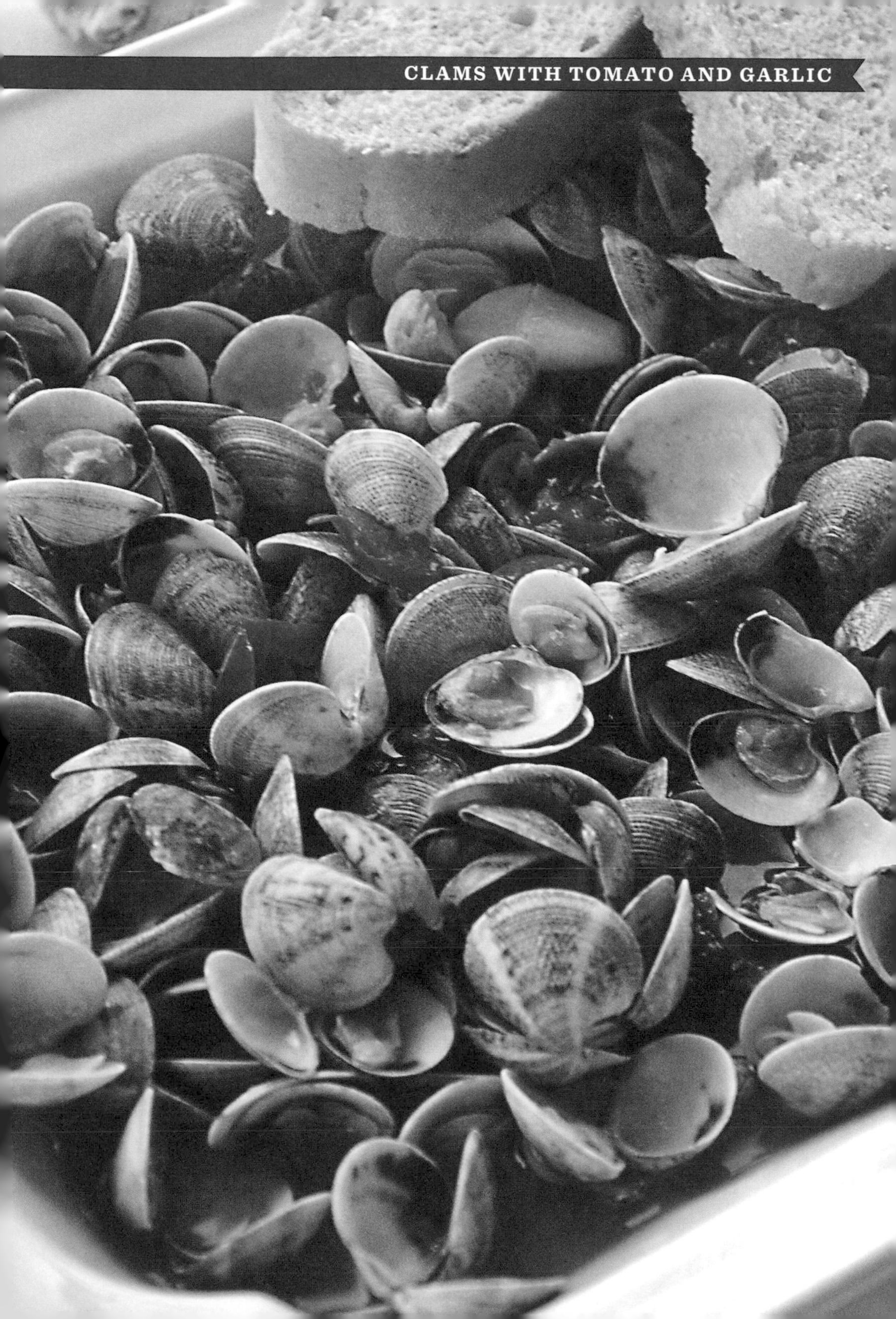

9 ounces (250 grams) broccoli
Extra-virgin olive oil for sautéing and drizzling
2 cloves garlic
2 to 3 anchovy fillets in oil, chopped
Chile pepper flakes to taste
Salt to taste
Breadcrumbs for topping

Preheat the oven to 425° F (220° C). Line a baking pan with parchment paper and set aside. Bring a pot of water to a boil and boil the soaked salt cod and the bay leaves for 10 minutes. Drain, discard the bay leaves, and cut the salt cod into slices. Steam the broccoli and then cut into florets and chop the stalks. In a large pan, heat a small amount of oil and add the garlic, anchovy fillets, and chile pepper. Add the broccoli and cook, stirring frequently, for 5 minutes. Remove and discard the garlic, season with salt, then puree the broccoli in a food processor fitted with the metal blade or a blender. Place the salt cod slices in the prepared pan. Spread the broccoli puree on top of the salt cod. Sprinkle with the breadcrumbs, then drizzle with a little additional oil. Bake until browned on top, about 5 minutes. Serve immediately.

« CAPPON MAGRO »
TRADITIONAL LIGURIAN SEAFOOD SALAD

Though *cappon magro* is a traditional dish from the coastline in Liguria, I first tasted it in Sauze d'Oulx, in the mountains of the Piedmont region. Carlo Bergamo, top-notch cook and fisherman, couldn't resist preparing this dish, even up in the mountains. I can therefore testify that this tastes good no matter where you eat it! This is impressive looking: a pyramid of fish and shellfish layered with vegetables.

SERVES 6

10 ounces (300 grams) green beans, trimmed and chopped
1/2 small head broccoli, broken into florets
2 carrots, sliced into rounds
1 zucchini, sliced into rounds
1/2 red bell pepper, sliced into rounds

1 slice bread
2 tablespoons white wine vinegar plus more for serving
2 to 3 anchovy fillets in oil
1 teaspoon capers, rinsed and drained
1 teaspoon pine nuts
Parsley leaves to taste
$1/2$ cup (100 milliliters) extra-virgin olive oil
3 dorade fillets
3 sea bass fillets
5 shrimp
3 friselle or other rusks

Bring a pot of water to a boil. Separately blanch the green beans, broccoli, carrots, zucchini, and bell pepper until slightly tender but still crisp. Toss to combine. Reserve the cooking water. In a food processor fitted with the metal blade or a blender, process the bread, 2 tablespoons white wine vinegar, anchovy fillets, capers, pine nuts, and parsley. Thin with the oil and enough of the cooking water to make a pourable sauce that's not too oily. Set aside. Steam the dorade and sea bass fillets until opaque. Boil the shrimp until opaque, about 1 minute. Briefly hold the rusks under running water and place them on a large serving platter. Sprinkle with some white wine vinegar. Arrange the fish fillets in a single layer on top of the rusks. Add a layer of the vegetables scattered on top of the fillets. Top that with some of the sauce. Continue creating layers in this order from the bottom up: fillets, vegetables, sauce. Make each layer a little smaller to form a pyramid. Arrange the shrimp decoratively on the top of the pyramid and drizzle with the remaining sauce. Serve at room temperature.

BREADS, SIDE DISHES, SALADS, AND SNACKS

« FILONE DI PANE ALLE ERBE E FETA »
BREAD WITH HERBS AND FETA

This is a sandwich bread, baked in a loaf pan.

MAKES 1 LOAF, ABOUT 4 TO 6 SERVINGS

4 cups (500 grams) unbleached all-purpose flour
1 envelope instant yeast
Salt to taste
Extra-virgin olive oil for oiling pan
3 $\frac{1}{2}$ ounces (100 grams) feta, crumbled
Snipped fresh chives to taste

In a bowl, combine the flour and yeast with a little salt. Stir in enough warm (not hot) water to create a soft dough. Knead until smooth, 5 to 10 minutes, then place in a bowl, cover with plastic wrap or a dish towel, and set aside to rise for about 1 $\frac{1}{2}$ hours.

Preheat the oven to 400° F (200° C). Oil a loaf pan and set aside. Divide the dough into 2 equal pieces and roll them into rectangles about the size of the pan or slightly smaller. Distribute the feta and chives on one rectangle of dough and cover with the other piece. Pinch the edges together to seal. Place the dough in the prepared pan, tucking the edges underneath. Bake until golden, 30 to 35 minutes. Cool in the pan on a rack for 10 minutes, then unmold and allow to cool completely before slicing.

« CIABATTINE AL ROSMARINO »
ROSEMARY CIABATTA ROLLS

These *ciabattine*—which literally means "little slippers," as these long, flat breads resemble footwear—were actually the result of an error. I was making breadsticks, but I added too much water to the dough. These are a great accompaniment to salami, prosciutto, and cheese—and proof that it pays to make mistakes.

MAKES 6 TO 8 ROLLS

2 1/2 cups (300 grams) unbleached all-purpose flour
1 1/2 teaspoons instant yeast
Leaves of 1 sprig rosemary, minced
2/3 cup (60 grams) grated Parmesan
1 tablespoon salt
1/4 cup (50 milliliters) extra-virgin olive oil

In a bowl, combine the flour, yeast, rosemary, Parmesan, and salt. Drizzle in the oil and stir to combine. Stir with a wooden spoon while adding enough warm (not hot) water to create a soft dough. Knead until smooth, about 5 minutes, then place in a bowl, cover with plastic wrap or a dish towel, and set aside to rise in a warm, draft-free place for 40 minutes.

Preheat a convection oven to 350° F (180° C). Line a jelly-roll pan with parchment paper and set aside. Cut off pieces of dough about the size of a ping pong ball and shape them into rectangles, then gently pull them until they are long and fairly flat. Set on the prepared baking sheet and bake until golden, 10 to 12 minutes.

« PANINI AL BASILICO »
BASIL ROLLS

Don't be intimidated by baking bread—it's a fairly easy process, and the results are so rewarding. Serve these with a variety of cold cuts.

SERVES 4 TO 6

4 cups (500 grams) unbleached all-purpose flour
3 tablespoons (30 grams) instant yeast
Salt to taste
Sugar to taste
2 tablespoons pine nuts
1/4 cup (50 milliliters) extra-virgin olive oil
1 cup tightly packed (50 grams) basil leaves
1 large egg, lightly beaten
1/2 cup (50 grams) grated Parmesan

In a bowl, combine the flour, yeast, salt, sugar, and pine nuts. Drizzle in the oil and stir to combine. Stir with a wooden spoon while adding enough warm (not hot) water to create a soft dough, about 1 1/4 cups (300 milliliters). Tear the basil leaves into rough pieces and add to the dough. Knead until smooth, 5 to 10 minutes.

Preheat the oven to 400°F (200°C). Cut the dough into small pieces, form the pieces into rolls, and place them on a jelly-roll pan. Cover loosely with a dishtowel and set aside to rise for 30 minutes. Brush the rolls with the egg wash and sprinkle them with the Parmesan. Bake until golden, about 20 minutes.

« CHIOCCIOLE AL GRANA »
CHEESE ROLLS

These rolls couldn't be easier to prepare, and as an added bonus, they look nice, too.

SERVES 4 TO 6

2 cups (250 grams) unbleached all-purpose flour
1 envelope instant yeast
1/2 cup (50 grams) grated Parmesan
2 teaspoons sugar
2 teaspoons salt
2 tablespoons extra-virgin olive oil

In a bowl combine the flour, yeast, Parmesan, sugar, and salt. Drizzle in the oil and stir to combine. Stir with a wooden spoon while adding enough warm (not hot) water to create a soft dough. Knead on a work surface until smooth, 5 to 10 minutes. Cut the dough into pieces and form the pieces into ropes, then roll them into spirals. Fit the spirals into a round cake pan or a springform pan. They should fit comfortably, and as they rise, they will puff up and touch each other. Cover with a dish towel or plastic wrap and set aside to rise for 1 hour. When the rolls are almost risen, preheat the oven to 350°F (180°C). When the rolls are ready, make some small cuts on the surface with a paring knife and bake until golden, about 15 minutes. Let the rolls cool in the pan briefly, then unmold, separate, and serve warm.

« PANINI PATATE E SPECK »
POTATO AND SPECK ROLLS

There are dozens of ways to liven up the bread basket on your table. Potatoes make this dough moist and fluffy, while speck makes them sing with flavor.

SERVES 4

9 ounces (250 grams) potatoes
4 cups (500 grams) unbleached all-purpose flour
1 envelope instant yeast
Salt to taste
3 $1/2$ ounces (100 grams) thickly sliced speck, diced
3 $1/2$ ounces (100 grams) smoked scamorza, diced
1 egg yolk
Extra-virgin olive oil for egg wash

Bring a pot of water to a boil. Boil the potatoes until tender, then peel and crush them through a potato ricer (or peel then crush them with a fork). Let the potatoes drop into a bowl and then add the flour, yeast, and some salt. Stir with a wooden spoon while adding enough warm (not hot) water to create a soft dough. Place the dough on a work surface and scatter the speck and scamorza on top. Knead until the dough is smooth and the speck and scamorza have been incorporated, 5 to 10 minutes. Divide the dough into rolls. Form the rolls and place them on a jelly-roll pan. Cover loosely with a dish towel and set aside to rise until they are puffy, about 2 hours. When the rolls are almost risen, preheat the oven to 425° F (220° C). When the rolls are ready, lightly beat the egg yolk with a little oil. Brush the tops with the beaten egg yolk mixture and bake until golden, 10 to 15 minutes. Serve warm.

« PANINI DI PATATE E POMODORINI SECCHI »
POTATO ROLLS WITH SUN-DRIED TOMATOES

While I maintain that bread isn't particularly difficult to make, bread dough made with potatoes is particularly forgiving. These will be moist on your first try—promise. Your friends are bound to ask where you bought these delicious rolls. They won't believe you made them.

SERVES 4 TO 6

9 ounces (250 grams) potatoes
3 1/2 cups (400 grams) unbleached all-purpose flour
3/4 cup (100 grams) bread flour
1 envelope instant yeast
3 1/2 ounces (100 grams) sun-dried tomatoes in oil, minced
3 1/2 ounces (100 grams) smoked scamorza, diced
Minced fresh thyme leaves
Salt to taste
1 egg yolk
Extra-virgin olive oil for egg wash

Bring a pot of water to a boil. Boil the potatoes until tender, then peel and crush them through a potato ricer (or peel then crush them with a fork). Let the potatoes drop into a bowl and add the all-purpose and bread flours, and the yeast. Stir with a wooden spoon while adding enough warm (not hot) water to create a soft dough. Place the dough on a work surface and knead until the dough is very smooth, with no large pieces of potato, about 10 minutes. Sprinkle with the minced tomatoes, scamorza, thyme, and a little salt (you may not need much if the tomatoes are salty). Knead until the scamorza, tomatoes, and thyme are incorporated and the salt has dissolved, an additional 4 to 5 minutes. Divide the dough into rolls. Form the rolls and place them on a jelly-roll pan. Cover loosely with a dish towel and set aside to rise until they are puffy, about 2 hours. When the rolls are almost risen, preheat the oven to 400°F (200°C). When the rolls are ready, lightly beat the egg yolk with a little oil. Brush the tops with the beaten egg yolk mixture and bake until golden, about 15 minutes. Serve warm.

« GRISSINI RIPIENI »
STUFFED BREADSTICKS

I was at the Cairo airport one day, coming back from vacation, when a nice Italian lady struck up a conversation with me. Naturally, our talk turned to recipes, and before I knew it she'd given me this excellent recipe. These are wonderful with a meal, with appetizers, or as a snack, and you really can stuff them with anything. I also like the combination of mortadella, rosemary, and onions. Let your imagination run wild.

SERVES 4

Swiss cheese to taste
1 package puff pastry
1 large egg, lightly beaten
Grated Parmesan to taste
2 to 3 thick slices salami, minced
Unbleached all-purpose flour for work surface and dough

Preheat the oven to 350° F (180° C). Grate the Swiss cheese on the large holes of a four-sided box grater and set aside. Place the puff pastry on a lightly floured work surface. Brush the top with the beaten egg, leaving a 1-inch margin on all sides. Cover the entire egg-brushed area with the grated Parmesan. Sprinkle the salami over half of the area. Sprinkle the Swiss cheese over the same half. Fold the empty half of the puff pastry over the half with the salami and cheese and seal the edges. Lightly flour the top and press gently with a rolling pin to seal and to roll out, but not too thin. Cut the puff pastry into 3/4-inch strips. Transfer 1 strip to a jelly-roll pan or cookie sheet. As you set it down, place one end on the pan or sheet and twirl the other end so that the breadstick is attractively twisted. Repeat with remaining strips. Bake for 10 minutes, turning the breadsticks over halfway through the baking time to guard against burning. Serve warm or at room temperature.

« LE PUCCE »
PUGLIESE FOCACCIA ROLLS

For years my close friend Francesca La Torre told me about these tasty little rolls filled with tomatoes, onions, and olives, but I would always forget the name of them and lose the recipes she wrote down for me. When I finally made them, I could have kicked myself for missing out on all those years due to my own flakiness.

SERVES 4

3 $^2/_3$ cups (450 grams) unbleached all-purpose flour
1 $^1/_4$ cups (150 grams) semolina flour
1 tablespoon salt, plus more to taste for the filling
1 envelope active dry yeast or instant yeast
1 teaspoon sugar
1 teaspoon honey
5 green onions, thinly sliced
$^1/_4$ cup (100 milliliters) extra-virgin olive oil
10 cherry tomatoes, halved
1 cup (200 grams) pitted taggiasca olives
Pepper to taste

In a bowl, combine the all-purpose and semolina flours with the salt. Dissolve the yeast, sugar, and honey in 2 cups (500 milliliters) warm (not hot) water. (If you prefer to use instant yeast, combine the yeast with the flour.) Add the liquid to the dry ingredients while stirring with a wooden spoon, then transfer the dough to a work surface and knead until soft and smooth, 5 to 10 minutes. Transfer the dough to a clean bowl, cover, and set aside to rise for 1 hour.

Meanwhile, sauté the onions in the olive oil over low heat until very soft and golden. Add the tomatoes and olives, season to taste with salt and pepper, and cook until the tomatoes are soft. Set aside to cool. When the dough has risen for 30 minutes, preheat the oven to 400° F to 425° F (200° C to 220° C). When the dough is completely risen, add the onion mixture and knead by hand in the bowl until the mixture is incorporated. The dough will be very wet. Drop heaping tablespoons of the dough onto a jelly-roll pan. Bake until golden, 15 to 20 minutes. Serve warm.

« FOCACCIA AI CARCIOFI CROCCANTI »
FOCACCIA WITH CRISPY ARTICHOKES

This focaccia is topped with very thinly sliced baby artichokes. Thanks to Marta Vittadini, passionate home cook and my colleague when I was a television reporter, for this recipe.

SERVES 4

Juice of 1 lemon
2 baby artichokes
Unbleached all-purpose flour for work surface
1 readymade focaccia or pizza crust
Breadcrumbs for sprinkling
2 fresh mozzarella balls, 8 ounces (225 grams), diced
Salt to taste
Extra-virgin olive oil for dressing artichokes
Pepper to taste

Preheat a convection oven to 400° F (200° C). Fill a bowl with ice water and add the lemon juice. Trim the artichokes: Working one at a time, remove any leaves from the stem, and then cut off the stem, leaving an inch or two. Pull off and discard any hard, dark-colored leaves. When you have revealed the light green portion of the artichoke, peel off any tough skin off from the outside of the stem. Cut off the top of the artichoke completely. Cut the artichoke in half the long way and use the tip of a paring knife to dig out the fuzzy part in the center. Slice the cleaned artichoke very thinly (use a mandoline if you have one) and drop the slices into the bowl with the lemon juice. Repeat with remaining artichoke.

On a lightly floured work surface, roll out the focaccia or pizza crust a little thinner. (You can skip this step if you're really in a hurry.) Transfer to a jelly-roll or pizza pan. Sprinkle breadcrumbs over the dough and distribute the mozzarella on top of the breadcrumbs. Salt to taste and bake until the bottom is golden, 15 to 20 minutes. Meanwhile, drain the artichokes and dress with oil and salt. Cut the baked dough into slices or rectangles, distribute the artichokes on top, season with pepper, and serve immediately.

« TIGELLE MODENESI »
MODENA TIGELLE FLATBREADS

Tigelle are just one of the many flatbreads made on a stovetop throughout Italy. These hail from the Modena area. They're not the flattest of flatbreads—more like an English muffin than a cracker. Traditionally, these are split in half and then filled with a spread of fatback and rosemary and served with various types of salami and prosciutto. They're a really fun addition to a rustic supper with friends and family. My friend Marco Miana shared the recipe.

SERVES 4

4 cups (500 grams) unbleached all-purpose flour
Salt to taste
1 envelope instant yeast
$1/2$ cup (100 milliliters) whole milk, at room temperature
2 tablespoons extra-virgin olive oil
2 ounces (50 grams) fatback
2 tablespoons grated Parmesan
Minced fresh rosemary leaves to taste
Unsalted butter for greasing cooking surface
Cold cuts for serving

In a bowl combine the flour, salt, and the yeast. Stir in the milk and oil and enough water to make a smooth but not sticky dough. Transfer to a work surface and knead until smooth, 5 to 10 minutes. Place the dough in a clean bowl, cover, and set aside to rise for 40 minutes.

Meanwhile, in a food processor fitted with the metal blade, process the fatback, Parmesan, and rosemary until smooth. Transfer to a small bowl or ramekin and set aside. Lightly flour the work surface and roll out the dough to about 1 inch (3 centimeters) thick. With a cookie cutter or the rim of a glass, cut out circles of dough. Reroll scraps and repeat. Heat a griddle or cast-iron pan and grease with a small amount of butter. Cook the *tigelle* until browned on both sides, cooking in batches and greasing the cooking surface with additional butter if necessary. Transfer the *tigelle* to a serving platter as they are finished and serve with the fatback spread and the cold cuts. Encourage guests to split the *tigelle* in half (or slice each one in half with a serrated knife) and serve themselves.

« CIAMBELLA RUSTICA »
SAVORY RUSTIC RING CAKE

This lovely cake not only tastes terrific, but it makes a nice centerpiece, too. Just place it on a raised cake stand, already cut into slices. Arrange something decorative in the middle and set it on the table. Prompt your guests to eat it or no one will have the nerve to dismantle your masterpiece! You can add any savory bits and pieces you like to this cake: salami, cheese, even chopped up cooked hot dogs.

SERVES 4 TO 6

Unsalted butter for coating the pan
Breadcrumbs for coating the pan
1 cup (250 milliliters) plain yogurt
1 heaping cup (100 grams) grated Parmesan
3 cups (375 grams) unbleached all-purpose flour
1 tablespoon baking powder
3 large eggs
Salt to taste
$1/2$ cup (100 milliliters) vegetable oil
3 $1/2$ ounces (100 grams) prosciutto cotto, diced
2 ounces (50 grams) Gruyère, grated on the large holes of a four-sided
    box grater

Butter a ring pan, then coat with breadcrumbs. Shake out the excess and set pan aside. In a large bowl, combine the yogurt, Parmesan, flour, baking powder, and eggs. Add salt and the oil and stir to combine. Stir in the prosciutto and then the Gruyère. Cover the bowl with a dish towel and set aside to rest for 40 minutes.

Preheat the oven to 350° F (180° C). Pour the batter into the prepared pan and bake until it is golden on top and springs back when pressed with a finger, 30 to 40 minutes. Allow to cool before unmolding. Serve warm or at room temperature.

« PURÈ DI FAGIOLINI E MANDORLE »
GREEN BEAN PUREE WITH ALMONDS

This interesting side dish pairs wonderfully with meat or cheese.

SERVES 4

Salt to taste
14 ounces (400 grams) potatoes, peeled
7 ounces (200 grams) green beans
2 green onions
Extra-virgin olive oil for puree and sautéing
Grated nutmeg to taste
1/2 cup (100 milliliters) whole milk, at room temperature
1 clove garlic
Sliced almonds to taste
Cayenne pepper to taste
Grated Parmesan to taste

Bring a large pot of salted water to a boil. Boil the potatoes, green beans, and onions until very tender, 15 to 20 minutes. Reserve a few whole green beans and place the rest of the vegetables in a food processor fitted with the metal blade or a blender and process into a puree. Transfer the puree to a bowl and by hand whisk in a generous drizzle of oil, salt, nutmeg, and the milk until smooth and silky. Transfer to a serving bowl. Heat a small amount of oil in a pan and sauté the garlic clove until golden. Remove and discard the garlic and add the reserved green beans, almonds, and cayenne pepper. Sauté, stirring frequently, until golden. Sprinkle this mixture over the top. Sprinkle on Parmesan, and serve immediately.

« CUPOLETTE DI ZUCCA E BIETA »
SQUASH PUREE WITH CHARD

This colorful vegetable dish can also be served as a light vegetarian entrée.

SERVES 4

1 ⅓ pounds (600 grams) winter squash, such as butternut or acorn
    squash
2 leeks, sliced
Extra-virgin olive oil for sautéing
2 pounds (1 kilogram) Swiss chard, roughly chopped
Salt and pepper to taste
Unsalted butter for puree
Grated Parmesan to taste

Preheat the oven to 350° F (180° C). Seed the squash, cut into wedges, and place the wedges on a parchment-lined jelly-roll pan. Bake until soft, 30 to 35 minutes. Meanwhile, in a large pan sauté the leeks in a small amount of olive oil. Add the chard, season with salt and pepper, add enough water to come about ½ inch (2 centimeters) up the side of the pan, and braise, covered, over low heat until tender. When the squash is cooked, peel it and, in a food processor fitted with the metal blade or a blender, puree the squash flesh with a generous amount of butter, grated Parmesan, and salt to taste. Transfer the squash puree to a platter and top with the chard mixture and a little additional Parmesan. Serve immediately.

« GRATIN DI CAROTE E CATALOGNA »
BAKED CARROTS AND ENDIVE WITH BREADCRUMBS

Even I get a little tired of the same side dishes—sautéed greens night after night can be a drag. Everything tastes good under a coating of crispy breadcrumbs, though.

SERVES 4

Extra-virgin olive oil for sautéing and drizzling
2 cloves garlic
1 pound (500 grams) endive, chopped
Salt to taste
1 shallot, minced
1 pound (500 grams) carrots, cut into matchsticks
1/2 cup (50 grams) grated Parmesan
1/2 cup (50 grams) breadcrumbs
Minced fresh thyme leaves to taste
Pepper to taste

Preheat the oven to 400° F (200° C). Heat a small amount of oil in a pan and sauté the garlic, tilting the pan to keep it submerged. Add the endive, season with salt, and cook until wilted. In another pan, heat a small amount of oil and cook the shallot and carrots until just beginning to color, then add about 1/4 cup (50 milliliters) water and braise over medium heat until the carrots are soft and most of the liquid has evaporated. (Add more water if necessary.) In a small bowl, combine the Parmesan, breadcrumbs, and thyme. Spread the cooked endive in the bottom of a baking pan. Top with the cooked carrots. Sprinkle the breadcrumb mixture on top. Season with pepper, drizzle with a little more oil, and bake until the breadcrumbs are crisp, about 30 minutes. Serve hot or warm.

« FINOCCHI GRATINATI »
BROILED FENNEL WITH BREADCRUMBS

I like fennel, but I tend to forget about it. It sits in the back of the vegetable drawer in my refrigerator until finally I notice it one day—only it's so sad by then that I end up throwing it away. This is one dish that prompts me to use that fennel quickly and to give it a short but happy life!

SERVES 4

Salt to taste
4 bulbs fennel, cut into wedges
Extra-virgin olive oil for oiling pan and drizzling
$1/2$ cup (50 grams) breadcrumbs
$1/2$ cup (50 grams) grated Parmesan
$1/2$ cup (100 milliliters) whole milk

Preheat the broiler to 350° F (180° C). Bring a pot of salted water to a boil and boil the fennel until tender but not falling apart. Drain and set aside. Lightly oil a baking pan and arrange the cooked fennel in a single layer. Sprinkle with the breadcrumbs and Parmesan. Drizzle on the milk and a little additional olive oil and season with salt. Broil until the surface is browned and crisp, about 10 minutes. Serve immediately.

« GRATIN DI FINOCCHIO E CAPRINO »
BROILED FENNEL AND GOAT CHEESE

The goat cheese adds a savory edge to the fennel, which is quite mild when cooked. Even people who claim they don't like fennel go for this dish.

SERVES 4 TO 6

Extra-virgin olive oil for coating pan and drizzling
1 $1/2$ pounds to 1 $3/4$ pounds (700 to 800 grams) fennel, cut into wedges
Salt and pepper to taste
7 ounces (200 grams) soft goat cheese

¼ cup (25 grams) grated Parmesan
¼ cup (25 grams) breadcrumbs
½ cup (100 milliliters) whole milk

Preheat the broiler to 400° F (200° C). Oil a baking pan and set aside. Bring a large pot of water to a boil and boil the fennel until tender but not overly soft. Drain the fennel and arrange in the prepared baking dish. Season with salt and pepper. Dab spoonfuls of the goat cheese on top of the fennel. In a small bowl, mix the Parmesan and breadcrumbs to combine. Sprinkle this mixture on top of the fennel. Drizzle with the milk and a generous amount of olive oil and broil until the surface is golden, watching closely to guard against burning, 5 to 10 minutes. Serve hot.

« SPINACI GRATINATI »
BROILED SPINACH WITH SCAMORZA CHEESE

Pair this hefty side dish with some cheese and cold cuts and you've got dinner.

SERVES 4

Extra-virgin olive oil for coating pan and sautéing
1 yellow onion, sliced
¼ cup (40 grams) pine nuts
2 (10-ounce) boxes (600 grams) frozen spinach, thawed, squeezed dry, and chopped
Salt to taste
3 ½ ounces (100 grams) scamorza, grated on the large holes of a four-sided box grater
Grated Parmesan to taste

Preheat the broiler to 400° F (200° C). Lightly oil a baking pan and set aside. In a medium pan, sauté the onion in a small amount of oil until golden. Add the pine nuts and, as soon as the pine nuts are toasted, add the spinach. Cook, stirring frequently, over high heat for 3 minutes. Season with salt and transfer to the prepared baking pan. Scatter the grated scamorza on top, then sprinkle with the Parmesan and broil until cheese is melted and browned, about 5 minutes. Serve hot.

« POMODORINI GRATINATI »
BAKED CHERRY TOMATOES

This light side dish goes with any kind of meat.

SERVES 4

7 ounces (200 grams) cherry tomatoes, halved
Salt to taste
1/2 cup (50 grams) grated Parmesan
1/2 cup (50 grams) breadcrumbs
Minced fresh rosemary leaves
Minced fresh thyme leaves
Pepper to taste
Extra-virgin olive oil for drizzling

Preheat a convection oven to 350° F (180° C). Line a jelly-roll pan with parchment paper. Arrange the tomatoes on the pan and season lightly with salt. In a bowl, mix the Parmesan, breadcrumbs, rosemary, and thyme. Sprinkle the breadcrumb mixture over the tomatoes. Season with pepper and drizzle with a generous amount of oil. Bake until soft and charred in spots, 10 to 15 minutes. Serve immediately.

« PEPERONI ABBRUSTOLITI »
ROASTED PEPPERS

There are two kinds of people in the world: those who eat bell peppers with no problem whatsoever, and those who find them difficult to digest. Not only is this the tastiest way to prepare peppers, but even people who have issues with peppers often find that, once they are roasted, they go down quite easily. Additionally, these will keep in the refrigerator for several days. With several slices of fresh buffalo-milk mozzarella, they form the perfect summer lunch. If you like, you can also add a couple chopped anchovy fillets along with or in place of the olives.

SERVES 4

4 red and yellow bell peppers
Minced pitted black olives to taste
Salt to taste
3 cloves garlic, sliced
Minced leaves of 1 bunch parsley
Extra-virgin olive oil for dressing

Preheat the oven to 350° F (180° C). Place the peppers on a jelly-roll pan and roast, turning occasionally, until they are soft and spotted with brown and black marks, about 30 minutes. Allow the peppers to cool in the oven, then peel them and cut them into strips. In a jar or container (preferably glass) with a tight-fitting lid, alternate layers of pepper strips with olives, salt, the garlic slices, and minced parsley. Pour in enough oil to cover the peppers completely. Store in the refrigerator and serve cold.

« PADELLATA DI LATTUGA AL CIPOLLOTTO »
SAUTÉED LETTUCE WITH ASPARAGUS AND EGGS

I recently discovered that the butcher near our country house in Carpeneto sells fresh eggs laid only hours earlier by his chickens. This sauté of vegetables topped with fried eggs is one of the dishes I invented to really highlight the flavor of those eggs. Seek out fresh eggs at a farmer's market near you—you won't believe the difference. This can be either a light entrée or an interesting side dish. Be sure to serve some bread for dipping into the egg yolks.

SERVES 4

Salt to taste
1 1/2 pounds (700 grams) asparagus
3 green onions, sliced
Extra-virgin olive oil for sautéing
1 head lettuce, cut into ribbons
4 large eggs
Grated pecorino to taste
Pepper to taste

Bring a pot of salted water to a boil. Snap off the fibrous ends of the asparagus and boil them until they are tender but still have some bite, about 3 minutes. In a large pan, sauté the onion in a small amount of oil. Add the lettuce and cook just until wilted, which will happen quickly. Remove from the heat and add the asparagus. Add the eggs to the pan, being careful not to break the yolks. Sprinkle with grated pecorino. Return the pan to medium heat, cover, and cook just until the whites of the eggs are set, about 2 minutes. Season with a generous amount of pepper and serve immediately.

« PEPERONATA »
SAUTÉED PEPPERS

Roast chicken cries out for a side dish of sautéed peppers. This is easy, quick, and always a hit.

SERVES 4

1 yellow onion, sliced
Extra-virgin olive oil for sautéing
3 red bell peppers, cut into strips
Salt to taste
1/2 cup (100 milliliters) tomato puree
Fresh basil leaves to taste

In a large pan, sauté the onion in the oil until golden. Add the peppers and cook until soft. Season with salt and then add the tomato puree, 1/2 cup (100 milliliters) water, and basil leaves, tearing the leaves into pieces if they are large. Simmer, covered, over medium-low heat until the peppers are soft and the tomato sauce has thickened, about 20 minutes. Serve immediately.

« PADELLATA DI ZUCCHINE E FORMAGGIO »
SAUTÉED ZUCCHINI WITH CHEESE

In spring and summer when zucchini are in season, I could subsist on nothing else! This versatile dish can be served as an appetizer, a side dish, or even a vegetarian entrée.

SERVES 4

Extra-virgin olive oil for sautéing and drizzling
1 clove garlic
2 zucchini, sliced into rounds
5 sun-dried tomatoes in oil, drained
Minced fresh thyme leaves to taste
Minced fresh marjoram leaves to taste
Salt to taste
2 slices sandwich bread
Parmesan shavings to taste
Pepper to taste

In a pan, heat a small amount of oil with the garlic. Add the zucchini and sauté over medium-low heat until golden, only 5 minutes total. Mince 4 sun-dried tomatoes and add them to the zucchini. Season with thyme, marjoram, and salt. Remove from the heat when the zucchini are still crunchy, but leave in the pan. In a food processor fitted with the metal blade, process the bread with the remaining sun-dried tomato and a small amount of oil. In a small pan, toast this breadcrumb mixture until browned and crisp. Add the breadcrumb mixture and the Parmesan shavings to the pan with the zucchini. Season with pepper and serve immediately.

« CAPONATA DI PEPERONI E MELANZANE »
SICILIAN SWEET AND SOUR PEPPERS AND EGGPLANT

Caponata is a delicious side dish, something like a relish. But it takes its time and tastes even better if prepared a day ahead and allowed to rest and mellow.

SERVES 4

Vegetable oil for pan-frying
1 eggplant, diced
1 red bell pepper, diced
1 yellow onion, sliced
5 cherry tomatoes, halved
$^1/_4$ cup pine nuts
$^1/_4$ cup raisins
$^1/_2$ cup (100 milliliters) white wine vinegar
2 tablespoons sugar
Salt to taste
Fresh basil leaves for garnish

Heat 3 to 4 inches of vegetable oil and fry the eggplant and pepper. Drain on paper towels, changing the paper at least twice to ensure that any excess oil is absorbed. In another pan, braise the onion in a small amount of water (no oil) until soft. When the water has evaporated and the onion is soft, add the fried eggplant and pepper, tomatoes, pine nuts, and raisins. Stir in the vinegar and sugar and season with salt. Adjust seasoning, adding additional vinegar if the mixture is too sweet or additional sugar if it is too acidic. Cook, stirring, until the flavors have combined. Before serving, let the dish cool completely, or refrigerate overnight and bring to room temperature. Garnish with basil leaves just before serving.

« CIPOLLE CARAMELLATA »
CARAMELIZED ONIONS

Onions appear in almost everything you make, but here they are the star of the show. Chef Davide Oldani taught me this recipe, or rather, he makes a much more elevated version of this dish, which I've simplified for the home cook.

SERVES 2

1 white onion
2 slices bread
Extra-virgin olive oil for brushing bread
Grated Parmesan to taste
Unsalted butter for sautéing
3 tablespoons sugar
1/2 cup (100 milliliters) red wine vinegar

Steam the onion until soft but not falling apart. Cut in half and set aside. Cut 2 circles out of the center of the 2 slices of bread and place the circles on a jelly-roll pan lined with parchment. (Discard outer ring of bread or save to make breadcrumbs.) Brush a generous amount of oil onto the bread circles, sprinkle with some grated Parmesan, and broil (or place in a toaster oven, which is ideal for this) until the cheese has melted and the bread has toasted. Place the toasted bread circles on individual serving plates. In a pan large enough to hold the 2 onion halves, melt a small amount of butter, then add the sugar. Cook, stirring constantly, to make a caramel. When the caramel begins to color, place the onion halves in the pan, cut side down. Add the vinegar to the pan and let it evaporate. Cook the onion halves, turning once, until they are browned on both sides, then transfer them to the plates on top of the toasted circles of bread and serve immediately.

« RICCIOLI D'ORO »
POTATO CURLS WITH SQUASH PUREE

This creamy, rich puree is so good, and it's suitable for everything from a simple dinner with kids to a fancy dinner party.

SERVES 1

1 potato
2 1/2 ounces (70 grams) peeled and seeded winter squash, such as
     butternut or acorn squash (about 1 large wedge)
1 bay leaf
1 tablespoon crescenza cheese
1/2 cup (50 grams) grated Parmesan, plus more for serving (optional)
Extra-virgin olive oil for puree and drizzling
Salt to taste

Bring 2 pots of water to a boil. In one boil the potato, and in the other boil the squash with the bay leaf. Cook each until tender, about 20 minutes. Drain the potato and set aside. Remove the squash with a strainer or slotted spoon and reserve the cooking water. Discard the bay leaf and place the cooked squash in a food processor fitted with the metal blade or a blender, along with the crescenza and Parmesan. Process, drizzling in some oil and enough of the cooking water to make a silky puree that is on the loose side. Transfer the squash puree to a soup bowl. Place the cooked potato in a potato ricer and squeeze the potato to make curls, letting them drop directly onto the squash puree. (The ricer should remove the peel.) Drizzle with a little more oil and season with salt. Sprinkle with additional Parmesan if desired and serve immediately.

« GÂTEAU DI PATATE »
POTATO CAKE

This unique potato cake is extra crunchy. For this recipe, I'm grateful not to Lorenzo Boni, but to his mother, Maria Josè Buccigrossi.

SERVES 4

Unsalted butter for coating pan and for sauce
4 potatoes
3 1/2 ounces (100 grams) Gruyère, diced
3 1/2 ounces (100 grams) stracchino cheese
3 1/2 ounces (100 grams) smoked scamorza, diced
Salt to taste
Grated Parmesan to taste
Grated nutmeg to taste
Fresh sage leaves to taste
1 clove garlic

Preheat the oven to 350° F (180° C). Butter a baking dish and set aside. Bring a pot of water to a boil, boil the potatoes until easily pierced with a fork, then drain. Peel the potatoes, and pass 2 of the cooked potatoes through a potato ricer into the prepared pan. Flatten the potatoes with a fork to make a compact layer. Distribute the Gruyère, stracchino, and scamorza on top. Season with salt and sprinkle with some grated Parmesan. Pass the other 2 potatoes through the ricer and let them fall on top of the potatoes already in the pan so that all the cheese is covered. Leave these as they fall (in other words, don't flatten them). Sprinkle with additional Parmesan and grated nutmeg. In a small pan, melt some butter and brown the sage and the garlic clove, then remove the sage and garlic and drizzle the flavored butter over the top of the potatoes. Bake until the top is browned and the cheese has melted, about 20 minutes. Allow to settle for 5 to 10 minutes before serving.

« INSALATA TIEPIDA DI PATATE »
WARM POTATO SALAD

This fragrant salad is wonderful as a side dish to meat or fish. I also like to serve it with a rustic plate of cold cuts.

SERVES 2

2 pounds (1 kilogram) potatoes
2 tablespoons (20 grams) pine nuts, plus more for garnish
1/2 cup (100 milliliters) extra-virgin olive oil
30 fresh basil leaves, plus more for garnish
2 sun-dried tomato halves in oil, drained
Salt to taste
1/2 cup (100 grams) pitted black olives, preferably taggiasca olives

Bring a pot of water to a boil and boil the potatoes until tender. In a food processor fitted with a metal blade or a blender, process the 2 tablespoons pine nuts with the oil, basil, and sun-dried tomatoes until smooth. When the potatoes are cooked and have cooled enough that you can handle them, peel them and then crush them with a fork. They shouldn't be perfectly smooth—you want a few larger chunks. Toss the basil mixture with the potatoes until combined. Season with salt, add the olives, and toss. Garnish with pine nuts and basil leaves and serve warm.

« INSALATA PRIMAVERA »
ARTICHOKE AND FAVA BEAN SPRING SALAD

When spring arrives and fava beans start filling the shelves of my local fruit and vegetable seller, I go nuts. I just love them! I eat them with salami, with sheep's cheese, and all by themselves. Serving big green pods and letting guests shell their own is a great way to start a meal. For this recipe, you need to shell the beans yourself, and take off the skin that covers the individual beans as well. It's a little tedious, but it's worth it. If you absolutely can't bring yourself to do it, just make the salad with artichokes alone—it's still delicious.

SERVES 2

Juice of 1 lemon, plus more for dressing
3 baby artichokes
1 pound ($^{1}/_{2}$ kilogram) fava beans in the pods
Extra-virgin olive oil for dressing
Salt and pepper to taste
Parmesan shavings to taste

Squeeze the lemon juice into a bowl of ice water and set aside. Trim the artichokes: Working one at a time, remove any leaves from the stem, and then cut off the stem, leaving an inch or two. Pull off and discard any hard, dark-colored leaves. When you have revealed the light green portion of the artichoke, peel any tough skin off of the outside of the stem. Cut off the top of the artichoke completely. Cut the artichoke in half the long way and use the tip of a paring knife to dig out the fuzzy part in the center. Slice the cleaned artichoke into thin slices and drop them into the bowl of lemon water. Repeat with the remaining artichokes. Shell the fava beans, remove the hard skin around individual beans, and place in a serving bowl. Drain the artichoke slices and add to the bowl with the fava beans. Make a dressing by whisking together olive oil and lemon juice and seasoning with salt and pepper. Pour over the salad and toss to combine. Add a generous amount of Parmesan shavings and serve.

« INSALATINE DI CASTAGNI »
CHESTNUT SALAD

Winter can be a bit dreary when it comes to salad. After all, there aren't a lot of vegetables available during the season. This is a great solution to that. The warm dressing wilts the spinach just the right amount.

SERVES 4

10 ounces (300 grams) baby spinach
7 ounces (200 grams) pancetta, diced
Extra-virgin olive oil for sautéing
3 $^{1}/_{2}$ ounces (100 grams) cooked chestnuts, diced

1 tablespoon mustard
White wine for dressing
Balsamic vinegar for dressing
Salt to taste

Place the spinach in a salad bowl. In a pan, sauté the pancetta in a small amount of oil. Add the chestnuts and cook over low heat until the flavors have melded. Transfer the pancetta and chestnuts to the salad bowl and, without cleaning the pan, add the mustard to the pan. Place over low heat and whisk in a small amount of white wine and a small amount of balsamic vinegar to make a dressing. Season with salt. Pour the warm dressing over the chestnuts and spinach, toss, and serve warm.

« INSALATA DI SPINACI »
SPINACH SALAD

Baby spinach makes a wonderful salad, and to me the perfect accompaniments are walnuts, cheese, and pears. Abate fetel pears (named for the monk who created them) are tall and narrow; anjou or Bosc pears will also work. Choose a pear that's not too ripe so that it will hold its shape when sliced.

SERVES 2

3 ¹/₂ ounces (100 grams) baby spinach
¹/₄ cup walnuts, roughly chopped
2 ounces (60 grams) Gruyère or Fontina cheese, cut into cubes
Extra-virgin olive oil for dressing
Salt to taste
1 abate fetel or anjou pear
Balsamic vinegar for dressing

In a salad bowl, combine the spinach, walnuts, and cheese. Dress with olive oil and salt to taste. Cut the pear into quarters, core the quarters, and then slice them very thin. (Leave the peel on the pear.) Add the pear slices to the salad and toss. Dress with a small amount of balsamic vinegar and serve immediately.

« INSALATA DI ASPARAGI CROCCANTE »
CRISPY ASPARAGUS SALAD

This salad of both cooked and raw ingredients is very refreshing—not to mention colorful.

SERVES 2

3 large eggs
5 ounces (150 grams) asparagus
3 to 4 (about 2 ounces/50 grams) cooked shelled shrimp
1 small light green zucchini, thinly sliced into rounds
1 teaspoon mayonnaise
$1/2$ cup (100 milliliters) extra-virgin olive oil
Salt to taste
Lemon juice to taste

To hard-boil the eggs, place the eggs in a small pot of water, bring to a boil, then lower the heat to a simmer and cook for 10 minutes. Run under cold water, peel, and slice. Blanch the asparagus in boiling water for 5 minutes. Chop the asparagus and place in a serving bowl with the shrimp and the zucchini. In a small bowl, whisk the mayonnaise with the oil. Season the salad with salt and drizzle with lemon juice. Toss with the mayonnaise dressing. Garnish with the hard-boiled egg slices and serve.

« INSALATA RADICCHIO, MOZZARELLA, E MELAGRANA »
RADICCHIO, MOZZARELLA, AND POMEGRANATE SALAD

The word "salad" hardly does justice to this dish, which is fit for a holiday meal. Do your best to find late-season Treviso radicchio—the kind with the long thin leaves—or it just won't be the same. This must be made at the last minute, just before serving.

SERVES 4 TO 6

4 heads late-season Treviso radicchio
1 pomegranate, seeds removed

Salt to taste
Extra-virgin olive oil for dressing
Balsamic vinegar for dressing
1 fresh mozzarella ball, 8 ounces (225 grams), preferably buffalo-milk
  mozzarella

Cut the radicchio into 1- to 1 $\frac{1}{2}$-inch pieces. Transfer the pieces to a bowl with half the pomegranate seeds. Season with salt, then make a dressing by whisking together oil and balsamic vinegar. Pour the dressing over the salad and toss to combine. Arrange the mixture on a serving plate with raised sides. Cut the mozzarella into cubes and scatter them on top of the salad. Add the other half of the pomegranate seeds, drizzle with a little more balsamic vinegar, and serve immediately.

« INSALATA RUSSA »
RUSSIAN SALAD

No one is certain where the dish of mayonnaise and vegetables, similar to coleslaw, that Italians label "Russian salad" originated. It may be Italian, it may be Russian, or it may even be French. In any case, children universally love it.

SERVES 4

Salt to taste
1 (14-ounce/400-gram) bag frozen peas
2 potatoes, peeled and cut into small dice
1 (5-ounce/150-gram) can tuna in oil, drained
1 cup (200 grams) mayonnaise
Juice of $\frac{1}{2}$ lemon
Extra-virgin olive oil for dressing

Bring a pot of salted water to a boil and boil the peas and potatoes until tender. Drain and transfer to a bowl. Add the tuna, breaking it up with a fork, and the mayonnaise and toss to combine. Make a dressing by whisking together the lemon juice with oil. Pour the dressing over the salad and toss to combine. Serve immediately.

« INSALATA MIMOSA »
MIMOSA SALAD

Mimosa flowers are bright yellow blossoms with small puffs like pom poms that are traditionally given to women in Italy to celebrate International Women's Day, March 8. This recipe cleverly uses egg yolk to mimic them.

SERVES 1

1 large egg
1 cup mixed salad greens
$1/2$ tomato, sliced
3 radishes, sliced
$1/2$ cucumber, sliced
3 tablespoons canned corn, rinsed and drained
1 (5-ounce/150-gram) can tuna in oil, drained
Extra-virgin olive oil for dressing
Vinegar for dressing
Salt to taste

To hard-boil the egg, place the egg in a small pot of water, bring to a boil, then lower the heat to a simmer and cook for 10 minutes. Run under cold water and peel. In a salad bowl, combine the salad greens, tomato, radishes, and cucumber. Add the corn and the tuna, flaking it with a fork. Make a dressing by whisking together the olive oil, vinegar, and salt to taste and toss the salad. Remove the egg white and discard or use for another purpose. Press the hard-boiled egg yolk through the holes of a strainer or colander, letting it fall onto the salad. Serve immediately.

« INSALATINA LOMBARDA »
PEAR AND GORGONZOLA SALAD

This salad uses Lombardy's creamy Gorgonzola cheese. It's not exactly light, but it is satisfying. I often serve this with rice.

SERVES 4

10 ounces (300 grams) mixed salad greens
1 abate fetel or Anjou pear
10 walnut halves, roughly chopped
Extra-virgin olive oil for dressing
Vinegar for dressing
Salt to taste
3 $\frac{1}{2}$ ounces (100 grams) Gorgonzola, cut into cubes

Place the salad greens in a salad bowl. Cut the pear into quarters, core the quarters, and then slice them very thin. (Leave the peel on the pear.) Add the pear slices and walnuts to the salad bowl. In a small bowl, whisk together oil and vinegar to make a dressing. Season with salt and pour over the salad. Toss to combine. Sprinkle with the Gorgonzola and serve.

« INSALATA DI CARCIOFI E CALAMARI »
ARTICHOKE AND CALAMARI SALAD

Delicious flavors and textures unite in this salad: tender grilled calamari, crisp thin slices of artichoke, and tart lemon.

SERVES 4

Juice of 1 lemon, plus more for dressing
3 baby artichokes
Extra-virgin olive oil for dressing, griddle, and drizzling
2 calamari bodies, cut into rings
Salt to taste
Balsamic vinegar for drizzling (optional)

Squeeze the lemon juice into a bowl of ice water and set aside. Trim the artichokes: Working one at a time, remove any leaves from the stem, and then cut off the stem, leaving an inch or two. Pull off and discard any hard, dark-colored leaves. When you have revealed the light green portion of the artichoke, peel off any tough skin from the outside of the stem. Cut off the top of the artichoke completely. Cut the artichoke in half the long way and use the tip of a paring knife to dig out the fuzzy part in the center.

Thinly slice the cleaned artichoke and drop the slices into the bowl of lemon water. Repeat with the remaining artichokes. Heat a griddle over high heat. Lightly brush the griddle with oil and cook the calamari on it until nicely browned, about 2 minutes. Season the calamari with salt. Drain the artichoke slices and transfer to a bowl. Whisk together lemon juice and olive oil to create a dressing, season with salt, and toss with the artichokes. Make a bed of artichokes on a serving platter. Arrange the calamari on top. Drizzle with a little more oil and balsamic vinegar, if using. Serve immediately.

« INSALATA CON FRITTI »
SALAD WITH FRIED SEAFOOD

Salad and fried food are a wonderful match, as they balance each other out. Some crisp apple incorporates yet another texture into this delicious and unique dish.

SERVES 4

1 apple, peeled, cored, and diced
9 ounces (250 grams) arugula and mâche
Balsamic vinegar for dressing
Extra-virgin olive oil for dressing
Salt to taste
Vegetable oil for deep-frying
1 zucchini, cut into julienne
1 potato, cut into julienne
3 1/2 ounces (100 grams) baby calamari
3 1/2 ounces (100 grams) whitebait
Unbleached all-purpose flour for dredging

In a salad bowl, mix the apple with the greens. Whisk together vinegar and olive oil to create a dressing, season with salt, and toss with the salad. In a pan, heat a generous amount of vegetable oil for frying. Lightly dredge the zucchini, potato, baby calamari, and whitebait in flour and fry until browned and crisp. Transfer to paper towels to drain. Scatter the fried vegetables and seafood on top of the greens and serve immediately without tossing.

« ARANCINE »

RICE BALLS

There are two types of fried rice balls in Italy: Rome's *supplì* are filled with mozzarella, while Sicily's *arancine* instead have meat sauce and peas in the middle. Which are better? It would be impossible to say!

SERVES 4

5 ounces (150 grams) frozen mirepoix (minced carrots, onion, and celery)
Extra-virgin olive oil for sautéing
9 ounces (250 grams) ground beef
1 cup (250 milliliters) white wine
2 tablespoons tomato paste
3 1/2 ounces (100 grams) frozen peas
Salt to taste
7 ounces (200 grams) saffron risotto
2 large eggs, lightly beaten
Breadcrumbs for dredging
Vegetable oil for deep-frying

To make the meat sauce, in a pan, sauté the mirepoix in a small amount of olive oil. Add the beef and cook over low heat until it loses its raw red color, then add the wine and allow most of it to evaporate. Stir in the tomato paste and peas and season with salt. Cook, covered, over low heat for 20 minutes, then remove from the heat and allow to cool. When the meat sauce has cooled, in a pan, heat a generous amount of vegetable oil for frying. Take a handful of risotto, about 1/4 cup, in the palm of one hand, create an indentation, and fill the indentation with the meat sauce. Close up the rice around it as if it were a meatball. (Add a little additional rice if necessary to seal the meat sauce inside the rice.) Repeat with the remaining risotto and sauce. Dredge the balls first in the beaten eggs, and then in the breadcrumbs. Fry until golden and crisp. Serve hot.

« MOZZARELLE IN CARROZZA A SORPRESA »
FRIED MOZZARELLA WITH A SURPRISE

Mozzarella in carozza are little mozzarella sandwiches that are dipped in egg and then fried. They're pretty terrific in their original version, but I like to slip a little savory surprise into each one. Feel free to use something else as a surprise—I find strongly flavored savory items work best.

SERVES 4

2 slices sandwich bread, crusts removed
1 slice mozzarella
8 small pieces of one or more of the following: anchovy, sun-dried
    tomato, prosciutto, cooked bacon
Vegetable oil for deep-frying
Lightly beaten eggs for dredging
Breadcrumbs for dredging

Place one slice of bread on the work surface. Place the mozzarella slice on top. Trim the mozzarella to fit if it overhangs the bread. Place the second slice of bread on top. Cut the sandwich into 4 squares, and then cut each square diagonally into 2 triangles. Open each little triangular sandwich and add a piece of anchovy, sun-dried tomato, prosciutto, or cooked bacon. Replace the bread. In a pan, heat a generous amount of oil for deep-frying. Dredge each little sandwich first in the beaten eggs, then in the breadcrumbs. Squeeze firmly and pinch the edges to seal. Fry just until golden. If any mozzarella looks ready to leak out, remove the sandwich from the oil immediately. Serve hot.

DESSERTS

« TORTA MARGHERITA »
YELLOW CAKE

Soft, plain yellow cake is so delicious! It can be flavored either with lemon or with vanilla. It can also be used to make dozens of different desserts: Try it spread with pastry cream or even Nutella.

MAKES 1 CAKE

4 large eggs
$2/3$ cup (150 grams) granulated sugar
1 stick plus 6 tablespoons (200 grams) unsalted butter, melted
$1/2$ teaspoon vanilla extract (optional)
$3/4$ cup (100 grams) unbleached all-purpose flour
$2/3$ cup (100 grams) potato starch
1 tablespoon baking powder
Grated zest of 1 lemon (optional)
Confectioners' sugar for finishing

Preheat the oven to 350° F (180° C). Line a cake pan with parchment paper and set aside. With an electric mixer or wooden spoon, beat the eggs with the sugar until they are light and foamy. Add the butter and the vanilla extract, if using, and mix to combine. In a small bowl, whisk together the flour, potato starch, baking powder, and lemon zest, if using. Gradually add the dry mixture to the batter and beat to combine. Transfer the batter to the prepared pan. Bake until a toothpick inserted in the center comes out clean, about 30 minutes. Allow to cool completely, then sprinkle with confectioners' sugar.

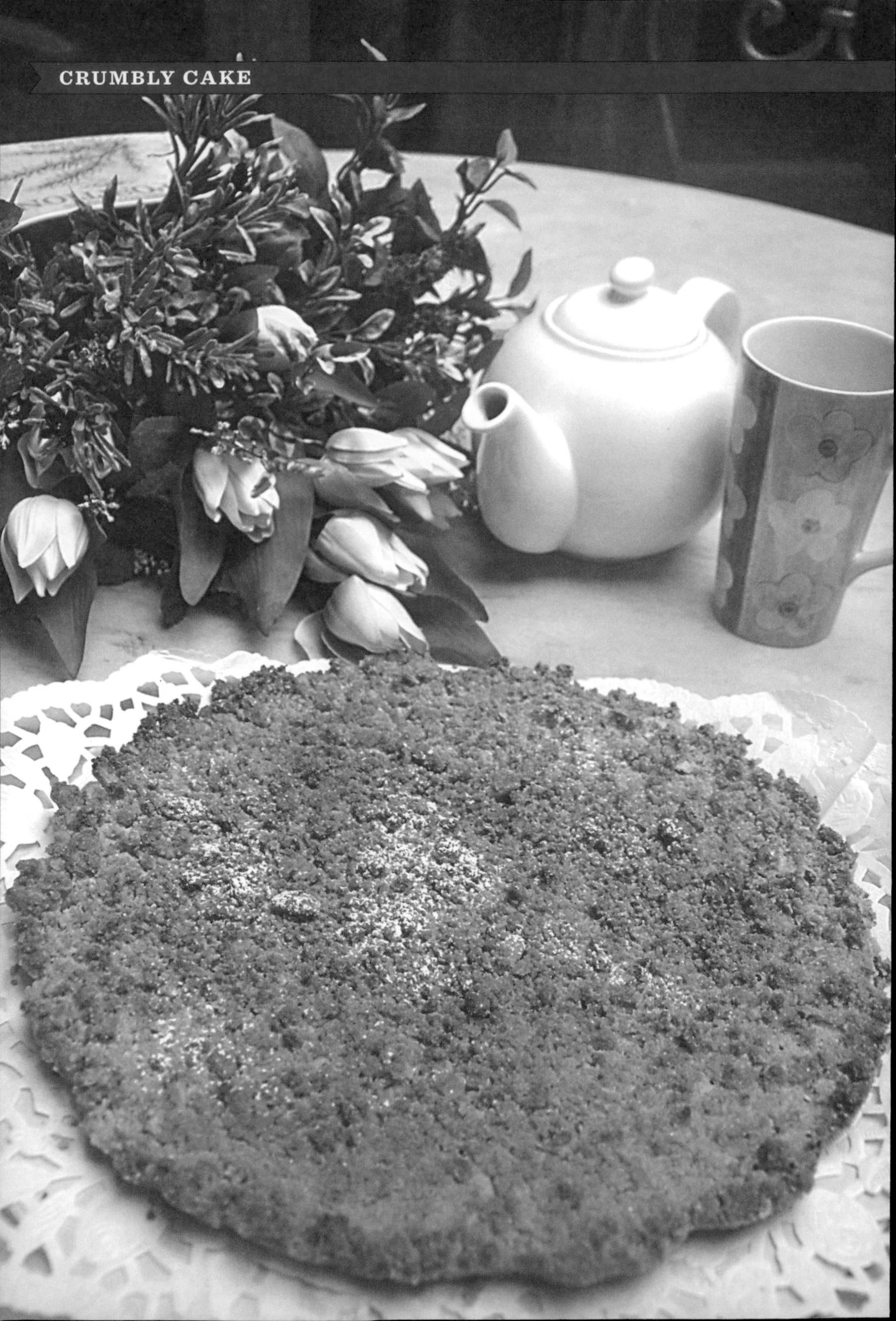
CRUMBLY CAKE

« SBRISOLONA »
CRUMBLY CAKE

This traditional cake hails from the Lodi area in Lombardy. It's crunchy, buttery, and irresistible. It's also very easy to make. It should be truly crumbly—so crumbly that you can't cut it with a knife. Everyone just breaks off pieces with their hands. Be sure to use very finely ground cornmeal for this recipe.

SERVES 6

1 $\frac{1}{2}$ cups (200 grams) almonds, ground
1 $\frac{2}{3}$ cups (200 grams) unbleached all-purpose flour
1 $\frac{1}{3}$ cups (200 grams) finely ground cornmeal
1 cup (200 grams) granulated sugar
Grated zest of 1 lemon
1 pinch salt
2 egg yolks
$\frac{1}{2}$ teaspoon vanilla extract
1 stick plus 6 tablespoons (200 grams) unsalted butter, melted
Confectioners' sugar for finishing

Preheat the oven to 350° F (180° C). Line a springform pan with parchment paper and set aside. In a large bowl, with a wooden spoon, combine the almonds, all-purpose flour, cornmeal, sugar, lemon zest, and salt. Add the egg yolks and vanilla and mix to combine. Stir in the butter. The mixture will not be a smooth batter—it will look like wet sand. Transfer to the prepared pan and bake until golden and crisp, 40 to 45 minutes. Allow the cake to cool completely. Remove the ring from around the pan and slide the cake onto a serving platter. Sprinkle with confectioners' sugar.

« CIAMBELLONE AI FRUTTI DI BOSCO E MASCARPONE »
CIAMBELLONE CAKE WITH BERRIES AND MASCARPONE

Ciambellone is a plain round cake that is often eaten for breakfast in Italy, but I like it any time of day. This version is a little richer than usual due to the mascarpone (the same creamy cheese that goes into tiramisù). Thanks to Francesca La Torre for this recipe.

SERVES 4 TO 6

Unsalted butter for coating pan
2 3/4 cups (350 grams) unbleached all-purpose flour, plus more for
    coating pan
1 cup (200 grams) granulated sugar
4 large eggs
1 tablespoon baking powder
1 (8-ounce/250-gram) tub mascarpone
1/4 cup (50 milliliters) whole milk
7 to 9 ounces (200 to 250 grams) frozen mixed berries

Preheat the oven to 350°F (180°C). Butter a ring pan. Add a little flour, shake the pan to coat, then dump out any excess flour and set aside. Beat the sugar with the eggs until pale yellow and smooth. Add the flour, baking powder, mascarpone, and milk and beat until smooth and well combined. Gently fold in the berries by hand with a spatula. Pour the batter into the prepared pan and bake until golden and well risen, about 30 minutes. Let the cake cool in the pan, then invert a platter over it, turn over the pan and the platter, and lift away the pan.

« TORTA DI FICHI »
FIG CAKE

Anyone who likes figs will adore this simple cake. It's great for dessert or to serve in the afternoon with coffee or tea.

MAKES 1 CAKE

1 stick plus 3 tablespoons (150 grams) unsalted butter, melted
$1/2$ cup (120 grams) granulated sugar
4 large eggs
$1/4$ cup (50 milliliters) whole milk
2 cups (250 grams) unbleached all-purpose flour
1 $1/2$ teaspoons baking powder
1 pinch salt
4 fresh figs
Confectioners' sugar for finishing

Preheat the oven to 350° F (180° C). Line a cake pan with parchment paper and set aside. In a bowl, beat together the butter and sugar, then add the eggs and milk and beat until creamy and smooth. In a small bowl, combine the flour, baking powder, and salt. Gradually add the dry ingredients to the wet, beating to incorporate between additions. Transfer to the prepared pan. Peel the figs, cut them into wedges, and arrange them neatly on top of the cake, pressing down slightly so that they are pressed into the batter but don't sink to the bottom. Bake until golden and firm, 20 to 30 minutes. Allow to cool, then sprinkle with confectioners' sugar.

« ROVESCIATA ALLA PERE »
SPICED PEAR UPSIDE DOWN CAKE

Intense spice flavors liven up this cake in the most delicious way. Even my kids, who usually complain about cloves, happily ate this and asked for seconds.

MAKES 1 CAKE

1/2 cup (150 milliliters) whole milk
1 large egg
1 stick (120 grams) unsalted butter
1/3 cup (100 grams) honey
1 teaspoon ground cinnamon
1 teaspoon ground ginger
1 whole clove, ground
1 2/3 cups (200 grams) unbleached all-purpose flour
1 pinch salt
1 teaspoon baking powder
1/2 cup (100 grams) turbinado sugar
3 pears
Juice of 1 lemon

Preheat the oven to 350° F (180° C). Line a cake pan with parchment paper and set aside. In a bowl, whisk together the milk and the egg. Place the butter and the honey in a small pot and melt over low heat, whisking to combine. Add the honey mixture to the milk and egg mixture and whisk to combine. In a small bowl, combine the cinnamon, ginger, ground clove, flour, salt, and baking powder. Add 1/3 cup (70 grams) turbinado sugar to the bowl with the spices and mix to combine. Gradually add the dry ingredients to the wet, beating to incorporate between additions.

Peel and core 1 pear, cut into thin slices, and fold into the batter. Peel and core the remaining 2 pears and cut into wedges. Place the pears in a bowl and toss with the lemon juice. Scatter the remaining turbinado sugar (about 3 tablespoons) in the bottom of the prepared cake pan. Arrange the pear wedges in a circle with their points in the middle of the pan. Gently pour the batter over the pears, smooth the top with a spatula, and bake until a tester comes out clean, about 40 minutes. Let the cake cool in the pan, then invert a platter over it, turn over the pan and the platter, and lift away the pan. If any of the pear slices come off with the pan, simply return them to the top of the cake.

« PLUM-CAKE LEGGERISSIMO CON PRUGNE E PERE »
LIGHT LOAF CAKE WITH PRUNES AND PEARS

This is one of the few desserts that my husband, Fabio, who doesn't have much of a sweet tooth, enjoys as much as I do. It's really satisfying and very light.

MAKES 1 CAKE

1 cup (240 milliliters) Marsala
$1/_2$ cup (100 milliliters) whole milk
10 pitted prunes, chopped
2 large eggs
$1/_2$ cup (100 grams) granulated sugar
$1/_3$ cup (70 milliliters) vegetable oil
1 $1/_2$ cups (180 grams) unbleached all-purpose flour, plus more for
    coating the prunes
1 $1/_2$ teaspoons baking powder
1 pinch salt
2 pears

Preheat the oven to 350° F (180° C). Line a loaf pan with parchment paper and set aside. In a small bowl, combine the Marsala and milk, then add the chopped prunes to soak. In a bowl, with an electric mixer or wooden spoon, beat the eggs with the sugar. Add the oil and beat again. Remove the prunes from the Marsala and milk mixture and set aside, then add the soaking liquid to the bowl. Beat to combine. Add the flour, baking powder, and salt, and beat until combined. Toss the chopped prunes in a little flour, then fold them into the batter. Pour the batter into the prepared pan. Peel and core the pears and cut them into thin slices. Push the pears into the batter so they are hidden completely. (It's fine if they sink all the way to the bottom.) Bake until a tester comes out clean, about 40 minutes. Let the cake cool completely in the pan, then invert it onto a serving platter, lift away the pan, and slice with a serrated knife.

« PLUM CAKE RICCO »
LOAF CAKE WITH DRIED FRUIT AND NUTS

Despite the name, plum cake (always referred to in English in Italy) doesn't contain plums. It's a loaf cake similar to a pound cake that may be plain or enriched with chocolate, flavorings, or—as in this case—dried fruit and nuts. It is served for breakfast and snacks as well as for dessert. Use any combination of fruit and nuts that you like.

SERVES 4 TO 6

1 stick plus 3 tablespoons (150 grams) unsalted butter, melted
¹/₃ cup (80 grams) granulated sugar
¹/₃ cup (50 grams) raisins
1 ²/₃ cups (200 grams) unbleached all-purpose flour
4 large eggs
2 tablespoons baking powder
¹/₃ cup (50 grams) chopped pitted dates, dried figs, and dried apricots
¹/₃ cup (50 grams) chopped walnuts, almonds, and hazelnuts
Confectioners' sugar for finishing

Preheat the oven to 350° F (180° C). Line a loaf pan with parchment paper and set aside. In a large bowl, with an electric mixer or wooden spoon, mix the butter and sugar. Toss the raisins with about 1 tablespoon of the flour. Add the eggs, baking powder, and remaining flour to the bowl and mix. With a spatula, fold in the raisins, chopped dried fruit, and chopped nuts. Transfer the batter to the prepared pan and bake until a tester comes out clean, about 30 minutes. Allow to cool completely in the pan, then unmold and sprinkle with confectioners' sugar.

« TORTA PARADISO DI MARIA CALLAS »
MARIA CALLAS'S TORTA PARADISO

I adore opera, but these days, if I dare to play a Maria Callas aria, my kids howl in protest. Our home is filled with the sounds of Hannah Montana and Lady Gaga. So, I bake La Divina's favorite cake instead. *Torta paradiso* is a traditional Italian cake that's extra-light due to the use of potato starch.

SERVES 4 TO 6

2 sticks plus 3 tablespoons (300 grams) unsalted butter, softened
$1/2$ teaspoon vanilla extract
3 large eggs
3 egg yolks
$1\,1/3$ cups (300 grams) granulated sugar
Grated zest of 1 lemon
$3/4$ cup (100 grams) unbleached all-purpose flour
1 tablespoon baking powder
$1\,1/4$ cups (200 grams) potato starch
Confectioners' sugar for finishing

Preheat the oven to 350° F (180° C). Line a cake pan with parchment paper and set aside. With an electric mixer, beat the butter, vanilla, eggs, and egg yolks. Add the sugar and mix until well combined, then add the lemon zest, flour, baking powder, and potato starch. When the batter is smooth and all the ingredients have been incorporated, transfer the batter to the prepared pan and bake until a tester comes out clean, about 40 minutes. Let the cake cool in the pan on a wire rack. Sprinkle with confectioners' sugar before serving.

BANANA-ALMOND CAKE

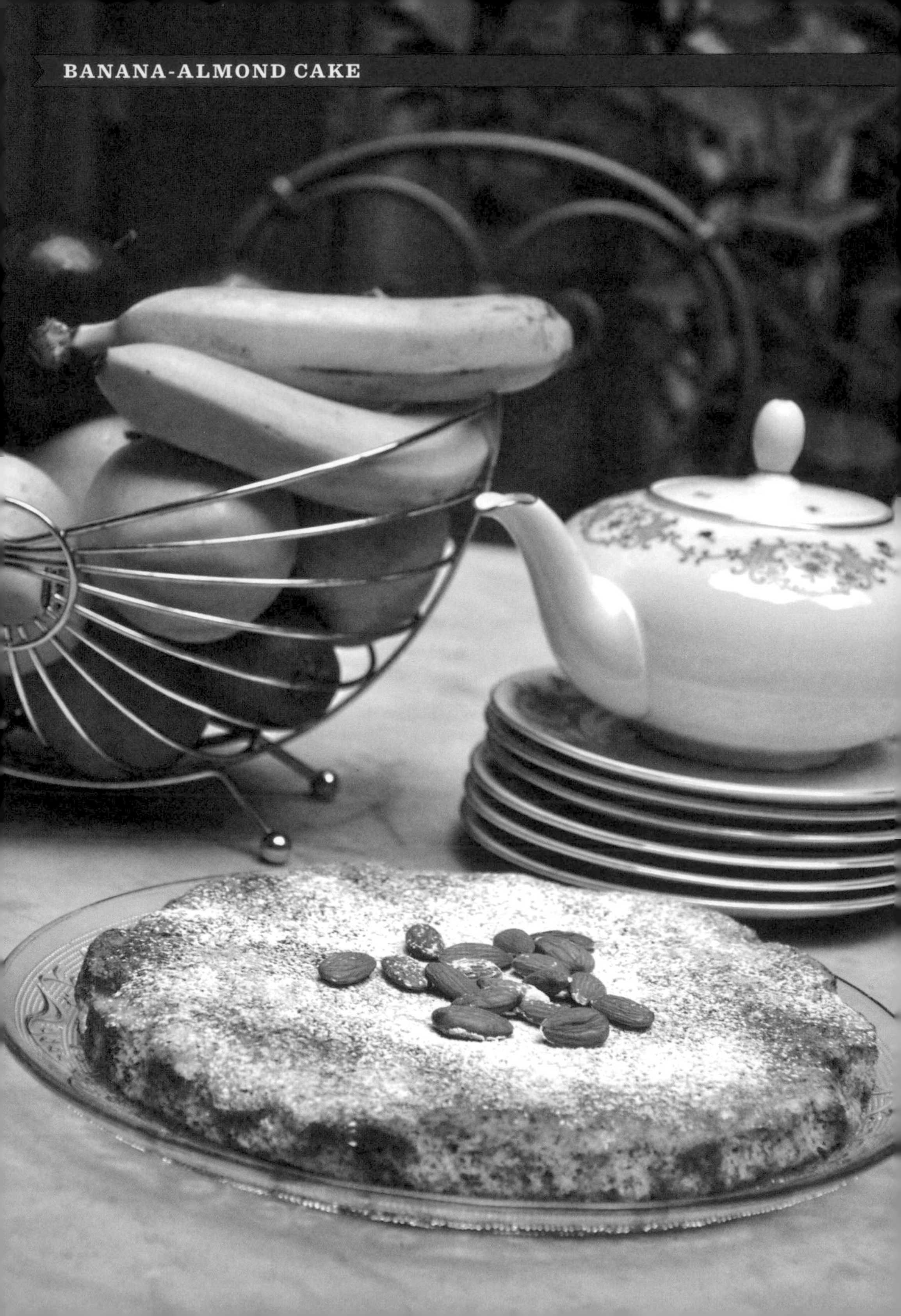

« TORTA DI BANANE E MANDORLE »
BANANA-ALMOND CAKE

This flourless cake recipe is from my colleague Michele Vanossi. In addition to the banana, you can fold raisins and chopped dried apricots (about 1/3 cup each) into the batter along with the egg whites if you like. I've also made it with walnuts in place of the almonds and it's just as good.

SERVES 4 TO 6

1 cup (150 grams) almonds
2 ripe bananas
2 large eggs
1/4 cup (60 grams) granulated sugar
2 tablespoons potato starch
1/4 teaspoon baking soda
Confectioners' sugar and almonds for finishing

Preheat the oven to 350° F (180° C). Line a cake pan with parchment paper and set aside. In a food processor fitted with the metal blade or a nut grinder, grind the almonds. In a small bowl, mash the bananas with a fork. Separate the eggs and, in a large bowl, with an electric mixer or wooden spoon, beat the egg yolks with the sugar until pale yellow. Add the bananas, ground almonds, potato starch, and baking soda and beat until smooth. Separately, beat the egg whites with an electric mixer until stiff peaks form. Fold the egg whites into the batter. Transfer the batter to the prepared pan and bake until a tester comes out clean, about 25 minutes. Allow to cool completely, then sprinkle with confectioners' sugar and a few whole almonds before serving.

« CIAMBELLA ALLE MELE DI FRANCI »
FRANCI'S APPLE CAKE

Who doesn't love an apple cake? Fragrant and soft, this cake from Franci is good for breakfast, an after-school snack, or with a cup of coffee or tea. I made it for the bake sale at Matilde's school this year, and her teacher bought it, which made me a little nervous. But apparently the cake passed with flying colors!

MAKES 1 CAKE

Butter for coating pan
2 1/2 cups (300 grams) unbleached all-purpose flour, plus more for
    coating the pan
5 apples
2 large eggs
1 cup (250 grams) granulated sugar
1 cup (250 milliliters) plain yogurt
1/4 cup plus 2 tablespoons (100 milliliters) olive oil
1 1/2 teaspoons baking powder
1 pinch salt
Pearl sugar for finishing

Preheat the oven to 350° F (180° C). Butter a ring pan, then coat with flour. Shake out the excess and set the pan aside. Peel and core the apples, cut them into small dice, and, in a small bowl toss them with about 1 tablespoon of the flour. Set aside. With an electric mixer (or by hand, but you'll need to work vigorously), beat the eggs with the sugar. Add the yogurt and olive oil and mix until smooth. Add the remaining flour, baking powder, and salt and beat until smooth. Fold the apples into the batter. Transfer the batter to the prepared pan, sprinkle with pearl sugar, and bake until a tester comes out clean, 40 to 45 minutes.

« TORTA CON ARANCE CARAMELLATE »
CARAMELIZED ORANGE CAKE

Just about any orange cake is good if you ask me, but this one is particularly tasty because it's baked upside down so the oranges caramelize beautifully. It's a real show-stopper.

SERVES 8

1 stick plus 1 tablespoon (130 grams) unsalted butter, melted
1 1/3 cups (290 grams) granulated sugar
3 large eggs
2/3 cup (80 grams) unbleached all-purpose flour
3/4 cup (120 grams) cornmeal
1 teaspoon baking powder
2 oranges
1 1/2 cups (200 grams) almonds, ground
Orange marmalade for glaze

Preheat the oven to 350° F (180° C). Line a cake pan with parchment paper and set aside. In a bowl, with an electric mixer or wooden spoon, beat the butter with 2/3 cup (145 grams) sugar. Add the eggs, flour, cornmeal, baking powder, and the juice and grated zest of 1 orange. Beat until smooth. Add the ground almonds and beat again until smooth. Peel and remove any white pith from the remaining orange and cut into slices. In a small pan, combine the remaining 2/3 cup (145 grams) sugar with a small amount of water and cook over low heat until caramelized. Pour the caramel into the prepared pan. Arrange the orange slices in a single layer on top of the caramel. (Be careful not to burn your fingers.)

Transfer the batter to the pan and bake until a tester comes out clean, 40 to 45 minutes. Place an inverted platter over the cake, then turn over the pan and the platter together and lift off the pan. If any of the fruit has stuck to the parchment in the pan, simply place it on top of the cake. Let the cake cool completely, then place some marmalade in a small pot, thin with a little water, and heat until warm. Brush the orange glaze on top of the cake, allow to cool briefly, and serve.

AMALFI CAKE WITH RICOTTA AND PEARS

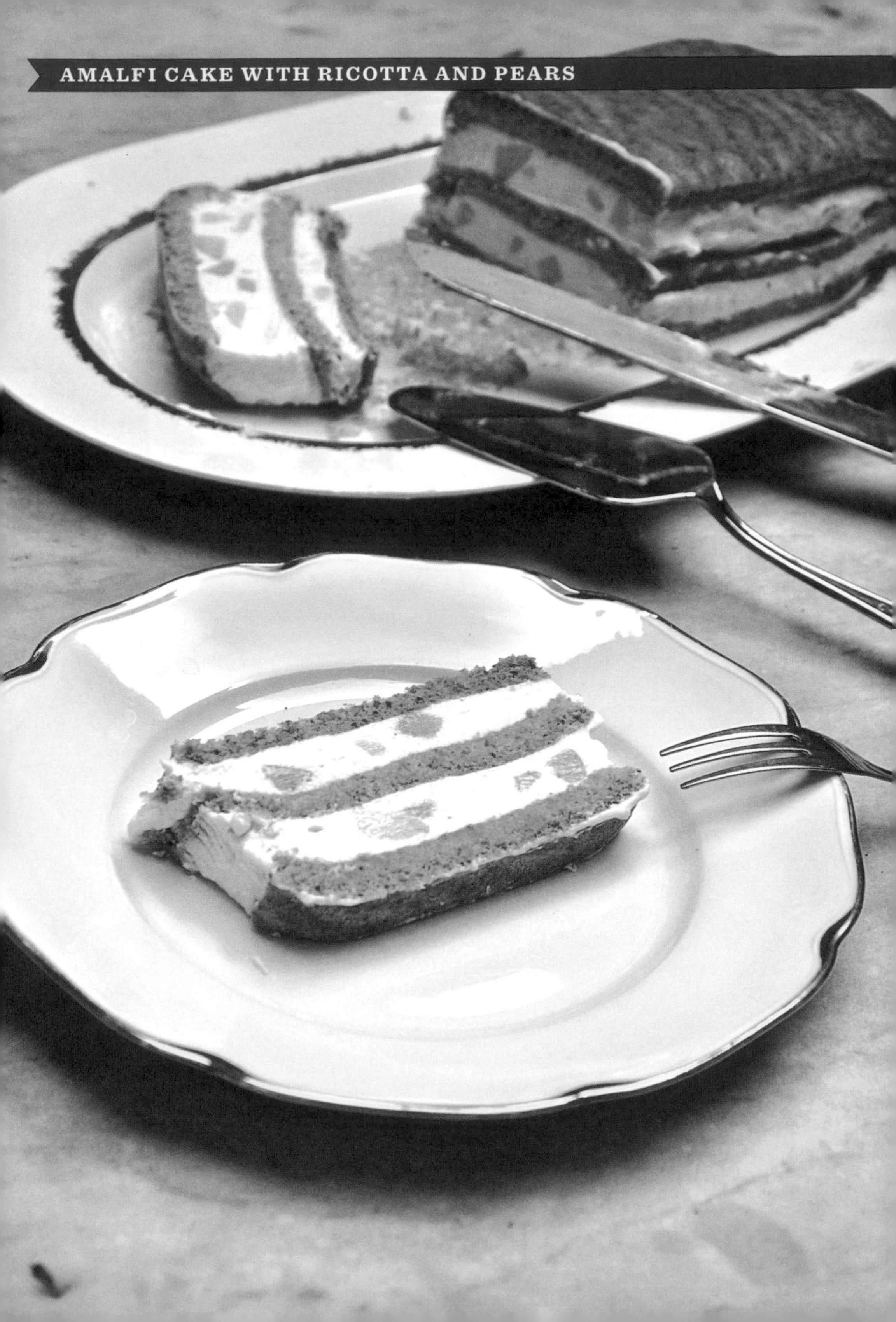

« TORTA AMALFITANA DI RICOTTA E PERE »
AMALFI CAKE WITH RICOTTA AND PEARS

This cake is truly special: three layers of hazelnut sponge cake—a little crunchier and more flavorful than a plain cake—alternate with ricotta cream and delicately flavored pears. If you want to get really fancy, garnish slices with some additional diced pears that you've cooked in liqueur right before serving, or drizzle with chocolate sauce.

SERVES 6 TO 8

Hazelnut Sponge Cake
1 cup (110 grams) hazelnuts, toasted and skinned
3 large eggs
$1/3$ cup (65 grams) sugar
$1/4$ cup (30 grams) unbleached all-purpose flour, sifted
3 $1/2$ tablespoons (50 grams) unsalted butter, melted

Filling
$1/2$ cup plus 2 tablespoons (150 milliliters) heavy cream
1 $1/2$ cups (400 grams) ricotta
$2/3$ cup (150 grams) sugar
$1/4$ teaspoon vanilla extract

Pears
1 large or 2 small (175 grams) pears
$1/4$ cup (50 grams) sugar
$1/2$ cup pear liqueur or other liqueur
1 teaspoon cornstarch
Pear juice for moistening cake (about $1/2$ cup/100 milliliters)

To make the cake, preheat the oven to 350° F (180° C). Line a jelly-roll pan with parchment paper and set aside. In a food processor with the metal blade or a nut grinder, grind the hazelnuts. Whip the eggs with the sugar until foamy. Gradually fold in the hazelnuts, flour, and butter, stirring up from the bottom with a spatula. Pour the batter into the prepared pan, gently smooth the top with a spatula, and bake until golden and firm, about 10 minutes. Set the pan on a wire rack to cool.

To make the filling, whip the cream. In a separate bowl, whisk together the ricotta, sugar, and vanilla, then fold the ricotta mixture gently into the whipped cream with a spatula. Peel and core the pears and cut them into medium dice. Toss the pear cubes in a pan with the sugar over medium heat until the sugar melts. Add the liqueur and allow it to evaporate. Meanwhile, dissolve the cornstarch in 1 tablespoon cold water and add the cornstarch mixture to the pan with the pears. Continue cooking until thickened, about 1 minute. Set aside to cool. When the cake has cooled, cut it into 3 equal-sized rectangles that will fit into a loaf pan. Brush the cake rectangles with the pear juice. Line the bottom and sides of the loaf pan with plastic wrap. Place a cake layer in the bottom of the pan. Very gently fold the cooled pears into the ricotta mixture to create the filling. Top the cake layer with half the filling and smooth with a spatula. Set a second cake rectangle on top, and spread the remaining filling on top of it. Smooth with a spatula. Top with the third cake rectangle. Allow the assembled cake to rest in the refrigerator overnight. To serve, invert the cake onto a platter, peel off the plastic wrap, and cut into slices.

« TORTA CON IL RIPIENO AL FONDENTE »
DARK CHOCOLATE TART

Chocolate and orange go beautifully together. If, like me, you find chocolate-dipped candied orange peel irresistible, this is the tart for you.

SERVES 8

Readymade short-crust pastry dough
$1/2$ cup brandy
11 ounces (300 grams) dark chocolate, finely chopped
2 large eggs
4 egg yolks
$3/4$ cup (100 grams) confectioners' sugar
$1/3$ cup (80 milliliters) heavy cream
Grated zest of 1 orange

Preheat the oven to 350° F (180° C). Place the pastry dough on a piece of parchment paper and roll out the dough. Transfer the dough round with the parchment still underneath to a tart pan. Line the crust with aluminum foil, fill with pie weights or dry

beans, and bake for 15 minutes. Meanwhile, in a small pot combine the brandy, chocolate, and 1 tablespoon water. Melt, whisking, over low heat. In a bowl, beat the eggs
and egg yolks with the confectioners' sugar. Add the cream and grated orange zest and
beat to combine. Add the melted chocolate and beat to combine thoroughly. Remove
the aluminum foil and pie weights from the crust, pour in the filling, and return to the
oven. Bake until set, about 30 minutes. Allow to cool before serving.

« TORTA AL CIOCCOLATO CON PINOLI E NOCCIOLE »
CHOCOLATE CAKE WITH PINE NUTS AND HAZELNUTS

Chocolate, nuts, and ricotta are a fantastic mix! This flourless (unless you count the
tiny amount tossed with the nuts to keep them from sinking to the bottom of the pan)
spice cake is a 100-percent grown-up dessert. I like to make this with dark chocolate,
but you can use any kind of chocolate you like.

MAKES 1 CAKE

4 large eggs
1 3/4 cups (500 grams) ricotta
1/2 teaspoon vanilla extract
1 cup (230 grams) granulated sugar
1 cup (150 grams) hazelnuts
1 cup (150 grams) pine nuts
1 teaspoon unbleached all-purpose flour
1/2 teaspoon ground cinnamon
1/2 teaspoon ground ginger
9 ounces (250 grams) chocolate, melted

Preheat the oven to 350° F (180° C). Line a cake pan with parchment paper and set
aside. Separate the eggs. In a large bowl, beat the ricotta with the egg yolks, vanilla
extract, and sugar. In a food processor or a nut grinder, grind the hazelnuts and pine
nuts. Toss the nuts with the flour, cinnamon, and ginger, and stir the ground nut mixture into the batter. Stir in the melted chocolate. With an electric mixer, whip the egg
whites until firm peaks form, then fold them into the batter. Transfer the batter to
the prepared pan and bake until a tester comes out clean, about 1 hour. Cool the cake
completely in the pan, then invert into onto a serving platter and serve.

« TORTA CIOCCOLATE E PEPERONCINO »
CHOCOLATE AND HOT PEPPER CAKE

This chocolate loaf cake is made truly exceptional with a spicy chocolate syrup that's poured over it while it's still warm.

SERVES 8

Juice of $1/2$ lemon
$1/3$ cup (80 milliliters) heavy cream
$1\,2/3$ cups (200 grams) unbleached all-purpose flour
1 teaspoon baking soda
$1/2$ cup (50 grams) plus 1 tablespoon unsweetened cocoa powder
$1\,3/4$ cups (375 grams) granulated sugar
2 large eggs
1 stick plus 4 tablespoons (175 grams) unsalted butter, softened
$1/2$ teaspoon vanilla extract
1 cup (175 grams) chocolate chips
Ground cayenne pepper to taste
2 ounces (50 grams) chopped dark chocolate for finishing

Preheat the oven to 340° F (170° C). Line a loaf pan with parchment paper and set aside. Whisk together the lemon juice and cream and set aside. In a food processor fitted with the metal blade, combine the flour, baking soda, $1/2$ cup cocoa powder, $1\,1/4$ cups (325 grams) sugar, the eggs, the cream with the lemon juice, the butter, and vanilla and process. With the machine running, through the tube, add $1/2$ cup (125 milliliters) boiling water. Add the chocolate chips, combine, and pour the batter into the prepared pan. Bake until the cake is risen and the top has split, about 1 hour.

Just before you take the cake out of the oven, prepare the syrup: In a small pot, combine $1/2$ cup (125 milliliters) water, the remaining $1/2$ cup sugar, the remaining 1 tablespoon cocoa powder, and cayenne pepper and bring to a boil. Boil until thickened slightly, about 5 minutes. Remove the cake from the oven and set the pan on a wire rack over a jelly-roll pan to catch any drips. With a toothpick, poke holes all over the warm cake and pour the syrup over it. Let the cake cool completely in the pan, then unmold and sprinkle with the chopped chocolate.

« TORTA SOFFICE RICOTTA E CIOCCOLATE »
RICOTTA AND CHOCOLATE CAKE

Whenever I make this cake, I feel like I'm in a commercial: smiling children gather around me, clamoring for a slice of this soft and fluffy chocolate cake. Ricotta is the secret to keeping it moist.

1 1/3 cups (300 grams) ricotta
1 cup (200 grams) granulated sugar
3 large eggs
1 2/3 cups (200 grams) unbleached all-purpose flour
1 tablespoon baking powder
2 tablespoons unsweetened cocoa powder
3/4 cup (150 grams) chocolate chips or chopped dark chocolate

Preheat the oven to 350° F (180° C). Line a cake pan with parchment paper and set aside. In a large bowl, mix the ricotta with the sugar. Add the eggs and mix to combine. Add the flour and baking powder and mix again until combined. Stir in the cocoa powder and chocolate chips. Pour the batter into the prepared pan and bake until a tester comes out clean, about 30 minutes. Cool in the pan on a wire rack.

« QUADROTTI AL CIOCCOLATO »
SIMPLE CHOCOLATE CAKE SQUARES

These little squares of plain cake are delightful any time—as a snack in the afternoon, as a nibble during a coffee break, or even right before bed with a glass of warm milk.

SERVES 4 TO 6

7 ounces (200 grams) dark chocolate, broken into pieces
1 stick plus 5 tablespoons (180 grams) unsalted butter
3 egg yolks
2 large eggs
1 cup (200 grams) granulated sugar

3/4 cup (100 grams) unbleached all-purpose flour
Confectioners' sugar for finishing

Preheat the oven to 350° F (180° C). Line a square baking pan with parchment paper and set aside. In the top of a double boiler, melt the chocolate with the butter. Whisk in 1 to 2 tablespoons water. Set aside to cool slightly. In a bowl, beat the egg yolks with the whole eggs. Add the sugar and the slightly cooled chocolate mixture and beat to combine. Add the flour and beat to combine. Pour the batter into the prepared pan and bake until a tester comes out clean. Cool in the pan on a wire rack. Sprinkle with confectioners' sugar just before serving.

« CUBOTTI AGLI AGRUMI »
CITRUS CAKE SQUARES

These cake squares are moistened with a delicious citrus syrup that keeps them tender for days.

SERVES 6 TO 8

7 tablespoons (100 grams) unsalted butter, melted
1/4 cup plus 2 tablespoons honey
3 large eggs
1/2 teaspoon vanilla extract
2 lemons
1 cup (200 grams) plain Greek yogurt
2 3/4 cups (350 grams) unbleached all-purpose flour
1 tablespoon baking powder
1/2 teaspoon baking soda
1 teaspoon ground cinnamon
1/2 cup (50 grams) ground almonds
1 cup (100 grams) whole almonds
1 orange
2/3 cup (150 grams) granulated sugar

Preheat the oven to 350° F (180° C). Line a rectangular baking pan with parchment paper and set aside. Beat the butter and honey. Beat in the eggs, vanilla, grated zest and juice of 1 lemon, yogurt, flour, baking powder and soda, and cinnamon. Stir in the ground almonds and pour the batter into the prepared pan. Sprinkle the whole almonds on top and bake until a tester comes out clean, about 40 minutes.

Meanwhile, prepare the syrup: Juice the remaining lemon and the orange and place the juices in a small pot with the sugar. Cook over medium-low heat until syrupy and caramelized, about 5 minutes. Pour the syrup over the baked cake (still in the pan) while it's warm. Set the pan on a wire rack to cool. Cut into squares just before serving.

« BIANCANEVE DI CIOCCOLATO BIANCO »
WHITE CHOCOLATE CAKE

Kids love this cake, which is also makes an excellent birthday cake since it's frosted with whipped cream and decorated with sprinkles. Thanks to Nicoletta Romanoff, who made this for me!

SERVES 6 TO 8

Oil for coating pan
2 sticks plus 5 tablespoons (300 grams) unsalted butter
11 ounces (300 grams) white chocolate, chopped
2 1/2 cups (300 grams) unbleached all-purpose flour
1 1/4 cups (150 grams) self-rising flour
1 3/4 cups (400 grams) granulated sugar
1 pinch salt
3 large eggs, lightly beaten
1 teaspoon vanilla extract
1 pint raspberries (optional)
2 cups (500 milliliters) heavy cream, a few drops red food coloring, and
    multi-colored chocolate candies (such as M&Ms) for finishing

Preheat the oven to 350° F (180° C). Oil a cake pan and line it with parchment paper on the bottom and about 1 inch up the sides. Set aside. Place the butter in the top of a double boiler with 1 cup (270 milliliters) water and melt. Remove the double boiler from the heat, but leave the melted butter in the pot. Add the white chocolate and whisk until the chocolate is melted. Sift both flours into a large bowl. Whisk the sugar and salt into the flour to combine, and then form a well in the dry ingredients. Pour the white chocolate mixture, eggs, and vanilla extract into the well and stir with a wooden spoon until thoroughly combined. If using the raspberries, fold them into the batter. Transfer the batter to the prepared pan and bake until a tester comes out clean, about 1 hour and 40 minutes. Let the cake cool in the pan on a wire rack. When the cake is cool, invert it onto a serving platter. To finish, lightly whip the cream and incorporate the food coloring. Frost the top and sides of the cake with the pink whipped cream. Sprinkle with the multi-colored candies, pressing them gently on the sides. Refrigerate until serving.

« PANE AL CIOCCOLATO »
CHOCOLATE BUNS

It's common for Italian kids to eat Nutella or chocolate melted onto a split roll as an afternoon snack or for breakfast. These buns take that idea one step further and include the chocolate right in the bread. The smell as they bake is intoxicating.

SERVES 6

1 large egg
1/4 cup granulated sugar
3 1/2 tablespoons (50 grams) unsalted butter, melted
1/4 cup (60 milliliters) vegetable oil
About 1/2 cup (100 milliliters) whole milk at room temperature
4 cups (500 grams) bread flour, plus more for work surface
1 envelope instant yeast
1 pinch salt
1/3 cup (75 grams) chocolate chips or chopped dark chocolate

Line a jelly-roll pan with parchment paper and set aside. In a bowl, beat the egg with the sugar. Beat in the butter, oil, and $1/2$ cup (100 milliliters) milk. In a separate large bowl, combine the flour, yeast, and salt. Pour the wet mixture into the dry ingredients and mix with a wooden spoon until combined. If the mixture seems dry, add a little additional milk.

Transfer to a lightly floured work surface and knead by hand until smooth and compact, about 10 minutes. Scatter the chocolate chips on the work surface, place the dough on top of it, and knead just until the chocolate is distributed throughout the dough. (This should only take a few turns of the dough—don't knead for too long or the chocolate will begin to melt.) Divide the dough into 12 equal-sized pieces, shape them into spherical rolls, and place them on the prepared pan. Cover with a dishtowel and set aside to rise for 1 hour and 30 minutes. After 1 hour, preheat a convection oven to 350° F (180° C). Bake the rolls in the preheated oven for 15 minutes. Serve warm or at room temperature.

« CAPRESE DI CIOCCOLATO BIANCO »
CAPRI CAKE WITH WHITE CHOCOLATE

This is one of my all-time favorites—creamy, rich with white chocolate, offset by lemon, and then there are the almonds that give the cake a distinctive texture. It all works. Don't rush this, though: It needs to cool completely before serving, and it benefits from being made the day before. Thanks to Francesca La Torre for this wonderful recipe.

SERVES 6 TO 8

1 $1/2$ cups (200 grams) almonds, ground
7 ounces (200 grams) white chocolate
5 large eggs
1 cup (200 grams) granulated sugar
1 stick plus 3 tablespoons (150 grams) unsalted butter, melted
Grated zest and juice of 1 lemon
$1/4$ cup (50 milliliters) limoncello cream liqueur
1 tablespoon baking powder
Confectioners' sugar for finishing

Preheat the oven to 340° F (170° C). Line a cake pan with parchment paper and set aside. In a food processor fitted with the metal blade, grind the almonds with the white chocolate and set aside. With an electric mixer, beat together the eggs, sugar, butter, lemon juice and zest, and liqueur. Add the ground almonds and chocolate mixture and baking powder and beat to combine. Pour the batter into the prepared pan and bake until the top is dark brown and a tester comes out clean, about 50 minutes. Set the pan on a wire rack and allow the cake to finish cooking on the rack. Serve 1 day after baking, if possible! Sprinkle with confectioners' sugar just before serving.

« TORTA GELATO ALLA FRUTTA »
FROZEN MOUSSE CAKE WITH FRUIT

This is the perfect summer dessert, as it makes use of both raspberries, which are in season in summer, and a frozen mousse that's very refreshing! For the crust use plain (no filling or nuts or chocolate chips), not-too-sweet cookies such as Oro Saiwa, or substitute graham crackers or arrowroot cookies.

SERVES 6 TO 8

4 1/2 ounces (130 grams) plain cookies
3 1/2 tablespoons (50 grams) unsalted butter, melted
2 large eggs
1/2 cup (100 grams) granulated sugar
3/4 cup plus 1 tablespoon (200 milliliters) whole milk
1/2 teaspoon vanilla extract
1 pinch salt
1/2 cup (130 milliliters) heavy cream
3 ounces (80 grams) white chocolate, finely chopped
1 pint (250 grams) raspberries
White chocolate curls for finishing

Line a springform pan with parchment paper and set aside. In a food processor fitted with the metal blade, grind the cookies. Add the melted butter and process until combined. Press into the prepared pan by hand, making an even layer in the bottom of the pan. Separate the eggs. Beat the yolks with the sugar, then add the milk and vanilla.

Cook this mixture, whisking constantly, over low heat until thickened to a custard. Transfer to a large bowl and set aside to cool. When the custard is cool, with an electric mixer, whip the egg whites with the salt until stiff peaks form, then fold them into the custard. Whip the cream to stiff peaks and fold it in as well. Fold in the white chocolate and about half the raspberries. Spread the white chocolate mixture over the cookie crust. Puree the remaining raspberries for finishing, strain the puree through a chinois or fine-mesh sieve, and discard the solids. Drizzle most of the raspberry sauce on top of the cake decoratively with a spoon, reserving a small amount of the sauce. Freeze the cake overnight. Before serving, unbuckle the ring from around the cake. Cut the cake into slices. (Run the knife blade under hot water between slices if necessary.) Top each serving with the remaining raspberry sauce and white chocolate curls.

« TORTA DIPLOMATICA »
LAYER CAKE WITH PASTRY CREAM

This is a classic Italian cake, sold in most bakeries. It has several components, but it's really not difficult to make at home.

SERVES 6 TO 8

2 packages readymade puff pastry
1 egg, lightly beaten
Confectioners' sugar for sprinkling
4 egg yolks
1/2 cup (100 grams) granulated sugar
1/4 cup (30 grams) unbleached all-purpose flour
1 1/2 cups plus 2 tablespoons (400 milliliters) whole milk at room temperature
1/2 teaspoon vanilla extract
1 cup (250 milliliters) heavy cream
1 readymade genoise or sponge cake layer
Peach juice (or peach liqueur) for brushing
1 1/4 cups (100 grams) toasted sliced almonds, 5 plain cookies ground into crumbs, and confectioners' sugar for finishing

Preheat the oven to 400° F (200° C). Cut 2 disks from the puff pastry and place them in a single layer on a cookie sheet with the parchment from the package underneath. Brush with the beaten egg, sprinkle lightly with confectioners' sugar, and pierce each disk all over with a fork. Bake until crisp, 20 to 25 minutes.

Meanwhile, in a bowl, beat the egg yolks with the granulated sugar. Beat in the flour, then transfer the mixture to a pot. Add the milk and the vanilla and cook, whisking constantly, over low heat until the mixture thickens into a pastry cream. Transfer to a bowl and set aside to cool. When the pastry cream is cool, whip the heavy cream until stiff peaks form, then fold it into the pastry cream a little at a time, using a spatula.

Trim the genoise layer into a disk the same size as the puff pastry disks. Place one of the puff pastry layers on a cake plate. Top with about $1/3$ of the cooled cream mixture, spreading it evenly with a spatula. Brush the genoise disk with the peach juice and place it on top of the custard. Spread another $1/3$ of the cream mixture on top of the genoise, and place the second disk of puff pastry on top. With an offset spatula, spread the remaining cream mixture on the sides of the cake. In a small bowl, mix the almonds and cookie crumbs, then gently press the mixture against the sides of the cake by hand. Sprinkle the top with confectioners' sugar. Refrigerate until serving time.

« PASTIERA NAPOLETANA »
NEAPOLITAN RICOTTA CAKE

Pastiera is one of the signature dishes of Naples and a must for any Easter celebration. Brothers Francesco and Marcello Bocci, winners of the Italian pastry and baking championships, were guests on my show and kindly shared this recipe with me and my viewers. Cooked wheat berries can be found sold in jars in Italian groceries—they are particularly easy to find in spring as Easter approaches.

SERVES 6 TO 8

1 stick plus 6 tablespoons (200 grams) unsalted butter, softened
2 cups (400 grams) granulated sugar
2 vanilla beans
4 large eggs

1 pinch salt
4 cups (500 grams) unbleached all-purpose flour
1 teaspoon (5 grams) baking powder
3/4 cup (200 grams) ricotta, drained in a sieve
7 ounces (200 grams) cooked wheat berries
2 to 3 drops orange flower water
1/3 cup (50 grams) candied orange and citron peel, chopped
Confectioners' sugar for finishing

Preheat the oven to 340° F (170° C). Line a 10-inch tart pan with parchment paper and set aside. To make the crust, in a bowl, combine the butter and 1 cup (200 grams) sugar. Scrape out the seeds of 1 vanilla bean into the bowl. Add 2 eggs and the salt and beat to combine. Add the flour and baking powder and mix by hand, pinching to create a ball of dough. Wrap the dough in plastic and refrigerate for at least 30 minutes. To make the ricotta filling, combine the ricotta and the remaining 1 cup (200 grams) sugar. Scrape in the seeds of the remaining vanilla bean along with the wheat berries. Whisk in the orange flower water and candied fruit peel. Lightly beat the remaining 2 eggs, then add to the ricotta mixture and whisk to combine.

Roll out the dough to about 1/4 inch thick and transfer it to the prepared pan. Cut away and reserve any excess dough for the lattice. Pierce the crust all over with a fork. Pour in the ricotta filling and smooth the top with a spatula. Roll out the reserved dough to about 1/8 inch thick and cut it into strips about 1/2 inch wide. Form a lattice on top of the ricotta filling with the strips. Pinch the lattice strips to the border and cut away any excess. Bake until the filling is set and the crust is browned, about 1 hour. Allow the cake to cool completely. Sprinkle with confectioners' sugar just before serving.

« TORTA DI ANTONIA »
ANTONIA'S CHOCOLATE RICOTTA CAKE WITH CHOCOLATE GLAZE

This is another great choice for a birthday cake. It has a delicious chocolate glaze. I've been asking my friend Antonia Maiello to give me this recipe for years, but she's such a masterful baker that she just does it by eye and has never written down the measurements. Finally, I invited her onto my show and handed her a scale and a set of measuring cups! You must follow the exact order for adding the ingredients given here.

MAKES 1 CAKE

^{2}/$_3$ cup (80 grams) unbleached all-purpose flour
1 tablespoon baking powder
1 cup (250 grams) ricotta
1 cup (250 grams) granulated sugar
3 large eggs
^{1}/$_2$ cup plus 2 tablespoons (75 grams) unsweetened cocoa powder
7 tablespoons (100 grams) unsalted butter, melted
3 ^{1}/$_2$ ounces (100 grams) dark chocolate
Colored sprinkles for finishing

Preheat the oven to 350° F (180° C). Line a cake pan with parchment paper and set aside. In a small bowl, combine the flour and baking powder. With an electric mixer, beat the ricotta and sugar until combined. Beat in the eggs, cocoa powder, flour and baking powder mixture, and butter, beating until smooth between additions. Continue beating until the mixture is light and fluffy. Pour the batter into the prepared pan and bake until a tester comes out clean, about 30 minutes. Set the pan on a wire rack and allow the cake to cool completely. For the glaze, unmold the cake and set it on a serving platter. Melt the dark chocolate in a double boiler, and then spread it on the cooled cake with a spatula. Top with colored sprinkles.

« TORTA ZEBRATA »
ZEBRA-STRIPED CAKE

This wonderful cake is not only tasty, but it looks great, too! You create the stripes by alternating portions of vanilla and chocolate batter. Thanks to Alessia, who always watches my show and has emailed me so many ideas. One of these days we're bound to meet in person!

MAKES 1 CAKE

4 large eggs
1 cup (250 grams) granulated sugar
^{3}/$_4$ cup plus 1 tablespoon (200 milliliters) vegetable oil
1 cup (250 milliliters) whole milk

¹/₂ teaspoon vanilla extract
2 ¹/₂ cups (300 grams) unbleached all-purpose flour
1 tablespoon baking powder
2 heaping tablespoons unsweetened cocoa powder

Preheat the oven to 350° F (180° C). Line a cake pan with parchment paper and set aside. With an electric mixer, beat the eggs with the sugar until pale yellow and smooth. Beat in the oil, milk, and vanilla. In a small bowl, combine the flour and baking powder. Add the dry ingredients to the batter and beat until very smooth and thick. Transfer half the batter to a clean bowl. Add the cocoa powder to one bowl of batter. Place 3 tablespoons of the yellow batter in the center of the prepared pan. Place 3 tablespoons of the cocoa batter on top of it. From there, create alternating concentric circles of the two types of batter until you've used up all the batter. Bake the cake until a tester comes out clean, about 40 minutes.

« SCHIACCIATA FIORENTINA »
FLORENTINE CARNIVAL CAKE

This is one of the few desserts made for Carnival that is not fried. But it really is a shame to restrict it to Carnival—it should be enjoyed year-round. In Florence, a fleur-de-lis, the city's symbol, is often stenciled on top of the cake.

SERVES 4 TO 6

2 large eggs
1 pinch salt
¹/₄ cup (50 milliliters) plus 1 tablespoon extra-virgin olive oil
¹/₃ cup (60 grams) plus 1 tablespoon granulated sugar
¹/₄ cup (50 milliliters) plus 1 tablespoon whole milk
Grated zest and juice of 1 orange
¹/₂ cup (60 grams) plus 2 tablespoons unbleached all-purpose flour
1 tablespoon baking powder
Confectioners' sugar for finishing

Preheat the oven to 340° F (170° C). Line an 8-, 9-, or 10-inch cake pan with parchment paper and set aside. Beat the eggs with the salt. Add the oil and continue beating while adding the sugar and the milk. Add the orange zest and juice. Then add the flour, about 1 tablespoon at a time, beating smooth between additions. Beat in the baking powder. Beat until all the ingredients are incorporated, then set aside to rest for about 10 minutes. Pour the batter into the prepared pan and bake until a tester comes out clean, about 15 minutes. Let the cake cool in the pan on a wire rack. When it is completely cool, sprinkle with confectioners' sugar.

« PANETTONE IMBOTTITO »
PANETTONE WITH CHESTNUT CREAM

This recipe takes a store-bought Italian Christmas cake, panettone, and gussies it up with candied chestnuts and a tasty glaze. It has to be made in advance and refrigerated. In season, you can buy panettone in Italian specialty stores and in many grocery stores. Candied chestnuts are sometimes labeled "marrons glacés."

SERVES 10

1 readymade panettone
2 large eggs
Granulated sugar to taste
2 (8-ounce/500 gram) tubs mascarpone
1/4 cup (50 milliliters) cognac
9 ounces or 12 to 13 pieces (250 grams) candied chestnuts, chopped
1 1/2 cups (200 grams) confectioners' sugar
1 egg white
Juice of 1/2 lemon
Silver dragées for finishing

Cut the top off the panettone, reserving the top. Hollow out the pannettone by carefully scooping out the crumb inside, leaving about 1/2 inch on the bottom and sides. Cut the crumb into small cubes and reserve. Separate the eggs. In a bowl, with an electric mixer, beat the yolks with enough granulated sugar to make a pale yellow and foamy mixture. Add the mascarpone and the cognac and beat to combine. Add the chopped candied chestnuts. Separately, whip the 2 egg whites until soft peaks form, then fold them into the mixture. Finally, fold in the cubes of panettone.

Place the pannettone on a piece of parchment paper. Fill the panettone with the mascarpone mixture, place the reserved top on it, and refrigerate for 2 hours. Mix together the confectioners' sugar with the egg white and lemon juice to make a glaze. Peel off the paper from the bottom of the panettone and place the cake on a serving plate. Pour the glaze over the top of the panettone and let it run down the sides, gently spreading it with a knife if necessary. When the glaze begins to harden but is still sticky, sprinkle with the dragées. Return the panettone to the refrigerator and refrigerate until just before serving.

« PANETTONE CON SALSA ALLA VANIGLIA »
PANETTONE WITH VANILLA SAUCE

This vanilla sauce is ready in an instant and helps make a store-bought panettone a little more special. Because the sauce is made with flour, there is no risk of it breaking. Just be sure to let it cool so that it thickens. If I have leftover sauce, I dip cookies in it, or just eat it with a spoon!

MAKES 1 CAKE, 8 TO 10 SERVINGS

1 ½ cups plus 2 tablespoons (400 milliliters) heavy cream
½ cup (100 milliliters) whole milk
1 teaspoon vanilla extract
5 egg yolks
½ cup (125 grams) granulated sugar
1 readymade panettone

In a pot, combine the cream, milk, and vanilla. Warm over low heat, but don't allow the mixture to boil—remove from the heat as soon as the first bubbles break the surface. In a bowl, beat the egg yolks with the sugar. Add the warmed milk and cream mixture and whisk vigorously, then return to the pot over low heat. Cook, whisking constantly, until the mixture is slightly thickened and coats a spoon. Transfer the sauce to a cold bowl and allow to cool. It should thicken further as it does. To serve, cut slices of panettone and top each one with a spoonful or two of sauce.

« MATTONELLA GLASSATA »
CHRISTMAS FRUIT AND NUT CAKE

This colorful and rich dessert is a Christmas tradition. Just a small square is very satisfying.

SERVES 6 TO 8

2 1/4 cups (300 grams) Brazil nuts, chopped
1 cup (150 grams) chopped walnuts
1 2/3 cups (250 grams) chopped pitted dates
1 1/4 cups (180 grams) dried apricots, chopped
3/4 cup (120 grams) raisins
1 cup (150 grams) chopped candied orange peel
1/2 cup (80 grams) chopped candied cherries
3/4 cup (100 grams) unbleached all-purpose flour
1 1/2 teaspoons baking powder
Juice of 1/2 orange
3 large eggs, lightly beaten
2 cups (250 grams) confectioners' sugar
2 egg whites
1/2 teaspoon lemon juice

Preheat the oven to 325° F (160° C). Line a rectangular baking pan with parchment paper and set aside. In a bowl, combine the nuts, dried dates, apricots, and raisins, candied orange peel, and candied cherries. In a small bowl, toss together the flour and baking powder. Add the dry mixture to the bowl with the nuts and toss to combine, then add the orange juice and eggs and stir to combine. Transfer the mixture to the prepared pan and bake until browned and dry to the touch, about 1 hour. When the cake is done, make the glaze by mixing the confectioners' sugar, egg whites, and lemon juice in a small bowl until combined. Unmold the cake and set it on a platter. Drizzle the glaze on top and allow the cake to sit for at least 2 hours. Cut into small squares to serve.

« STELLA DI NATALE »
CHRISTMAS STAR CAKE

A star-shaped dessert topped with silver dragées is a festive way to celebrate Christmas.

SERVES 6 TO 8

2 packages readymade puff pastry
1 egg yolk
Whole milk for egg wash
Granulated sugar for sprinkling and dredging
Silver dragées for sprinkling
1 1/4 cups (300 milliliters) heavy cream
1/2 cup (50 grams) confectioners' sugar
1 pint (340 grams) raspberries
1 pint fresh red currants
1 egg white, whisked

Preheat the oven to 350° F (180° C). Using a cardboard stencil as a guide, cut 2 stars out of the puff pastry and place them in a single layer on a cookie sheet. Whisk the egg yolk with a small amount of milk, then brush one of the stars with the egg wash. Pierce the egg wash–brushed star with a fork in several places and sprinkle the top with granulated sugar and silver dragées. Poke holes in the other star with a fork as well, but don't brush or decorate it. Place any scraps of puff pastry on the cookie sheet (or another cookie sheet) and bake both the stars and the scraps until crisp, about 20 minutes. When the puff pastry is done, set it aside to cool.

When the puff pastry is cool, in a bowl, with an electric mixer, whip the cream and confectioners' sugar until stiff peaks form. Fold in the raspberries. Place the undecorated star on a serving plate. Spread the whipped cream mixture with the raspberries on top of the star. Place the other star on top (with the decorated side facing up). Crumble the puff pastry scraps by hand and gently press the crumbs against the sides of the cake. Dredge the currants in the egg white and then in some sugar and place the currants on top of the cake. Refrigerate until serving time.

« TRONCHETTO DI NATALE »
YULE LOG CAKE

This cake is a challenge but so much fun to make. Luigi Biasetto, one of the best pastry chefs in Italy, provided this recipe.

SERVES 6 TO 8

3 tablespoons plus 1 teaspoon (25 grams) unsweetened cocoa powder
$1/4$ cup plus 2 tablespoons (65 grams) potato starch
$1/2$ cup (50 grams) almond flour
1 cup (125 grams) unbleached all-purpose flour
4 large eggs
1 $1/2$ cups (300 grams) granulated sugar
3 tablespoons (40 grams) unsalted butter, melted
4 egg yolks
10 ounces (290 grams) milk chocolate, melted
1 $3/4$ cups (400 grams) heavy cream
Confectioners' sugar and chocolate garnishes for finishing

Preheat the oven to 350° F (180° C). Line a jelly-roll pan with parchment paper and set aside. In a small bowl, whisk together the cocoa powder, potato starch, almond flour, and all-purpose flour. Separate the eggs. Lightly beat the yolks and set aside. In a large bowl, with an electric mixer, beat the whites until soft peaks form. Beat in $1/2$ cup (100 grams) sugar. Fold in the melted butter, the 4 egg yolks from the separated eggs, and the dry ingredients. Mix gently until combined, trying to deflate the egg whites as little as possible. Transfer this mixture to the prepared pan in an even layer, smooth the top with a spatula, and bake until it springs back when pressed with a finger, 10 to 15 minutes. Set the cake aside to cool.

Meanwhile, make the mousse. In a bowl, mix together $3/4$ cup plus 1 tablespoon (200 milliliters) water, the remaining 1 cup (200 grams) sugar, and the 4 egg yolks. Microwave on the highest setting for 2 minutes. Stir in the melted milk chocolate and set the mixture aside to cool. When the chocolate mixture has cooled, whip the cream and gently fold it into the chocolate mixture. Refrigerate until cool.

When the mousse is cool and the cake has cooled completely, slide the cake, still on the parchment paper, onto a work surface. With a spatula, spread about half the mousse in a thin layer on top. Roll up the cake jelly-roll style into a log, using the parchment to keep it even and peeling off the parchment as you go. Transfer the rolled cake to a serving platter and frost the top and sides with the remaining mousse. Refrigerate until serving. Sprinkle with confectioners' sugar and decorate with chocolate garnishes just before serving.

« PANETTONCINI FARCITI »
STUFFED MINI-PANETTONE

Christmas celebrations last several days in Italy, and it seems like panettone is served at every meal. Here's something a little different: mini-panettone cakes filled with coffee-flavored mascarpone and drizzled with white chocolate.

SERVES 4 TO 6

2 miniature panettone cakes
2 tablespoons mascarpone
1 to 2 tablespoons strong coffee
1 to 2 tablespoons sugar
2 tablespoons chopped hazelnuts
7 ounces (200 grams) white chocolate, melted
Silver dragées, *quanto basta*

Cut the tops off the panettone cakes and reserve. Hollow the cakes by scooping out the crumb inside. Crumble the interior of the cakes into a bowl. Mix with the mascarpone and coffee. Add the sugar and chopped hazelnuts. Fill the cakes with the mascarpone mixture and place the tops back on the cakes. Drizzle the white chocolate over the panettones and sprinkle with the dragées. Refrigerate until serving time.

« TORTA DELLA NONNA »
GRANDMA'S TART

This traditional Italian tart is made in slightly different ways in various parts of the country but always includes the zing of lemon. This recipe is from Antonia Mecacci.

SERVES 6 TO 8

3/4 cup (175 grams) granulated sugar
1 large egg
1 stick plus 1 tablespoon (125 grams) unsalted butter, softened
2 1/4 cups (280 grams) unbleached all-purpose flour
1 pinch salt
1 1/2 teaspoons baking powder
2 cups (500 milliliters) whole milk
Zest of 1 lemon
3 egg yolks
Pine nuts and confectioners' sugar for finishing

To make the crust, in a bowl, combine 1/2 cup (100 grams) sugar and the egg. Add the butter, 1 3/4 cups (220 grams) flour, salt, and baking powder and knead until you have a compact dough. Wrap the dough in plastic and refrigerate until firm, about 1 hour.

Meanwhile, make the filling. Combine the milk and lemon zest in a pot and scald the milk. In a bowl, combine the remaining 1/4 cup (75 grams) sugar, egg yolks, and remaining 1/2 cup (60 grams) flour. Remove and discard the lemon zest and add the scalded milk to the egg yolk mixture. Whisk to combine. Transfer the mixture to a pot (the pot you used to scald the milk is fine) and cook over low heat, whisking constantly, until thickened. Transfer to a bowl and refrigerate until needed.

Preheat the oven to 350° F (180° C). Place about three-fourths of the dough on the work surface between 2 pieces of parchment paper and roll into a disk with a rolling pin. Transfer the disk to a tart pan with the parchment paper still underneath. Peel off and discard the top piece of parchment. Fill the crust with the prepared filling, spreading it smooth. Roll out the remaining dough into a disk and place it on top of the filling. Pinch the edges together to seal. Sprinkle a few pine nuts on top and bake until the crust is golden, 20 to 25 minutes. Allow the tart to cool in the pan. Sprinkle with confectioners' sugar just before serving.

« TORTA DI AMARETTI E PESCHE »
AMARETTO COOKIE AND PEACH CAKE

Ripe peaches filled with amaretto cookie crumbs are a signature dessert in my native region of Piedmont. I've combined those flavors in this cake. Every year for his birthday, my brother, Roberto, invites friends out to the country and throws a big barbecue dinner. One year I made this cake and brought it out for the party, but I got there early to help out with the cooking and preparation. We started nibbling on this as we worked, and by the time the guests arrived that evening, my entire dessert contribution had been polished off!

MAKES 1 CAKE

3 $^1/_2$ ounces (100 grams) amaretto cookies
3 large eggs
$^2/_3$ cup (150 grams) granulated sugar
$^3/_4$ cup (100 grams) unbleached all-purpose flour
1 teaspoon baking powder
2 pounds (1 kilogram) peaches, peeled, pitted, and sliced
1 cup (100 grams) almonds, finely chopped

Preheat the oven to 350° F (180° C). Line a cake pan with parchment paper and set aside. Grind the cookies finely in a food processor fitted with the metal blade and set aside. Separate the eggs. In a large bowl, beat the yolks with the sugar. Add the flour and baking powder and beat to combine. Add the cookie crumbs. Whip the egg whites until soft peaks form, then gently fold into the mixture in the large bowl. Transfer the batter to the prepared pan. Arrange the peach slices on top in an attractive pattern. Press gently, if necessary, to partially submerge them in the batter. Sprinkle with the chopped almonds and bake until set, about 45 minutes. Cool at least slightly before serving.

« CROSTATA DI AMARENE E RICOTTA »
SOUR CHERRY AND RICOTTA PIE

Fabio loves a dessert made with ricotta. Sometimes I make this pie for him with chocolate chips, but when we're out in the country, where I make sour cherry jam all the
time, I bake this version instead.

SERVES 4 TO 6

1 3/4 cups (500 grams) ricotta
1 cup (200 grams) granulated sugar
1 large egg
1 1/2 packages readymade short-crust pastry dough
4 to 5 tablespoons sour cherry jam
Confectioners' sugar for finishing

Preheat the oven to 350° F (180° C). In a bowl, mix the ricotta and sugar together, then
mix in the egg and combine thoroughly. Roll out 1 package of short-crust pastry dough
into a disk and line a pie pan with high sides with the disk. Spread the sour cherry jam
on the crust and pour the ricotta mixture on top. Smooth with a spatula. Roll out the
remaining short-crust pastry dough into a disk and cut it into strips. Make a lattice on
top of the pie with the strips. Bake until the filling is set and the crust is golden, 40 to
45 minutes. Set aside to cool. Sprinkle with confectioners' sugar just before serving.

« CROSTATA AL LIMONE E PINOLI »
LEMON PINE NUT TART

My daughter Matilde continues to challenge me in the lemon tart department. She
insists that the cafeteria at her school serves the best one she's ever tasted, and I keep
trying to improve my version in order to change her mind once and for all. While I haven't succeeded yet, I think you'll find that my latest lemon tart is pretty great. If you
like it, let my daughter know!

1 package readymade short-crust pastry dough
2 large eggs

4 egg yolks
$^2/_3$ cup (140 grams) granulated sugar
$^1/_2$ cup (100 milliliters) lemon juice, or more to taste
3 $^1/_2$ tablespoons (50 grams) unsalted butter, cut into pieces
1 cup (100 grams) almond flour
$^1/_4$ cup pine nuts
Confectioners' sugar for finishing

Preheat the oven to 400° F (200° C). Line a pie pan with parchment paper. Roll out the dough into a disk and place it in the pie pan so that it lines the bottom and sides. Pierce the bottom of the crust all over with a fork. Line with aluminum foil and fill with pie weights or dry beans. Bake for 25 minutes.

Meanwhile, in a pot off the heat, whisk together the eggs, egg yolks, and sugar. Whisk in the lemon juice and butter and cook over low heat, whisking constantly, until thickened. Remove from the heat and whisk in the almond flour. Refrigerate until needed.

When the crust is done baking, remove the aluminum foil and pie weights from the crust and allow to cool completely. Preheat a broiler. When the crust is cool, transfer the filling to the crust and spread until smooth with a spatula. Sprinkle the pine nuts on top and put the pie under the broiler until the pine nuts turn golden, 1 to 2 minutes. Watch closely to guard against burning. Allow the tart to cool completely. Sprinkle with confectioners' sugar just before serving.

« TORTA AL LIMONE CON AMARETTI E TÈ »
TEA-FLAVORED LEMON TART WITH AMARETTO COOKIE CRUST

The crust for this lemon tart is flavored with some tea leaves, which add an interesting dimension. Tea sommelier Francesca Natali gave me the recipe.

SERVES 6 TO 8

7 ounces (200 grams) amaretto cookies
15 grams Darjeeling tea leaves
1 stick plus 6 tablespoons (200 grams) unsalted butter

2 tablespoons Earl Grey tea leaves
4 large eggs
1/2 cup (120 grams) granulated sugar
1 1/4 cups (120 grams) almond flour
Juice and grated zest of 2 lemons
Whipped cream and lemon slices for finishing

Preheat the oven to 350° F (180° C). In a food processor fitted with the metal blade, process the amaretto cookies and the Darjeeling tea leaves. Melt 4 tablespoons butter, add to the food processor, and process until you have a moist, finely ground mixture. Line a pie pan with parchment paper and press the cookie mixture into the pan to form a crust. Bake for 10 minutes.

Meanwhile, place the remaining 1 stick and 2 tablespoons butter in a small pot with the Early Grey tea. Place over low heat and cook, stirring frequently, until the butter has melted. Set aside. In a bowl, beat the eggs with the sugar. Beat in the almond flour, lemon juice, and lemon zest. Strain the melted butter, discard the Early Grey tea leaves, and beat the butter into the egg mixture. Pour the filling into the crust and bake until the filling is set, about 25 minutes. Allow to cool before serving. Just before serving, top each slice with a dollop of whipped cream and a lemon slice.

« TORTA NOCCIOLE E MELE »
APPLE HAZELNUT CAKE

The first time I made this cake, I knew as soon as I took it out of the oven that it was special. The batter is stuffed with hazelnuts and apples and contains very little flour, resulting in a soft cake that's perfect paired with a glass of sweet dessert wine.

MAKES 1 CAKE

1 cup (160 grams) toasted hazelnuts
1/2 cup (120 grams) granulated sugar
1 1/4 cups (150 grams) unbleached all-purpose flour
1 teaspoon baking powder
1 pinch salt

1 stick plus 3 tablespoons (150 grams) unsalted butter, melted
1 large egg
1 large or 2 small apples, peeled, cored, and sliced
Chopped hazelnuts, confectioners' sugar, and whipped cream or vanilla
    ice cream for finishing

Preheat the oven to 350° F (180° C). Line a cake pan with parchment paper and set aside. In a food processor fitted with the metal blade, grind the hazelnuts with $1/4$ cup (60 grams) sugar. Add the flour, baking powder, and salt and process briefly to combine. In a bowl, mix the melted butter with the remaining $1/4$ cup sugar and the egg. Stir in the hazelnut mixture. Transfer about half the batter to the prepared pan. Arrange the apple slices on top of the batter in the pan. Cover with the remaining batter and smooth the top with a spatula. (The apples should not be visible.) Sprinkle with chopped hazelnuts and bake until a tester comes out clean, about 30 minutes. Serve warm. To serve, sprinkle slices with confectioners' sugar and accompany each serving with a dollop of whipped cream or a scoop of ice cream.

« TORTA ROMANTICA »
ROMANTIC APPLE PIE

I call this apple pie with amarena sour cherries and amaretto cookies "romantic," because after I take a few bites I'm always in a much better mood! When I'm out in the country, I use fresh sour cherries from the tree in our yard, and I enlist the kids to pick them. In the city, I use amarena sour cherries in syrup, and I only use four or five of them. P.S. It's up to you whether to make your own sweet pastry dough or buy readymade dough from the refrigerator case or freezer of the grocery store.

SERVES 6 TO 8

2 apples
1 tablespoon sugar
Juice of $1/2$ lemon
2 packages readymade short-crust pastry dough, or 1 batch homemade
    sweet pastry dough (see below)
15 amaretto cookies

**³/₄ cup (100 grams) fresh amarena sour cherries, pitted, or 4 to 5
amarena sour cherries in syrup with 2 teaspoons syrup
Confectioners' sugar for garnish**

Preheat the oven to 350°F (180°C). Peel and core the apples and cut into thin slices.
Place the apples in a small bowl, sprinkle with 1 tablespoon sugar and the lemon juice,
and toss to combine. Set aside. Roll out one ball of pastry dough between two pieces of
parchment paper, lightly flouring if necessary to keep it from sticking. Peel off the top
piece of parchment and transfer the dough on the parchment to a pie pan. Pierce the
crust with a fork in several places. With your fingers, crumble the cookies and scatter
them over the crust. Add the apples and the cherries. Roll out the other ball of pastry
dough between two pieces of parchment paper. Remove the top piece of parchment
and invert the second piece of dough on top of the pie. Carefully peel off the parchment on top and discard. Pinch the edges of the two pieces of dough together. Trim
and discard any excess. Bake until golden and bubbling, about 40 minutes. Allow to
cool. Sprinkle with confectioners' sugar just before serving.

Sweet Pastry Dough
**2 sticks plus 2 tablespoons (250 grams) unsalted butter, cold, cut into
pieces
1 scant cup (200 grams) sugar
2 large eggs, lightly beaten
¹/₄ teaspoon vanilla extract
1 pinch salt
2 ¹/₂ cups (300 grams) unbleached all-purpose flour**

To make the sweet pastry dough, in a bowl, toss the butter pieces with the sugar. Stir
in the eggs and vanilla. Add the salt and flour, stir just to combine, then turn the dough
out to a lightly floured work surface. As quickly as possible, knead with your fingertips until the mixture forms a dough. (You're trying not to allow the dough to heat up,
as the butter will melt, resulting in a greasy crust.) Divide the dough into two pieces,
form each into a ball, wrap the balls of dough in plastic, and refrigerate for at least 1
hour or freeze for at least 20 minutes.

« TORTA ALLE NOCCIOLE DEL 2 »
HAZELNUT CAKE

Hazelnut cake is a great way to end a winter meal. A thin slice of this rich buttery cake goes a long way—and pairs beautifully with dessert wine.

MAKES 1 CAKE

1 cup (200 grams) granulated sugar
2 large eggs
1 stick plus 6 tablespoons (200 grams) unsalted butter, melted
1 $^2/_3$ cups (200 grams) unbleached all-purpose flour
1 teaspoon baking powder
$^1/_4$ cup (50 milliliters) whole milk
1 pinch salt
1 $^1/_2$ cups (200 grams) hazelnuts, toasted and chopped
Confectioners' sugar for finishing

Preheat the oven to 325° F (160° C). Line a cake pan with parchment paper and set aside. In a bowl, with an electric mixer, beat the sugar and eggs until pale yellow. Beat in the butter, then add the flour in small amounts, beating to incorporate between additions. Beat in the baking powder, milk, and salt. Beat in the hazelnuts. Pour the batter into the prepared pan and bake until a tester comes out clean, 30 to 40 minutes. Allow to cool. Sprinkle with confectioners' sugar just before serving.

« CROSTATA NUTELLA E RICOTTA »
NUTELLA AND RICOTTA TART

Who can resist Nutella, Italy's famous hazelnut and chocolate spread? Pair this tart with a big bowl of cut-up fruit for a balanced dessert that everyone will enjoy. If you're really pressed for time, use a store-bought crust rather than making your own.

MAKES 1 TART

1 1/4 cups (150 grams) unbleached all-purpose flour
6 tablespoons (80 grams) unsalted butter, cut into pieces
1/3 cup plus 1 tablespoon (60 grams plus 1 tablespoon) granulated sugar
1 large egg
1 pinch salt
1/2 teaspoon vanilla extract
1 jar Nutella or other hazelnut chocolate spread
1 1/2 cups (400 grams) ricotta

Preheat the oven to 350° F (180° C). To make the crust, in a bowl, combine the flour and the butter. Pinch together until the mixture resembles sand. Add 1/3 cup (60 grams) sugar, the egg, salt, and vanilla and knead just until combined. Form the mixture into a ball. Wrap the dough in plastic and freeze until firm, about 15 minutes. Place the dough on the work surface between 2 pieces of parchment paper and roll out into a disk with a rolling pin. Transfer the disk to a tart pan with the parchment paper still underneath. Peel off and discard the top piece of parchment. Spread the Nutella on the crust. Mix the ricotta and the remaining 1 tablespoon sugar and spread it on top of the Nutella in an even layer. Bake until the crust is golden and the ricotta is set, about 45 minutes. Allow to cool before serving.

« TORTA DI RISO »
RICE TART

This rice tart is crunchy on the outside and creamy in the center—not mushy, as I admit I do find some rice desserts to be.

SERVES 8

3 cups (750 milliliters) whole milk
1/4 cup (50 grams) short-grain rice
1/2 teaspoon ground cinnamon
1 pinch salt
1 cup (200 grams) granulated sugar
3 large eggs
6 tablespoons (80 grams) unsalted butter, melted

2 tablespoons pine nuts
Grated zest of 1 lemon
$1/3$ cup (50 grams) raisins
Confectioners' sugar for finishing

Combine the milk and rice in a pot with the cinnamon, salt, and $1/4$ cup (50 grams) sugar and bring to a boil, then reduce to simmer and simmer briskly until the rice is cooked and has absorbed the milk, about 15 minutes. Set the rice aside to cool.

Preheat the oven to 350° F (180° C). Line a tart pan with parchment paper and set aside. In a bowl, with a whisk, beat the eggs with all but 1 tablespoon of the remaining sugar. Stir in the butter, 1 tablespoon pine nuts, lemon zest, and raisins. Add the cooled rice to the egg mixture, then pour the rice mixture into the prepared pan. Sprinkle with the remaining 1 tablespoon sugar and 1 tablespoon pine nuts. Bake until set, 30 to 40 minutes. Allow to cool, then sprinkle with confectioners' sugar just before serving.

« CROSTATA CON ARANCIA E CIOCCOLATO »
ORANGE AND CHOCOLATE TART

The combination of orange and chocolate is always divine. Here the chocolate is in the crust and the orange is in the filling.

SERVES 6 TO 8

2 $1/4$ cups (275 grams) unbleached all-purpose flour
$1/3$ cup (45 grams) unsweetened cocoa powder
$2/3$ cup plus 2 tablespoons (150 grams plus 2 tablespoons) granulated
    sugar
1 stick plus 3 tablespoons (150 grams) unsalted butter, melted
1 pinch salt
4 oranges
5 large eggs
$1/2$ cup (120 milliliters) heavy cream
Chocolate shavings for finishing

In a bowl, combine the flour, cocoa powder, 2 tablespoons sugar, butter, and salt. Stir with a fork and add enough water to form a compact ball of dough. Form the dough into a ball, wrap it in plastic, and refrigerate until firm, about 30 minutes. Preheat the oven to 400° F (200° C). When the dough is firm, place on the work surface between 2 pieces of parchment paper and roll out into a disk with a rolling pin. Transfer the disk to a tart pan with the parchment paper still underneath. Peel off and discard the top piece of parchment. Line with aluminum foil and fill with pie weights or dry beans. Bake for 20 minutes. Remove the crust from the oven and lower the temperature to 325° F (160° C to 170° C).

To make the filling, grate the zest from 2 oranges and juice all 4 oranges. Beat the eggs with the remaining $2/3$ cup sugar, orange juice and zest, and cream until smooth and well combined. Remove the aluminum foil and pie weights from the crust, pour in the filling, and return to the oven. Bake until set, about 45 minutes. Allow to cool, then decorate with chocolate shavings just before serving.

« TORTA LAMPO CIOCCOLATO E PERE »
QUICK CHOCOLATE AND PEAR PIE

When it comes to cooking, I look for maximum results with the minimum of effort. This simple recipe is a prime example. You can also use puff pastry in place of the pie crust. And if you prefer the pears to be visible, pour in the pudding mixture first and top it with the pears.

SERVES 8

3 pears, peeled, cored, and sliced
1 readymade pie crust
$3/4$ cup plus 1 tablespoon (200 milliliters) heavy cream, cold
1 packet instant chocolate pudding
1 packet unflavored gelatin powder and 1 cup sugar (optional)

Preheat the oven to 350° F (180° C). Arrange the pear slices in concentric circles on the pie crust. Mix the cream with the contents of the pudding packet and pour the mixture over the pears. Bake for 35 minutes. Remove the pie from the oven and allow to cool, then refrigerate until serving time. If using the gelatin, combine the gelatin and the sugar and stir in the amount of boiling water indicated on the package. Pour the sweetened gelatin over the pudding (you may not need all of it) and refrigerate until firm.

« SCHIACCIATA ALL'UVA »
GRAPE FOCACCIA

Schiacciata all'uva is a Tuscan specialty that is a cross between a bread and a dessert. Serve squares of it along with plenty of apples and pears as a fitting conclusion to a rustic fall meal. Be sure to use seedless grapes!

SERVES 6

3 1/2 cups (400 grams unbleached all-purpose flour
1 envelope instant yeast
3/4 cup (200 grams) granulated sugar
1/4 cup extra-virgin olive oil, plus more for drizzling
1 pinch salt
2 pounds (1 kilogram) seedless red grapes, halved

In a bowl, combine the flour, yeast, 1/4 cup (50 grams) sugar, the olive oil, and salt. Stir in enough warm (not hot) water to make a soft dough—about 1 cup (240 milliliters). Transfer to the work surface and knead until compact, about 10 minutes. Place the dough in a clean bowl, cover, and set aside to rise for about 1 hour.

Preheat the oven to 350° F (180° C). Line a jelly-roll pan with parchment paper. When the dough has finished rising, roll out about 2/3 of the dough, or simply place it on the prepared pan and stretch it thin, using your fingertips. (If the dough resists, let it rest for 5 to 10 minutes and try again.) Sprinkle with about 1/2 of the grapes and sprinkle with 1/4 cup (50 grams) sugar. Place the remaining dough on the work surface (lightly floured, if necessary, to keep it from sticking) and stretch or roll it to roughly the same size as the first piece. Place it on top of the first piece of dough and pinch the edges together to seal. Sprinkle the remaining grapes on top and sprinkle with the remaining 1/4 cup (50 grams) sugar. Drizzle with a little oil and bake until golden, about 20 minutes. Serve warm or at room temperature.

« BACI DI DAMA »
CHOCOLATE NUT COOKIES

These cookies—the name literally translates to "ladies' kisses"—are a lot of fun to make. These are sandwich cookies, so don't make the cookie halves too large, especially because they expand as they bake. I did that the first time I made them, and the resulting cookies looked like hamburgers on buns rather than delicate morsels of pastry!

SERVES 6

1 cup (100 grams) almonds, toasted
1 cup (100 grams) hazelnuts
1 cup (200 grams) granulated sugar
1 ²/₃ cups (200 grams) unbleached all-purpose flour
1 pinch salt
1 stick plus 6 tablespoons (200 grams) unsalted butter, cut into pieces
2 egg yolks
3 ¹/₂ ounces (100 grams) dark chocolate, melted

Preheat the oven to 350° F (180° C). Line a cookie sheet with parchment paper. In a food processor fitted with the metal blade, grind the almonds, hazelnuts, and sugar. Add the flour and salt and process to combine. Add the butter and pulse briefly until the mixture resembles wet sand. Add the egg yolks and pulse until the dough forms a ball on top of the blade. Remove the dough from the food processor bowl and pull off a small piece of dough the size of a hazelnut. Roll between your palms to make it round, and place it on the prepared cookie sheet. Repeat with the remaining dough, leaving some space between the cookies. Bake in the upper part of the oven for 10 minutes. Remove from the oven and let the cookies cool completely on the cookie sheet. (Don't touch them until they're cool.) Using an offset spatula, spread the melted chocolate on the flat side of one of the cookies. Place another cookie flat-side down on top of the chocolate. Repeat with the remaining cookies and chocolate. Store in an airtight container.

Note: To keep these and other cookies from browning too quickly on the bottom, I sometimes place the top of a broiler pan or a cooling rack on the cookie sheet, line that with parchment paper, and bake the cookies on top of it. This keeps them from having too much contact with the cookie sheet and browning too quickly. There are many other ways to do this. You can ball up a few pieces of parchment paper and place those between the cookie sheet and the parchment underneath the cookies to keep them off the surface of the cookie sheet. You can also double up cookie sheets if you have enough, and when baking cookies, it's always best to turn the sheets front-to-back and switch them between the oven shelves during baking. Cookies bake best in the top two thirds or so of your oven.

« CANESTRELLI »
BUTTER COOKIES

Canestrelli are simple little butter cookies that could not be tastier. Once I start eating them, I find it hard to stop. When I'm putting together a buffet, I always like to include these for dessert. They allow guests to have a little something sweet without gorging.

SERVES 6

3 hard-boiled egg yolks
1 cup (125 grams) unbleached all-purpose flour
$3/4$ cup (125 grams) potato starch
1 stick plus 3 tablespoons (150 grams) unsalted butter, cut into pieces
$2/3$ cup (75 grams) confectioners' sugar, plus more for sprinkling
$1/2$ teaspoon vanilla extract
1 pinch salt

In a bowl, crush the egg yolks with a fork. Add the flour and potato starch and stir with the fork to combine. Add the butter and cut it in or pinch the mixture lightly with your fingertips until it resembles wet sand. Add the confectioners' sugar, vanilla, and salt and work them in. Continue kneading the dough with your fingertips until it forms a ball. Wrap the ball of dough in plastic and refrigerate until firm. When the dough is firm, preheat the oven to 350° F (180° C). Line cookie sheets with parchment paper. (See the Note at left for more on baking cookies.) On a lightly floured work surface, roll out the dough to about $1/2$-inch thick and cut out the *canestrelli* with a flower-shaped cookie cutter. Cut a small hole in the center of each. Transfer the cookies to a prepared cookie sheet. Reroll the scraps and cut out the remaining cookies. (Don't reroll more than once—simply bake any odd-shaped remaining scraps.) Bake until lightly golden, about 20 minutes. Cool on a wire rack. Sprinkle with confectioners' sugar before serving.

« CANTUCCI »
ALMOND BISCOTTI

These plain nut cookies are baked twice, which gives them their characteristic hard texture. They are perfect for dunking in coffee, tea, or vin santo. If you like your cookies extra-hard, you can leave out the baking powder. My friend Cristina Pistocchi gave me this recipe.

SERVES 6

4 large eggs
2 1/4 cups (500 grams) granulated sugar
1/2 teaspoon vanilla extract
7 tablespoons (100 grams) unsalted butter, melted
1 1/2 cups (200 grams) raw almonds
4 cups (500 grams) unbleached all-purpose flour, plus more for flouring
    work surface
1 pinch salt
1 teaspoon baking powder

Preheat the oven to 350° F (180° C). Line a cookie sheet with parchment paper and set aside. In a bowl, with a wooden spoon, beat the eggs with the sugar and the vanilla. Add the butter and the almonds. Gradually add the flour in small amounts, mixing to combine between additions. Switch to kneading by hand on a lightly floured work surface when the mixture becomes too dense for the spoon. Knead in the salt and baking powder. If the dough is still very sticky, add a small amount of flour. Divide the dough into two equal pieces and shape them into logs. Place the logs on the prepared cookie sheet and bake for 20 minutes. Remove the logs from the oven and raise the temperature to 400° F (200° C) on the convection setting. With a serrated knife, slice the logs at an angle. Place the cookies back on the prepared cookie sheet (they don't spread, so they can be fairly close together, but use a second cookie sheet if they don't fit in a single layer) and return to the oven until they are dark and crisp, about 5 minutes. Allow to cool completely. Store in an airtight container.

« BISCOTTI DA PUCCIARE »
COOKIES FOR DUNKING IN MILK

These cookies soak up milk like nobody's business. They're perfect for eating with milk for breakfast, or as a sweet note with a cup of tea.

SERVES 6

1 stick plus 6 tablespoons (200 grams) unsalted butter, softened
1 cup (200 grams) granulated sugar
1 large egg
1 egg yolk
3 tablespoons (40 milliliters) heavy cream
3 $^2/_3$ cups (450 grams) 00 flour or unbleached all-purpose flour
$^2/_3$ cup (100 grams) cornstarch
1 teaspoon baking powder
$^1/_2$ teaspoon vanilla extract
1 pinch salt

In a bowl, with an electric mixer or wooden spoon, beat together the butter and sugar. Add the egg, egg yolk, cream, flour, cornstarch, baking powder, vanilla, and salt and beat until thoroughly combined. Knead by hand until the dough is compact and soft. Wrap in plastic and refrigerate until firm.

Preheat the oven to 350° F (180° C). Line a cookie sheet with parchment paper and set aside. (See page 392 for more on baking cookies.) When the dough is firm, place on a work surface between 2 sheets of parchment paper and roll out about $^1/_2$ inch (1 centimeter) thick. With cookie cutters, cut out cookies and place them on the prepared cookie sheet. (Line another cookie sheet with parchment if necessary.) Reroll scraps once and cut out more cookies. Place any remaining scraps on the cookie sheets as they are. Bake until lightly browned, 10 to 15 minutes. Transfer cookies still on the parchment to a wire rack to cool.

« CIALDE NOCCIOLA E CIOCCOLATO »
HAZELNUT CHOCOLATE COOKIES

These thin, crisp cookies are perfect with coffee or liqueur. For an easy dessert, serve scoops of ice cream in pretty goblets with one or two of these as decoration.

SERVES 4

3/4 cup (100 grams) skinned hazelnuts, finely chopped
7 tablespoons (100 grams) unsalted butter, melted
1/2 cup (100 grams) granulated sugar
3/4 cup (100 grams) unbleached all-purpose flour
1 pinch salt
2 tablespoons unsweetened cocoa powder

Preheat the oven to 350° F (180° C). Line 2 cookie sheets with parchment paper and set aside. (See page 392 for more on baking cookies.) In a bowl, combine the hazelnuts, butter, sugar, flour, salt, and cocoa powder and knead by hand. If the dough is too soft to manipulate, wrap in plastic and refrigerate until firm, about 30 minutes. Pinch off a small piece of dough and flatten it between your palms to create a disk. Place on one of the cookie sheets. Repeat with the remaining dough. Bake until golden, 8 to 10 minutes. Watch closely, as the hazelnuts can burn easily. Let the cookies cool completely on the pans on a wire rack. Store in an airtight container.

« BISCOTTI AL CIOCCOLATO »
CHOCOLATE COOKIES

When I was growing up, I was wild about packaged chocolate cookies with a creamy chocolate center. These are a homemade version, courtesy of Francesca La Torre, my baking expert. Don't be tempted to bake these longer than indicated—they should remain undercooked in the center.

SERVES 6

8 ounces (220 grams) chocolate
1 stick (110 grams) unsalted butter

2 large eggs
1/2 cup (100 grams) granulated sugar
1 3/4 cups (220 grams) unbleached all-purpose flour
1 pinch salt
1/2 teaspoon baking powder
Confectioners' sugar for finishing

Place the chocolate and butter in a pot and melt over very low heat. Set aside to cool. In a large bowl, with an electric mixer or wooden spoon, beat the eggs with the sugar, then stir in the butter and chocolate mixture and beat until combined. In a small bowl, combine the flour, salt, and baking powder. Add the dry ingredients to the chocolate mixture in small amounts, beating to combine between additions. Place the mixture in the freezer or refrigerator until it is no longer sticky. Preheat the oven to 350° F (180° C). Line 2 cookie sheets with parchment paper. (See page 392 for more on baking cookies.) Pinch off pieces of dough and roll them between your palms into walnut-sized spheres. Place on the prepared cookie sheets. With the palm of one hand, flatten each cookie. Bake for 6 minutes. Let the cookies cool completely on the pans. Sprinkle with confectioners' sugar before serving.

« BISCOTTINI SPEZIATI »
SPICE COOKIES

This may sound funny, but I love Christmas afternoon. The presents are opened. All your hard work has paid off, and things have quieted down a little. I like to sit down with a cup of coffee and some cookies and think about how lucky I am. These spice cookies are perfect for that moment. I also like to cut them out with star-shaped cookie cutters, decorate them with silver dragées, and give little tins of them as gifts.

SERVES 6

1 2/3 cups (200 grams) unbleached all-purpose flour
3 tablespoons (40 grams) granulated sugar
1 pinch salt
1 tablespoon mixed spices, such as ground ginger, ground cinnamon, and
    nutmeg

1 stick plus 3 tablespoons (150 grams) unsalted butter, cut into pieces
1 large egg
1 tablespoon egg white
1/2 teaspoon lemon juice
1/2 cup (60 grams) confectioners' sugar

With an electric mixer, beat the flour, sugar, salt, spices, and butter. When the mixture looks like wet sand, add the 1 whole egg and beat until the dough forms a ball. Wrap in plastic and freeze until firm, about 30 minutes.

Preheat the oven to 350° F (180° C). Line 2 cookie sheets with parchment paper and set aside. (See page 392 for more on baking cookies.) Place the dough on the work surface between 2 pieces of parchment paper and roll out about 1/2 inch thick (this will take some effort). Cut out the cookies with cookie cutters and transfer to the cookie sheets. Reroll any scraps and cut out again. Bake until golden, about 10 minutes, then set aside to cool on the pans on a wire rack.

To make the glaze, mix the egg white with the lemon juice and enough of the confectioners' sugar to make a gluey mixture. Brush the tops of the cooled cookies with the glaze, allow to dry completely, and sprinkle with the remaining confectioners' sugar.

« OSSA DA MORTO »
BONES OF THE DEAD COOKIES

These no-bake cookies are meant to resemble bones, making them the perfect Halloween treat. Kids will love helping with these—they simply mold the dough as if it were clay.

SERVES 4 TO 6

2 cups (200 grams) almond flour
2 1/4 cups (300 grams) confectioners' sugar
1/2 cup (150 grams) sweetened condensed milk
1 egg white

In a bowl, combine the almond flour with 1 1/2 cups (200 grams) confectioners' sugar. Stir in the condensed milk. Knead the mixture in the bowl until it is the consistency of clay. Pinch off bits of dough and shape them like bones. Refrigerate the bones. For the glaze, mix the remaining 3/4 cup (100 grams) confectioners' sugar with enough of the egg white to form a smooth glaze. (You may not need all the egg white.) Brush the glaze on the bones and refrigerate until firm.

« BISCOTTI DI NATALE CON CRISTALLI COLORATI »
STAINED-GLASS CHRISTMAS COOKIES

My sister and I made these cookies last Christmas, and we had so much fun pulverizing the hard candies. Then we decorated the tree with the resulting cookies—beautiful!

SERVES 6 TO 8

1 stick (120 grams) unsalted butter, softened
3/4 cup (160 grams) granulated sugar
1 large egg
1 pinch salt
2 1/4 cups (280 grams) unbleached all-purpose flour, sifted
1 teaspoon baking powder
7 ounces (200 grams) translucent hard candies in different colors

In a bowl, with a wooden spoon, combine the butter and the sugar. Stir in the egg, salt, sifted flour, and baking powder. Knead until you have a soft dough. Wrap in plastic and refrigerate for 1 hour. Preheat the oven to 325° F (160° C). Line 2 cookie sheets with parchment paper and set aside. (See page 392 for more on baking cookies.) Place the dough on the work surface between 2 pieces of parchment paper and roll out about 1/4 inch thick. Cut out cookies with cookie cutters or the rim of a glass and transfer to the cookie sheets. Make a small hole in each cookie with the end of a drinking straw (for the string you will use to hang them on the tree). Make 2 or 3 larger holes in each cookie using a thimble or the cap of a small bottle (for the stained glass). Reroll the scraps and cut out more cookies. Refrigerate the cookies on the cookie sheets for 15 minutes. Meanwhile, in a food processor fitted with the metal blade, grind the hard candies, keeping the different colors separate. Fill the larger holes in each cookie with the crushed candies, keeping the colors separate. Bake until golden, about 10 minutes. Cool on the pans on a wire rack.

« SEADAS »

SARDINIAN HONEY PASTRIES

Seadas are a delicious Sardinian treat. In Sardinia, you can actually find them in the freezer section of the grocery store, all ready to go, but anywhere else you'll have to make your own—and it's nearly impossible to find the traditional Sardinian cheese used to make them. My friend Menica, a native of the island, helped me out with the brilliant suggestion to use low-moisture mozzarella as a substitute.

SERVES 4

3 1/2 ounces (100 grams) lard, melted
4 cups (500 grams) unbleached all-purpose flour
7 ounces (200 grams) low-moisture mozzarella, grated on the large holes
    of a four-sided box grater
Grated zest of 1 orange
Vegetable oil for deep-frying
Honey, *quanto basta*

In a bowl, combine the lard and flour and add enough hot water to make a soft dough. Let the dough rest for about 30 minutes, then roll it out as thinly as possible with a rolling pin. Cut out disks of dough. Place some of the grated mozzarella and some of the grated zest on one disk. Brush the edges with a small amount of water and place another disk on top. Pinch the edges to seal. Repeat with the remaining disks. When the disks have all been filled, fry them in a pan with a generous amount of hot vegetable oil. Serve piping hot, drizzled with honey.

« CANNOLI SICILIANI »
SICILIAN CANNOLIS

Pastry shops all over Sicily sell delicious cannoli, but you can make them at home, too. Don't fill them too far in advance or they'll get soggy.

SERVES 6 TO 8

3 $^1/_2$ cups (400 grams) unbleached all-purpose flour
1 large egg
1 pinch salt
3 tablespoons (40 grams) granulated sugar
1 $^1/_2$ ounces (40 grams) lard, melted
$^1/_3$ cup (90 milliliters) Marsala
Vegetable oil for deep-frying
1 $^3/_4$ cups (500 grams) ricotta, preferably sheep's milk ricotta, drained
$^1/_4$ cup plus 1 tablespoon (55 grams) confectioners' sugar
$^1/_2$ cup (90 grams) chocolate chips
Ground pistachios for finishing

In a bowl, form the flour into a well. In a small bowl, beat together the egg, salt, granulated sugar, lard, and Marsala. Pour this mixture into the well. Gradually pull flour in from the sides of the well with a fork and mix with the liquid. When you have a dry, crumbly dough, transfer to a work surface and knead until smooth. Roll out the dough, cut out disks, and wrap the disks around cannoli forms to shape. Pinch the overlap together to seal and fry in a pan in a generous amount of hot vegetable oil over low heat until golden and crisp. Set aside. To make the filling, in a bowl combine the ricotta, confectioners' sugar, and chocolate chips. Just before serving, fill each pastry tube with 1 to 2 tablespoons filling. Dip the ends in the ground pistachios and serve.

« PROFITTEROL CON SCORCIATOIA »
EASY PROFITEROLES

When I was young and my family went out to eat for pizza, I always wanted to order profiteroles—seemingly sold in every pizzeria in Italy in the 1980s—but my mother would never let me, because she said they were too heavy. These days, I make my own.

SERVES 4 TO 6

3 cups (750 milliliters) heavy cream
1/2 cup (150 grams) hazelnut chocolate spread, such as Nutella
8 to 12 (90 grams) readymade miniature cream puffs, halved
11 ounces (300 grams) dark chocolate, roughly chopped

Whisk 1/4 cup (60 milliliters) cream with the hazelnut chocolate spread and set aside. Whip 3/4 cup (190 milliliters) cream until stiff peaks form and fold it into the chocolate mixture. Fill the cream puffs with spoonfuls of this chocolate-cream mixture. Arrange the cream puffs in a pyramid on a serving plate. In a pot, combine the chocolate and remaining 2 cups (250 milliliters) cream. Place over low heat and cook, whisking constantly, until the chocolate is melted. Let the chocolate mixture cool, then pour the chocolate sauce over the cream puffs. Refrigerate until serving time.

« FAGOTTINI DOLCI DI RICOTTA »
SWEET FRIED RAVIOLI

These crisp phyllo pastries are filled with creamy ricotta.

SERVES 6 TO 8

1 3/4 cups (500 grams) ricotta
4 to 5 teaspoons honey
Grated zest of 1 lemon
1/2 teaspoon ground cinnamon, plus more for sprinkling
1/2 cup ground almonds
1 package readymade phyllo dough

1 large egg, lightly beaten
Vegetable oil for deep-frying

In a bowl, combine the ricotta, honey, lemon zest, and cinnamon, then stir in the almonds. Cut disks out of the phyllo dough with a cookie cutter or the rim of a glass. Brush each one with egg and top each with a spoonful of the ricotta mixture. Fold the disks in half to form semicircles and seal the edges. Brush again with egg. In a pan in a generous amount of hot vegetable oil, deep-fry the ravioli, then sprinkle them with additional cinnamon and serve piping hot.

« FRITOLE VENEZIANE »
VENETIAN RAISIN FRITTERS

All over Italy, Carnival is celebrated with fried pastries. These are the specialty of Venice.

SERVES 6 TO 8

3 1/2 cups (400 grams) unbleached all-purpose flour
1 envelope instant yeast
2 tablespoons granulated sugar
2 large eggs, lightly beaten
1 pinch salt
1 cup whole milk
Rum for dough
2/3 cup (100 grams) raisins
Vegetable oil for deep-frying
Confectioners' sugar for finishing

In a bowl, combine the flour, yeast, and sugar. Create a well and add the eggs and salt to the well. Gradually pull flour in from the sides of the well with a fork and mix with the liquid. Add the milk and enough rum to make a soft dough that clumps together when you squeeze a handful of it. Knead in the raisins. Transfer to a work surface and knead until smooth and soft. Cover the dough with a clean dish towel and set aside to rise for 2 hours. When the dough has risen, in a pan, bring a generous amount of vegetable oil to temperature for deep-frying. Use a wet spoon to pull off chunks of the dough and add them to the oil. Fry until puffed and golden, then drain briefly on paper towels. Sprinkle with confectioners' sugar and serve warm.

« STRUDEL DI PERE, CIOCCOLATO E CANNELLA »
PEAR, CHOCOLATE, AND CINNAMON STRUDEL

Purists may turn up their noses, but I think pears and chocolate are even better together than the traditional strudel filling of apples and raisins. Don't go overboard with the filling, though, or you won't be able to roll up the strudel. I speak from experience!

MAKES 1 STRUDEL

2 pears, peeled, cored, and diced
$1/4$ cup (45 grams) chocolate chips
$1/4$ cup plus 1 tablespoon (55 grams) granulated sugar
1 package puff pastry
1 egg yolk
1 tablespoon whole milk
Ground cinnamon to taste

Preheat the oven to 350° F (180° C). Line a jelly-roll pan with parchment paper and set aside. In a bowl, combine the diced pears, chocolate chips, and $1/4$ cup (50 grams) sugar. Unroll the puff pastry, spread the pear mixture on top, then roll up the pastry jelly-roll style, using the parchment paper underneath to guide you. Pinch the ends, seal well, and place seam-side down on the prepared baking sheet. In a small bowl, beat together the egg yolk and milk and brush it onto the strudel. Sprinkle with the remaining 1 tablespoon sugar and some cinnamon and bake until puffed and golden, about 30 minutes. Serve warm, sprinkled with a little additional cinnamon.

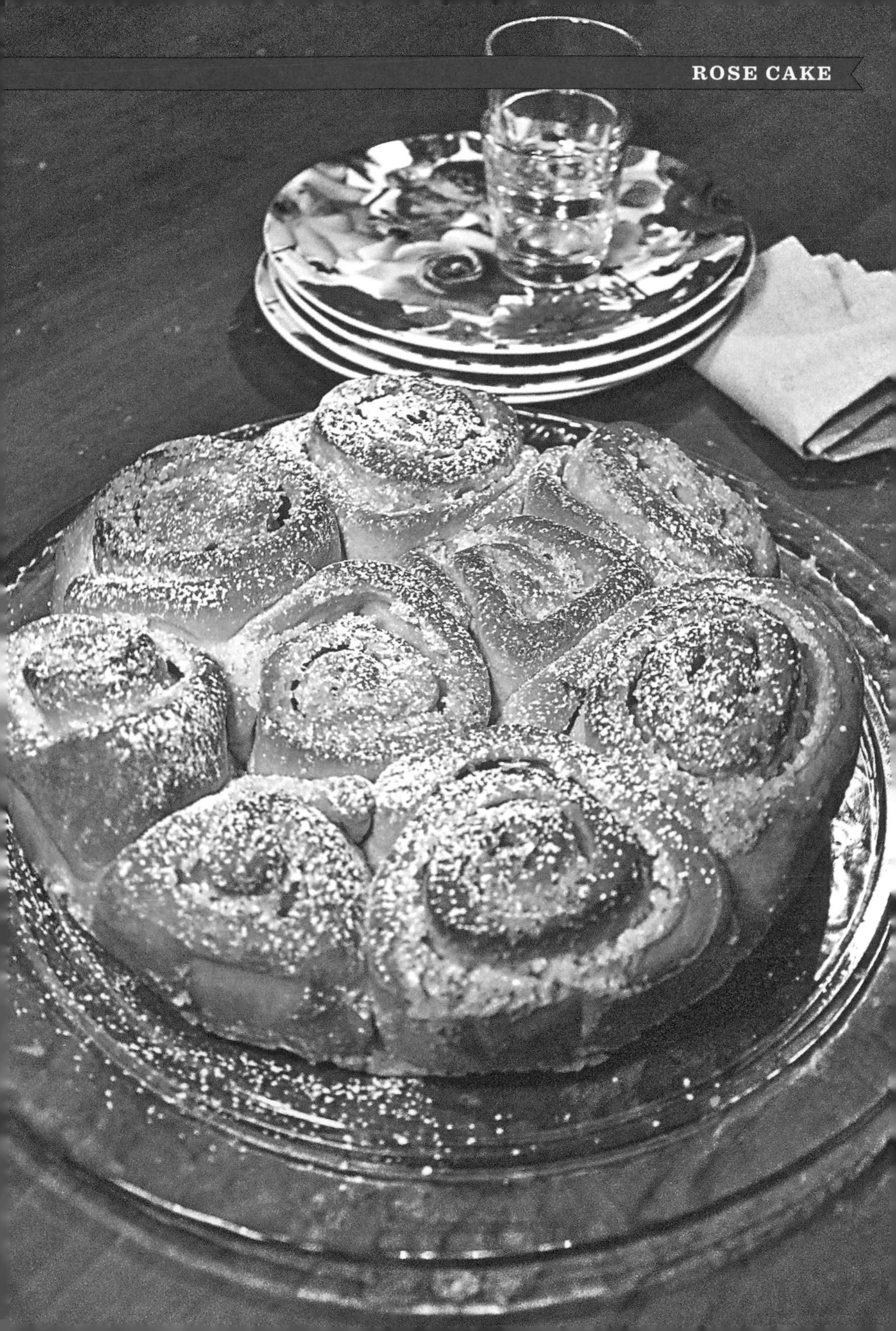

« TORTA DI ROSE »
ROSE CAKE

I'd seen this pretty cake around for years, but I never knew how to make it. My friend Francesca La Torre showed me the way.

SERVES 6 TO 8

1/2 cup (150 milliliters) whole milk at room temperature
3 tablespoons vegetable oil
2/3 cup plus 1 tablespoon (150 grams plus 1 tablespoon) granulated sugar
3 egg yolks
2 3/4 cups (350 grams) unbleached all-purpose flour, plus more for
      flouring the surface
1 envelope instant yeast
1 pinch salt
1 stick plus 3 tablespoons (150 grams) unsalted butter, softened
Grated zest of 1 lemon
Confectioners' sugar for finishing

Line a cake pan with parchment paper and set aside. In a large bowl, with an electric mixer, beat the milk, oil, 2/3 cup sugar, and egg yolks. In a separate bowl combine the flour, yeast, and salt. Add the dry ingredients to the wet ingredients and knead in the bowl to combine. Transfer the dough to a lightly floured work surface and knead until soft and compact. With a rolling pin, roll out the dough to a rectangle. (Don't roll extremely thin.) Place the butter in a bowl. Sprinkle with the remaining 1 tablespoon sugar and the lemon zest and knead together, working quickly to avoid melting the butter. Spread the flavored butter on top of the rectangle of dough and roll the dough jelly-roll style into a cylinder. Cut the cylinder into 1 1/2-inch slices. Arrange the slices cut side up in the prepared pan. Cover with a clean dish towel and set aside to rise for 1 hour. The pieces should expand to fit together. Preheat the oven to 400° F (200° C) and bake the cake for 25 minutes, then reduce the oven temperature to 350° F (180° C) and bake for an additional 25 minutes. If the cake begins to look too dark, cover with aluminum foil. Allow to cool slightly before serving. Sprinkle with confectioners' sugar and pull apart individual "roses" to serve.

« MILLEFOGLIE FRAGOLE E MERINGHE »
STRAWBERRY AND MERINGUE MILLEFEUILLE

This dessert is best made in summer, when berries are at their best. In winter, I make it with candied chestnuts in place of the strawberries.

SERVES 6 TO 8

1 package puff pastry
1 large egg, lightly beaten
3/4 cup (180 grams) granulated sugar, plus more for sprinkling
2 cups (1/2 liter) whole milk
Zest of 1 lemon
6 egg yolks
2/3 cup (60 grams) cornstarch
3 cups (700 milliliters) heavy cream
2 to 3 pints (800 grams) strawberries, chopped
4 to 5 meringues
Confectioners' sugar for finishing

Preheat the oven to 400° F (200° C). Line a cookie sheet with parchment paper. Cut the puff pastry into 3 equal-sized rectangles and place on the prepared pan. Brush with the egg, sprinkle with sugar, and bake until crisp, 5 to 10 minutes. Place the milk and lemon zest in a small pot and scald the milk. In a bowl, whisk together the egg yolks, cornstarch, and 3/4 cup (180 grams) sugar. Remove and discard the lemon zest from the milk and pour the scalded milk into the egg yolk in a thin stream, whisking constantly. Return the milk mixture to the pot and place over low heat. Cook, whisking constantly, until thick, then set aside to cool.

When the milk mixture has cooled, whip the cream and fold the whipped cream into the milk mixture. Place one of the puff pastry rectangles on a serving plate. Spread half the whipped cream filling on top and sprinkle with half of the chopped strawberries. Top with a second puff pastry rectangle, spread with the remaining filling, and sprinkle with the remaining strawberries. Place the third puff pastry rectangle on top. Crumble the meringues and gently press the crumbs against the side of the millefeuille. Refrigerate until serving. Sprinkle with confectioners' sugar just before serving.

« MELE IN GABBIA »
APPLES IN PUFF PASTRY

I filmed an episode of a television show in a famous bakery in Milan that sells this apple dessert. The bakery makes its own puff pastry, of course, but I promise you can achieve delicious results with packaged puff pastry. *Canestrelli* are perfect for the cookie crumbs.

MAKES 12 PORTIONS

1 apple
1 package puff pastry, rolled out to a rectangle
Strawberry jam for filling
5 to 6 *canestrelli* (see page 393), crumbled
1 egg yolk
$^{1}/_{2}$ cup (100 milliliters) whole milk
Sugar for sprinkling

Preheat the oven to 350° F (180° C). Line a cookie sheet with parchment paper and set aside. Peel and core the apple and cut into wedges, then cut each wedge into 2 or 3 pieces. Cut the puff pastry into 5-inch squares. Place about 1 teaspoon jam on each square. Add some cookie crumbs and a piece of apple to each. Bring 3 corners of one square together at the top and pinch along their sides to seal. Take the fourth corner and pull it up and all the way around the pastry to the bottom on the opposite side and pinch to seal. Place on the prepared pan. Repeat with the remaining squares. Beat the egg yolk with the milk and brush the pastries with this mixture, then sprinkle with some sugar. Bake until golden, about 10 minutes. Serve warm.

« DOLCETTI BURROSI ALLA BANANA »
INDIVIDUAL BUTTERY BANANA CAKES

These are as good for breakfast as they are for dessert.

SERVES 6

5 tablespoons (70 grams) unsalted butter, melted, plus more for
    buttering pan
$1/2$ cup (70 grams) unbleached all-purpose flour, plus more for flouring
    pan and tossing with fruit
1 large egg
$1/4$ cup (50 grams) granulated sugar
3 tablespoons (50 milliliters) whole milk
1 $1/2$ teaspoons baking powder
2 ripe bananas

Preheat the oven to 350° F (180° C). Butter and flour a muffin pan and set aside.
In a bowl, with an electric mixer, beat the egg with the sugar until pale yellow and
foamy. Add the melted butter and milk and beat until combined. Add the flour and
baking powder and beat until combined. Cut 1 $1/2$ bananas into small dice and toss
with a small amount of flour. Fold into the batter. Fill the muffin pan indentations
halfway with the batter. Cut the remaining banana into slices and drop 1 slice into
each muffin pan indentation, pushing it gently so that it sinks below the surface of
the batter. Bake until a tester comes out clean, about 20 minutes. Unmold to a wire
rack to cool.

« SFOGLIATELLE ALLE UVETTE »
MINIATURE APPLE RAISIN CAKES

These little cakes are a great last-minute dessert and a fitting end to any meal. Keep them in mind for when you have unexpected guests.

Serves 4 to 6

1 package puff pastry
2 Golden Delicious apples, peeled, cored, and thinly sliced
1/4 cup raisins, minced
1/4 cup pine nuts
Grated nutmeg to taste
24 pink peppercorns
Confectioners' sugar for sprinkling
Butter for dotting

Preheat a convection oven to 400° F (200° C). Line a cookie sheet with parchment paper. Roll out the puff pastry and cut into 8 equal-sized rectangles. Place the rectangles on the prepared pan. Spread the apple slices on the puff pastry rectangles. Sprinkle the raisins, pine nuts, some grated nutmeg, and 3 pink peppercorns on each. Sprinkle with the sugar, dot with butter, and bake until the tops are golden and the pastry is crisp, about 15 minutes. Serve warm.

« CESTINO CROCCANTE DI PERE E CIOCCOLATO »
ALMOND BRITTLE BASKETS WITH PEARS AND CHOCOLATE

Crisp brittle with chocolate-flavored whipped cream and cinnamon-scented pears—an amazing dessert that's beautiful to boot.

SERVES 4 TO 6

5 ounces (150 grams) dark chocolate
1/2 cup (100 milliliters) heavy cream
1/2 cup (100 grams) granulated sugar

Juice of $1/2$ lemon
$3/4$ cup (40 to 50 grams) almonds
1 abate fetel or Anjou pear
Butter for browning
Ground cinnamon for sprinkling
Confectioners' sugar for sprinkling

Place the chocolate and cream in a small pot over low heat, whisking constantly, until the chocolate has melted. Set aside to cool. Make a caramel by placing the sugar in a pan and whisking in the lemon juice and enough water to make a grainy mixture. Cook over low heat until the mixture turns golden. Add the almonds and toss vigorously. Pour the caramel mixture onto a sheet of parchment paper, cover with a second sheet of parchment paper, and roll thin with a rolling pin. Leaving the caramel mixture between the 2 pieces of parchment, cut it into squares with a knife and press the squares over upside-down bowls to form them into baskets. (Make sure to do this while the caramel is still warm and pliable.)

Once the caramel has cooled, peel off the parchment paper and set the baskets on individual plates or a serving platter. With an electric mixer, whip the chocolate-flavored cream until stiff peaks form and fill the baskets with the cream. Peel and core the pear and slice it. Melt some butter in a pan. Add the pear slices and brown them. Sprinkle with ground cinnamon. Top the baskets with the pears and drizzle with any juices left in the pan. Sprinkle with confectioners' sugar. Leave at room temperature until serving.

« STRUFFOLI »
FRIED DOUGH DRIZZLED WITH HONEY

Struffoli are typically served at Christmastime in Naples and throughout Southern Italy.

SERVES 6 TO 8

4 $3/4$ cups (600 grams) unbleached all-purpose flour, plus more for
   dredging

4 large eggs
1 egg yolk
2 tablespoons granulated sugar
Grated zest of $1/2$ lemon
6 tablespoons (80 grams) unsalted butter, melted
1 pinch salt
$1/2$ cup rum
Vegetable oil for deep-frying
1 $1/4$ cups (400 grams) honey
Multi-colored nonpareils for finishing

Place the flour in a bowl. Form a well and add the eggs, egg yolk, sugar, lemon zest, butter, salt, and rum to the well. Beat with a small fork, gradually drawing in flour until you have a dry, crumbly dough. Turn out onto a work surface and knead until smooth. Divide the dough into 2 equal pieces and roll them out into long ropes. Cut the ropes into small pieces and form the pieces into balls. In a pan, bring a generous amount of vegetable oil to temperature for deep-frying and fry the balls of dough. Remove them from the oil with a skimmer and transfer to paper towels to drain. Place the fried dough on a platter. Warm the honey in a small pot until liquid, then pour it over the fried dough. Sprinkle with nonpareils. Serve warm or at room temperature.

« GELATINE DI FRUTTA »
FRUIT GELATIN SQUARES

These little squares of gelatin are a revelation. I had no idea it was so easy to make your own. The only problem with them is that without any additives or preservatives, they don't last long. It's best to polish them off soon after you've dredged them in the sugar. You can use any type of fruit juice you like for these, and you can cut the gelatin into different shapes, or even pour the gelatin liquid into candy molds to cool.

MAKES ABOUT 50 GELATIN CUBES

1 ounce (24 grams) gelatin sheets
1 $1/4$ cups (300 milliliters) orange juice
1 $1/4$ cups (280 grams) granulated sugar, plus more for coating

Grated zest of 1 orange
1 $^1/_2$ ounces (40 grams) pectin
3 tablespoons (40 grams) butter
1 teaspoon orange extract

Line a pan at least $^1/_2$ inch deep with parchment paper and set aside. Soak the gelatin sheets in cold water. Meanwhile, strain the orange juice through a fine-mesh sieve, place it in a pot, and add the sugar, grated zest, pectin, and butter. Place over low heat and bring to a boil, mixing constantly. Squeeze the gelatin sheets and add them to the pot, stirring to ensure that the gelatin sheets have dissolved completely. Remove from the heat and mix in the orange extract. Pour the gelatin liquid into the prepared pan and allow to cool to room temperature, then cover the pan with plastic wrap and refrigerate for at least 3 hours or until gelled. Once the gelatin is firm, unmold it, cut it first into strips and then into cubes, and roll the cubes in the sugar to coat them on all sides. Store in the refrigerator.

« ASPIC DI FRUTTI DI BOSCO »
BERRIES IN ASPIC

This pretty dessert couldn't be simpler to prepare. You just have to make it far enough ahead of time that it has a chance to firm up in the refrigerator. Thanks to Annalisa Benzi and Caterina Varvello, who made it with me on my show.

SERVES 6 TO 8

4 gelatin sheets
14 ounces (400 grams) mixed berries
$^2/_3$ cup (150 grams) granulated sugar
$^1/_2$ cup (100 milliliters) orange juice, strained
Rum to taste (optional)

Soak the gelatin sheets in cold water. Place the mixed berries in a loaf pan or mold. In a pot, combine the sugar with 1 $^3/_4$ cups (400 milliliters) water and bring to a boil. Remove from the heat, stir in the orange juice and the rum, if using. Squeeze the gelatin sheets and add those to the pot. Stir until the sheets are dissolved. Let the mixture cool to a warm but no longer hot temperature, then pour it into the pan over the berries. Refrigerate until firm, 4 to 5 hours. To serve, place the pan in a bowl of hot water for a few seconds, then place a platter upside down on the pan, turn over the pan and platter together, and lift off the pan. Slice and serve.

« MOUSSE AI TRE AGRUMI »
CITRUS MOUSSE

The ideal light dessert—a fluffy mousse. Be sure to remove all the white pith and membrane from your limes, oranges, and grapefruits, as it can add a bitter undertone and an unpleasant consistency.

SERVES 6

$1/3$ ounce (10 grams) gelatin sheets
2 oranges
2 limes
2 pink grapefruits
1 cup (200 grams) granulated sugar
2 cups (500 milliliters) heavy cream

Soak the gelatin sheets in a small amount of cold water. Juice 1 orange, 1 lime, and 1 grapefruit into a pot and add $1/2$ cup (100 grams) sugar. Section the remaining orange, lime, and grapefruit and add them to the pot. Bring to a boil over low heat, stirring frequently. When the juice mixture begins to boil, remove from the heat, squeeze the gelatin, and add to the pot, stirring until the gelatin dissolves. Set aside to cool.

To make the mousse, whip the cream and fold it into the juice mixture. Divide the mousse among individual dessert cups or goblets and refrigerate. Meanwhile, cut the zest from 1 orange and 1 lime and add to a pot with water to cover. Bring to a boil and boil for 30 seconds. Drain the zest, add fresh water to the pot, and repeat. Do this 3 times total, then cut the zest into thin strips. In a pan, combine the remaining $1/2$ cup (100 grams) sugar and $1/2$ cup (100 milliliters) water and cook, stirring, until golden. Add the blanched zest to the caramel and toss to combine, then set the zest directly on a wire rack to cool. Garnish the servings of mousse with candied zest before serving.

« LATTE FRITTO »
FRIED MILK

This Genoese classic is a mild finish to any meal and always popular with kids. Fried milk is also sometimes served as part of an antipasto platter with other fried foods.

SERVES 4

Vegetable oil for deep-frying and oiling a plate
1 cup (250 milliliters) whole milk
$1/4$ cup plus 2 tablespoons (50 grams) unbleached all-purpose flour
$1/4$ cup (50 grams) granulated sugar
$1/2$ teaspoon vanilla extract
2 large eggs
Breadcrumbs for dredging
Confectioners' sugar for finishing

Oil a large, flat platter and set aside. Place the milk in a small pot over low heat. Gradually whisk in the flour in small amounts to make a very thick mixture with no clumps. Remove from the heat and whisk in the sugar and the vanilla. Transfer to a bowl and whisk in 1 egg. Spread evenly on the prepared plate and allow to cool completely. When the milk mixture is cool, it will be solid. Cut it into diamonds. In a pan, bring a generous amount of vegetable oil to temperature for deep-frying. Lightly beat the remaining egg. Dredge the diamonds in the egg and then in breadcrumbs and fry. Sprinkle with confectioners' sugar and serve hot.

« TIRAMISÙ CROCCANTE »
CRISPY TIRAMISÙ

Lorenzo Boni came up with this really appealing tiramisù recipe, which uses flaky puff pastry cookies in place of the usual ladyfingers.

SERVES 4 TO 6

1 egg yolk
3 tablespoons granulated sugar

2 (8-ounce/500 gram) tubs mascarpone
2 tablespoons brewed espresso
1 package puff pastry cookies, such as palmiers
Unsweetened cocoa powder for finishing

In a bowl, beat the egg yolk with 2 tablespoons of the sugar. Add the mascarpone and beat until combined. Sweeten the coffee with the remaining 1 tablespoon sugar and stir it into the mascarpone mixture. Spread some of this mixture in the bottom of a 1-quart baking dish or trifle dish. Top with a layer of cookies, and continue, alternating layers, until you've used up all the ingredients. End with a layer of the mascarpone mixture on top. Sprinkle with cocoa powder and refrigerate for at least 10 minutes before serving.

« PANNA COTTA AL CIOCCOLATO »
CHOCOLATE PANNA COTTA

Panna cotta can be a little bland, but when it's paired with chocolate it really sings. I use very little gelatin in my version, because rather than putting the panna cotta in molds and then unmolding it, I simply place it in glasses or teacups and serve it that way. This results in a much creamier panna cotta.

SERVES 4 TO 6

2 gelatin sheets
1 cup (250 milliliters) whole milk
2 cups (500 milliliters) heavy cream
$2/3$ cup (150 grams) granulated sugar
3 $1/2$ ounces (100 grams) dark chocolate, roughly chopped
Berries and confectioners' sugar for finishing

Soak the gelatin sheets in cold water. Meanwhile, in a small pot combine the milk, cream, granulated sugar, and chocolate. Place over low heat, whisking constantly, and remove from the heat when thickened, before it boils. Squeeze the gelatin and add it to the pot. Stir to dissolve. Pour the mixture into individual serving cups or glasses. Refrigerate for at least 3 hours. Garnish with berries and sprinkle with confectioners' sugar just before serving.

« CREMA DI YOGURT CON FRAGOLE »
YOGURT AND CREAM WITH STRAWBERRIES

Yogurt adds a nice tart edge to this dessert, keeping it from being cloying. If you prefer a sweeter version, you can add a little sugar to the yogurt.

SERVES 4 TO 6

1 to 2 pints (400 grams) strawberries
^{2}/$_3$ cup (150 grams) plain yogurt
^{2}/$_3$ cup (150 grams) heavy cream

In a food processor fitted with the metal blade or a blender, puree about $1/2$ pint (100 grams) strawberries. Whisk the strawberry puree and yogurt together in a bowl. Whip the cream until stiff peaks form and fold the whipped cream into the yogurt mixture. Slice the remaining strawberries and place in a separate bowl. Either present the two bowls separately and allow guests to serve themselves, or dish a little of the strawberries and a little of the yogurt mixture into individual serving dishes just before serving.

« SEMIFREDDO AL CAFFÈ »
COFFEE SEMIFREDDO

Semifreddo is halfway between ice cream and mousse—and completely delicious.

SERVES 6

2 cups (500 milliliters) heavy cream
$1/4$ cup instant espresso powder
2 egg yolks
$1/2$ cup (170 grams) condensed milk
Unsweetened cocoa powder and coffee beans for finishing

In a pot over low heat, scald $1/4$ cup (125 milliliters) cream and then dissolve the espresso powder in it. Whip the remaining 1 $3/4$ cups (375 milliliters) cream until stiff peaks form. In a bowl, beat the egg yolks with the condensed milk. Beat in the cream with the espresso powder dissolved in it, and then gently fold in the whipped cream. Transfer the mixture into a loaf pan, smooth the top until even, and freeze for several hours or overnight.

To serve, set the loaf pan in hot water for a few seconds, then invert a platter on top and flip over both the pan and the platter. Lift away the pan. Slice the semifreddo, wetting your knife in hot water between slices if necessary. Serve 1 to 2 slices per person. Sprinkle with cocoa powder and coffee beans just before serving.

« SEMIFREDDO AL TORRONE »
NOUGAT SEMIFREDDO

Bars of *torrone*, nut-studded nougat, are a classic Christmas treat in Italy. This semifreddo can be made year-round, of course, but it offers a handy way to use up any leftover *torrone* as the holidays come to an end.

SERVES 8

1 pound (450 grams) *torrone* (Italian nougat candy)
4 large eggs
1/3 cup (80 grams) granulated sugar
1/2 cup brandy
1 1/4 cups (300 milliliters) heavy cream
Whipped cream and chocolate shavings for finishing

Line a loaf pan with parchment paper and set aside. (Or use a silicone loaf pan if you have one.) Mince the nougat in a food processor fitted with the metal blade. Separate the eggs. In a bowl, beat the yolks with the sugar, then add the minced nougat and the brandy and stir to combine. Separately, whip the egg whites and the cream to stiff peaks and gently fold both into the yolk mixture. Transfer to the prepared pan and freeze until firm, 5 to 6 hours. About 30 minutes before you want to serve the semifreddo, move it from the freezer to the refrigerator. To serve, invert a platter on top and flip over both the pan and the platter. Lift away the pan. Decorate with whipped cream and chocolate shavings just before serving.

The Seattle Public Library
Central Library
Visit us on the Web: www.spl.org

Check out date: 08/21/14

xxxxxxx7002

Everyday cooking from Italy /
0010082491688   Due date: 09/11/14
book

Revolutionary French cooking /
0010083678697   Due date: 09/11/14
book

TOTAL ITEMS: 2

Renewals: 206-386-4190
TeleCirc: 206-386-9015 / 24 hours a day
Online: myaccount.spl.org

* *
Pay your fines/fees online at pay.spl.org

« MINI CASSATINE »
INDIVIDUAL CASSATA

Sicily's famous cassata is a silky dessert made with ricotta. It's one of my favorites. Make these simplified individual versions in disposable aluminum baking pans or ramekins.

SERVES 2

Unsalted butter for coating pans
3/4 cup (200 grams) ricotta
2 to 3 tablespoons confectioners' sugar
1 pinch ground cinnamon
2 to 3 tablespoons chocolate chips
1 package readymade short-crust pastry dough

Preheat the oven to 350° F (180° C). Butter individual-sized aluminum baking pans or ramekins. In a bowl, mix the ricotta with the confectioners' sugar and cinnamon, then stir in the chocolate chips. Roll out the pastry dough and cut 4 disks, 2 larger and 2 smaller. Line the prepared pans with the larger disks. Fill the crusts about 3/4 full with the ricotta mixture. Place the smaller disks on top and pinch the edges to seal. Bake until the crust is golden, 10 to 15 minutes.

« ZUCCOTTO DI RIBES »
ZUCCOTTO WITH CURRANTS

Zuccotto is a bombe—a dome of cake with a creamy filling. This version is a brilliant ruby red because of the currants and currant jelly. Make sure to have lots of currant jam on hand—you want to coat the entire exterior surface of the dessert.

SERVES 2 TO 3

1 1/2 cups plus 2 tablespoons (400 milliliters) heavy cream
4 egg yolks
3/4 cup (100 grams) confectioners' sugar

1 2/3 cups (400 grams) mascarpone
1/2 cup (100 milliliters) rum
1/2 cup (100 milliliters) Maraschino cherry liqueur
2 readymade genoise or sponge cake layers
Red currant jam and fresh currants for finishing

Line a bombe mold or a round bowl with plastic wrap. (Or use a silicone mold if you have one.) Whip the cream to stiff peaks and set aside. In a large bowl, beat the egg yolks with the confectioners' sugar, then beat in the mascarpone. Fold the whipped cream into the mascarpone mixture. In a small bowl, mix the rum and the Maraschino together and brush the genoise layers with the mixture. From one cake layer, cut a disk the same diameter as the rim of the mold or bowl. Cut the remaining cake layer into 1-inch strips. Line the interior of the mold or bowl with the strips so that the entire surface is covered. (Cut strips to fit if necessary.) Fill the lined bowl with the mascarpone mixture, and place the disk of cake on top. Freeze until the filling is firm, 2 to 3 hours. To serve, invert a platter on top and flip over both the mold and the platter. Lift away the mold and peel off the plastic wrap. Spread a generous amount of currant jam on the outside of the *zuccotto* and sprinkle with a generous amount of currants. Cut into wedges at the table.

« ZUPPA INGLESE »
TRIFLE

Zuppa inglese (which literally means "English soup") is a popular homemade Italian spoon dessert. It's traditionally made with Alchermes, a scarlet-colored liqueur, but I prefer to use fruit juice to achieve that same color.

SERVES 6 TO 8

Unsalted butter for coating pan
1 1/4 cups (275 grams) granulated sugar
2 large eggs
6 egg yolks
3 tablespoons (20 grams) unbleached all-purpose flour
1 1/4 cups (300 milliliters) whole milk

Grated zest of 1/2 lemon
5 ounces (150 grams) dark chocolate
40 ladyfingers
Cranberry juice, *quanto basta*

Butter a large rectangular dish, sprinkle with 2 tablespoons sugar, and set aside. To make the custard, in a small pot, lightly beat the eggs and egg yolks together. Add the remaining 1 cup plus 2 tablespoons (250 grams) sugar. Add the flour 1 tablespoon at a time, whisking to combine between additions. Whisk in 1 cup (250 milliliters) milk and the grated lemon zest. Place over medium heat and bring to a boil. Lower the heat to low and cook for 5 minutes, whisking constantly, then remove from the heat and set aside to cool. Place the chocolate and the remaining 1/4 cup (50 milliliters) milk in another small pot. Over low heat, whisking constantly, melt the chocolate. Divide the cooled egg custard in half. Stir the chocolate mixture into one half.

Moisten the ladyfingers with the cranberry juice and place one layer of cookies in the bottom of the prepared pan. Top with a layer of the chocolate mixture, spreading smooth with a spatula. Make a second layer of ladyfingers moistened with cranberry juice, and top with a layer of the egg custard without chocolate. Continue to fill the pan with alternating layers of cookies and custard—alternating the two types of custard as well and finishing with a layer of the egg custard without chocolate—until you have used up all the ingredients. Refrigerate until serving time.

« LATTE IN PIEDI ALLA LIQUIRIZIA »
LICORICE PUDDING

Latte in piedi (the name means "milk standing up" and dates back to the days when gelatin was a novelty) is similar to panna cotta. I first tried making this by infusing the milk with a licorice stick. It didn't have any discernible flavor, though. Frustrated, I tried melting a black licorice wheel in the milk instead. Perfect!

SERVES 10

1/3 ounce (10 grams) gelatin sheets
1 1/2 cups (350 milliliters) whole milk

11 black licorice wheels
2 to 3 tablespoons granulated sugar
Mint syrup and fresh mint leaves for finishing

Soak the gelatin sheets in cold water. Meanwhile, place the milk in a pot over medium heat. Chop 1 licorice wheel, add it to the pot, and whisk until dissolved. Whisk in the sugar. Remove the pot from the heat. Squeeze the gelatin and add it to the pot. Stir until the gelatin is completely dissolved. Divide the mixture among 10 small serving bowls or drinking glasses and refrigerate until firm, 5 to 6 hours. Just before serving, drizzle a little mint syrup over each portion and garnish with 1 licorice wheel and a few mint leaves.

« MARQUISE AL CIOCCOLATO »
CHOCOLATE MARQUISE

A marquise is a rich chocolate terrine that is usually unmolded and then sliced. I prefer to cut down on the risk of less-than-pretty results by chilling it in a bowl and then scooping it out at the table.

MAKES 1 MARQUISE

6 egg yolks
$2/3$ cup (80 grams) vanilla confectioners' sugar
14 ounces (400 grams) dark chocolate, melted
1 stick (125 grams) unsalted butter, melted
$1/2$ teaspoon ground cinnamon
2 cups (500 milliliters) heavy cream
Multi-colored nonpareils or ground pistachios for finishing

With an electric mixer, beat the egg yolks with the sugar until pale yellow and foamy. Beat in the melted chocolate, melted butter, and cinnamon until thoroughly combined. Whip the cream until stiff peaks form. Fold the whipped cream into the chocolate mixture. Transfer the chocolate and whipped cream mixture to a pan or shallow bowl and refrigerate until firm, 12 to 24 hours. Sprinkle on nonpareils or pistachios just before serving.

« CREMA DI CIOCCOLATO CON CARPACCIO DI LAMPONI »
CHOCOLATE MOUSSE ON RASPBERRY "CARPACCIO"

Gianluca Fusto, one of Italy's top pastry chefs, shared this brilliant concept with me.

SERVES 4

1 gelatin sheet
1/2 cup (130 milliliters) whole milk
7 ounces (195 grams) milk chocolate
1 cup (260 milliliters) heavy cream, cold
1/2 pint (200 grams) raspberries
3 to 4 *canestrelli* (see page 393), crumbled

Soak the gelatin in cold water. Meanwhile, place the milk in a small pot and bring to a boil. Remove from the heat, squeeze the gelatin, and add it to the pot with the milk, whisking to dissolve completely. Melt the chocolate in the top of a double boiler (or in the microwave) and pour in the hot milk mixture in a thin stream, whisking constantly. Whisk in the cream until thoroughly combined. Refrigerate until firm, 2 to 3 hours.

Meanwhile, place the raspberries in a plastic freezer bag and pound with a meat pounder or the side of a rolling pin so that they form a thin sheet. Freeze the raspberries until very hard. To serve, handling the sheet of raspberries as little as possible, peel off the plastic bag and place the sheet of raspberries on a work surface. With a cookie cutter, cut out disks of raspberry "carpaccio." Place one disk of carpaccio on each serving dish, top with a generous spoonful of the mousse, and sprinkle with some of the cookie crumbs. Serve immediately.

« RAVIOLI AL CIOCCOLATO »
CHOCOLATE RAVIOLI

I invited a bunch of my daughters' friends to come on my show and make these ravioli with me. You can imagine the chaos in the kitchen that day! They were flinging flour in all directions and eating the Nutella instead of putting it in the ravioli. But the results tasted delicious and looked great—kids have a way of making things work out. These are meant to be eaten with your hands.

SERVES 6

1 1/4 cups (150 grams) unbleached all-purpose flour
3 tablespoons granulated sugar
2 tablespoons (30 grams) unsalted butter, melted
1 large egg, lightly beaten
1/4 teaspoon vanilla extract
Nutella or jam for filling
Vegetable oil for deep-frying
Confectioners' sugar for finishing

In a bowl, combine the flour and sugar. Add the butter, egg, and vanilla. Stir with a fork, and when you have a dry, crumbly dough, knead by hand until smooth and compact. Divide the dough into 4 equal pieces and use a pasta machine to roll each into a thin sheet. (If you are an expert pasta maker, you can roll the dough with a rolling pin.) Place about 1 teaspoon of your chosen filling down one side of 1 strip of dough. (Leave a border and space between each spoonful.) Fold the other side of the strip over the filling. With your fingertips, seal the dough along the border and between the spoonfuls of filling. Cut the filled strip into ravioli with a knife or ravioli cutter. Repeat with the remaining strips of dough. In a pan, bring a generous amount of vegetable oil to temperature for deep-frying and fry the ravioli until golden and crisp. Sprinkle with confectioners' sugar before serving.

« BACI CON LE NOCCIOLE E IL CIOCCOLATO DELLE UOVA DI PASQUA »
CHOCOLATE HAZELNUT KISSES

Here's a quick confection that you can serve any time. I always make these after Easter is over to use up any leftover chocolate eggs.

MAKES ABOUT 2 DOZEN CHOCOLATES

1/2 cup (70 grams) skinned hazelnuts
5 ounces (150 grams) dark chocolate
1 tablespoon confectioners' sugar

Line a jelly-roll pan or cookie sheet with parchment paper and set aside. Roughly chop most of the hazelnuts, leaving some of them whole. In a double boiler, melt the chocolate with the confectioners' sugar, whisking to combine. Add the hazelnuts and stir to combine. Drop spoonfuls of the chocolate and hazelnut mixture onto the prepared pan. Refrigerate until firm, about 30 minutes.

« FRAGOLE E CIOCCOLATO »
CHOCOLATE-DIPPED STRAWBERRIES

Strawberries and chocolate are an unbeatable combination. My friend Alessandra isn't very confident in the kitchen, but I suggested that she make this as dessert for an anniversary dinner. Her husband, who is practically a professional chef, was suitably impressed.

MAKES 20 STRAWBERRIES

7 ounces (200 grams) dark chocolate
20 large strawberries, green leaves attached

Line a jelly-roll pan or cookie sheet with parchment paper and set aside. Roughly chop the chocolate and melt it in the top of a double boiler. Stick toothpicks in each of the strawberries, inserting them vertically through the leaves on top. One at a time, dip the strawberries into the melted chocolate so that about $2/3$ of each berry is covered and transfer to the prepared pan. Remove the toothpicks and set aside (in the refrigerator if it is very warm, at room temperature if it is not) to allow the chocolate to cool and harden. Serve these the day they are made; they do not keep.

INDEX OF RECIPES

INDEX